D0847781

THE TIE GOES TO FREEDOM

THE TIE GOES TO FREEDOM

Justice Anthony M. Kennedy on Liberty

HELEN J. KNOWLES

ROWMAN & LITTLEFIELD PUBLISHERS, INC.

Lanham • Boulder • New York • Toronto • Plymouth, UK

ROWMAN & LITTLEFIELD PUBLISHERS, INC.

Published in the United States of America
by Rowman & Littlefield Publishers, Inc.
A wholly owned subsidiary of The Rowman & Littlefield Publishing Group, Inc.
4501 Forbes Boulevard, Suite 200, Lanham, Maryland 20706
www.rowmanlittlefield.com

Estover Road
Plymouth PL6 7PY
United Kingdom

British Library Cataloguing in Publication Information Available

Library of Congress Cataloging-in-Publication Data:

Knowles, Helen J., 1973–
The tie goes to freedom : Justice Anthony M. Kennedy on liberty / Helen J. Knowles.
p. cm.
Includes bibliographical references and index.
ISBN-13: 978-0-7425-6257-8 (cloth : alk. paper)
ISBN-10: 0-7425-6257-3 (cloth : alk. paper)
ISBN-13: 978-0-7425-6608-8 (electronic)
ISBN-10: 0-7425-6608-0 (electronic)
1. Kennedy, Anthony M., 1936– 2. Civil rights—United States. 3. Privacy, Right of—United States. 4. Freedom of speech—United States. I. Kennedy, Anthony M., 1936– II. Title.
KF4749.K59 2009
342.7308'5—dc22 2008037891

Printed in the United States of America

∞™ The paper used in this publication meets the minimum requirements of American National Standard for Information Sciences—Permanence of Paper for Printed Library Materials, ANSI/NISO Z39.48-1992.

In memory of
Ralph Knowles and Paul Donovan

Epigraph

The law is what we live with. Justice is sometimes harder to achieve.

—Sherlock Holmes
(Arthur Conan Doyle, *The Adventure of the Red Circle*)

Justice is the end of government. It is the end of civil society. It ever has been and ever will be pursued until it be obtained, or until liberty be lost in the pursuit.

—James Madison, *Federalist* No. 51

Contents

List of Figures

List of Tables

Preface

"WHAT DO YOU LIKE ABOUT JUSTICE KENNEDY?" During the course of writing this book, numerous people have asked me this question. It used to catch me off guard, because it is not something I ever thought about asking myself. I never stopped to consider whether the person, whose judicial opinions, speeches, and confirmation testimony I would spend years studying, was someone I "liked." What fascinated me, from the beginning, was not the person, but the work product. Admittedly, understanding Justice Anthony M. Kennedy's jurisprudence has required me to try and understand the justice himself; and, on the one occasion when I did have the opportunity briefly to speak to him (he did not respond to requests to be interviewed for this project), I gained the impression that he was the gracious, mild-mannered individual that others report him to be. However, it was the subject of our short conversation—the importance and value of education, which served to confirm one of my conclusions about his judicial philosophy, which I consider to have been far more informative than any insight into his personality.

What, then, do I find interesting about Justice Kennedy's jurisprudence, and why have I written this book? In order to answer this, it is instructive to employ the following hypothetical. Imagine that it is oral argument day at the U.S. Supreme Court.

"Oyez! Oyez! Oyez! All persons having business before the Honorable Supreme Court of the United States are admonished to draw near and give their attention, for the Court is now sitting. God save the United States and this Honorable Court!" Following some administrative announcements, the chief justice clears his throat and indicates that the Court will now hear arguments in the first case of the day. As the attorney rises, proceeds to the lectern, and nervously sets down his papers, he feels the palpable sense of tension within the courtroom begin to rise. Perhaps this change in atmosphere is a figment of his imagination. Yet, for this "one-shotter"[1]—who is arguing his first case, on this particular first Monday in October, before a Court that recently welcomed two new members whose views (judicial or otherwise) about gay marriage (the subject of the case at hand) are as yet unknown—this is probably an accurate perception. "Mr. Chief Justice, and may it please the court." Instead of following this obligatory opening statement with a question mark, which seemed all too appropriate, but at the same time distinctly inappropriate, the attorney makes the following observation. "I understand that this will be a difficult case for this Court to decide. If a majority of this Court believes that the correct interpretation of the word 'liberty,' in the due process clause of the Fourteenth Amendment, is a narrow one defined by closely consulting the nation's history and traditions, then my client will not prevail in this case." In the months since the Court had granted certiorari in the case, if Court watchers—both scholarly and journalistic—were to be believed, then the votes of only two of the justices were truly "up for grabs." However, on this occasion the attorney's opening sentence prompted all nine members of the Court to sit up and take notice. Encouraged, the attorney continued: "If, on the other hand, a majority of this Court affords 'liberty' a more expansive interpretation—embodying the concepts of individual autonomy, dignity, and responsibility (balanced against legitimate state interests)—then the government faces a far greater burden of justifying its actions in this case." Afterward, several of the justices would remark to their clerks that it was refreshing not to hear an advocate step forward and say: "This will clearly be an easy case for you to resolve, because it is clearly obvious that my client should win because the other side wrongly interprets the Constitution"—or words to that effect. As one of the justices said to her secretary afterward: finally, a lawyer who does not think the justices have an easy job.[2]

Although this scene is fictional, it addresses a current jurisprudential reality—that the constitutional boundaries of individual liberty, as defined by the U.S. Supreme Court in the twenty-first century, will most likely be drawn by reference to one of the two sets of interpretive guidelines described by my imaginary attorney. And, in the immediate future in closely divided cases, the prevailing interpretation will likely be "what Anthony Kennedy says it is."[3] It is this that I find interesting. Therefore, in the chapters that follow, I do not provide a comprehensive, analytical breakdown of all of the opinions written and votes cast by Kennedy during his, thus far, two decades on the Court.[4] Rather, what you will find is an examination of the justice's understanding of the content and boundaries of constitutionally protected liberty, as it pertains to four areas of the law—freedom of expression, equal protection of the law, race-based classifications, and noneconomic, individual decision making and autonomy. In other words, the question that I try to answer is: What meaning has Kennedy, whose vote has been determinative in so many landmark cases, given to the constitutional "Blessings of Liberty"?

Acknowledgments

When I came to the United States, I brought with me a passion for the pursuit of knowledge about the constitutional foundations and principles of the American governmental system and the work of the U.S. Supreme Court. This book represents part of the fulfillment of that American dream, but it is a goal that could not have been achieved without the input, advice, and encouragement from a great many people whose paths I consider myself incredibly lucky to have crossed.

Ever since the first day of graduate school, I have been able to call upon the wisdom and experience of Mark Silverstein. His passion for teaching and studying judicial politics and constitutional theory is infectious; it was his enthusiasm and knowledge about law and courts that converted me into a student of public law; and it was he who ensured that I chose a dissertation topic in which someone, other than myself, would be interested. Mark has always been exceedingly generous with his time, graciously answering my endless requests to review article and manuscript drafts. I could not have asked for a better person with whom to discuss both the Supreme Court and horses—an unlikely, but to the both of us I suspect, quite logical pairing of subjects.

I was attracted to Boston University because the political science program explicitly encouraged interdisciplinary study; after all, I had never been, and knew I would never really be, a true political scientist. I was equally adamant, however, that I never wanted to be a lawyer. Upon reflection, therefore, I find it more than slightly amusing that I chose, of my own free will, to pursue the interdisciplinary option by enrolling in a class at BU Law School. Had I not done so, I would not have met Randy Barnett, the second person to have a profound influence on the way I think about jurisprudence. His seminar Liberty and the Constitution was intellectually inspirational. Like Mark, Randy is blessed with wonderful teaching and mentoring skills, and he has always ensured that I push the bounds of my scholarly curiosity.

Randy has played several important roles in the evolution of this book, and it would be remiss of me not to give each of them the credit that is due. On one of the many occasions that I made use of his office hours, he initially gave me the idea of exploring the jurisprudence of Justice Kennedy (although I do not think he thought I would take the idea quite this seriously). Additionally, during a three-hour coffee meeting when we sketched out the framework for this book, something I said prompted the reply (with Randy's characteristic enthusiasm), "There's the title for the book." I never imagined that the inspiration for the name of my first book would be something written in a judicial opinion in a case in which the victorious party was Playboy Entertainment.

Finally, I have Randy to thank for introducing me to the Institute for Humane Studies (IHS), an organization that played a very important role in my dissertation and book research, namely, funding. Time and again, the wonderful community of the IHS—particularly Nigel Ashford—welcomed me into its fold and helped by providing the financing necessary to make repeated trips to Washington, D.C., to use the papers of Justices Harry Blackmun, William J. Brennan Jr., and Thurgood Marshall. During the summer of 2006, an IHS Summer Graduate Research Fellowship provided the time and resources necessary to finish my dissertation.

For the final summer of book research in Washington, I received a Small Research Grant from the American Political Science Association. Spending countless hours poring over the justices' papers was an enjoyable exercise made that much easier by the expert guidance of the staff at the Manuscript Division of the Library of Congress, particularly Jeffrey Flannery. I would also like to thank Bill Davis at the Center for Legislative Archives of the National Archives and Records Administration for providing me with copies of Kennedy's preconfirmation speeches, and the literary executors of Justice Brennan's papers for granting me access to the restricted files of his manuscripts. During these trips to D.C., I consider myself extremely fortunate that Sarah and Brian Riedl acted as such gracious hosts, opening their home to me and providing excellent conversation about baseball and politics and superb food to which the weary researcher eagerly returned at the end of the day.

In addition to the individuals mentioned above, my work has greatly improved because of the comments and suggestions made by panelists and discussants at the annual meetings of the American Political Science Association, the New England Political Science Association, the Northeastern Political Science Association, and the Southern Political Science Association. Participants at the research colloquia of the Institute for Humane Studies and the Université Laval in Quebec City, the 2006 Institute for Humane Studies Social Change Workshop, and the Boston University Department of Political Science, Graduate Student, and Faculty Seminar Series have provided me with valuable advice and feedback. Chapters 2 and 5 contain significantly revised sections of the following articles: Helen J. Knowles, "The Supreme Court as Civic Educator: Free Speech According to Justice Kennedy," *First Amendment Law Review* 6 (2008): 252; and Helen J. Knowles, "From a Value to a Right: The Supreme Court's Oh-So-Conscious Move from 'Privacy' to 'Liberty,'" *Ohio Northern University Law Review* 33 (2007): 595–621.

Singled out for special mention are the following individuals who have all provided useful feedback on different aspects of my work: Beau Breslin, Keith Bybee, David Mayers, Chris Rossell, Jim Schmidt, Mark Tushnet, and Eugene Volokh. The following individuals read and provided extremely useful comments on the entire manuscript—Mark Graber, Steven Lichtman, and Art Ward. I am also very grateful to Chris Anzalone, my original editor at Rowman & Littlefield, for having faith in this project and finding a really first-rate group of anonymous reviewers who were able to prevent me from going seriously astray in the thoughts I put into words. Of course, I remain responsible for the occasions that I have gone astray.

My colleagues at the State University of New York (SUNY) Oswego provided an excellent environment in which to work during the process of converting my dissertation into this book, and my students helped me to refine some of my thoughts about the arguments made in the chapters that follow (especially the students in my Rehnquist Court seminars). I am particularly grateful to my research assistants, Joe Rogers and Greg Zak (both members of the SUNY Oswego class of 2008), for their invaluable help in preparing the final draft of the manuscript—and to the SUNY Oswego Committee on Scholarly and Creative Activity for providing generous funding for hiring Joe and Greg.

Malteser, Bearito, Nick, and Kaya helped to keep me sane while I was writing my dissertation; and as I finished work on the book manuscript I benefited immensely from the intellectual company of Doc and Kiss. These six equines constantly proved that Houyhnhnms are a whole lot smarter than the average Yahoo thinks.[1] My mother deserves special recognition for acting as the unpaid and overworked editor of my writing assignments. One month before completion of the final manuscript, my father was killed in a tragic accident. He had developed a far greater interest in the Supreme Court than he probably ever expected to. I will always carry with me in my heart the love and support he gave me, knowing, with the greatest of sorrow, that he will never see this book in print. I am eternally grateful that he and my mother gave me the inner strength to finish this project. Without my parents' support, I would not be in a position to write these acknowledgments. Thank you!

This book is dedicated to the memory of my father and to the memory of Paul Donovan, a wonderful uncle who also sadly did not live to see its completion, but whose passion for political and historical inquiry will always serve as a source of inspiration.

HJK
Lysander, New York, July 2008

Introduction: Shall We Call it the Kennedy Court?

> All in all, Kennedy leads the kind of life that you might expect a Supreme Court Justice to lead if you were constructing your impression of the Court from a civics textbook: diligent, earnest, gracious, gentlemanly, a little bland, patriotic, uncynical, and full of official parties with important dignitaries. He is a man whose only visible personal vice appears to be a weakness for innocent pomp.[1]
>
> —Jeffrey Rosen

SPEAKING TO THE CONSERVATIVES WHO GATHERED for an April 2005 conference sponsored by the Judeo-Christian Council for Constitutional Restoration, author-lawyer Edwin Vieira proposed a solution to the problem of "judicial tyranny," the conference theme. Josef Stalin had said it best, suggested Vieira: "No man, no problem." In the context of "judicial activism," this translated into "No Justice Kennedy, no problem." On another occasion, Dr. James C. Dobson, of the conservative evangelical group Focus on the Family, described Kennedy as "the most dangerous man in America."[2] Two years later, in the cover story of the June 18, 2007, edition of the traditionally liberal *New Republic*, law professor Jeffrey Rosen mounted his own attack on the justice. Kennedy, argued Rosen, viewed the Supreme Court as a pulpit from which to preach to the American people about his own, preferred brand of morality.

Justice Kennedy has been able to please all of the people some of the time, and he has even been able to please some of the people all of the time. However, as these criticisms from across the ideological spectrum suggest, he has not pleased all of the people all of the time.

The bipartisan criticisms are indicative of the fact that, after two decades as an associate justice of the United States Supreme Court, Anthony M. Kennedy continues to baffle those who comment on the judicial behavior of the men and women appointed to sit on America's highest court. Since he took his seat in February 1988, the votes he has cast and the opinions he has written have consistently frustrated observers' attempts to affix ideological labels to him. For the most part, they have had to be content with describing him as a judicial centrist—an enigmatic "Man in the Middle."[3] To be sure, Justice Kennedy's penchant for crafting broad, sweeping opinions that avoid excessive legalese and jurisprudential "clutter" means that "the gist of the arguments" that he makes could "read . . . well in the *New York Times* and the *Sacramento Bee*" (Sacramento is Kennedy's hometown).[4] However, this juridical trait has failed to placate Court watchers who instead focus on the idiosyncrasies that they see as evidence to support the charge that Kennedy's jurisprudence is wrapped in a cloak cut from the cloth of inconsistency and pomposity. A judge who is famous for "try[ing] on different ideas 'kind of like a hat,'"[5] and keeping a whiteboard in his chambers in order to debate approaches with his law clerks is unlikely to write opinions that demonstrate well-defined legal doctrine. This book challenges that conclusion.

It is not a book that claims to have found the definitive key to unlocking the mysteries that surround many of the justice's judicial decisions. Nor does it represent an effort to provide a comprehensive analysis of the jurisprudential content of every opinion authored by Kennedy. Such an undertaking would require a Herculean effort, the labors of which would almost certainly not be justified by the finished product. What this book seeks to do is simply to try to identify some of the most prominent and important philosophical and legal threads that are woven into the cloth from which Justice Kennedy's jurisprudence is cut. Kennedy's opinions in many areas of the law are widely considered to be doctrinally weak and lacking significant reference to and use of the judicial tests that the Court traditionally employs to decide many cases. I demonstrate that in cases involving freedom of speech, equal protection law, and individual liberty and privacy rights this is an unfair reading of the justice's opinions.

Justice Kennedy's *Modest* Libertarianism

There is a certain amount of definitional baggage attached to the ideological labels "conservative," "liberal," and "libertarian." Justice Kennedy has expressed his discomfort at the tendency to attach these appellations to his jurisprudence because of all that those terms usually connote.[6] On numerous occasions, he has also said that he neither has a comprehensive, overarching judicial philosophy, nor subscribes to a jurisprudence that is heavily influenced by political theory.[7] As he explained during his Supreme Court nomination hearings in 1987, his jurisprudence does not revolve around an all-encompassing theory because "I am searching, as I think many judges are," he said, "for the correct balance in constitutional interpretation. So many of the things we are discussing here are, for me, in the nature of exploration and not the enunciation of some fixed or immutable ideas."[8] He sees the inflexibility of tying oneself to a particular interpretive methodology as a judicial vice, a trait that actually conflicts with the judicial duty to judge each case on its merits.[9] Absent an overarching judicial philosophy, what is this modest libertarianism that plays an important role in Justice Kennedy's judicial decision making? While this is a question that will be answered in detail in chapter 1, here I want to touch upon some of its highlights and to explain my decision to label the justice's libertarian jurisprudence as modest.

Modest: "moderate or restrained in amount, extent, severity, etc.; not excessive or exaggerated."[10] Even though, as this book demonstrates, libertarian principles play prominent roles in Justice Kennedy's judicial opinions in several areas of the law, it is no wonder that, in a 2005 interview with the *New York Times* reporter Jason DeParle, the justice said: "People say I'm a libertarian. I don't really know what that means."[11] This reaction is unsurprising, because all too often the adjective "libertarian" and/or the noun "Libertarian" are bandied about by commentators and critics without accompanying efforts to delve into their meaning, beyond a basic observation that they stand (up) for limited government. The libertarianism (note that nowhere in the pages that follow will the reader find me saying that Kennedy is a Libertarian) that influences Justice Kennedy's understanding of the law is modest because it avoids much of the radicalized, unrestrained, and polarizing rhetoric and policy proposals that are frequently associated with this political philosophy. In other words, Justice Kennedy's modestly libertarian jurisprudence gets us back to the basic, fundamental principles of this particular approach to relationships between individuals and their governments.

Writing for the majority in *United States v. Playboy Entertainment* (2000), Justice Kennedy concluded that the government had not met its burden of demonstrating that its regulation of speech was constitutional because it was the least restrictive, effective manner of achieving the stated goal. The Court found that the failure of an alternative regulation to remedy the problem of children's exposure to adult programming was just as likely to result from the absence of this problem as from the statute's ineffectiveness. "The case, then," wrote Kennedy, "was at best a draw. Unless the District Court's findings are clearly erroneous, the tie goes to free expression."[12] In other words, an individual's liberty is too valuable to be sacrificed at the altar of government regulation unless there is actually a problem that the regulation can address in a constitutionally legitimate manner. This conclusion embodies the spirit of the three intertwined components that make up Kennedy's modestly libertarian jurisprudence. As we will see in chapter 2, the first element's defining characteristic is the toleration of diverse views. The second element, explored in opinions discussed in chapters 3 and 4, emphasizes preserving and protecting human dignity. The third and final element, one that is extremely important for understanding the justice's controversial opinions regarding abortion rights—discussed in chapter 5—focuses on personal responsibility.

Judicial Activism and Libertarianism: Strange Bedfellows?

In terms of its use of judicial review, the Rehnquist Court was the "most activist" Court in history. Over the course of its nineteen-term existence (1986–2005), it struck down, on constitutional grounds, over 40 federal laws and over 130 state and local statutes.[13] At the same time, it was a deeply divided Court that was, as the political scientist Nancy Maveety has written, prone to generate decisions of an "ad hoc and *ipse dixit* nature" that in large part reflected the jurisprudential divisions between its members.[14] The Rehnquist Court always contained a majority of Republican appointments, but these men and women never predictably voted as one. This meant that a considerable amount of power could be accrued by a justice who was (1) not shy about using the power of judicial review, and (2) situated at the ideological center of the Court. This perfectly describes Justice Kennedy.

Justice Kennedy does not like the label "swing vote" because he believes that rather than either the justices or the law, it is the "cases [that] swing."[15] However, there is no escaping the fact that for most of his two decades on the Supreme Court Kennedy has been the model of a median justice. As defined by political scientists Andrew Martin, Kevin Quinn, and Lee Epstein, this is a justice who is "in the middle of a distribution of justices, such that (in an ideological distribution, for example) half the justices are to the right of (more 'conservative' than) the median and half are to the left (more 'liberal' than) the median."[16] When the Supreme Court is particularly ideologically divided and activist, as was the case with the Rehnquist Court, there is great potential for this median justice to position him- or herself to don the cape of what Professor Epstein and Tonja Jacobi, another political science-trained law professor, call a "super median": a member of the Court "so powerful that they [are] able to exercise significant control over the outcome and content of the Court's decisions."[17] Kennedy clearly fits this description.

It is well known that Kennedy has few qualms about vigorously and expansively using the Court's power of judicial review. Michael Dorf, a law professor and former Kennedy clerk, concludes that the justice is "probably the most confident of all the justices in the court's power."[18] This is supported by data showing that, more than any of his Rehnquist Court colleagues, Kennedy was willing to cast votes striking down both federal and state laws.[19] It was an all-purpose and evenhanded activism that led him away from using the power of judicial review in such a way as to either significantly discriminate between federal and state laws, or only to favor states or individuals.[20] It may seem paradoxical to describe Kennedy's expansive use of judicial review as consistent with libertarianism, which prescribes a limited role for government. However, his requirement that governmental actions pass far more stringent tests when they impinge upon liberty in ways that demean the individual, negatively affect a person's dignity, diminish personal responsibility, or treat in a particular way because of their race is entirely consistent with the tenets of libertarian thought. This holds true even if the means to achieving the goal of greater individual freedom and respect is bold use of the authority vested in a governmental institution. And it is unaffected by whether or not the right that an individual is claiming lies within his or her constitutional liberty is actually enumerated in the text of the Constitution. As we will see in the pages that follow, this is an understanding of jurisprudence that is infused with the Western conservative values shaped by Kennedy's upbringing in northern California.

A Sacramento Californian on Chief Justice Rehnquist's Court

In the fall of 1987, as the ideologically charged confirmation of Robert Bork to replace Lewis Powell on the Supreme Court was turning out to be an unmitigated disaster, and as it became increasingly likely that the nomination would not secure the affirmative votes of fifty senators, the Reagan administration drew up another shortlist of nominees. By most accounts, Anthony McLeod Kennedy was always in the top three. Although their understandings of the law were not identical, Kennedy was known to, and liked by, both President Reagan and Attorney General Edwin Meese. They knew him for what he was (and still is)—a mild-mannered and studious Californian deeply committed to the rule of law. After education at Stanford University, London School of Economics, and Harvard Law School, Kennedy returned to northern California, coming home to Sacramento to continue his late father's law practice and the proud family tradition of involvement in the political and civic scene of the state capital.[21] These activities made it inevitable that during the late 1960s and early 1970s, when Reagan was governor of the Golden State and Meese was his executive assistant and chief of staff, Kennedy, a member of a well-connected Republican family, would many times cross paths with the two men who would eventually hold the key to his nomination to the U.S. Supreme Court.[22]

Whether or not Kennedy "wanted to be a judge virtually all the time" he was at law school, the extent to which he was immersed in the worlds of legal and governmental service at a very young age (when he was ten he spent a year away from school serving as a page in the California State Senate, and he often worked as his father's legal aide when the elder Kennedy was working a trial) certainly increased the probability that he would enter the judicial profession. As Kennedy has said: "I wasn't sure I wanted to be a judge. But some of the people I admired most in the community were judges. I loved the law. I thought I could best contribute to the law as a judge."[23] The first such opportunity came in 1975, when at the age of thirty-eight, Kennedy became, at the time, the nation's youngest federal judge when President Ford appointed him to the U.S. Court of Appeals for the Ninth Circuit, headquartered in northern California. In October 1987, he was on the shortlist for a seat on the highest court in the land, but the opportunity to make a "contribution to the law" by being at the "center of the storm" appeared to have passed him by. When the Bork nomination went down in flames, it was not Kennedy who was "struck by lightning" (as Kennedy has described the rare honor of a Supreme Court nomination).[24]

Chosen over him was Douglas H. Ginsburg, the former law clerk to Thurgood Marshall and a Harvard Law School professor whom President Reagan, a year earlier, had appointed to the U.S. Court of Appeals for the D.C. Circuit. However, Ginsburg's nomination lasted less than ten days. The judge decided to withdraw himself from the process because information generated by background inquiries led him publicly to acknowledge that he had smoked marijuana "once as a student in the 1960s and on a few occasions in the '70s"—a revelation that did not sit well with social conservatives and the antidrugs messages of the Reagan administration.[25] So, like Harry Blackmun before him, Kennedy was destined to become the third choice to fill a seat on the Supreme Court. Nominated in November 1987 and confirmed by a 97–0 Senate vote after relatively uncontroversial judiciary committee hearings, Kennedy took his seat on the Court in February 1988.

When Kennedy formally became a member of the "good old #3 club" (as Blackmun liked to describe the small group of justices who were neither the first nor second selections of their nominating president), his appointment "ushered in a period of uncertainty about the Supreme Court's direction."[26]

To be sure, by 1987 the Reagan administration had enjoyed opportunities to appoint over 50 percent of the federal judiciary, including elevating William H. Rehnquist to chief justice and appointing three new associate justices (Sandra Day O'Connor, Antonin Scalia, and Kennedy) to the Supreme Court. However, a president can never guarantee political and ideological consonance between his views and those of his federal judicial appointments. As political scientists Mark Silverstein and William Haltom suggest, instead of "getting what they *want*" presidents usually have to settle for "what they *need*" (which is to see that their judicial nominees are confirmed).[27] On November 11, 1987, during the press briefing in which he introduced the country to Judge Kennedy, his (next) nominee to replace Justice Powell, President Reagan made a number of references to the "domestic tranquility" of the country and "keeping our cities and neighborhoods safe from crime." The only area of Kennedy's jurisprudence that Reagan mentioned was criminal justice. In the two sets of "Talking Points" prepared by the White House Office of Public Affairs, this emphasis was made very clear. These documents focused on Kennedy's "firm committment [*sic*] to vindicating the victims of crime and protecting the rights of society from vicious criminals."[28] It is clear that in terms of its law and order policies, the Reagan administration got what it *wanted* in the Kennedy appointment. In many other areas of the law, however, it had to settle for what it truly *needed*—a clean-cut, "not Bork" compromise.[29]

Jurisprudence, Sunny-Side Up

President Reagan might have hoped that his fellow Californian would take to the Court the type of very conservative jurisprudence that directed Chief Justice Rehnquist's decision making. However, Kennedy turned out to have a judicial personality far more like that of another westerner, and Reagan appointee, Justice Sandra Day O'Connor, whom law Professor Mark Tushnet categorized as an "old-fashioned Republican."[30] Rehnquist, O'Connor, and Kennedy all brought important degrees of western optimism to their work in Washington, D.C., but all three of these justices demonstrated that the American West is very large and diverse. Phoenix, Arizona (where Rehnquist settled after law school), was a world apart from the Lazy B ranch (also in Arizona) where O'Connor grew up; and both stood in sharp contrast to the environment of Sacramento where Kennedy was raised.

"It was a wonderful town and a wonderful time. What's the movie with Jimmy Stewart? *It's a Wonderful Life.*" This is how Justice Kennedy recalls Sacramento, the at-the-time economically booming city in which he was born and raised. This is the city in which he had always lived (with the exception of a few years)—"in the same white colonial-style house . . . behind a camelia [*sic*] bush and a neat row of gardenias"—before moving to Washington, D.C.[31] One might point to these fond recollections of his Californian upbringing as evidence that Kennedy has brought an air of pomposity, elitist morality, and an unrealistically sunny disposition to the Court.[32] Criticism or praise of the justice aside, it cannot be denied that his jurisprudence has been significantly shaped by his western roots and his "approach to life [that] suggests a small-town innocence."[33] His conservatism is "personal," "respectable," embodies "small-town traditional values," and is "a conservatism of character"; his Republicanism can be described as "country club" or "affluent country-club."[34]

When he became president in 1981, Ronald Reagan brought many of these facets of conservatism to Washington. He sought to unify conservatives and to offer a social and economic agenda that would appeal to as many Americans as possible. He was very successful at selling a brand of Republicanism that created "one big Republican tent" that was welcoming to not only conservatives but also the moderate, middle-class, and primarily white voters who would be dubbed "Reagan Democrats."[35] As Joseph Bottum has written:

> There was a period in the 1980s in which nearly every article in the ostensibly liberal *New Republic* opened with something like: "I'm not one of those horrible conservatives, and I'd never vote for a Republican, but, gosh, there actually seems to be some merit to the idea of welfare reform"—or a strengthened military, or a mistrust of the United Nations, or any of a dozen other conservative topics.[36]

Although this "Big Tent" approach proved to be a formidable political (and vote winning) strategy, its ability to maintain unity among conservatives has inevitably been weakened by the existence of numerous different conservative responses to one of the most fundamental differences between liberalism and conservatism as traditionally understood. When one considers the relationship between the individual and the government, it is necessary to distinguish between the private and the public spheres of actions. Establishing the boundaries of these spheres requires one to account for several different factors. For liberals, just what constitutes the public sphere is predominately, if not solely, determined by the rights held by individuals. In this respect, the main goal of modern conservatism in America, as it evolved in the 1930s in reaction to the ascendancy of liberalism in national politics, was to emphasize the existence of "'other' elements" that affected the relationships between individuals, and between individuals and their governments.[37] By the 1950s, conservatives had begun to identify tradition as the primary point of reference for identifying these other elements.[38] It was not, however, the only point of reference. Consequently, by the 1980s votes were won by adopting a Big Tent approach, but this did not guarantee that once under this tent everybody would or could agree to any one particular response to the rights-based public sphere parameters set by liberals. These differences have manifested themselves in the judicial opinions of the conservative members of the Rehnquist Court.

Taking Opinions Seriously

Speaking at an American Bar Association symposium in 2005, Justice Kennedy made the following observation about the work of Supreme Court justices (he was joined on the dais by Justices O'Connor and Breyer). "We teach," he said, "that our court is based on the reasons that we give in our opinions. We will be judged by what's in these opinions in the books that are on the wall."[39] This is an explanation that this book takes seriously.

Within the field of political science, one will find numerous different schools of thought ready and willing to offer explanations of judicial behavior and decision-making processes. Every approach has its own set of distinct virtues and shortcomings, which have been extensively documented elsewhere. It would be wrong to try and identify common bonds that unite the different approaches. Nevertheless, there is much truth to the observation, made by a quartet of political scientists led by Wayne McIntosh, that members of their profession are frequently inclined to emphasize votes, leaving legal researchers to focus on language.[40] The methodological approach that I take in this book was not chosen out of ignorance of the value that can be gained from bringing the best of these two fields together. However, my interdisciplinary instincts lead me to make more use of the insights into judicial behavior provided by strategic and new institutional schools of thought than the knowledge that we gain from the research undertaken by members of the behavioralist school of judicial politics. Why? The answer lies in the fact that this is a book underpinned by a firm belief that C. Herman Pritchett was absolutely right when, in 1969, he issued a classic, but unfortunately still often unheeded, warning to members of his profession. They were admonished, he said, to remember: "Political scientists who have done so much to put the 'political' in 'political jurisprudence' need to emphasize that it is still 'jurisprudence.'"[41] To be sure, we have learned much from the quantitative analysis of behavioralist (later called attitudinal) studies that question the extent to which the justices base their decisions on legal principles rather than their own philosophical, political, and moral beliefs (it is this model of decision making that does the vote counting).[42] However, to a large degree I am one of the aforementioned legal researchers. Consequently, my work is influenced by the strategic and new institutionalist schools of thought, whose members are, to a far greater degree than the attitudinalists, interested in asking why justices vote the way they do and how they are constrained and/or influenced by the broad political, historical, and cultural contexts within which they work.[43] Consequently, I am primarily concerned with analyzing judicial opinions, not counting the votes in different cases.

The Importance of Legal Education

In terms of Justice Kennedy's jurisprudence, a focus on opinions is a particularly appropriate methodological approach because of the justice's high regard for legal education, and the fact that he "think[s] of judges as teachers"—who, as we saw above, teach through their written opinions.[44] In a speech delivered to a bar association meeting in 1885, future Supreme Court Justice Oliver Wendell Holmes Jr. famously described the law as "a magic mirror, [in which] we see reflected, not only our own lives, but the lives of all men that have been!"[45] Over a century later, at an American Bar Association (ABA) dinner, Justice Kennedy explained that the law *and the legal profession* could be described as "mirrors of America," as "mirror[s] of the nation's heritage, its present condition, and its destiny." Commenting, Judge Louis H. Pollack said that Kennedy "plainly had more than professional good manners in mind." He "was speaking to the members of the association in their *dual roles—as lawyers and as citizens*."[46] This is a very astute observation, because it recognizes the justice's belief in the importance of the educational roles that the bar and legal academia must play, roles that, as chapter 1 will show, are important to his modestly libertarian jurisprudence.

Kennedy has a longstanding interest in educating young people; "I love to teach," he says.[47] Before he became a federal judge on the Ninth Circuit Court of Appeals, he was a law professor at the McGeorge School of Law, at the University of the Pacific in Sacramento. This was a job he continued to do (albeit for night-school sessions) after his judicial appointment. Every year, since joining the Supreme Court, he has taught the course "Fundamental Rights in Europe and the United States" for the McGeorge summer program in Salzburg, Austria. By all accounts, Kennedy's enthusiasm for teaching (he was once described by Gordon D. Schaber, the dean at McGeorge, as "a human hydroelectric project"[48] in the classroom) makes him a very popular professor. At the beginning of his teaching career, Kennedy felt he knew he was doing well when his night-school students would forgo *Monday Night Football* to attend his lectures.[49]

It is unsurprising that the importance of legal education is a recurring theme in Kennedy's speeches and opinions. Addressing members of the graduating class at McGeorge Law School in 1981, he noted that they were joining a profession with "the principal responsibility for defending freedom and the rule of law in our society."[50] Similarly, in a farewell speech to his McGeorge students when he left to join the Supreme Court, Kennedy said: "I hope I've been able to teach you that rules alone don't make the law and that knowledge of the rules doesn't make you a lawyer."[51] Kennedy considers civic education to be very valuable because "you don't take a DNA test to see if you believe in freedom; it's taught. . . . You cannot preserve what you don't understand, you cannot defend what you do not know."[52] This is particularly important vis-à-vis constitutional interpretation. For, as he noted in a 1987 (pre-Supreme Court nomination) speech to the Sacramento Rotary Club: "We are still in a stage of evolution under a Constitution that is potentially fragile."[53]

At his Supreme Court confirmation hearing in 1987, he elaborated upon this when responding to questioning from Senator Robert Byrd (D-WV). Explaining how he understood the relationship between historical inquiry and constitutional interpretation, Kennedy said:

> Senator, the Court can use history in order to make the meaning of the Constitution more clear. As the Court has the advantage of a perspective of 200 years, the Constitution becomes clearer to it, not murkier. The Court is in a superior advantage to the position held by Mr. Chief Justice Marshall when he was beginning to stake out the meanings of the Constitution in the great decisions that he wrote. And this doesn't mean the Constitution changes. It just means that we have a better perspective of it. This is no disparagement of the Constitution. *It is no disparagement of the idea that the intentions and the purposes of the framers should prevail. To say that new generations yield new insights and new perspectives does not mean the Constitution changes. It just means that our understanding of it changes.*[54]

The forces of globalization and the changes brought about by the events of September 11, 2001, have, says Kennedy, made it that much more important to remember that the nation's "fundamental" principles of constitutionalism are "transmitted . . . handed down from one generation to the next"—a process that "was the whole idea of the framers."[55] Kennedy is very proud that his former students are scattered across the globe, sitting, for example, on the Supreme Court of Hungary and working in the Justice Ministry of the Czech Republic. "The American law school system," he observed during congressional testimony in 2008, "gives us a language, it's the language of the law, it's a great national resource. I can pick up a telephone and talk to a young person, a couple of generations removed, and a continent away and I've never met him, never been introduced to her, but I know them because we talk this common language, and this is what we preserve in the legal academy."[56] In his Supreme Court opinions, Justice Kennedy often attempts to strip the legalese away from his arguments in order to educate the "next generations" about the values embodied in this language. In so doing, he frequently uses rhetoric that demonstrates his tendency to wear his principled passions on his sleeve. This presents another important reason to focus on Kennedy's opinions.

The Myth of Judicial Consistency (Or, Why We Should Learn to Stop Worrying About Judicial Agonizing)

Justice Kennedy is often described as a "rudderless and unpredictable" individual because of the perception that his rhetorical flourishes represent his inability to adopt consistent and predictable positions on issues.[57] In 1990, in a letter to Justice Blackmun, Justice Kennedy explained to his colleague, the author of *Roe v. Wade*, that he was "struggling with the whole abortion issue." He was trying "to convey this" in the language he used in his opinion for the Court in *Ohio v. Akron Center* (discussed in chapter 5), an opinion that generated some divisive exchanges of memoranda between the justices (including between Blackmun and Kennedy).[58] There is every reason to believe that today Kennedy is still struggling,[59] not just with the legal and moral issues raised by abortion cases, but also with the issues that his job requires him to confront in many other areas of the law. Indeed, Kennedy has made no secret of the fact that he agonizes over many of his judicial decisions, and that oftentimes the "right" answers do not come as easily as they do for some of his colleagues. For example, he has been quoted as saying that "the clear legal philosophy of Scalia and Brennan 'does seem to yield them an answer a little more quickly.'"[60]

Most famously, in June 1992, on the morning of the Court's announcement of the decision in the landmark abortion case *Planned Parenthood v. Casey* (also discussed in chapter 5), Kennedy brought an interview with a journalist to an end by saying that he needed to go away and "brood" about the impending decision. He also observed that there were often occasions when he had trouble deciding whether he was "Caesar about to cross the Rubicon or Captain Queeg cutting [his] own tow line."[61] Understandably, this tendency to agonize has led many commentators to accuse Kennedy of judicial inconsistency. However, it is important to note that this conclusion is implicitly underpinned by a belief that judicial agonizing is a bad thing.

This prompts the question: Why assume that judicial agonizing is bad? Were I to "take my case to the Court," I would rather hope that a pivotal judge, such as Kennedy, would agonize over his or her decisions. For example, I would like judges to enter an oral argument with relatively open minds. After all, as Kennedy describes oral argument, it "has to make a difference. That's the poetry of the law. A rhetorical case can make a difference because abstract principles have to be applied in a real-life situation, and that's what the lawyer is there to remind the Court about."[62] The chances of the rhetorical case actually making a difference are surely reduced when the judges are so certain they know what the law is. Of course, the attractiveness of having one's case considered by reasonably open-minded men and women might be undercut if those jurists are not at all anchored in their views. It is this characterization of his jurisprudence that has often followed Kennedy. Admittedly, there is something disquieting about the statement that Kennedy made to the reporter in 1992. One might use this self-acknowledged habit of agonizing to support the argument that the ideologically centrist and unmoored Kennedy is the model of an inconsistent jurist. Only, however, if one assumes that there is something inherently wrong with judicial agonizing.

Regardless of whether one sees this trait as problematic, it is important to remember that, as Judge Michael Boudin says, the patterns in a judicial career usually "reflect likelihoods, not certainties."[63] This is a commonsense statement that the literature frequently overlooks. However, increasingly, political scientists are producing data that are making it all but impossible for their colleagues to ignore the conclusion, implicit in Judge Boudin's words, that judicial consistency is a myth. For example, in an important article published in 2007 in the *Northwestern University Law Review*, a quartet of prominent scholars from the law and courts subfield of political science demonstrated that, over the long term, ideological drift among Supreme Court justices is actually the norm rather than the exception.[64] Also of importance is the nascent Digital Docket Project—"Applying Computational Linguistics to the Study of Law and Courts"—based at the University of Maryland. Using a more qualitative approach than that taken by the authors of the *Northwestern University Law Review* article, this has already begun to produce valuable data about the content of Supreme Court opinions. These data have enabled researchers to show that there is not always as much methodological consistency to the jurisprudence of "predictable" justices as many commentators would like us to think, let alone those, such as Justice Kennedy, who are widely viewed as anything but predictable.[65]

Finally, it bears mentioning that numerous scholars have written about the problems inherent in (often futile) quests to try and put forward one overarching method of constitutional interpretation. As the philosopher Ronald Dworkin wrote, "there are hard cases, both in politics and at law, in which reasonable lawyers will disagree about rights, and neither will have available any argument that must necessarily convince the other."[66] The Constitution's broad, ambiguous language inevitability leads judges to make subjective, "constitutional choices." Maintaining the institutional integrity of the judicial system and the dictates of the rule of law (discussed at some length in chapter 1) does constrain judges—when deciding cases, they are not free to impose any choice they wish. They are unlikely, however, to feel compelled to adhere to one jurisprudential approach in every case. Justice Kennedy is no different.

Methodological Musings

Of course, a focus on Justice Kennedy's opinions inevitably generates the following question. Just how much of the opinions are written by Kennedy himself, and/or contain material that reflects his own jurisprudential ideas? In order to arrive at the best possible answer to this question, I supplemented my analysis of the justice's opinions with several different sources of material. Every year, Justice Kennedy accepts many speaking engagements, often choosing to address audiences of lawyers or students. Consistent with generally accepted judicial norms, he rarely remarks about cases in which he has participated. Therefore, the primary sources of information for explaining his votes in his own words are inevitably his written judicial opinions.[67] Nevertheless these speeches have proven to be rich sources of data. Information has been collected from the set of prenomination speeches in the Judiciary Nominations Files of the Center for Legislative Archives at the National Archives and Records Administration, and from video recordings and media reports of many of the speeches the justice has given since joining the Supreme Court. I have also made use of the small number of articles authored by the justice and an extensive collection of newspaper and magazine articles that feature remarks from the rare interviews the justice has granted to journalists. As my use of this research will show, collectively these materials are extremely good evidence that there is a considerable amount of Justice Kennedy in his opinions. Time and again pivotal language will appear in both the opinions and the speeches, language that serves to demonstrate that the commitment to a modestly libertarian jurisprudence is the justice's, and the justice's alone.

Of course, it is worth considering whether Justice Kennedy's law clerks played a hand in directing both his votes in cases and the content of his opinions. However, my analysis of the data does not substantiate an affirmative outcome to this inquiry.[68] Generally, what we do know is that it is the justice, not the clerk, whose name appears on the finished product. And we would not expect a justice to claim responsibility for written work with which he or she patently disagrees. Additionally, as the political scientist Corey Ditslear has shown, arriving at concrete conclusions about the jurisprudential and ideological similarities between a justice and his or her clerks is methodologically messy. To be sure, throughout his Supreme Court tenure Justice Kennedy has consistently hired clerks who, from many different perspectives, can be considered "conservative."[69] Kennedy makes no secret of the fact that he discusses cases with these clerks. He employs an adversarial method of debate that mirrors the work environment of some English barristers.[70] It is well known that Kennedy is one of the members of the Court who will "more often than not give their clerks considerable leeway in drafting opinions."[71] Given the dialogical dynamics of his chambers, this is to be expected. However, this is a long way from saying that clerks can control an opinion's content. Instead, it has usually been the case that out of Kennedy's dialogue with his clerks there would emerge an "[explanation of] the basic thrust of the analysis and arguments he wanted to use; it would be obvious anyway from long prior discussions of the case with him."[72]

Ultimately, only Justice Kennedy knows the extent to which, over the course of his two-decade Supreme Court tenure, he has delegated opinion-writing duties to his clerks. Only he knows how much of his own jurisprudence is written into the pages of the *U.S. Reports*. Not even the extensive papers of Justice Harry Blackmun tell us the precise nature and extent of clerkish influence on a justice's opinion-writing process. That said, these manuscripts of the former justice—who was Kennedy's Supreme Court colleague from 1988 through 2004—have proven to be another valuable source of information for helping to understand Justice Kennedy's jurisprudence.[73] Together with material from the papers of former Justices William J. Brennan Jr. and Thurgood Marshall (Kennedy's colleagues between 1988 and 1990, and 1988 and 1991 respectively), they have given me a deeper appreciation of the ways in which Kennedy constructed his opinions.

Finally, it is important to bring brief attention to two other sources that confirm that the modestly libertarian jurisprudence that I ascribe to his opinions is actually composed of Kennedy's own views. My analysis confirms that the content of the briefs filed in cases (whether by the parties or by *amici curiae*) and the exchanges during oral arguments do influence the justice's thoughts, as the literature suggests should be the case.[74] However, again these sources of information play only supporting roles for a jurisprudence predominantly shaped by Kennedy's own approach.

The Roadmap of This Book

For the readers who have come this far, it is my hope—perhaps best described as modest—that you will continue on the journey that has brought you to this point. For, in the chapters that follow, I show that, contrary to popular wisdom, many of Justice Kennedy's Supreme Court opinions clearly demonstrate that he is a highly principled jurist. He does not simply look to the editorial pages of major national newspapers, rather than the U.S. Constitution, for guidance in the "hard cases" that his job requires him to confront.

In chapter 1, we will take a close look at the fundamental principles of libertarianism and then examine the ways in which these principles manifest themselves in Justice Kennedy's jurisprudence. Guiding the analysis will be sections examining the aforementioned three main elements of this modestly libertarian jurisprudence: the universal, humane, and responsible elements. I do not contend that either these elements or the conclusions in this book that are constructed using them can explain Justice Kennedy's judicial behavior in every case decided in the areas of the law upon which the chapters focus. However, what they can do is to provide us with a good understanding of some of the most important jurisprudential and doctrinal elements of Kennedy's opinions. This understanding will help to explain the crucial centrist role that Kennedy played on the Rehnquist Court, a role he is expected to reprise as a member of the Roberts Court. In this respect, the three elements are best viewed as the main points of the justice's jurisprudential compass. As with any compass, while these points are fixed, there exist, between each of them, many degrees of divergence in one direction or the other. And so it is with Justice Kennedy's jurisprudence. In the areas of the law discussed in chapters 2 through 5, we will see the guiding influence of libertarian considerations of tolerance, dignity, and responsibility.

There are two reasons why my analysis of specific areas of Kennedy's jurisprudence—the application of these principles to the resolution of particular cases—begins, in chapter 2, with the justice's opinions about the First Amendment's guarantee of freedom of speech. First, this area of the law accounts for approximately 10 percent of all of Justice Kennedy's opinions, far exceeding the percentage of cases dealing with any other constitutional provision. Significantly, Kennedy has been a member of the majority in approximately 85 percent of these decisions; 40 percent of his opinions were for the Court, and 37 percent were concurrences. Justice Kennedy has a clearly defined understanding of the scope and content of First Amendment speech protection. In the chosen cases, we will see that when the government seeks to restrict speech based on its content or the viewpoint of the speaker, Justice Kennedy consistently votes to strike down the action. He also writes in defense of revising strict scrutiny so that very few of these restrictions are ever upheld. In so doing, he is protecting far more than just expressive freedom, and this gives us the second reason why the First Amendment is the initial area of analysis for this book. The right of the people to express their thoughts is crucial to a libertarian jurisprudence, such as Kennedy's, that emphasizes concepts of tolerance and individual dignity. As the justice has written, there is no escaping the fact that "speech is the beginning of thought."[75]

Chapters 3 and 4 both deal with the egalitarianism that is evident in Kennedy's libertarian philosophy. With regard to the way in which he reads both the Fourteenth Amendment's Equal Protection Clause and the Constitution in its entirety, Kennedy does not believe that equality and liberty make competing claims. Rather, they are two parts of a philosophical–constitutional whole. In chapter 3, this will be demonstrated by examining the justice's majority opinions in *Romer v. Evans* (1996) and *Lawrence v. Texas* (2003). These two cases involve limits on the freedom of individuals to live their lives without discrimination because of their sexual orientation. In non-race-based equal protection cases such as these, Kennedy wrote opinions providing for extensive protection of the liberty and dignity of "unpopular minorities" and the rejection of animus-based legislative justifications for discriminatory laws. In chapter 4, Kennedy's views about the relationship between equality and liberty translate into a sharp rejection of government policies that classify individuals using race, even for the purpose of enacting programs designed to aid minorities. Kennedy considers such laws demeaning because they treat people not as individuals but as members of a group. Such policies *must*, he argues, be judged using strict judicial scrutiny.

Analysis of Justice Kennedy's libertarian views in action is brought to a close in chapter 5 with discussion of some of the most controversial opinions he has written in his two decades on the nation's highest court. In cases addressing the personal decision-making freedom of individuals, Kennedy led the Court away from the rhetoric of "privacy." Instead, it now uses the language of "liberty." In abortion cases, however, Justice Kennedy has been careful to remind us that his enthusiasm for an expansive understanding of constitutionally protected liberty is sharply tempered by a strong belief that the freedom of a woman to seek an abortion can be restricted using a personal responsibility rationale.

Before proceeding to these chapters, it should be noted that they do contain discussions of some cases in which Justice Kennedy has authored opinions that seem to challenge this book's thesis. The reader will find that even in the areas of the law where the light of Kennedy's modestly libertarian jurisprudence seems to shine brightest, there are occasions when it would appear that the justice is definitely not giving the tie to freedom. With a justice such as Kennedy, who does agonize over his decisions and who is sometimes guilty of using flowery rhetoric in place of crystal clear legal analysis, the identification of such opinions is inevitable. Therefore, with each example of the limitations of my thesis, I do not try and shoehorn it into the book. Rather, I use the opinion to gain the best possible understanding of how Justice Kennedy decides the really hard cases that his job requires him to pass judgment on.

1

Justice Kennedy, On Liberty

> There is a zone of liberty, a zone of protection, a line that is drawn where the individual can tell the Government: Beyond this line you may not go. Now, the great question in constitutional law is: One, where is that line drawn? And, two, what are the principles that you refer to in drawing that line?[1]
>
> —Anthony M. Kennedy

THERE ARE CERTAIN BROAD, ABSTRACT CONCEPTS that appeal to most people. In the United States there is a general consensus of opinion that freedom of choice and association, personal autonomy and dignity, and individual rights are valuable. There is also agreement that they all, in some shape or form, reside within a "zone of liberty" free from undue government interference. Yet, as soon as we attempt to explore these concepts at anything other than this level of abstraction, it becomes clear that consensus gives way to contention and confusion. Just what do we have the freedom to choose to do? Must we play by certain rules of fairness when exercising our associational freedom, and is the government permitted to step in and impose a certain level of order in the name of this fairness? Indeed, how do we know what individual "dignity" and "rights" are? When libertarians address these questions, they favor answers prescribing (or describing) a limited role for the government and, concurrently, expansive conceptions of individual liberty. However, as this chapter will show, we can only reach an understanding as to why the jurisprudence of Justice Anthony M. Kennedy can be described as libertarian by (1) identifying the core beliefs held by all libertarians, and (2) appreciating that libertarians employ a diverse range of theoretical points of departure.

It would be quite wrong to suggest that there is a definitive legal libertarianism. There are many different and distinctive threads woven into this particular philosophical blanket. For example, some theorists take an empirical approach, while others produce strictly normative works. Then there are those whose work is a mixture of the two. Quite simply, libertarians do not all address and analyze the relationship between government and the individual in the same way. This multitude of approaches tends to create the confusion that fuels the arguments of many of libertarianism's critics. Therefore, it is important to discuss the different "libertarianisms" before attempting to understand the nature of the modest libertarian jurisprudence that, this book argues, is practiced by Justice Kennedy.

Deconstructing Libertarianism: Principles

What we now know to be libertarianism was, until as late as the early part of the twentieth century, traditionally referred to as liberalism.[2] Indeed, to this day libertarians remain torn about whether to call their body of principles and beliefs libertarianism or "classical liberalism." Although arguments can be made for and against both terms, there is much philosophical hesitancy about "classical liberalism." "Classical" makes it sounds like something that is musty, old-fashioned, and of decidedly limited relevance to life in the twenty-first century. More problematic, though, is the fact that, particularly in modern America, "liberalism" has come to be associated with a relatively high level of government involvement in individuals' lives. This might give the concept of "classical liberalism" more mainstream appeal than libertarianism, but it can also make some of its advocates wary about using the term.[3] This hesitancy reflects the fact that the three basic libertarian principles can be summarized as emphasizing that the individual is the primary political unit in society, and has fundamental, unenumerated rights that are protected by a government whose powers are limited.

Individual Self-Ownership (Self-Sovereignty)

During the nineteenth century, prior to the Civil War and the 1865 ratification of the Thirteenth Amendment, opponents of slavery often spoke about and constructed their abolitionist arguments around the idea of "self-ownership." It was something that no form of government could legitimately "deny."[4] It was entirely natural to find libertarianism playing an important role in the abolitionist movement. Slavery was a "denial of the humanity and individuality of African Americans," and at the heart of the pursuit of the eradication of slavery was the belief in self-ownership.[5] After all, the most fundamental property that one owns is oneself, and the enslaved individual is deprived of this personal sovereignty and all the rights of self-determination that are inherent in it. When the Thirteenth Amendment imposed a constitutional ban on the enslavement of human beings, there was a subtle terminological shift from talking about "self-ownership" to emphasizing "sovereignty of the individual."[6] However, the same basic point remained—the individual cannot be free to exercise the liberty to which he or she is rightfully (legally) entitled unless he or she enjoys the freedom to make the choices that this liberty permits, unencumbered by outside interference. In other words, whether described as "self-ownership" or "sovereignty of the individual," the first core principle of libertarianism emphasizes individual decision-making autonomy.

To be sure, some of the libertarian arguments made by the philosopher Robert Nozick include the claim that a free society would permit an individual to sell himself into slavery if that were his wish.[7] However, it would seem that enslavement—whether forced or voluntary—is the most obvious example of an action that lies beyond the legitimate boundaries of an individual's authority. Consequently, slavery is anathema to libertarianism, which is a theory at whose intellectual heart is the argument that:

> The only relevant consideration in political matters is individual liberty: that there is a delimitable sphere of action for each person, the person's "rightful liberty," such that one may be forced to do or refrain from what one wants to do only if what one would do or not do would violate, or at least infringe, the rightful liberty of some other person(s).[8]

Slavery is a wholesale violation of this, because when an entity—such as an individual—has the "authority" to do something (when it is within his or her liberty), implicit is the argument that he or she has a legitimate right, just as international law tells us that states do, to prohibit outside interference with the choice that liberty affords the individual. "In a sovereignty system . . . States uphold their rights by attempting to exclude foreign influence over their decision-making procedures."[9] This is precisely why the global society could not be formed while countries were still under colonial rule—and did not have supreme authority.[10] In terms of the basic concepts of sovereignty, this idea of supreme authority applies just as equally to human beings—for whom slavery, not colonial rule, is the mortal enemy. This supreme authority of an individual, this supreme autonomy, includes moral self-ownership.

As we will see, identifying the boundaries of morality is something that governments frequently try to do, but this is something to which libertarianism adamantly objects, for the simple reason that "individuals are moral agents."[11] Our freedom to choose to act in a particular way involves making decisions about right and wrong and what is best for us. If we are deprived of this freedom, we are no longer free to make of ourselves what we wish—we are no longer free to make moral decisions about our "holdings" (as Nozick described them), the property that is our body and mind.[12] This takes on particular importance when we talk about the relationship between morality and the law. Its emphasis on *self*-ownership leads libertarians to conclude that the only entity legally entitled to make morality-based decisions and judgments is the individual, not the majority, and certainly not the government. This is because, at its heart, "moral sentiment is an interest incapable of refutation."[13] Therefore, asking individuals to abide by the stated "moral sentiment" of others is asking them to give up part of their freedom to make choices about the direction of their lives. It is asking them to abide by the choices of others who have passed judgment about the morality of some of the choices that the individual should have been free to make.

Bounded Liberty (Not License)

It is the "distinctiveness" of this individual liberty that leads us to the second core principle of libertarianism. Liberty is bounded by a rights-based theory of individual relations. And this is a theory that tells us that as much as one rights-holder—A—is able to limit the actions of another rights-holder—B, it is equally important that A cannot ask B to do something that would violate the rights of B. In other words, the individual liberty that libertarianism holds up as "the fundamental and only legitimate concern of any just society" is *bounded* liberty—it is not a license to engage in whatever one wants. It is "those freedoms which people ought to have" and, as such, liberty is very different from "license," because this "refers to those freedoms which people ought *not* to have and thus those freedoms which are properly constrained."[14] Quite simply, society could not function if its citizens had unbridled freedom to do anything, anytime, anyhow. Liberty necessarily (and inevitably) involves some restraints on one's actions and is actually stronger for these restraints.

Libertarianism often encounters criticism and resistance because its expansive understanding of liberty is misconstrued as placing very few limits on individual behavior. To be sure, it imposes *fewer* limits than most theories, but it does nevertheless impose limits. As law professor Richard A. Epstein, who has written extensively from a libertarian perspective (we will hear more about his specific approach in the pages that follow), notes:

> The reason for the dominance of the autonomy principle is not any belief that people live in small social islands uninfluenced by and unconcerned with the interests and the behavior of others. It is that no other principle matches power with interest to the same degree.[15]

Now, the big question that is generated by libertarianism's focus on rights is: what rights? Libertarianism certainly does seem to offer several different ways of thinking about this question.

The most appropriate place to begin is with the concept of natural rights, because as the following discussion demonstrates, it is easy to place natural rights at the heart of libertarianism. These are rights that no government determines; they are neither listed nor limited by the written lawful dictates (positive laws) of a legal system. Such a system can be created to secure and/or protect them, and natural rights can be used to establish the boundaries for the creation of further legal rights. Natural rights will *always*, however, precede any such system—they are, in other words, *prepolitical* rights. They are "more original" than government, and because they are the actual "end or purpose of government" they are considered "more fundamental than government." Individuals possess natural rights by virtue of being human beings—by virtue of their individual sovereignty. Indeed, natural rights actually help to define the "'space' over which . . . [a person] has sole jurisdiction of *liberty* to act and within which no one else may rightfully interfere."[16] Possession of these rights is not contingent upon adherence to any particular moral code of behavior (religious or secular). To be sure, recognition and respect for natural rights needs to exist for society to function justly, but it is equally important that any attempt at systematic enforcement of natural rights–respecting behavior not violate any of these natural rights in the process. Simply put, "for human laws to be obligatory, they should not violate natural rights."[17]

This sounds fine, but it now generates the question: what are these natural rights? Are they just "out there"? Do we, to paraphrase U.S. Supreme Court Justice Potter Stewart, "know them when we see them"?[18] The English philosopher Jeremy Bentham probably had a point when he derisively described them as mere "nonsense upon stilts."[19] What should we say of natural rights today, in the twenty-first century? This question becomes all the more pressing when libertarians attempt to apply their political theory to the process of interpreting the Constitution. The author James Jones ably captured this problem in *From Here to Eternity*, in which two of the characters discuss the relationship between "certain rights" and the Constitution:

> "I understand it."
>
> "No you don't. Every man's supposed to have certain rights."
>
> "Certain inalienable rights," Starke said, "to liberty, equality and the pursuit of happiness. I learnt it in school, as a kid."
>
> "Not that," Prew said. "That's The Constitution. Nobody believes that any more."
>
> "Sure they do," Starke said. "They all believe it. They just don't do it. But they believe it."
>
> "Sure," Prew said. "That's what I mean."
>
> "But at least in this country they believe it," Starke said, "even if they don't do it."[20]

Not since the 1940s have Supreme Court opinions referred to "natural rights" with any frequency. The Court has on occasion suggested that "fundamental rights" is the modern linguistic substitute. However, the Court has not really treated the two terms as synonymous. As we will see in the chapters that follow, the justices have, particularly since the 1930s, used a variety of interpretive justifications for their decisions that a right is "fundamental." Tradition, morality, and societal consensus have all been invoked to delineate the boundaries of fundamental rights. This is clearly not the same as a natural rights methodology, whose focus is on a social structure whose boundaries are defined by individuals' pre-political liberty jurisdictions. Therefore, we can reach the conclusion that a language of "fundamental rights" is not terribly helpful for libertarians engaging in constitutional interpretation. To be sure, libertarians have used this term when discussing their understanding of individual rights. For example, in *Libertarianism: A Primer*, David Boaz says:

> Fundamental rights *cannot* conflict. Any claim of conflicting rights must represent a misinterpretation of fundamental rights. That's one of the premises, and the virtues, of rights theory: because rights are universal, they can be enjoyed by every person at the same time in any society.[21]

As useful as this might be for understanding some of the boundaries of liberty identified by libertarianism, it becomes problematic when used in discussions of constitutional interpretation.

Where, then, does that leave us? The Constitution contains broad language, and in the Ninth Amendment—"The enumeration in the Constitution, of certain rights, shall not be construed to deny or disparage others retained by the people"—James Madison explicitly set forth an understanding of (1) limited government and (2) expansive individual rights above and beyond those enumerated in the document's text (this is discussed in more detail below).

Therefore, libertarian readings of the Constitution will inevitably focus on its "glittering generalities"—those discussed by Prew and Starke.[22] The best that can be said, then, about the philosophical approach that libertarianism brings to the table is that the rights the government has no business violating are best understood as property rights. Indeed, the rights that libertarians care about "can [all] be understood as property rights."[23] Why? The answer lies in the concept of self-ownership. Above all else, the property that we have—that we own—that is our body and mind, cannot be violated unless we are enslaved, a scenario that no libertarian should endorse.

Limited Government (Not Anarchy)

One way in which we can try to identify the rights that we, as rights-bearing individuals have, and which others cannot take away without abrogating our liberty, is to look at the arguments made by the seventeenth-century English philosopher, John Locke, in the *Second Treatise of Government* (1689).[24] Locke's theory, as we shall see, also helps us to understand the third of the three core principles of libertarianism. Many discussions of libertarian theory, particularly as it applies to American constitutional theory, begin by recalling the arguments made by Locke, who heavily influenced the political thought of the Constitution's Framers. And, Locke's theory tells us something very important about libertarianism. It tells us that libertarianism is not an anarchical political theory. We can see why this is so by considering the fact that central to Locke's *Second Treatise* arguments is the understanding that some government regulation is needed in order to protect individuals' rights. This, in other words, is the principal reason why government should exist.

Locke theorized that individuals would decide to leave a (hypothetical) state of nature in order to establish a civil (political) society with governing institutions. This meant giving up some individual freedom, but the negative consequences of this were considered outweighed by the benefits attached to the creation of formal structures. This is because these formal structures—which were created by individuals for individuals—were designed to protect individual rights (Locke placed a special emphasis on property rights). This decision to establish a civil society, said Locke, resulted from the capacity of individuals to make reasoned judgments about the necessity of creating political arrangements (this set him apart from Thomas Hobbes, another English philosopher, whose 1651 publication *Leviathan* famously portrayed people as far more selfish beings).[25] Locke's arguments were constructed using social contract theory—people agreed, or contracted, to form a political society, on the understanding that this society's institutions would not violate their fundamental rights.

On the one hand, ensuring that the powers of the government are limited is central to libertarianism. This is because unfettered or expansive state authority often leads to the abrogation of individual liberty—even if the government thinks that it is acting in your best interests. Government is not all bad, however. Libertarianism recognizes that often individuals need to turn to the power of the government to help remedy rights violations. For example, as philosophy professor Craig Duncan observes:

> The state's power can be used to make . . . private forms of power more accountable, by (among other things) enabling some form of sexual harassment suits; enabling the formation of employee organizations (e.g., unions); and by passing anti-discrimination laws, health and safety laws, minimum-wage laws, and mandatory overtime-pay laws. The abuses of economic power listed above are abuses in virtue of being acts of exploitation, which we can define as taking unfair advantage of a person's vulnerabilities.[26]

While libertarians generally frown upon such government intervention, the point should be made that if such action is taken in response to rights violations, then one might well find libertarian legitimacy in it.

More important to this book, however, is the observation touched upon in the introduction. It may seem paradoxical to describe an expansive use of judicial review—such as Justice Kennedy's—as consistent with a theoretical tradition that prescribes a limited role for government. However, imagine a libertarianism that uses the authority of the state's judges—neutral decision makers—to ensure that governmental actions (by the other branches of government) pass far more stringent tests when they impinge upon liberty. Now imagine that this libertarianism takes an especially dim view of government actions that demean the individual, negatively affect a person's dignity, or diminish personal responsibility. This, it seems, would be a modest libertarianism that is entirely consistent with the tenets of libertarian thought. This holds true even if the means to achieving the goal of greater individual freedom and respect is vigorous use of the authority vested in a governmental institution.[27]

The Harm Principle

As many readers of this book will no doubt have already surmised, part of the subtitle is a reference to one of the most famous works by the nineteenth-century British philosopher John Stuart Mill. Although as a whole Mill's political philosophy is rightly understood as utilitarian rather than libertarian, some of what he wrote in *On Liberty* (first published in 1859) is theoretically attractive to most libertarians. It is here that we find perhaps the most famous (certainly the most widely recognized) formulation of what might be considered a basic principle of libertarianism—limiting actions only if these actions cause *harm* to a rights-bearing person. As we will see, however, this harm principle is controversial and is best used as an explanatory tool for bringing together the basic principles outlined above. According to Mill, the harm principle is "very simple." It states: "the only purpose for which power can be rightfully exercised over any member of a civilized community, against his will, is to prevent harm to others."[28]

Professor Epstein describes the concept of harm as the "gateway to liability." As he says, "in virtually all civilizations, harm operates as the gateway through which disputes enter the legal system."[29] As shown in figure 1.1, in terms of the legal claim that an individual might have when *another individual* causes them harm, this can be explained in the following way. Imagine that there is a person—Alice—who, like every other human being, enjoys a sphere of individual liberty that represents the activities over which she has complete sovereign control. For the reasons outlined above, this sphere is bounded—it is not limitless. Built into the boundaries of Alice's liberty is a gate. Usually this gate remains closed, preserving and protecting her sovereignty. However, imagine that Alice violates the harm principle by causing harm to Belinda, another rights-bearing person. Now we have a situation wherein Belinda, whose *liberty* was harmed by Alice's actions, is lawfully entitled to ask for that gate to be opened—by, for example, a neutral decision maker such as a judge—in order to impose penalties upon Alice for the causing of harm. While this penalty can take many different forms, in essence the punishment begins when the gate is opened, because it is at this point that Alice's individual liberty is now exposed to third-party control. Finally, notice that upon arriving at a decision that Belinda has been harmed, the gate is simply returned to it starting position. When it is closed it is not pushed further inward—which would reduce Alice's liberty—because the ruling in Belinda's favor was simply that it was not within Alice's liberty to harm Belinda.

As shown in figure 1.2, when the party that causes the harm is the government rather than an individual, the same basic situation exists. However, what differs is that this formulation generates several important questions. They arise in both the private and public situations, but take center stage when the actor causing the harm is the government. This time, imagine that another individual, Charlotte, goes to the judge and says that she has been harmed by the government—specifically, an executive agency headed by Doris. Now the laws of the land tell us the public powers of Doris are limited. Therefore, if Charlotte prevails and is found to be the victim of government harm—by Doris—then the harm gateway is closed again without any reduction in the government's powers because what Doris did to Charlotte was not something she had the power to do in the first place.

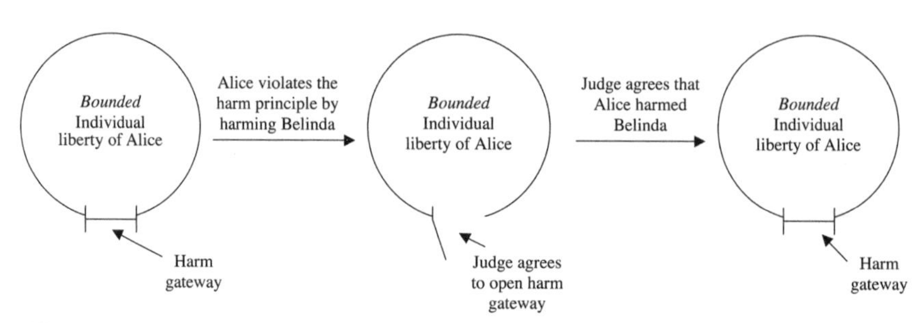

FIGURE 1.1
Demonstration of the harm principle in action when the actor causing the harm is the individual (rather than the government).

The first question that arises is: who is lawfully entitled to open the gate? The answer may initially seem obvious—the individual who has been harmed. However, take another look at figures 1.1 and 1.2. There you will find that only a judge opens the gate. As we will see in chapters 2 through 5, in the world of American constitutional law, an individual only really has a chance of getting the gate open and winning his or her case when certain requirements are met—and if we employ the harm principle then the primary requirement is a demonstration that there has been harm. This raises the following question: what constitutes harm? Within libertarianism there is much disagreement about the proper answer to this question—in large part because there are many different libertarian approaches to studying the relationship between the government and the individual (as discussed below). This disagreement ultimately fails to provide protection for individual liberty. For when a rule that limits the ability of the government to infringe upon an individual's rights is very flexible, it is not much of a rule at all.

This can be further understood by considering what is known as the "police power." This is the government's authority to impose regulations that help to

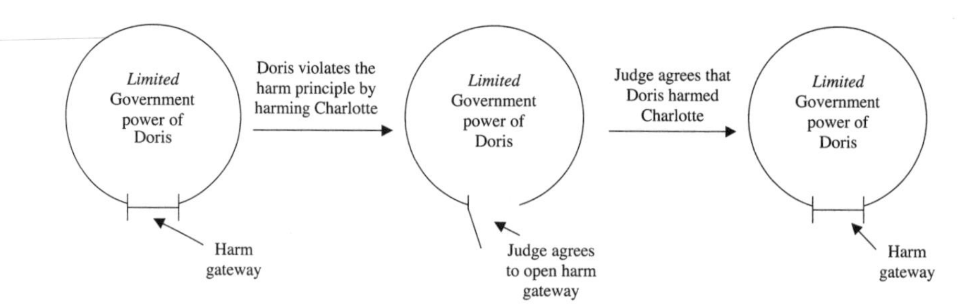

FIGURE 1.2
Demonstration of the harm principle in action when the actor causing the harm is the government (rather than the individual).

preserve and protect the health, safety, and welfare of its citizens. In that respect, *when properly employed* the police power is something that libertarians view as entirely legitimate. After all, the harm principle states that the primary limitation on individual freedom is the requirement that no individual be harmed by another's actions. Therefore, the police power helps to *police* this boundary of liberty. "When properly employed" is, however, a major qualification of this observation, and it is important to note that libertarians are by no means in agreement about what constitutes a valid exercise of the police power. There is little libertarian disagreement with the argument that this power is a necessary way to check the excesses that will inevitably arise because of human interaction. However, when competing interpretations of the scope of the police power are offered controversy abounds. For example, one libertarian might conclude that abortion can be strictly regulated by the state because "the state has to protect the lives of unborn children, which could fall easily . . . within the general health and safety rationales." Conversely, another libertarian could conclude: "the police power of a state is its power to *protect the liberties of the people*," therefore "the proper scope of that power is a function of and limited by those same liberties."[30] And this is a conclusion that places far greater restrictions on the police power, restrictions that would most likely prohibit the abortion regulations advocated above. These differences demonstrate that there is not one single libertarianism. Instead, it is a political philosophy claiming adherents that adopt numerous different approaches.

Deconstructing Libertarianism: Approaches

In the postscript to his influential 1960 book *The Constitution of Liberty*, the libertarian theorist-economist (and future Nobel Laureate) Friedrich A. Hayek wrote of the reasons why he did not consider himself a "conservative." A commitment to liberty, he explained, should not be characterized as either conservative or liberal. It was only accurate and appropriate to describe it as an *individualist* endeavor.[31] If this is the case, might it actually be inappropriate to try and place libertarianism on an ideological spectrum somewhere between conservatism and liberalism? Faced with the profound difficulties associated with reaching comfortable definitions of these two competing positions, one might be tempted to opt for the middle path that libertarianism seems to offer. Although he was critical of libertarianism, writing in *Liberalism at Wits' End* political scientist Stephen Newman acknowledged that it would be such an option because "it offers a critical perspective on the putatively benign paternalism practiced by liberals and the aggressive militarism advocated by conservatives."[32] Similarly, in *Libertarianism: A Primer*, the Cato Institute's David Boaz, one of the leaders of the modern libertarian movement in the United States, argues:

> Conservatives want to be your daddy, telling you what to do and what not to do. Liberals want to be your mommy, feeding you, tucking you in, and wiping your nose. Libertarians want to treat you as an adult.[33]

There is nothing wrong with positing that, on the ideological spectrum, libertarianism is located somewhere between conservative and liberal viewpoints. However, when it is contrasted with political perspectives that are described using such straw-man rhetoric, the result is a very weak definition that actually provides us with little substantive information about what this political theory stands for. Additionally, such characterizations are problematic because of something that is common to libertarianism, conservatism, and liberalism. None of these ideological perspectives can be described as a unified theory evincing only one approach. There are many different types of libertarians, conservatives, and liberals. Therefore, it is more profitable to consider the ideological status of libertarian thought by comparing its own variations rather than setting it up against these other ideological perspectives.

Consequentialist Arguments

Some libertarian theories are underpinned by considerations drawn from broader moral theories—an emphasis might, for example, be placed on the positive *consequences* of limited government. Those who work from this theoretical foundation tend to emphasize the economics of libertarianism; within legal theory they are usually members of what is known as the law and economics school of thought, which argues that markets are inherently efficient tools for allocating goods in society. To be sure, law and economics theorists recognize that market freedom will generate disparities—most obviously, some people will have more material goods than others; however, the consequences of such a system are considered preferable to those that would emerge from a system of extensive government regulation, and these are consequences that a limited government can adequately address. As is demonstrated by the work of Richard Epstein—the most prominent law and economics member of the group of law professors who tackle constitutional theory from a libertarian perspective—this view assigns high value to personal property rights.[34] Yet, it is also important to remember that these libertarians prefer markets to governments because they draw theoretical inspiration from another political theory—utilitarianism—a theory that is far more concerned, than traditional libertarianism, with the *societal* benefits of individual actions (I will have more to say about the libertarianism-utilitarianism relationship below).[35]

It might seem strange to describe the work of some libertarians, who prize individual liberty, as being quite heavily influenced by a political theory constructed around a central belief that the morality of an action is to be judged by asking whether it helps to maximize utility, whether it produces "the greatest good for the greatest number." However, this philosophical relationship becomes easier to understand if we remember, as noted above, that some libertarianism is essentially consequentialist. This is particularly evident in the work of "mutual advantage" libertarians—most notably, the writings of David Gauthier and Jan Narveson. As nicely summarized by Will Kymlicka, social contract theory is employed by mutual advantage libertarians, but not because, as Locke argued, each human being is of equal moral worth with equal, unalienable, natural rights. Rather:

> For them, [moral advantage libertarians] there are no natural duties or self-originating moral claims. . . . The modern world view, they say, rules out the traditional idea that people and actions have any inherent moral status. What people take to be objective moral values are just the subjective preferences of individuals. . . . So there is nothing naturally "right" or "wrong" about one's actions, even if they involve harming others.[36]

How, then, do they account for the limits that individuals choose to place on their actions? In other words, how do mutual advantage libertarians explain that, absent the "self-originating moral claims," individuals still know where to draw the line because of an understanding of moral duty? The answer, says Gauthier, lies in the fact "that reason has a practical role related to *but transcending individual interest*, so that principles of action that prescribe duties overriding advantage may be rationally justified." What he and Narveson conclude is that there "are rules that *everyone* has good reason for wanting everyone to act on, and thus to internalize in himself or herself, and thus to reinforce in the case of everyone."[37]

Pluralist Arguments

This chapter consciously avoids the temptation of describing Justice Kennedy's jurisprudence as derived from, resembling, or representing a reformulation of the work or approach of any particular libertarian theorist. However, here it is important to note that the libertarian elements of his legal philosophy that are described in the pages that follow bear little resemblance to the quasi-utilitarian approaches of either the law and economics libertarians, or those whose theoretical foundations lead to a favoring of mutual advantage or rational choice approaches. There are far greater similarities between the justice's jurisprudence and the school of libertarian legal thought that emphasizes the pluralistic nature of society. As the work of the legal theorist Randy E. Barnett demonstrates, libertarian constitutional theory built on these theoretical foundations emphasizes that because society is composed of diverse individuals we cannot assume that it has one overarching moral identity.[38] In this respect, libertarianism is not considered to be a *moral* theory. This is not to say that a society cannot have a universal moral code that states, in normative terms, the ways in which people *should* act. However, pluralistic libertarianism sees no legal legitimacy in a law that says that the government shall have the power to make you behave in a certain way because such behavior is consistent with the morality of society. A government cannot legitimately prevent you from doing something simply because it determines that what you, the individual, wishes to do is "immoral."

Legal theorists who subscribe to this libertarian approach say that theirs is a *political* theory—individuals may form governments to order their lives, but the authority that a government is given cannot be justified by morality alone, because that government is not free to assume that there is only one moral code by which we should all live.[39] We see this in Justice Kennedy's observation that while the law may be "designed to vindicate a moral and ethical code," vindication is quite different from dictation. And it is the "obligation" of a judge, who interprets that law, "to define the liberty of all [individuals]" rather than "to mandate our own moral code."[40] To understand how this fits into American constitutional democracy, it is useful to think about the "Madisonian dilemma," which is something that then-Judge Kennedy was questioned about during his Supreme Court confirmation hearing. The dilemma is something that results from a tension inherent in America's constitutional democracy. The country's system of government recognizes the importance and the need to place faith in the ability of individuals to engage in self-government; however, it concurrently places limits on the rule of majorities in order to preserve and protect the rights and liberties of individuals. But just what are those limits? Can they be imposed to prevent a majority from enacting a law that imposes morality-based restrictions on a minority?

In his book, *The Tempting of America*, published three years after his failed Supreme Court nomination hearing, Robert Bork devoted a chapter to this dilemma and described it as meaning that "neither majorities nor minorities can be trusted to define the proper spheres of democratic authority and individual liberty."[41] During the hearing, Senator Arlen Specter (R-PA) asked Judge Bork to explain whether the Supreme Court was authorized to play a role in resolving, or at least adjudicating, disputes that grow out of this dilemma, and if so, to identify the nature of that role. Bork began by offering a broad response. "The Supreme Court," he observed, "must, by applying the Constitution, define what things the majority may rule and what things the majority may not rule, where the individual or the minority must be left freedom." When he began to flesh out the details of this statement, he encountered senatorial hostility because it was clear that what he really envisioned was limiting the judicial role and placing, in the hands of legislative majorities, considerable power to determine the boundaries of individual liberty—including permitting morality-based decisions.[42]

By contrast, when members of the Senate Judiciary Committee asked the same questions of then-Judge Kennedy, the new Supreme Court nominee was careful to emphasize that the most important aspect of the Madisonian dilemma is that it is unavoidable. This trait, said Kennedy, should be extolled as one of the dilemma's virtues.[43] As he explained at an earlier point in his testimony, Justice Robert Jackson had been right to criticize those who described the nation's constitutional "choice" as being "between order and liberty." Creating this distinction was nothing more than "an act of desperation" because "we can have both," said Kennedy, because "without ordered liberty, there is no liberty at all."[44] After all, it is relatively easy to arrive at the conclusion that individual liberty, when exercised responsibly, will not lead us down either an anarchical or a lawless path.[45] Liberty and order can peacefully coexist. One might reply, of course, that "when exercised responsibly" is a very large qualification. However, what we would do well to remember is the recognition, made by Hayek, that "liberty and responsibility are inseparable" (an idea that is central to Kennedy's jurisprudence, as we will see below).[46] This is important to keep in mind because it is underpinned by the libertarian argument that a commitment to liberty is a personal, individual commitment.[47] It is not a commitment whose boundaries and ideals may permissibly be determined by a majority's morals. To ascribe such a meaning to personal liberty is actually to demean it by overlooking the pluralistic nature of society. As the political scientist Stephen Macedo has astutely observed, "To recognize the moral force of individuality is to recognize that intelligent, responsible persons can and do pursue widely divergent personal goals and projects."[48]

Remember the Rule of Law

Next, we will proceed to a discussion of the ways in which libertarian theory manifests itself—in a modest form—in Justice Kennedy's jurisprudence. This will be done by dividing his judicial philosophy into three constituent elements that focus on toleration, individual dignity, and personal responsibility. Before doing so, it is worth considering where the concept of the "rule of law" fits into our discussion.

Is it possible to say what the "rule of law" is? After all, it is a concept that throughout history has derived its enduring status and respect in large part from the fact that its diverse adherents have not found it necessary to provide a definition that goes beyond a few key principles.[49] On occasion, in his Supreme Court opinions Kennedy has offered generalized statements of what he believes the rule of law means.[50] In 2006, however, Justice Kennedy devoted his address to the annual meeting of the ABA to explaining why he believes it is important to give a specific definition of the rule of law. He told the audience that recently he sat down and set himself this task and that he had identified three key elements of the concept.[51] The first component of the rule of law, Kennedy said, is the enforcement-acceptance element that requires government to be bound by the law so as to ensure that there is a bond of legitimacy between it and the people in whose "consciousness" the law "moves." This is central to the rule of law: the requirement that "law is binding on the government and all of its officials." As law professor Brian Tamanaha explains in *On the Rule of Law*—a concise, but comprehensive treatment of the concept—it is this broad understanding that historically described ways of thinking about the rule of law. The focus of its meaning, he explains, was on the simple idea that "the sovereign, and the state and its officials, are limited by the law." Unsurprisingly, it is this quality of the rule of law that is emphasized by the majority of legal theorists—regardless of whether they are libertarians.[52]

As Professor Tamanaha further explains, with the ascendancy of liberal thought came a change in focus. Definitions of the rule of law now began to emphasize "formal legality." Libertarians often assume that "personal liberty" is the primary goal of a system of "legally enforceable rights" secured by the rule of law. The strength of this assumption tends to lead to an emphasis on procedural requirements.[53] For example, Professor Hayek intended the rule of law to protect individual liberty, but he rarely considered it necessary to explicitly state this. He instead preferred to let the reader assume the rule of law would achieve this goal. The second element of his definition of the rule of law demonstrates that, by contrast, Justice Kennedy feels it is very important to state this goal. The rule of law, said Kennedy, incorporates the idea that "the law must recognize that in each person there is a core of spirituality, and dignity, and humanity, and within that broad general formulation you can begin to define those rights that are fundamental to our own humanity."[54]

By his own admission, Justice Kennedy was surprised when he wrote the following, which is the third and final element of his definition of the rule of law: "Every person has a right to know what the laws are and to enforce them without fear of retaliation or retribution."[55] It is not clear why Kennedy found this surprising. It is the rare commentator who offers a definition of the rule of law without referencing the importance of knowable laws. After all, the authority with which governments are entrusted is threatened by actions that are made for the people but impose restrictions on those people in ways that are unknown. Why? Under a system of government, the individual would cease to be the primary political unit.

One aspect of debates about the rule of law that Professor Tamanaha explores is the set of competing answers to the question, "Is the rule of law a moral good?"[56] Legal philosophers, such as Joseph Raz and Lon Fuller, can agree about the basic components of the rule of law but reach very different conclusions about the inevitability of, or likelihood that, "just" laws and/or moral goods will be produced by its existence. Raz draws a sharp distinction between the rule of law—defined as requiring that "the government shall be ruled by the law and subject to it"—and a system of "good" laws dedicated to the achievement of morally admirable goals, such as the protection of human rights. He believes that it is possible to identify a set of constituent principles of the rule of law that emphasize procedure over substance and that it is through "observance" of the structurally sound and stable rule of law generated by these principles that such moral values as the "respect [of] human dignity" can be pursued.[57] By contrast, Fuller argues that the rule of law is not morally neutral. He concludes that a legal system cannot be legally legitimate unless it meets the eight "desiderata" that constitute the law's inner morality.[58] These eight requirements are designed to ensure that individuals and institutions bound by the rules of the system know and understood what these rules are. This knowledge is crucial because knowing what our moral duties are does not first require us to search for and/or believe in a "comprehensive" and "aspirational" concept of morality. We do not need to know what "perfect justice" is in order to be able to judge whether actions are just. A rule of law has an inner morality that informs us about our moral duties and therefore makes the generation of just laws more likely.[59]

Tamanaha sees virtues in both of these approaches. On the one hand, Raz is correct that "like a knife, which is neither good nor bad in itself, but can be used to kill a man or to slice vegetables, the morality of law is a function of the uses to which it is put." On the other hand, he says, "A sensible resolution accepts the insights of both sides." This is because "formal legality enhances the dignity of citizens by allowing them to predict and plan, no doubt a moral positive."[60] As the following discussion of the key libertarian elements of his jurisprudence demonstrates, there is little doubt that Justice Kennedy agrees with Fuller's conclusions about the moral worth of a rule of law.

The Universal Element: Toleration

When Justice Kennedy addressed the annual meeting of the American Bar Association in 2003, he made references to something about which he had grown increasingly concerned in recent years. "The problem," he lamented, "is that all too many young people seem to equate the idea of tolerance with the concept of relativism."[61] He found it heartening that the concept of tolerance found a place in the hearts and minds of the nation's youth. At the same time, though, it was disheartening to find that this was not tied, as he believed it should be, to "a belief in universal rights." This is because, as Kennedy has repeatedly stated, the concept of toleration is "derived" from this belief.[62] As we will see in chapter 2, in Justice Kennedy's free speech jurisprudence, this universal element leads him to reject most government attempts to discriminate between different viewpoints, because these attempts represent a fundamental interference with individual sovereignty.

Thinking Globally

In *The Nine*, a best-selling effort to take readers into "the secret world" that is the U.S. Supreme Court, Jeffrey Toobin pays considerable attention to Justice Kennedy's judicial decision making. For example, he alerts readers to the justice's keen interest in human rights law, and he discusses Kennedy's desire to understand more about American constitutionalism by listening to and learning from the views of the international legal community. Toobin argues that this interest, and the justice's penchant for judicial opinions that incorporate such perspectives, became particularly noticeable following the terrorist attacks of September 11, 2001.[63] While there is some truth to this, it would be wrong to emphasize this at the expense of an understanding that Kennedy has always been particularly interested in hearing what foreign lawyers have to say. At the American Bar Association's annual meeting in London in 2000, after Lord Lester of Herne Hill QC took aim at the U.S. Supreme Court, Justice Kennedy took what might be interpreted as being a rather isolationist stance when he defended the institution of which he is a member. Lord Lester argued that the Court's failure to cite European court decisions in its opinions demonstrated that it was "turning its back on the Continent." As part of their colloquy, Kennedy offered the following response: "If you delegate authority to courts so remote and so unknown that the public doesn't know . . . who they are, you risk losing the allegiance of the people." This accounted for the lack of citations, as did the Supreme Court's "uncertainty whether those courts are referring to the same issue the justices are ruling on."[64] This is not an isolationist perspective because its emphasis is on something of *universal* relevance—using the rule of law to protect "those universal moral precepts that all free people share."[65] In an emotion-laden speech at the ABA's annual meeting in San Francisco in August 2007, Kennedy lamented the existence of legal injustices around the world. However, when—as it should—America steps up to the plate and addresses this situation, he said it must not adopt an arrogant, exceptionalist attitude because: "We've learned that we cannot say to some foreign country, 'Here's a red-white-and-blue package, the rule of law.'"[66]

Justice Kennedy has actually made very few references to international law in his judicial opinions. However, there are occasions when his attempts to legitimize his consideration and citation of the opinions (judicial or otherwise) of the international community seem not to be persuasive, thereby generating criticism from his colleagues. In *Roper v. Simmons*, for example, Kennedy's majority opinion relied heavily on international opinion to justify the Court's "determination that the death penalty is disproportionate punishment for offenders under 18." This conclusion, he wrote, "finds confirmation in the stark reality that the United States is the only country in the world that continues to give official sanction to the juvenile death penalty." Kennedy was quick to point out that "this reality does not become controlling, for the task of interpreting the Eighth Amendment remains our responsibility."[67] In this respect, therefore, international views on the death penalty are, as Justice Ginsburg has described them, "ornaments. . . . No foreign decision attracts the deference we give to U.S. precedent. But we do look abroad to *be enlightened by the fine minds existing on other benches.* We read what they write on *norms we share.* If the writing is persuasive, it may help us in formulating or confirming our own view."[68]

Kennedy's justification might, however, be considered unpersuasive because of his subsequent observation that "at least from the time of the Court's decision in *Trop* [*v. Dulles*]," the Court has referred to the laws of other countries and to international authorities as *instructive* for its interpretation of the Eighth Amendment's prohibition of "'cruel and unusual punishments.'"[69] Should not the Court, for "instruction" on the meaning and interpretation of the *United States* Constitution, consult the "judgment of the American people" rather than the views of "like-minded foreigners"?[70] While this might be a legitimate criticism, it fails to see the forest for the trees. In terms of Justice Kennedy's jurisprudence, his use of the word "instructive" is, for want of a better description, instructive. It suggests that international views play an educational role for the justices, and this is not because "like-minded foreigners" know more about the meaning of the Constitution than the "American people," but rather because of the common *human* principles involved. International law plays a "confirmatory role" when there is "congruence between domestic and international values, especially where the international community has reached clear agreement . . . that a particular form of punishment is inconsistent with fundamental human rights."[71] This is completely consistent with all of the major libertarian elements of Justice Kennedy's jurisprudence, as the following passage from *Roper* indicates:

> The document sets forth, and rests upon, innovative principles original to the American experience. . . . These doctrines and guarantees are central to the American experience and remain essential to our present-day self-definition and national identity. Not the least of the reasons we honor the Constitution, then, is because we know it to be our own. It does not lessen our fidelity to the Constitution or our pride in its origins to acknowledge that the express affirmation of certain fundamental rights by other nations and peoples simply underscores the centrality of those same rights within our own heritage of freedom.[72]

To be sure, Kennedy's work is focused on interpreting *American* legal provisions, but he recognizes that enshrined in these *provisions*, even if they are specifically articulated in an *American* legal text, are fundamental *principles* that are representative of universal human values and rights. Values and rights which can only be freely enjoyed and exercised when a government is not permitted to step in and exhibit intolerance for certain perspectives and viewpoints that do not violate the rights of others and do not cause harm.

The Dialogue on Freedom[73]

In a 2005 interview, Kennedy responded to a question about second chances in life by saying that he "would like to begin teaching more students. I've taught many, many students, I wish that I could have taught more. I wish I could find a way to reach more young people."[74] In the aftermath of the terrorist attacks of September 11, 2001, this is exactly what Kennedy set out to do when he created the Dialogue on Freedom, a program that he very much hoped would also reduce the aforementioned moral relativism that he believed to be a dangerous influence on the next generation of Americans. A few commentators have taken notice of this civic educational initiative, but they have not argued that it can inform our understanding of Kennedy's jurisprudence.[75] This is unfortunate, because as one journalist has observed, the Dialogue gives us an "unusual tour of a Supreme Court justice's mind."[76] As Judge Alex Kozinski, Kennedy's close friend and former clerk, has remarked, "There are those who might say the 'Dialogue' is corny or hokey, but it's really him."[77] At the time, the Dialogue was seen by some as a politically driven effort by Kennedy to curry favor with the Bush administration in case a vacancy for chief justice should open up; after all, it did allow Kennedy to spend "quality time" with First Lady Laura Bush.[78] The program has also been held up as an extrajudicial example of the justice's efforts to impose his own "arrogant" moral agenda on the country.[79] These interpretations of the Dialogue on Freedom overlook the fact that the program reflects the universal element of the justice's judicial thought, which contains principles that began to inform his decision making much earlier than September 11, 2001.

The Dialogue on Freedom program, which is administered by the American Bar Association, is designed to encourage student discussion of civic participation and democratic values. Its goal is, says Kennedy, "to foster among our nation's youth the identification and understanding of fundamental American values and those universal moral precepts that all free people share." Collaboration with the ABA reflects the justice's belief that "the bar ought to step up from time to time and say there are certain values that unite us."[80] As Justice Kennedy has said:

> I want lawyers to be once again advocates for the rule of law. And this involves a re-assessment by lawyers of very fundamental principles of democracy and of our culture and of our history, freedom. So I think of this [Dialogue on Freedom] in part as a way to re-energize the bar so that the bar can reaffirm and rededicate itself to these first principles.[81]

Dialogues have been established at schools across the nation, with students and prominent judges and politicians engaging in the discussions envisioned by Kennedy.[82] The high school and college students who participate in this program are asked to think about how they would address the disparities between their American political and cultural beliefs and those held by three individuals who live in a very different society. The program has a uniting rather than dividing goal. It seeks to celebrate and promote an understanding of the "rights and responsibilities that are universal," rather than to generate "a series of little debates" from which would emerge a relativistic attitude to cultural and political values.[83] This can be discerned not only from newspaper reports and ABA literature, but also from viewing the nationally televised Dialogues in which Justice Kennedy has participated.

The Dialogue is based around a hypothetical that asks the program's participants to assume that the following has occurred. Imagine that "on a trip to a popular tourist destination . . . your plane has engine trouble. You make an unscheduled landing in Quest and find that you must remain there for three days while the repairs are completed." Quest is a country of very high unemployment; the few people who do work are paid very low wages; and a government dominated by corruption seldom respects the written constitution. The most charismatic speaker in Quest is Drummer. He:

> preaches hatred of the United States and the necessity to destroy American power and influence. There is a religious component to Drummer's doctrine, and he proclaims that the United States is evil. The government often arrests its opponents, but it is reluctant to detain Drummer or be too hard on him because of his popularity, particularly among the poor.

You encounter two citizens of Quest—W and M; they both exhibit hostility toward Western and, in particular, American culture and values. W blames the "decadence" of this culture for the degradation of her country. She would be willing to put her trust in an authoritarian and nondemocratic regime that subjugates women, "resists American culture," and is led by someone like Drummer. M is a teenager who receives ten dollars a week for hard labor at the "bottom of a pit." He "needs the money to help support his family. He has few prospects for a different or better job. For all M knows, he might spend most of his life doing this kind of work at a low wage." How would you respond to W's political beliefs and her support for opposition to American culture? What is your answer when, during a discussion of the terrorist attacks of September 11, 2001, M says: "Why should I care what happens in New York or Washington?" When you leave Quest you have the opportunity to give W and M three books or movies "that best capture what America means to you." Which works would you choose?[84]

Kennedy was present at the inaugural Dialogue on Freedom, at the School Without Walls in Washington, D.C., in January 2002. His remarks prompted some of the student participants to complain that they felt the program was more a monologue of Kennedy's views than a true dialogue. This tells us a great deal about the justice.[85] One might interpret the students' comments as evidence that the Dialogue was born out of a righteous indignation at the ignorant and apathetic masses' reaction to the terrorist attacks. Similarly, the outside observer might be tempted (not unreasonably) to view Kennedy's dialogical initiative as somewhat pompous.[86] However, for the purpose of understanding the importance to his jurisprudence of the libertarian value of tolerance, such external observations misrepresent the justice's motivations for creating the program. His numerous oral interjections at the first Dialogue were evidence of his libertarian belief that the delicate balance between governments and individuals can only be sustained through a continuing awareness of, and commitment to, the rights that the former may not force the latter to surrender—in other words, the structure and scope of individual liberty.

To be sure, Justice Kennedy's comment at the first Dialogue—that "governments are most dangerous when they try to tell people what to think"—certainly prompts one to consider whether here Kennedy is betraying his libertarianism.[87] The Constitution protects individual freedom and autonomy and has an intellectual core of limited government. Therefore, one might legitimately wonder how a justice of the United States Supreme Court, a federal government employee, can take the normative position that governments should not be in the business of "try[ing] to tell people what to think." After all, he took this position while at the same time vigorously using the power of judicial review to defend the concept of tolerating diverse views. An initial reading of the Kennedy quotation might raise these questions and concerns. However, the universal element of his jurisprudence tells us that what Kennedy meant was that government will inevitably fail in its attempts to direct the thought (and, as we will see in chapter 2, speech) processes of its citizens. In Kennedy's opinion, government toleration of diverse views is essential, because otherwise a government will be free to strip individuals—the primary political units in society—of one of the most important elements of their existence—expressive freedom. A government that tolerates the (often critical) views of a diverse population will be one that does not act as though its citizens are "instruments or resources." Rather, it regards them as "persons having individual rights with the dignity this constitutes."[88]

The Humane Element: Individual Dignity

In July 1986, then-Judge Kennedy addressed the Canadian Institute for Advanced Legal Studies at Stanford University. He spoke at length about unenumerated rights and the proper role of the judiciary in interpreting such rights. Of all the speeches he gave prior to his Supreme Court nomination, this one attracted the greatest attention of the members of the Senate Judiciary Committee during his confirmation hearings in December 1987. Senator Patrick Leahy (D-VT) was just one of several senators who took a particularly active role in questioning Kennedy about the content of the speech. For example, Leahy wanted to know what the judge meant when he said that the Court's authority to hold—as it had done in several landmark cases—that certain unenumerated rights are "substantive, judicially enforceable right[s] under the Constitution" was authority that could not be derived solely from public acceptance of the Court's conclusions. "What," asked Leahy, "do you look for beyond just the feeling that our people accept these rights to make them such fundamental rights that they are judicially enforceable?"[89] To this inquiry, Kennedy offered the following response:

> Well, there is a whole list of things, and one problem with the list is that it may not sound exhaustive enough. But, essentially, we look to the concepts of individuality and liberty and dignity that those who drafted the Constitution understood. We see what the hurt and the injury is to the particular claimant who is asserting the right. We see whether or not the right has been accepted as part of the rights of a free people in the historical interpretation of our own Constitution and the intentions of the framers.[90]

This was, Kennedy observed, "hardly an exhaustive list." And it was important to remember that it was necessary to "balance that [list] against the rights asserted by the State, of which there are many."[91] How that drawing of liberty's boundaries takes place within Justice Kennedy's jurisprudence is, to a large extent, determined by the responsible element discussed below.

When Senator Gordon Humphrey (R-NH) later asked questions designed to press Kennedy further on this view of unenumerated rights—in particular the "standards" he believed were "available to a judge, a Justice in this case"[92] who should not betray the substance of the Constitution—the nominee again pointed to "the essentials of the right to human dignity, the injury to the person, the harm to the person, the anguish to the person, the inability of the person to manifest his or her own personality, the inability of a person to obtain his or her own self-fulfillment, the inability of a person to reach his or her own potential."[93]

The importance of protecting human dignity—a goal that he believes can and must be realized by the Constitution—is something about which Justice Kennedy cares deeply. For, as he asked the audience at a 2005 ABA symposium to remember, it is essential that "the law . . . recognize" and respect that "in each person there is a core of spirituality, and dignity" within which reside "those rights that are fundamental to our own humanity."[94] This emphasis on dignity constitutes the humane element of Kennedy's jurisprudence and can be clearly seen in his Supreme Court opinions—particularly, as we will see in chapters 3 and 4, those which address the Fourteenth Amendment's requirement that no state shall "deny to any person within its jurisdiction the equal protection of the laws."

Justice Kennedy's description of the centrality to an individual's humanity (and that individual's personal sovereignty) of the concept of dignity is something with which few people will disagree. His *use* of it in his judicial decision making generates much controversy, but the idea of human dignity is, in and of itself, uncontroversial. The importance of protecting human dignity is something upon which most liberals—however one defines that word—agree. Indeed, in a speech accepting the Democratic Party's presidential nomination in 1960, John F. Kennedy placed human dignity at the center of his description of what it meant to be a liberal:

> I believe in human dignity as the source of national purpose, in human liberty as the source of national action, and the human heart as the source of national compassion, and in the human mind as the source of our invention and our ideas. It is, I believe, this faith in our fellow citizens as individuals and as people that lies at the heart of the liberal faith, for liberalism is not so much a party creed or a set of fixed platform promises as it is an attitude of mind and heart, a faith in man's ability through the experiences of his reason and judgment to increase for himself and his fellow men the amount of Justice and freedom and brotherhood which all human life deserves.[95]

Therefore, it is important to understand why this aspect of the justice's jurisprudence can accurately be described as the *humane* element. After all, one might argue that this label suggests other nonlibertarian understandings of individual dignity are "inhumane."[96] When defining "humane," the dictionary emphasizes "benevolence" and "compassion."[97] It would be wrong to portray those who do not subscribe to Kennedy's interpretation of constitutionally protected human dignity as merciless and uncharitable. Rather, as chapters 3 and 4 will show, what makes Kennedy's conception of dignity "humane" is its emphasis on enabling people to be benevolent and compassionate individuals by enabling them to pursue their own constitutional visions.

"The Right to Search for Dignity"[98]

This humane element of Justice Kennedy's jurisprudence is in tension with government policies that seek to categorize individuals, in the name of equality, as members of a group (rather than leaving them alone, as individuals). This tension remains in place regardless of whether the government seeks to enact these policies to help or hinder (in its view) personal liberty. It is a libertarian approach that seeks to minimize the ability of the government to affect the equal status of persons (positively or negatively) by treating them in a particular way because they "belong" to a specific class of individuals. In other words, the belief that Kennedy expressed in *Metro Broadcasting v. FCC* (discussed in chapter 4)—that it is "demeaning" to assume that "certain 'minority views'" are inevitably held by those individuals who happen to possess a certain "minority characteristic"—is just as applicable to cases involving homosexuals or women as it is to racial minorities, with whom that case was concerned.[99]

In his 2003 speech to the annual meeting of the ABA, Justice Kennedy explained that "liberty means the right to search for dignity."[100] This indicates that Kennedy's definition of liberty is an active one. The mere equating of liberty with dignity would permit individual passivity, something that is inconsistent with the roles Kennedy believes that the American constitutional democracy assigns to its citizens. Democracy requires an active citizenry. "Embedded in democracy," says Kennedy, "is the idea of progress"; yet, it does not follow that a democracy will automatically generate progress; "it requires a sustained exercise of political will."[101] Phrased another way, the preservation and protection of dignified individual liberty is not something that persons can simply assume they have. As Professor Nozick observed in his famous libertarian work *Anarchy, State, and Utopia* (1974), requiring others—including the government—to "treat . . . us with respect by respecting our rights" helps us "to choose our life and to realize our ends and our conception of ourselves, insofar as we can, aided by the voluntary cooperation of other individuals possessing the same dignity."[102] Yet, in Kennedy's mind, our individual dignity is not going to be terribly secure unless we, ourselves, work at it by understanding what it is and what we can do with it. This is because "you don't take a DNA test to see if you believe in freedom. . . . You cannot preserve what you don't understand, you cannot defend what you do not know." And, while some of the knowledge that is required to engage in this exercise in preservation is "taught," the individual on his or her own learns a large part of it. But, this can only happen if the individual is afforded the "liberty [that] means the right to search for dignity."[103] The humane element of Justice Kennedy's jurisprudence argues that this cannot happen when the government is free to restrict persons' behavior based on their possession of certain immutable characteristics. This is because such classifications place a fundamental obstacle in the path of individuals who, by virtue of being human beings, have human dignity, dignity that they should have the liberty to search for in their own particular way (within the boundaries of that liberty).[104]

The humane element of Justice Kennedy's judicial decision making has gained him a lot of attention. It often engenders criticism because the justice has not been shy about using his Court opinions as vehicles for expressing his firm conviction that "broad provisions to secure individual freedom and preserve human dignity" can actually be found in the Constitution.[105] The criticism comes from the fact that the word "dignity" *cannot* actually be found in the Constitution. We might praise Justice Kennedy for affording individual liberty significant protection by concluding, as did Justice Brennan, that, as a central component of an individual's humanity, dignity is something that is *automatically* protected by the Constitution, even if that word is absent from the text (in this respect, "dignity" should be compared to "privacy" which, as chapter 5 will show, is in Kennedy's opinion a *constituent value* of the *right to liberty*). However, this raises questions about whether the humane element of Kennedy's jurisprudence is truly libertarian. Does the absence of easily definable limits make it difficult to reconcile with a commitment to limited government? For an understanding as to why the answer to this inquiry is "no," we need to examine the third and final element of the justice's judicial philosophy—the responsible element.

The Responsible Element: Personal Responsibility

In 1981, when he gave the commencement address at McGeorge Law School, Justice Kennedy told the audience of new graduates that they were about to enter a profession whose members "have the principal responsibility for defending freedom and the rule of law in our society."[106] The humane and universal elements of his jurisprudence remind us, however, that he believes that the freedom he refers to is neither boundless nor really free. In order to aid in the delineation of freedom's boundaries, some libertarians, such as Jan Narveson, reach the following conclusion:

> It is often said that rights entail responsibilities, but that is an indirect point. So far as a right is a right, and no more, it does not entail responsibilities, but rather, freedom on the part of the right-holder and responsibilities and duties on the part of other people. It is their rights that, in turn, impose duties and responsibilities on the rightholder himself or herself.[107]

Justice Kennedy's modestly libertarian jurisprudence indicates that he disagrees with a separation of rights and responsibilities. Kennedy's is, as chapter 5 demonstrates, a controversial approach, the consequences of which do not sit well with many libertarians. Nevertheless, it can be argued that it is actually an approach that has at its center a commitment to a principle that is consistent with libertarianism—the concept of personal responsibility. Kennedy uses this concept to place what are, in his mind, definable and legitimate limits on his interpretation of liberty. He does this by attempting to explain to Americans that their individual freedom to make decisions about their lives can only peacefully coexist with social order if that liberty is exercised in a consciously responsible manner. Sometimes this might require the government to step in and restrain our behavior because it considers it irresponsible. To be sure, this could be the result of a government decision that seemingly flies in the face of individual sovereignty. That, Kennedy is sometimes apt to conclude, has to be the price of freedom, because rights do, in his mind, entail responsibilities.

Marking the "Outer Limits" of Liberty

In a speech to the Ninth Circuit Judicial Conference three months before he was nominated to the Supreme Court, Kennedy said that he thought of American constitutional law as consisting of positive (written) law—the U.S. Constitution—*and* a small "c" unwritten constitution. The latter, he said, acts as "an additional restraint" on the actions of governments. "It's not a source of authority to interpret," but, rather, it "consists of our ethical culture, our shared beliefs, our common vision, and in this country, the unwritten constitution counsels the morality of restraint, and it applies to each branch of the government."[108] Kennedy regularly takes opportunities to discuss this subject. He elaborated upon it in 2005 during a session of his course on Fundamental Rights in Europe and the United States (which he teaches every year as part of the McGeorge Law School's summer program in Salzburg, Austria). Kennedy explained to his students that the U.S. Constitution could be neither understood nor appreciated without simultaneous consideration of the "constitution with a small 'c,' the sum total of customs and mores of the community." Why? "The closer the big 'C,' and the small 'c,'" he said, "the better off you are as a society."[109]

While Kennedy considers this absolutely vital to keep in mind if one wishes to appreciate the true nature of American constitutionalism (and constitutional law), he also concedes that it is an inherently controversial subject because it suggests that constitutional interpretation means much more than simply reading and analyzing the text of the formal legal document that is the nation's "supreme law."[110] References to the small "c" constitution bring to mind the concept of "unenumerated constitutional rights under the United States Constitution." As Kennedy observed in a 1986 speech, this is a subject irreparably tangled up with the thorny "question [as to] whether the judiciary has the authority to announce them."[111] The responsible element of his jurisprudence—which emphasizes personal responsibility—is an important part of Kennedy's judicial effort to find a way to address this question by giving legitimacy (in a libertarian manner) to the expansive understanding of liberty of which the concept of unenumerated constitutional rights is a part.

At his Supreme Court confirmation hearings, numerous senators pressed Kennedy to clarify and elaborate upon his understanding of the unwritten constitution. Did it include legally enforceable "rights"? "Yes," Kennedy immediately replied. What might these rights be? As I noted above, Kennedy pointed to "a whole list of things"—which included "the concepts of individuality and liberty and dignity that those who drafted the Constitution understood." He also observed, however, that there was little reason to think that it would be either possible or be a worthwhile exercise to try to create a definitive "list."[112] This, as the senators recognized, brought to mind the wording of the Ninth Amendment, which, as a reminder, reads: "The enumeration in the Constitution, of certain rights, shall not be construed to deny or disparage others retained by the people." One of the most controversial statements made by Judge Robert Bork, during his failed nomination hearing that immediately preceded Judge Kennedy's, came in response to questioning about the meaning of this provision of the Bill of Rights. Stating that its meaning and scope were a mystery to him, Bork famously described the amendment as obscured—by what, it was not clear—but obscured it was. Said Bork:

> I do not think you can use the Ninth Amendment unless you know something of what it means. For example, if you had an amendment that says "Congress shall make no" and then there is an ink blot and you cannot read the rest of it and that is the only copy you have, I do not think the court can make up what might be under the ink blot if you cannot read it.[113]

Although at the time this was the prevalent interpretation of the amendment—an inaccurate understanding since corrected by several scholars[114]—it was one that then-Judge Kennedy disagreed with when he testified at his Supreme Court nomination hearing three months later. He explained that, in his opinion, James Madison, the amendment's author, "wanted to make it clear that the first eight amendments were not an exhaustive catalogue of all human rights."[115] The Ninth Amendment, therefore, acted as an additional limit against government activity and an additional protection of individual liberty.

It has been suggested that Justice Kennedy deserves praise for integrating both the spirit and the original meaning of the words of the Ninth Amendment into his jurisprudence. The most prominent example of this usage came in *Planned Parenthood v. Casey* (a 1992 abortion decision which I discuss in detail in chapter 5), in which Kennedy wrote: "Neither the Bill of Rights nor the specific practices of States at the time of the adoption of the Fourteenth Amendment marks the outer limits of the substantive sphere of liberty which the Fourteenth Amendment protects. See U.S. Const., Amdt. 9."[116] To be sure, libertarians are right to find much to like in the justice's invocation of this particular constitutional addition. After all, it supports an expansive and liberating understanding of individual autonomy—against which Justice Scalia railed in his *Casey* dissent. Scalia was clearly offended by his colleague's belief that the amendment was a "charter for action"—"a literally boundless source of additional, unnamed, unhinted-at 'rights,' definable and enforceable by us, through 'reasoned judgment.'" This conclusion, argued Scalia, flew in the face of two centuries of Court rulings and seemed to give justification to an unbridled exercise of judicial power.[117] However, those seeking to understand his jurisprudence would do well to remember that Justice Kennedy is not a fan of "boundless" liberty. Instead, he favors individual liberty, responsibly exercised.

In his 1986 Stanford lecture, Kennedy extolled the virtues of constitutional provisions, such as the Ninth Amendment, whose virtues included their "flexible language." At the same time, however, he cautioned against courts employing them to such an extent that the political branches are able to avoid the "responsibility" of "[determining] the attributes of a just society."[118] Why is this so? The answer, says Kennedy, is that the liberty embraced by such provisions is not boundless. There are "certain rights and responsibilities that are universal,"[119] and unless we afford *both* responsibility and liberty adequate respect, neither of them will be secure, and the dignity that liberty gives us the right to search for will indeed be threatened.

The "Utopian" Objection

Before proceeding in the next four chapters to analyze the ways in which these three libertarian elements of Justice Kennedy's jurisprudence affect the opinions he writes in cases addressing several areas of constitutional law, we need briefly to address one more thing. Can it be credibly argued that *any* attempt to marry American constitutional theory and the principles of libertarianism is completely inconsistent with the Constitution? This inquiry must be confronted and considered in advance of this book's analysis that focuses on the work of only one particular member of the Supreme Court.

Strong Libertarianism

The type of libertarian political society that Professor Nozick once envisioned was one in which there was an extremely limited role for government and extensive rights protections for individuals. "Individuals have rights," wrote Nozick, "and there are things no person or group may do to them (without violating their rights). So strong and far-reaching are these rights that they raise the question of what, *if anything*, the state and its officials may do."[120] Nozick never argued that his normative libertarian philosophy, with its emphasis on how governments should be limited, was an empirical description of the government structure that was actually put in place by the U.S. Constitution. It is clear that neither Nozick nor any other libertarian could make an argument that the United States Constitution is such a "strong libertarian" document that the text cannot accommodate this type of interpretation.[121] However, at the center of one of the challenges most frequently leveled at libertarian constitutional theory is the contention that this is precisely the sort of reading of the Constitution in which it engages—a reading often described as utopian.

It is clear that the document really does evince an ideological commitment to libertarian principles of limited government and the reciprocal protection of individual liberty. The text demonstrates that it is founded on an ideology—a "set of [consistent] idea-elements"[122]—that reflects the impulse to rein in government power. It builds on the American Declaration of Independence and incorporates John Locke's quintessentially classical liberal arguments about the reasons why rational human beings come together to form a political society. Attempts to apply the principles of libertarian political theory to constitutional interpretation start to run into problems when talk turns from the Constitution in general to provisions—such as the Takings Clause in the Fifth Amendment—that permit the government to use its power in ways that are anathema to libertarianism. The Takings Clause gives the government the power of eminent domain—the power to appropriate private property. The government is limited to taking property for public use and is required to ensure that property owners receive just compensation for the taking. However, it does permit the taking of private property, which is definitely inconsistent with libertarian theory.[123] Such provisions are, though, few and far between. The argument that the Constitution is not strongly libertarian certainly does not mean that it is not modestly libertarian.

Utopian Ideology

It is similarly unhelpful to condemn legal libertarianism by focusing one's critical attention on those arguments situated at the radical fringes of the philosophy, or those composed of proposals perceived as seeking to "turn back the clock" and to bring unwanted and revolutionary disruption to modern American constitutional law. Just like the emphasis on strong libertarianism, this analytical approach results in libertarianism being mischaracterized as "suggest[ing] idealistic visions of social and political reconstruction often lacking in realism."[124] Sometimes these interpretations are the result of libertarians' political desires to put their ideas into practice without being sufficiently sensitive to the ease with which it is possible to mischaracterize calls for reducing the size of government.[125] Other times they are simply reflective of the hostile, liberal reaction to the most prevalent component of the last few decades' calls for a more libertarian constitutional law. This component is focused on the economic and property rights arguments of libertarianism.[126]

In 1938, Justice Harlan Stone wrote the Court's opinion in *United States v. Carolene Products*, a decision upholding the Filled Milk Act of 1923—which prohibited the manufacture and/or shipment of filled condensed milk, a cheaper condensed milk that contained vegetable oil, a substitute for the natural milk butter fat. Carolene Products, the manufacturer of Milnut, a filled milk product, argued that the law's blanket ban on the shipping of this product exceeded Congress's power to regulate commerce. The decision was then, and today remains significant because of its rejection of this argument that the Constitution's Commerce Clause only permits the federal government to regulate *interstate* commercial activities—those that, as the language of the clause states, take place "with foreign Nations, and among the several States, and with the Indian Tribes." *Carolene Products* was an indication that the Court had begun to adopt an attitude far more permissive of federal government regulation of the nation's economy than that which it had held during the past decades.[127]

In this respect, it is inevitable that libertarians frown upon the decision. However, for most of its history the attention that Stone's opinion has received has primarily been directed at its fourth footnote, in which Stone suggests that the Court adopt a stricter level of judicial review for cases involving alleged infringements on noneconomic, as opposed to economic, rights.[128] This has since evolved into a judicial double standard whereby the Court usually defers to the legislature when a statute deals with economic liberty. By contrast, when a law is seen as affecting a noneconomic right the government usually has to defend its actions by demonstrating that they address a "compelling governmental interest." Admittedly, some of the libertarians who object to this double standard do champion the importance of economic liberty by offering radical readings of the Constitution. However, when doing so they often admit that they are—to use Professor Epstein's words—"'way off the scale' of modern constitutional doctrine."[129] It is entirely possible to engage in libertarian criticism of the legacy of *Carolene Products* without adopting a "radical" or "utopian" approach. For example, Professor Barnett rejects the post-Footnote Four "presumption of constitutionality" that is applied in economic rights cases by focusing on the broad rights protections afforded by the Ninth Amendment. Barnett finds that the Amendment's "plain and original meanings . . . require the strict construction of any power that restricts the exercise of individual liberty, *whether that liberty is enumerated or unenumerated*."[130] This libertarian interpretation of the Constitution simply says that protection of liberty should not be discriminated against when the rights at stake are economic.

This book does not suggest that Justice Kennedy has made modestly libertarian jurisprudential decisions that consciously result in individual liberty being protected from government intrusion regardless of whether that liberty is concerned with the noneconomic or economic spheres of a person's life. However, it has been important briefly to consider some of these utopians objections to libertarian constitutional theory in order to underline a point of direct relevance to the analysis that will appear in the following chapters. As we proceed, it is essential to remember that there are multiple libertarianisms. Therefore, while readers are welcome (and, in the spirit of enlightened dialogue, are encouraged) to criticize my conclusion that some areas of Justice Kennedy's judicial philosophy are imbued with elements of modest libertarianism, they would do well not to repeat the errors of the past. These are the errors that were committed when one formulation (often the most radical) of libertarianism was used to condemn a different (and less radical) version of this particular political philosophy.

Conclusion

As we have already seen, Justice Kennedy cannot be described as a member of the Supreme Court reluctant to exercise the power of judicial review. Libertarianism prescribes a limited role for government; therefore, it may seem paradoxical to describe Kennedy's expansive use of judicial review as consistent with this theoretical tradition. In this respect, law professor Mark Tushnet was undoubtedly right when he made the following observation:

> Kennedy . . . understood, probably because of his work as a lobbyist, that the libertarian yearning for a *sharply* reduced government was entirely utopian. Big government was here to stay, and Kennedy knew it. [And] his years of teaching constitutional law taught him about the limits on the role of judges. The limits were practical; if judges went too far, the political system would slap them down. The limits were rooted in democratic theory as well; a sensible people ought to be allowed to make their own decisions without the close supervision of judges enforcing the Constitution.[131]

However, it would be misleading to say that there is a seemingly irreconcilable tension between libertarian "impulses" and modern American government, a tension that made it "impossible" for Kennedy to form "a coherent jurisprudence" that harmoniously married the two. Rather than resorting to "rhetoric alone," as Tushnet contends has been the justice's solution, what Kennedy's jurisprudence demonstrates is something fundamentally important about libertarian constitutional theory—something that often gets overlooked in debates about its merits.[132] This is the fact that while libertarians believe in limited government, within constitutional theory the mainstream libertarian view does not prescribe the "sharply reduced government" of which Tushnet wrote. Instead, its adherents are quite willing to embrace a relatively strong use of the power of judicial review—a governmental power. It is a modest type of this "traditional" libertarianism that is infused into Kennedy's jurisprudence.

2

"Speech is the Beginning of Thought"

> The First Amendment is often inconvenient. But that is beside the point. Inconvenience does not absolve the government of its obligation to tolerate speech.[1]
>
> —Justice Kennedy, *International Society for Krishna Consciousness v. Lee*

DURING THEN-JUDGE KENNEDY'S SUPREME COURT NOMINATION HEARING, Senator Dennis DeConcini (D-AZ) asked several questions about one particular standard of judicial review frequently used by the justices. This standard—strict scrutiny—is something about which we will hear much more in chapters 3 and 4. This is because it plays a central role in the Court's equal protection jurisprudence. In this respect, it is unsurprising that Senator DeConcini referred to it when inquiring about Kennedy's views on sex- and race-based discrimination. Yet, much of Kennedy's response did not focus on the Fourteenth Amendment's guarantee that "no State shall . . . deny to any person within its jurisdiction the equal protection of the laws." Instead, the nominee talked about the First Amendment. Specifically, he directed the Senator's attention to that amendment's expressive freedom clause—which reads: "Congress shall make no law . . . abridging the freedom of speech." Kennedy said that "one of the essential features" of this was the declaration "that we cannot engage in censorship." This gave "the first amendment . . . its own foundation." Therefore, Kennedy found "it . . . sometimes puzzling" that the Court used "equal protection analysis in . . . cases" involving free speech. Why, he wanted to know, did the justices really think it necessary to draw on tests derived from other constitutional provisions?[2]

These views expressed by Kennedy have played an important role in his decision making in free speech cases. He has not gone so far as to subscribe to Justice Hugo Black's absolutist reading of "no law" as meaning "no law."[3] However, Kennedy has made it obvious that he is unwilling to tolerate any decision that provides the government with an opportunity to engage in content-based restriction of speech—unless the expression falls into a very small number of "historic and traditional categories long familiar to the bar."[4] And he has sought to move the Court away from its traditional usage of strict judicial scrutiny for content-based laws, the test which asks whether the regulation (1) furthers a compelling government interest, (2) is narrowly tailored to meet that interest, and (3) is the least restrictive means of achieving the government's goal. As Kennedy noted at his nomination hearing, this is a test that does not have its jurisprudential roots in First Amendment law.

To be sure, some of Kennedy's early Supreme Court opinions do suggest that what is now a clear commitment to limiting government regulation of expression needed time to evolve during his first few years on the Court.[5] Indeed, it is possible that it took time for Kennedy to reach a certain level of comfort with the power of the institution of which he was now a part.[6] However, as we will see below, it would be wrong to say that Kennedy has been jurisprudentially inconsistent. Rather, it is better to understand that even in this area of the law—where his libertarianism is well defined—Justice Kennedy has encountered cases that have led him to agonize over his opinions. This will become particularly clear when we examine his writings in cases involving speech in what the law designates as "public forums." In this process of agonizing, however, Kennedy has never strayed far from the principle that if the Constitution's free speech provision protects anything, it protects the right of the individual to be free to choose to say what he or she wishes. This is important because, as Kennedy has said, speech is the "beginning of thought." In speech cases, the tie most definitely goes to freedom.[7]

The Obvious Libertarianism

On its own, the argument that Justice Kennedy takes a libertarian approach to freedom of expression is neither new nor remarkably insightful. Despite the "limitations of labeling," this is an area of Kennedy's decision making about which there is a relatively large amount of academic agreement regarding the applicability of the label "libertarian."[8] Indeed, one need only look at the data for confirmation of Kennedy's ideological tendencies in First Amendment cases. Data about the freedom of speech voting patterns of the Rehnquist Court justices leave us with little doubt about two things. First, as political scientists Lee

Epstein and Jeffrey Segal accurately observe, "Unadulterated support for freedom of expression is hardly the lodestar of liberalism assumed by political scientists." This was particularly true for the divided Rehnquist Court. The members of that Court reached free speech decisions, the voting patterns in which belied traditional "conservative" and "liberal" labels. Additionally, far more than their predecessors they heard and resolved "value-conflict" cases—involving expressive freedom and other constitutional values—in favor of the litigants who brought the free speech challenges.[9] Second, as figure 2.1 shows, Justice Kennedy, who is generally considered a conservative justice, was the most libertarian member of that Court in free speech cases. He voted against the government in almost three-quarters of those cases. Justices Clarence Thomas and David Souter also had a libertarian bent to their free speech jurisprudence, but statistically they trailed Kennedy by a long way. In speech cases they voted to protect the individual's rights about 60 percent of the time. At the other end of the spectrum were Chief Justice Rehnquist and Justice Stephen Breyer, who supported the individual's position in only 40 percent of cases. The First Amendment created some very strange jurisprudential bedfellows.

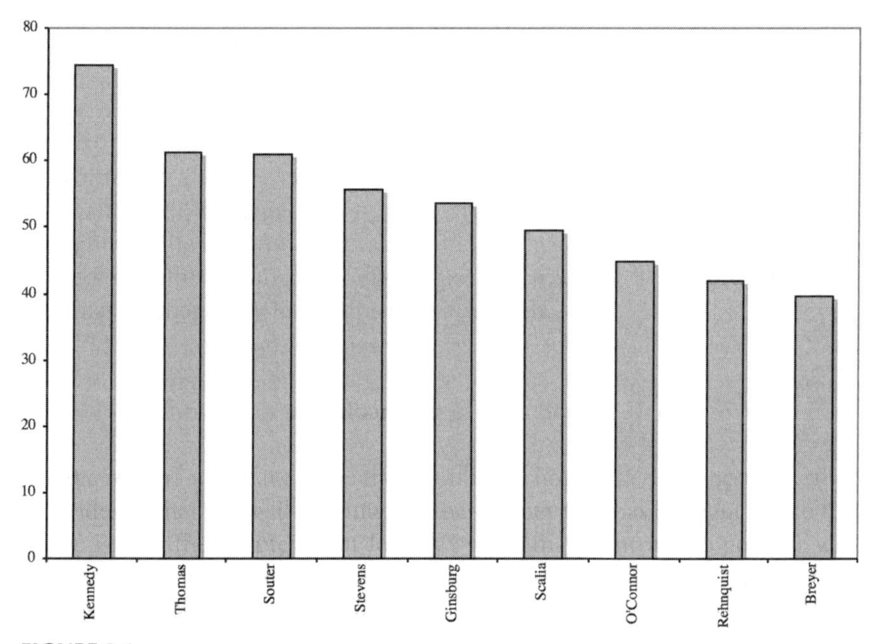

FIGURE 2.1
Percentage of cases in which members of the Rehnquist Court took the speech-protective position in First Amendment cases (1994–2002 terms).

Data taken from Eugene Volokh, "How the Justices Voted in Free Speech Cases, 1994–2002," www.law.ucla.edu/volokh/howvoted.htm (7 June 2006). This is an updated version of Eugene Volokh, "How the Justices Voted in Free Speech Cases, 1994-2000," *UCLA Law Review* 48 (2001).

Constitutional law professor Suzanna Sherry concludes that the free speech divisions on the Rehnquist Court, divisions that have had a tendency to generate multitudinous, fractured opinions, are evidence that this Court's justices took a pragmatic approach to First Amendment interpretation. She argues that pragmatism, rather than ideology, was the dominant force.[10] Admittedly, Rehnquist court data suggest that while there emerged a majority of the Court committed to the Constitution's libertarian protection of speech, describing this coalition[11] of justices in terms of "conservatism," "liberalism," or even "libertarianism" is, on its own, not very helpful. However, this does not take ideology out of the equation, at least not if one uses the very useful definition of "an ideology" provided by political scientist John Gerring, who describes it as a distinct "set of [consistent] idea-elements."[12] After all, as law Professor Eugene Volokh, who has written extensively about the First Amendment, has explained, Sherry's argument overlooks the fact that the Constitution's protection of free expression is *based* upon an ideology. "To resolve First Amendment questions," writes Volokh, "one cannot avoid making ideological judgments." After all, when the Framers wrote that "Congress shall make no law . . . abridging the freedom of speech," they drew on an ideology. Therefore, it is inevitable that the justices who interpret this clause will make ideological decisions.[13] This begs the question: Precisely what type of ideological interpretive decisions does Justice Kennedy make?

The First Amendment: "An American Doctrine"[14]

The "story of American freedom" is, as the noted historian Eric Foner reminds us, "a tale of debates, disagreements, and struggles rather than a set of timeless categories or an evolutionary narrative toward a preordained goal."[15] The Constitution is a product of such debates, its vague and ambiguous language speaking to the compromises and agreements struck in Philadelphia in 1787. However, it is also a document built upon certain fundamental political principles and ideas—ideas that are too important to be left to the "normal political debate and resolution" of majoritarian politics.[16] Justice Jackson famously observed in *West Virginia v. Barnette* (1943) (in which the Court held that the state cannot constitutionally require schoolchildren to salute the American flag) that freedom of speech is one such principle:

> If there is any fixed star in our constitutional constellation, it is that no official, high or petty, can prescribe what shall be orthodox in politics, nationalism, religion, or other matters of opinion or force citizens to confess by word or act their faith therein.[17]

This is reflected in the fact that the First Amendment's requirement that "Congress shall make no law . . . abridging the freedom of speech" is one of the less ambiguous clauses of the Constitution. To be sure, there could have been greater specificity to this provision. For example, as political scientist Michael Munger has observed: "The framers of the Constitution could have written the First Amendment this way: 'Congress shall make no law . . . restricting freedom of speech, *unless of course the speech is self-interested, in which case Congress can make any darned laws they feel like!*'"[18] Of course, the Framers did not choose this approach to the first provision of the Bill of Rights. Consequently, we have a broadly worded constitutional provision—which is unsurprising given that it embodies the Constitution's central concern for limited government.

As we saw in chapter 1, the Constitution is not a "strong libertarian" document, because it authorizes—among other things—the taking of private property. It is possible, however, to identify provisions that can accurately be described as "strongly libertarian." The First Amendment's free speech clause is one such provision—it has, as law professor Richard Epstein describes it, an "essentially libertarian cast."[19] This becomes clear if one steps back for a moment and looks at the First Amendment in its entirety:

> Congress shall make no law respecting an establishment of religion, or prohibiting the free exercise thereof; or abridging the freedom of speech, or of the press; or the right of the people peaceably to assemble, and to petition the Government for a redress of grievances.

There are two aspects of the amendment's content that tell us that placing limits on the government is at the heart of its ideology, its "idea-elements"; and, both aspects are strongly reminiscent of the Lockeian social contract theory discussed in the previous chapter. First, the amendment reminds the government that it was established—as the Constitution's Preamble says—by "the People of the United States" in order to, among other things, "secure the Blessings of [their] Liberty." John Locke made it very clear that individuals would choose to leave the state of nature and form a political society because they considered it a better way to protect their natural rights. It was not a move they would make with either the desire or expectation that they would be surrendering these rights. Consequently, if individuals do not consent to government violations of their natural rights, there must always remain a right for them to resist a government that does act in this way.[20] The First Amendment secures for the people a vital mechanism for such resistance. It prevents the government from interfering with individuals' desires "to petition the Government for a redress of grievances." Were such a right left unprotected, the government would have far greater ability to block its citizens' efforts to say "enough is enough."

Second, and of greater importance to this chapter, is the First Amendment's recognition of individual humanity and autonomy, central to which is freedom of conscience. Individuals must retain the ability to make their own unimpeded judgments about what they believe and think. As Justice Kennedy has said on several occasions, individuals will forever have their liberty harmed—and their "right to search for dignity" threatened—if they are deprived of the "right to think" what they will.[21] In other words, the law professor and prominent civil liberties advocate Burt Neuborne was absolutely right to say: "The first amendment is not the preserve of a particular political enclave. It is not a liberal doctrine. It is not a conservative doctrine. It is an American doctrine."[22] This doctrine is fundamentally challenged when the government discriminates between viewpoints. For, as Justice Kennedy reminds us, the aforementioned "right to think is the beginning of freedom," and "governments are most dangerous when they try to tell people what to think."[23] The alternative, which is to have the government tell us what to think by selecting the views that it considers "desirable," is inconsistent with the principles underpinning the First Amendment, the principles that place a premium on individual autonomy. Nowhere is protection of this more apparent in the Court's free speech jurisprudence than in its hostility to laws that engage in content- and/or viewpoint-based discrimination—laws that single out, for particular treatment, certain speech because of its subject matter.

"Above All Else": This is What "the First Amendment Means"[24]

The Supreme Court takes a dim view of content-based discrimination and works from the presumption that such regulatory efforts will most likely be difficult for the government to justify in a manner that satisfies the Constitution. The justices frown even more upon viewpoint discrimination, which they almost always afford the "most exacting [judicial] scrutiny."[25] The justices have adopted a multitude of approaches to the task of distinguishing content discrimination and viewpoint discrimination, leaving one to wonder whether only they know it when they see it. However, the distinction usually operates as a variation of the following general principle. Imagine that a school district adopts a law prohibiting civics teachers from including anything in their classes about political parties. Although it would be difficult to imagine covering the basics of the American political system without including this component, the school district has concluded that parties are elitist organizations that are rife with corruption—and it does not want its students to learn about such principles. Putting aside any questions about its constitutionality, this law would appear to discriminate against speech based on content, because it excludes discussion of a particular subject. Now imagine that, for whatever reason, exempted from the law's coverage are classes that cover the policies and strategies of the Green Party. In this respect, preferential treatment has been given to one *view*—appearing to make this law an example of viewpoint discrimination.

I use "appears to be" in this hypothetical because, as we will see, even though the justices agree that viewpoint discrimination is "an egregious form of content discrimination," they are far from settled on definitions of this distinction. As the law professor Daniel Farber wants us to remember, "Perhaps the only thing that is truly clear is that the Court has not yet found a satisfactory definition of viewpoint regulation."[26] In this respect, Justice Kennedy's approach to the subject is relatively well defined. As the opinions analyzed below demonstrate, Kennedy has repeatedly written strongly worded, separate opinions opposing such regulation. In so doing, he has carved out a position at whose heart is a libertarian emphasis on expanding the liberty of all by tolerating the views of all.

This is, it should be noted, neither a new approach nor one that has found its expression only in Kennedy-authored Supreme Court opinions. It is an approach that made its first significant appearance in 1972, in *Police Department of Chicago v. Mosley*. In this case the Court struck down a city ordinance that prohibited individuals from picketing or demonstrating "on a public way within 150 feet of any primary or secondary school building while the school is in session." It was enacted seven months after Earl Mosley, a postal employee, had begun frequently engaging in a solitary, peaceful protest outside one of the city's schools; he was protesting what he viewed as the racially discriminatory policies of the school. Although the Court declined to make a broad ruling on the constitutionality of such restrictions on peaceful protest, Mosley was still victorious. A majority of the justices agreed that the ordinance violated the Fourteenth Amendment's Equal Protection Clause because it specifically excluded from its coverage "peaceful picketing of any school involved in a labor dispute." The city failed to persuade the justices that it had a constitutionally legitimate reason for this unequal treatment of speech.[27]

Laying the groundwork for the judicial disagreement that besets content discrimination jurisprudence, within his opinion for the Court in *Mosley* Justice Thurgood Marshall failed to provide one hard and fast rule about how strongly this type of speech regulation would be scrutinized by the Court. Nevertheless, Marshall's opinion remains important because it is the starting point for the content discrimination doctrine. As Marshall recognized, "Above all else, the First Amendment means that government has no power to restrict expression because of its message, its ideas, its subject matter, or its content." Why is this so important? Using language and invoking principles of individual autonomy and viewpoint toleration that we will see playing prominent roles in Justice Kennedy's opinions analyzed below, Marshall wrote: "The essence of this forbidden censorship is content control. Any restriction on expressive activity because of its content would completely undercut the 'profound national commitment to the principle that debate on public issues should be uninhibited, robust, and wide-open.'"[28]

Insisting Upon "Scrupulous Protection" and Toleration of Speech Diversity[29]

Professor Farber has identified several main arguments made by scholars in opposition to content discrimination. First, it is argued that the government often uses this type of restriction in a paternalistic manner. These efforts should be constrained so that individuals are free to choose what to hear, say, and think. The government should not be in the business of making decisions for us about what views it would be harmful to be exposed to. Second, an individual's liberty and autonomy is similarly threatened by government attempts to direct and/or "distort" public discourse by preventing people from being exposed to certain expression. Finally, any effort to discriminate based on content should lead us to ask: why is the government doing this? Oftentimes, the answer exposes a suspicious government motive.

As Farber explains, while it is useful to break a discussion of content discrimination into these different categories, doing so shows us the limitations of each argument. The antipaternalism argument only really applies when speech might be seen to cause harm. The discourse-distortion emphasis is limited to government efforts to permit only one side of a debate. Finally, it is not always the case that a bad government motive is present.[30] Justice Kennedy's opinions do not overcome some of these concerns about trying to create a coherent content discrimination jurisprudence. However, they do demonstrate a quest for doctrinal synthesis that is based on the libertarian principles that make up the universal element of his judicial decision making.

We Don't Want (or Need) Your Paternalism

One of the most prevalent defenses of government actions that restrict expression based on the speaker's views rests on the fear of the "communicative impact" of speech. The two most common types of communicative impact are

(1) audiences having "undesirable or unlawful" reactions to the speech; and (2) audiences reacting because material offends them. A government that decides to restrict speech because of such fears is a government that is demonstrating very little faith in the personal responsibility or levels of tolerance of its citizens.[31] To be sure, the Framers recognized the fallibility of humans and knew that it was unrealistic to expect individuals to act responsibly and to tolerate their fellow citizens at every turn. However, their solution was to establish a system that limited the actions of the *government*; they did not envision a set of paternalistic restrictions on individuals' thought processes, because such restrictions would be derived from distrust held not by the governed, but rather by the governors. Such an approach would reverse the constitutional relationship between the people and their elected representatives. And it would deprive individuals of the informational value of knowledge and weaken the sovereign authority of which knowledge is an important part.

It is important to remember that there is general informational value in providing people with the greatest possible access to diverse knowledge and opinions. As described by law professor Randy Barnett in *The Structure of Liberty*, the problem of knowledge is a "pervasive social problem." We all have personal knowledge that is unique to ourselves; at the same time, though, we all have personal knowledge that we may value equally. Therefore, when we make use of our knowledge we must do so with the awareness that we are ignorant of so much of the knowledge and opinions of others.[32] The nature of the problem of knowledge suggests that collective and social decisions (such as those made by groups of political decision makers) should not be grounded in perceptions that the negative effects of an action or view warrant prohibiting or suppressing it. Of course, this might prompt one to reply that all actions negatively affect something or somebody and that there will always be dissenters from some views. Although there is much truth to this, it still does not legitimize a solution marked by intolerance. Instead, a libertarian resolution—such as that provided by Kennedy's jurisprudence—that meets the ultimate requirement of preserving the maximum amount of individual liberty, will provide a role for *some* restrictions on speech and actions. Indeed, just as it would be wrong to say that a democratic government of limited powers can legitimately respond to citizens' claims and concerns when it delineates the nature and defines all of the boundaries of the claims and concerns that it hears, it would be misleading to say that the corollary of this is the argument that we should place our trust not in the government's but, rather, solely in the citizens' expressive judgments. One need not follow this to its logical consequence to see the problems associated with, as Richard Epstein has described it, relying on the "good citizens to reach the right result every time."[33] It is for this reason that the First Amendment, and judicial review of its protection of free speech, exists: to provide a point of departure, expressed by the Framers and interpreted by the Supreme Court, for the country's "good citizens" to engage in an expressive dialogue defined by viewpoint diversity.

When Only a Dialogue Will Do

Dialogue: "a discussion, esp. one between representatives of two political groups."[34] It is difficult to have a meaningful discussion or dialogue—especially when the goal of the dialogue is to benefit from someone else's knowledge—when your interlocutor does not possess the "political principles which enable him to work with people whose moral values differ from his own." Absent these principles, there is no desire to work toward a "political order in which both can obey their convictions."[35] It is even more difficult to carry on an enlightened discourse when the government "distort[s] public discourse" by regulating one side of a debate because it disagrees with the message or view that is being expressed.[36] The speech clause of the First Amendment is underpinned by an argument for pluralism—that one should combat the speech with which one disagrees not by censoring it but instead by offering a competing opinion, an alternative perspective designed to *persuade* your audience that the position expressed by your interlocutor (or opponent) is worthy of reconsideration. This is the principle of persuasion, perhaps most eloquently articulated by Justice Brandeis in *Whitney v. California* when he wrote: "If there be time to expose through discussion the falsehood and fallacies, to avert the evil by the processes of education, the remedy to be applied is more speech, not enforced silence."[37]

Rather than defending the principle on consequentialist grounds—as a means to achieving the goal of "good" long-term consequences—in other words, arguing that more diverse views will be good for *society*, law professor David Strauss suggests that we should justify it as a way to maintain the *individual's* autonomy over his or her "reasoning processes."[38] This is precisely the approach taken by Justice Kennedy. It reflects the fact that protecting free speech is a fundamental component of the constitutional project because when government chooses to censor speech, it makes a statement not just about the speech but also about the way of life of the speaker. And, "validation of a way of life through its public expression," the philosopher Joseph Raz reminds us, "is of crucial importance for the well-being of individuals whose way of life it is."[39] In this respect, as Kennedy emphasized at his Supreme Court confirmation hearing, the speech protection of the First Amendment extends to "all ways in which we express ourselves as persons. It applies to dance and to art and to music. These features of our freedom are to many people as important or more important than political discussions or searching for philosophical truth. The first amendment covers all of these forms of speech."[40]

Texas v. Johnson: "Sometimes We Must Make Decisions We Do Not Like"[41]

In 1989, in one of his earliest Supreme Court opinions, Justice Kennedy provided a strong indication of his hostility to governmental attempts to regulate the content of speech. This indication came in an opinion that, even at the time, can have left little doubt in the minds of his new colleagues that his free speech jurisprudence was underpinned by libertarian values. *Texas v. Johnson* involved constitutional questions about which most people, both then and now, hold strong views.[42] It is a decision that has been described by Kennedy as "a great teaching case" because "it teaches that the Constitution has meaning in your own times." This, says Kennedy, is significant, because law is something that "moves in the consciousness of people." Its "work," though, "is never done"; as he reminded the American Bar Association in 2007, "the work of freedom has just begun."[43] For the work of freedom of *expression* to continue, the individuals for whom the First Amendment exists must be free to engage in educational and enlightening dialogues on the diversity of topics upon which they hold and form views. Otherwise, says Kennedy, the government will be telling us what to think—which is precisely what Texas tried to do to Gregory Lee Johnson.

A "Difficult and Distasteful Little (Big?) Case"[44]

During a political demonstration outside the 1984 Republican National Convention in Dallas, Texas, Johnson set fire to an American flag. Nobody was injured, but several onlookers later testified that they were "seriously offended" by the incident. One person returned to the site to collect the remains of the flag; he took them home and buried them in his backyard. The offense that Johnson's actions generated was sufficient to convict him under a Texas statute that made it a crime to "intentionally or knowingly desecrate . . . a state or national flag." This is because the state defined "desecrate" as to "deface, damage, or otherwise physically mistreat in a way that the actor knows will seriously offend one or more persons likely to observe or discover his action."[45] The five-justice majority that voted to strike down this law on First Amendment grounds was composed of Justice Brennan (who wrote the opinion) and Justices Marshall, Blackmun, Scalia, and Kennedy.

The Court concluded that Johnson's flag burning was a form of expression because it was conduct undertaken with "an intent to convey a particularized message . . . and the likelihood was great that the message would be understood by those who viewed it."[46] The conduct fell into a category of expression known as symbolic speech (nonverbal speech) that receives First Amendment protection because there is no clear line between speech and conduct. Those who wave (or burn) American flags are viewed as expressing themselves or attempting to communicate a particular message just as much as those who read speeches about Old Glory. The First Amendment protects both methods of expression. This does not mean, however, that governmental efforts to regulate speech that is harmful are evaluated under the same standard as those aimed at harmful conduct. The government has greater latitude to regulate the latter, even if it is conduct that is held to be expressive.

Since 1968, the standard of judicial review for governmental efforts to regulate expressive conduct has depended upon whether or not the regulation is related to the suppression of expression. If it is, then strict scrutiny is applied; if not, then the Court applies the "*O'Brien* test." The Court conceived this test in *United States v. O'Brien* (1968). This case was the result of David Paul O'Brien's decision in 1966 to burn his draft card on the steps of the South Boston Courthouse. O'Brien was arrested and subsequently convicted of violating a federal law which, as amended in 1965, made it a crime to "forge, alter, knowingly destroy, knowingly mutilate, or in any manner change" a draft card.[47] The Court upheld the law by crafting and applying a test that led it to conclude that the purpose served by the law was to prevent the destruction of draft cards, an action unrelated to free expression. The *O'Brien* test begins with the Court asking whether the government has a constitutional power to regulate in the manner it has chosen (the government usually satisfies this requirement). Next, the question becomes whether the regulation furthers an "important or substantial interest" and is "unrelated to the suppression of free expression." Even if the regulation conforms to both of these components of the test, it can still be held unconstitutional if the restriction it imposes on First Amendment freedoms is "greater than is essential to the furtherance of that interest."[48]

In *Johnson*, Texas defended its flag desecration law by arguing that it served two purposes—(1) preventing the breaches of the peace that would result when witnesses to flag burning were offended by that action, and (2) maintaining national unity. The Court summarily rejected the first argument; the facts of the case did not suggest that any such social disturbances had occurred. The second goal, of maintaining national unity (and the related aim of preserving the symbolic integrity of the flag), had to be viewed as directly related to the suppression of free expression. Texas, wrote Justice

Brennan, was worried that flag burning would "lead people to believe either that the flag does not stand for nationhood and national unity, but instead reflects other, less positive concepts, or that the concepts reflected in the flag do not in fact exist, that is, that we do not enjoy unity as a Nation." These concerns, said Brennan, "blossom only when a person's treatment of the flag communicates some message." Strict judicial scrutiny was the required standard of review because the *O'Brien* test was clearly inapplicable. Ultimately, Brennan concluded that the Texas law could not withstand strict scrutiny, because "if there is a bedrock principle underlying the First Amendment, it is that the government may not prohibit the expression of an idea simply because society finds the idea itself offensive or disagreeable."[49] This generated passionate dissenting views, expressed in two opinions written by Chief Justice Rehnquist and Justice Stevens—both World War II veterans—that detailed the patriotic history and special symbolic value of the American Flag. It "was not," wrote Rehnquist, an item that merely conveyed "another 'idea' or 'point of view'" that was "competing for recognition in the marketplace of ideas." Rather, it is something which many "Americans regard . . . with an almost mystical reverence."[50] And as such, it should be treated in a special way; it is the flag, rather than Johnson's burning of it, that needs and deserves governmental protection, concluded Rehnquist.

Justice Kennedy's Concurrence: "Judicial Hand-Wringing"

Although he joined Justice Brennan's opinion "without reservation,"[51] Justice Kennedy chose to pen a two-page concurrence in *Johnson*. In six short paragraphs, Kennedy explained why he felt compelled to write separately and offer his own, personal defense of the Court's protection of the First Amendment—which he described as "a pure command of the Constitution."[52] Kennedy has since (somewhat apologetically) described his opinion as "judicial hand-wringing," perhaps because in it he said: "The hard fact is sometimes we must make decisions we do not like. We make them because they are right, right in the sense that the law and the Constitution, as we see them, compel the result."[53] Whatever misgivings he may have had about the decision to write in *Johnson*, there is no doubt that collectively his words were a powerful statement of his First Amendment views.

The first draft of Justice Kennedy's concurrence contained passages that expressed his disdain for Johnson's actions. However, as table 2.1 shows, the language of the second and final version was noticeably toned down. Perhaps this was in response to comments from Justice Blackmun, whose marginalia on the first draft include objections to certain phrases that did not appear in the final opinion. What is clear is that it was also in recognition of the essential First Amendment principles of tolerance and viewpoint diversity at stake in the case.

For example, in the concurrence Kennedy wrote: "The flag is constant in expressing beliefs Americans share, beliefs in law and peace and that freedom which sustains the human spirit." Originally, he referred to beliefs "*all* Americans share." That the "all" was gone from his final opinion marked his awareness that the beliefs to which he was referring were not, and should not be interpreted as, the beliefs that a majority hold. In other words, in the eyes of the Constitution, it is just as American to burn the flag as it is to "wave it."[54] Indeed, in the final opinion Kennedy took pains to emphasize that this was not a case in which the justices could allow their decision to be affected by their "distaste for the result." Doing so would result in "undermining a valued principle that dictates the decision." He respected the passionate and heart-felt dissenting objections of his colleagues, but felt compelled to say: "I do not believe the Constitution gives us the right to rule" in this way, "however painful this judgment is to announce."[55] Kennedy emphasized that the essence of the First Amendment is governmental toleration of even the most distasteful views. This includes the views of Mr. Johnson. Kennedy initially described these views as given with "vengeful insolence," but in the final draft of his concur-

TABLE 2.1
Passages from the first and final versions of Justice Kennedy's concurrence in *Texas v. Johnson* (the changes are indicated in bold type)

First Draft	*Final Version*
"I agree that the flag holds a lonely place of honor in an age when absolutes are distrusted and **hard** truths are burdened by unneeded apologetics."	"I agree that the flag holds a lonely place of honor in an age when absolutes are distrusted and simple truths are burdened by unneeded apologetics."
"Though symbols often are what we ourselves make of them, the flag is constant in expressing beliefs **all** Americans share, beliefs in law and peace and that **special** freedom which sustains the human spirit."	"Though symbols often are what we ourselves make of them, the flag is constant in expressing beliefs Americans share, beliefs in law and peace and that freedom which sustains the human spirit."
"Whether or not he could appreciate the enormity of the offense he gave **with such vengeful insolence**, the fact remains that his acts were speech, in both the technical and the fundamental meaning of the Constitution."	"Whether or not he could appreciate the enormity of the offense he gave, the fact remains that his acts were speech, in both the technical and the fundamental meaning of the Constitution."

Source: *Texas v. Johnson*, Justice Kennedy concurrence, first and final drafts, Box 533, Harry A. Blackmun Papers, Manuscript Division, Library of Congress, Washington, D.C.

rence they were simply noted as acts that constituted "speech, in both the technical and the fundamental meaning of the Constitution."[56]

When they made references to Kennedy's separate opinion, the newspapers covering *Johnson* tended to focus upon the "personal toll" aspects of the justice's concurrence. This is a misleading approach. There is, of course, truth in the argument that "the authors [of concurrences] keep a careful eye on their own judicial identities to assure they remain intact for future battles."[57] However, to use the apt phrase coined by Justice Ginsburg (when she was a member of the U.S. Court of Appeals, D.C. Circuit), Kennedy's opinion did not constitute a "solo performance."[58] Rather, it illustrated that his First Amendment jurisprudence cannot be correctly labeled as "conservative" or "liberal" because this is not the way in which he views the principles embodied in this first section of the Bill of Rights. His concurrence was not "the first public sign that Kennedy might feel some conflicts about the court's conservative agenda."[59] Rather, *Johnson* stood (up) for the libertarian principle that encourages the toleration of all views.

Simon & Schuster: The Accidental Test

His decision to write separately in *Texas v. Johnson*, and the concurrence that this decision generated, left little doubt that Kennedy had brought with him to Washington, from California, well-developed and distinctly libertarian views about the First Amendment's protection of free speech. However, the *doctrinal* impact of these views did not become apparent until two years later. Beginning with his opinion concurring in the judgment in *Simon & Schuster v. Crime Victims Bd.* (1991), and continuing throughout his time on the Court, Kennedy has staked out a lonely but brave position vociferously objecting to content-based regulations of speech. The Rehnquist Court frequently mustered majorities willing to protect individuals' expressive freedom rights. Kennedy could often be found, however, writing separate opinions. In these, he took positions that provided individuals with even greater protection from government efforts to limit their speech because of disagreement with the viewpoints offered. *Simon & Schuster* was the first example of this endeavor.

Unanimity in Result Only

The Court did not have difficulty deciding *Simon & Schuster*. It unanimously concluded that New York's "Son of Sam" law was unconstitutional.[60] As its name suggests, the state enacted this law in the wake of the 1977 serial killings by David Berkowitz (popularly known as the "Son of Sam"). The law was designed to prevent criminals from profiting from their crimes through the publication of descriptions of their illegal activities. If an individual who was accused or convicted of a crime entered into a contract for any depiction of that crime, he or she was required to provide the New York Crime Victims Board with a copy of the contract and any income earned from the communication of the information. The money would be placed in escrow and would, for a five-year period, be made available to any victim of the crime who was awarded monetary damages in a related civil action. The coverage of the law extended to individuals who were neither accused nor convicted of a crime, but who admitted to such activity in a work (such as a book). Simon & Schuster brought a First Amendment challenge to the law after it published a book containing the admissions of such an individual—the organized crime figure Henry Hill.[61]

The Court did not hesitate to strike the law down. It was clearly a content-based regulation of speech because it only penalized those who engaged in expression on a particular subject (the commission of criminal activities). In her opinion for the Court, Justice O'Connor sharply criticized New York for enacting a law that "establishes a financial disincentive to create or publish works with a particular content."[62] Having established that the regulation was content-based, O'Connor proceeded to apply the strict judicial scrutiny test which required the state to prove that passage of the law furthered a compelling state interest, was narrowly tailored to further that goal, and was the least speech-intrusive option. O'Connor concluded that such an interest—compensating crime victims—did exist, but that it could be achieved in a way that resulted in less intrusion upon First Amendment speech rights. As it stood, the law was "significantly overinclusive" because of the breadth of its coverage. She noted that at oral argument even the attorney for the Crime Victims Board had conceded that, as O'Connor put it, "the statute applies to works on any subject, provided that they express the author's thoughts or recollections about his crime, however tangentially or incidentally."[63] Such a law could not be described as narrowly tailored.

Although there were no dissenters from the judgment in *Simon & Schuster*, Justice O'Connor's opinion only spoke for herself and five other justices. In a short, three-sentence concurrence in the judgment, Justice Blackmun suggested that the Court should have gone further. Many other states had in place similar laws, and Blackmun believed that it behooved the Court to draw attention to the constitutionally redeeming features of these statutes. The Court had an opportunity to provide "guidance" to a state, like New York, that might wish to enact a revised version of a constitutionally flawed law. Additionally, the "Son of Sam" law was underinclusive as well as overinclusive, meaning that

Blackmun concluded it was important to explain that there were many other types of speech that the government could restrict in order to meet the goal of compensating victims. This became an important part of Blackmun's judgment that the New York law was unconstitutional, because this statutory flaw was additional evidence that thc state was making a content-based decision about targeting speech.

Justice Kennedy's Concurrence: This Is "Raw Censorship"[64]

On December 1, 1991, eight days before the announcement of the Court's decision in *Simon & Schuster*, Jeff Meyer penned a memo to Justice Blackmun, for whom he was clerking. Blackmun had not yet decided whether to write separately in the case, and Meyer wrote to inform him that he had "heard from AMK's [Justice Kennedy's] chambers that he might be writing separately to address the underinclusiveness issue." Four days later, when Kennedy circulated the first draft of his concurrence, he did not focus on this flaw of the New York statute.[65] Like Blackmun, he refused to join O'Connor's opinion, but Kennedy did not believe that he needed to focus on anything very complex. His passionate opposition to the law was clear from the outset. The regulation, wrote Kennedy, "imposes severe restrictions on authors and publishers, using as its sole criterion the content of what is written." This should have terminated *any* discussion or use of strict judicial scrutiny because this "content has the full protection of the First Amendment." Given the egregious nature of the violation of freedom of expression that was the New York law, it was "unnecessary" and indeed "incorrect" to ask whether it addressed any compelling state interests.[66] Just as he had done at his confirmation hearing, Kennedy explained that the origins of the test lay not in First Amendment jurisprudence but rather in the Court's body of decisions about equal protection of the law. Kennedy then proceeded to make clear his views about the limited role that the test should play in First Amendment cases. It "has no real or legitimate place," he wrote, "when the Court considers the straightforward question whether the State may enact a burdensome restriction of speech based on content only." Indeed, concluded Kennedy, using the test in this case was dangerous to individual liberty because it "might be read as a concession that States may censor speech whenever *they* believe there is a compelling justification for doing so."[67]

To be sure, as every constitutional law student knows, there are certain categories of content-based speech that fall beyond the protection of the First Amendment, but Kennedy saw no need to add to them using a test producing results akin to "ad hoc balancing."[68] Why would this "inquiry" be irrelevant?

The answer, indicated Kennedy, was that in such cases "the *sole* question is, or ought to be, whether the restriction is in fact content-based." If the answer to *this* inquiry is "yes," then the regulation *cannot be constitutionally sustained.*[69] Kennedy was fully aware that this compelling interest test was a staple of First Amendment law, but its "familiarity" did not serve to make its presence in speech cases justifiable, because it owed its existence not to constitutional wisdom, judicious foresight, or "considered judgment," but rather to "accident."[70]

Hill v. Colorado: When Freedom of Speech Met Responsible Liberty

Justice Kennedy has a clear jurisprudential commitment to protecting individuals' expressive freedom; he aggressively seeks to limit government efforts to regulate the content of their speech. Can the same be said, however, about his approach to cases involving individuals who do not wish to be spoken to? What does he conclude in cases that ask whether the First Amendment establishes a right *not to be spoken to*? In recent years, this subject has surfaced in debates over hate speech and campus speech codes.[71] However, in *Hill v. Colorado* (2000) this question was confronted primarily from what one might describe as the traditional perspective—viewing it as an individual privacy question—epitomized by a "right to be let alone."[72]

This case involved a First Amendment challenge to a 1993 Colorado law that established 100-foot zones around "heath care facilities," zones within which a person was prohibited from "knowingly" coming within eight feet of another person, without their consent, "for the purpose of passing a leaflet or handbill to, displaying a sign to, or engaging in oral protest, education, or counseling with such a person."[73] This restriction on what is known as "sidewalk counseling" was challenged by individuals who wanted to participate in peaceful pro-life demonstrations outside abortion clinics. These expressive activities included "efforts 'to educate, counsel, persuade, or inform passersby about abortion and abortion alternatives by means of verbal or written speech, including conversation and/or display of signs and/or distribution of literature.'" Oftentimes, this involved coming within close proximity of people entering and exiting the clinics.[74] Writing for the six-justice majority that was willing to uphold the Colorado law, Justice Stevens acknowledged that the competing desires to (1) preserve "the constitutionally protected rights of law-abiding speakers," and (2) protect "the interests of unwilling listeners" raised "legitimate and important concerns."[75] He nevertheless considered it particularly important to remember that in this case the "unwilling listeners" would be primarily individuals seeking medical treatment. Stevens explained that in previous cases the

Court had "recognized that 'the First Amendment does not demand that patients at a medical facility undertake Herculean efforts to escape the cacophony of political protests.'"[76]

Justice Kennedy's Dissent: "Neutrality . . . Must be the First Principle of the First Amendment"[77]

Unlike the refined rhetoric of his concurrence in *Texas v. Johnson*, the passion of Kennedy's dissent in *Hill* was exhibited through his expressions of contempt for the damage that the First Amendment had sustained at the hands of the justices who voted to uphold the Colorado statute. Kennedy argued that the majority's "assumptions" were "erroneous," "disturbing," and underpinned by "grave errors of analysis" that "contradict[ed] more than half a century of well-established First Amendment principles."[78] Most significant, he disagreed with the Court's conclusion that the Colorado law did not discriminate against content and did nothing more than affect "the places where some speech may occur."[79]

One of the arguments that the petitioners put forward in defense of their conclusion that the law was content based was the contention that "an individual near a health care facility who knowingly approaches a pedestrian to say 'good morning' or to randomly recite lines from a novel would not be subject to the statute's restrictions." In his majority opinion, Stevens noted that none of the opinions penned in the decisions of this case by the Colorado courts mentioned this argument.[80] Stevens was convinced that the arguments put forward by Justice Kennedy were constructed upon equally weak foundations. "Under the most reasonable interpretation of Colorado's law," wrote Kennedy, "if a speaker approaches a fellow citizen within any one of Colorado's thousands of disfavored-speech zones and chants in praise of the Supreme Court and its abortion decisions, I should think there is neither protest, nor education, nor counseling." Not so, observed Stevens; this hypothetical individual would appear to be a hardcore violator of the law.[81] Continuing their dialogue,[82] Kennedy offered another example: "If a citizen approaches a public official visiting a health care facility to make a point in favor of abortion rights. If she says, 'Good job, Governor,' there is no violation; if she says, 'Shame on you, Governor,' there is."[83] This was a telling choice of hypothetical, because it introduced into Kennedy's discussion references to political speech, which is "the primary object of First Amendment protection" because of its "central[ity] to the civic discourse that sustains and informs our democratic processes."[84] Even though some of his hypotheticals were subject to the criticism—as Stevens indicated—that they did not accurately reflect the actual content of the Colorado law, there is no doubting the fact that in

Kennedy's view, upholding the Colorado law was a very dangerous path for the Court to take. It was a path that he believed was inconsistent with the First Amendment's protection against viewpoint discrimination.

A justice can choose to intensify the power of the message that he/she seeks to convey through a separate opinion by delivering it from the bench on decision day, reading it in either its entirety or by selecting particularly important passages. When a justice chooses the excerpts approach, Court watchers are provided with another source of data to analyze. Considering the passages that Justice Kennedy chose to read when he delivered his *Hill* dissent from the bench demonstrates this.[85] He chose carefully, using sections that expressed the most basic principles of free speech theory that the First Amendment exists to protect. He offered, as an example, the following analogy:

> If, just a few decades ago, a State with a history of enforcing racial discrimination had enacted a statute like this one, regulating "oral protest, education, or counseling" within 100 feet of the entrance to any lunch counter, our predecessors would not have hesitated to hold it was content based or viewpoint based.[86]

In his opinion, the First Amendment did not excuse the Court from "apply[ing] the same structural analysis when the speech involved is less palatable to it."[87] Justice Kennedy invoked memories of a period in American history plagued by intolerance in order to expose the intolerance of the modern Court's decision in *Hill.*

Why *Hill* Was Not Just "Nominally a Free Speech Case"[88]

Although Colorado's law applied to all types of health facility, it was no secret that the law was primarily directed toward protests outside abortion clinics.[89] This is why in his dissent (which Justice Kennedy did not join) Justice Scalia referred to the decision in *Hill* as part of the Court's "whatever-it-takes proabortion jurisprudence."[90] Scalia reasoned that because *Roe v. Wade*[91] was still good law, the ability of individuals to oppose abortion was limited to the exercising of their First Amendment right to "persuade women, one by one."[92] Scalia was additionally critical of the chilling effect of the Court's decision. Colorado defended the law as a means for ensuring the safety of persons entering "health care facilities." Scalia responded to this by saying that the law could not hope to accomplish this goal because the imposition of an eight-foot zone would be least likely to dissuade from expressive activities those most likely to threaten the safety of individuals, protesters using "bullhorns and screaming from eight feet away." Instead, those whose speech would probably be chilled—those who might choose not to express their antiabortion views for fear of prosecution—would be those "who would accomplish their moral and religious objectives by peaceful and civil means."[93] In this respect, Scalia concluded, the Court's decision represented a grave threat to the First Amendment, ignoring what the Framers recognized: "that the freedom to speak and persuade is inseparable from, and antecedent to, the survival of self-government."[94]

This First Amendment analysis has a distinctly libertarian tone to it. Therefore, it is unsurprising that, in the opening paragraph of his dissent, Kennedy noted that he agreed with Scalia's examination of the free speech principles at stake in the case. What raised more eyebrows was Kennedy's observation that his colleague was also correct to remind Americans that abortion is a "profound moral issue."[95] As I explain in chapter 5, this statement—which the justice has since reiterated—should not be read either apocalyptically (by abortion rights advocates) or triumphantly (by abortion opponents). Rather, as Kennedy views it, this is a rather benign statement of the obvious, which is neither indicative nor determinative of his judicial decision making in abortion rights cases. Here, it is important to draw attention to this aspect of Kennedy's *Hill* dissent because at least one commentator has reached the conclusion that this is an opinion that shows that for Kennedy this was only "nominally a free speech case." Writes the political scientist Frank Colucci, Kennedy's *Hill* dissent is best understood "as an explicat[ion]" of the justice's "view of the moral nature of the abortion decision under the Constitution, and the extent to which both government and other individuals have the liberty to influence that decision."[96] To be sure, Kennedy does try to achieve this goal, but this in no way makes his opinion only nominally about freedom of speech. In order to understand this, we need briefly to consider the fact that *Hill* was decided on the same day as *Stenberg v. Carhart* (striking down a state ban on so-called partial-birth abortions).[97] Kennedy's dissent in this case suggested to many that his support for abortion rights had weakened since the famous decision in *Planned Parenthood v. Casey* (1992), in which he joined Justices O'Connor and Souter to create the decisive joint opinion maintaining the "central holding" of *Roe*.[98] In *Stenberg*, as I explain in more detail in chapter 5, Kennedy took care to explain that as individual as the decision to abort a fetus may be, it is a decision that has consequences for, and impacts parties other than the pregnant woman.

A similar emphasis on personal responsibility was written into Kennedy's dissent in *Hill*, but it is clear that the justice considered this case to be primarily about the First Amendment rather than abortion. This became apparent when Kennedy turned to the subject of *Casey* in the last section of the opinion, which explained why the Court's decision in *Hill* violated the understanding of individual liberty for which both *Casey* and the First

Amendment stand. The only passage that he quoted from the 1992 decision was the following:

> [Abortion] is an act fraught with consequences for others: for the woman who must live with the implications of her decision; for the persons who perform and assist in the procedure; for the spouse, family, and society which must confront the knowledge that these procedures exist, procedures some deem nothing short of an act of violence against innocent human life; and, depending on one's beliefs, for the life or potential life that is aborted.[99]

This is the essence of the responsible element of Justice Kennedy's jurisprudence. The decision whether or not to have an abortion is a decision that, while constitutionally protected, is part of a liberty that the individual must exercise responsibly. In *Hill*, the focus of Justice Kennedy's opinion is freedom of speech, because providing women with information about views on abortion—whether in favor or in opposition to the procedure—makes a fundamental contribution to their ability to responsibly exercise their liberty. This is because "a leaflet can," wrote Kennedy, have the potential to make a "profound difference . . . in a woman's decision-making process."[100]

Listening to Justice Kennedy read excerpts of his *Hill* dissent, one is struck by the increased measure of passion with which he spoke the words of the entire final paragraph of his opinion. When he said this was a case involving individuals seeking to express their opinions about what was, "in their view," "a grievous moral wrong," one cannot help but think that he shared their view about "what they consider to be one of life's gravest moral crises."[101] Indeed, one can criticize Kennedy's inclusion, in his opinion, of a lengthy quotation from a woman's testimony before the Colorado State Senate about the extent to which her decision not to have an abortion was influenced by the receipt of antiabortion literature from a clinic protester. After all, Kennedy merely tipped his hat to the possibility that one could no doubt find "women who would testify that abortion was necessary and unregretted."[102] However, such criticism misses the most important point of Kennedy's First Amendment dissent in *Hill*: that "*speech makes a difference*."[103] This is the emphasis on viewpoint toleration at the heart of the universal element of Justice Kennedy's modestly libertarian jurisprudence.

A Particular Problem: The Public Forum Doctrine

We have seen that in the Kennedy-authored opinions examined above, the justice has taken a very dim view of governmental attempts to limit speech based on the content of, or the views contained in certain expression. While

Kennedy expresses particularly strong opposition to content discrimination, it is clear that most of his colleagues agree that the Court should generally evaluate this type of speech suppression very carefully. There remains, however, one area of the Court's free speech jurisprudence in which content-based laws have a better chance of succeeding—and even sometimes winning the vote of Justice Kennedy to uphold them. This is the area of the law addressing expression in "public forums" (where the government is acting as landlord). Here, the Court has been more deferential to governments that place limits on speech that may occur on their property.

In a series of opinions in the 1970s, the Court created a "public forum" doctrine specifically to address the ability of the government to restrict speech when acting as the landlord of public property.[104] This is a special role that affords the government greater regulatory freedom than it would otherwise have were it seeking to exert more generalized control over the actions of its citizens. The Court has identified four main types of places that are forums. The traditional, or "quintessential," public forum consists of those "places which, by long tradition or by government fiat have been devoted to assembly and debate."[105] At such locations—sidewalks, for example—the government's ability to restrict expression is greatly restricted; regulatory attempts are subject to high judicial scrutiny because they bear a striking similarity to the aforementioned generalized governmental actions. For the same reasons, this enhanced scrutiny is also applied to government actions within the second category of locations—"designated" public fora. These are public properties that the government has decided to make available for *some* expressive activities—usually only the speech for which the forum was opened up. Here, the Court is careful to ensure that once the government has decided to open a forum, the one thing it must not do is to then direct the debate by engaging in viewpoint discrimination. The government has far more flexibility in regulating speech when the forum falls into one of the remaining two categories. In a nonpublic forum—public property that the government does not use for speaking—a regulation must be reasonable and viewpoint neutral (this rule reflects the government's interest in preserving the property for the non-speech-related uses by preventing speech from interfering with these uses). Finally, property that the government owns and uses for government speech (such as a government-owned and operated television channel) is not considered a public forum; therefore, the government is free to choose which speech it permits.

The public forum doctrine requires that the government (1) permit speakers to use its property as venues from which to express their views; and (2) refrain from imposing undue discriminatory regulation on the views or content of these expressions. These requirements make this a doctrine that creates a "form of subsidy." This is because it makes it easier—it reduces the costs involved—for individuals to exercise their free speech rights.[106] This suggests that the doctrine poses a special challenge to a libertarian understanding of the First Amendment, because it explicitly endorses the concept of the government playing a role in supporting the marketplace of ideas. It is founded on the belief that a free market alone cannot guarantee expressive freedom and diversity—primarily because of the likelihood that a ruling majority will suppress the views of unpopular minorities. The resulting establishment of a public forum doctrine—rightly described as an "affirmative" reading of the requirements of the First Amendment[107]—should, at first glance, be impossible to reconcile with standard libertarian theory, which is constructed on the belief that private choices about speech should be made free of government interference.

Now, to be sure, governmental subsidizing of speech should not be entirely condemned as inconsistent with libertarianism. After all, one could argue that some state intervention might be needed to ensure adequate venues for a diversity of expressive views to flourish. That is, however, not a debate into which this chapter delves. Rather, the modern public forum doctrine merits our attention because of the fact that using public forums to protect access for speakers is undermined if the resulting doctrine exhibits too much deference to the government. It is this fear that drives Justice Kennedy's opposition to the Court's approach to this area of First Amendment law. As we will see below, Justice Kennedy has been very outspoken about the categorical approach to the public forum doctrine, because a jurisprudence of categories exposes individuals (and their liberty) to greater opportunities for the government to persuade the Court to adopt a deferential approach to its efforts, as landlord, to restrict speech. This can be seen in Kennedy's opinions in *United States v. Kokinda* (1990), and *ISKCON v. Lee* and *Lee v. ISKCON* (1992).

United States v. Kokinda: "Political Advocacy [Beyond] the Village Green"?[108]

In August 1986, Marsha Kokinda and Kevin Pearl decided to set up a table on the sidewalk that ran between the parking lot and the entrance of the post office in Bowie, Maryland. They intended to solicit contributions for and sell the political advocacy literature of the National Democratic Policy Committee, for which they were volunteering. When they refused to remove the table, postal inspectors arrested them. Kokinda and Pearl were convicted of violating a United States Postal Service regulation that prohibited persons from "soliciting alms and contributions, campaigning for election to any public office, collecting private debts, commercial soliciting and vending, and displaying or distributing commercial advertising on postal premises."[109] At every stage of the judicial process, the fate of the resulting First Amendment challenge to this regulation initially depended upon determining whether the sidewalk, which was wholly owned by the federal government (the postal service), was a public forum.

It was their chosen location for this expressive activity that determined how much constitutional protection Kokinda and Pearl's speech would enjoy. The government's regulation would be subjected to far greater judicial scrutiny if the sidewalk were found to be a public forum. After a district court ruling that the sidewalk was not such a place, and a Fourth Circuit appellate decision that it was, only a plurality of the Supreme Court was able to agree with the conclusion of the district court. In her opinion that spoke for herself and three of her colleagues, Justice O'Connor carved out an exception to the conventional practice of holding that public sidewalks are traditional public forums. The sidewalk in question was, she concluded, built for one purpose only—"the passage of individuals engaged in postal business." Not all public sidewalks were the same, even if they consisted of the same "physical characteristics."[110] Kokinda and Pearl had set up their table on a sidewalk at one end of which was the post office, and at the other end was the parking lot for the post office. O'Connor therefore concluded that the sidewalk was designed for the exclusive use of post office patrons (in large part because of the specific design and location of the building). Applying past case law, O'Connor found that the determination that the sidewalk was a nonpublic forum meant that the regulation only needed to be reasonable and viewpoint neutral, which it was.

Writing for the four dissenters, Justice Brennan attacked O'Connor's "strained and formalistic" logic, pointing out that she was guilty of applying exactly the type of reasoning whose relevance she said she rejected—judging the sidewalk's legal status by its "physical characteristics." The "architectural idiosyncrasies of the Bowie Post Office," he wrote, "are . . . not determinative of the question whether the public area around it constitutes a public forum. Rather, that the walkway at issue is a sidewalk open and accessible to the general public is alone sufficient to identify it as a public forum." This was a conclusion, he observed, that was entirely consistent with the Court's past decisions, even allowing for the fact that the state of the public forum doctrine was not terribly clear.[111] Justice Brennan also wanted to know how the regulation could be considered reasonable when it illogically prohibited the solicitation of funds but did not address the multitude of other expressive activities, many of which were much more likely to cause the sidewalk disruption that the post office sought to avoid.[112] This was an important section of his opinion, because it demonstrated Brennan's frustration with the final position upon which Justice Kennedy had settled.

For Justice Kennedy, this was always a close case. It was not until ten days before the decision in *Kokinda* was announced that Justice O'Connor's opinion, originally destined to be a dissent, ended up becoming the judgment of the Court. This is when Kennedy said he was prepared to join her in upholding the regulation. Indeed, Kennedy appears to have switched from his initial conference vote to affirm the Fourth Circuit's decision. Despite this change in vote, Kennedy remained convinced—as he had expressed at conference—that the Court did not need to reach the public forum question.[113] He wrote this argument into his *Kokinda* opinion that concurred only in the judgment. This opinion helps us to understand why, even though he voted to uphold the federal postal regulation, he was still making a concerted effort to remain faithful to the key principles that underpin the universal element of his jurisprudence.

At the *Kokinda* conference, Kennedy explained to his colleagues that he had reservations about the public forum doctrine.[114] In his concurrence, however, he discussed why he felt that the legal issues of the case could be resolved without the need to address these doctrinal misgivings. He wrote separately because his "analysis differ[ed] in essential respects" from O'Connor's.[115] Kennedy placed a great deal of emphasis on the fact that by its very nature a post office is used by the public for "communicative purposes." Indeed, Kennedy expressed much sympathy toward the "powerful argument" that the walkway was, for these reasons, "more than a nonpublic forum." Nevertheless, he believed the Court's decision correctly reflected the "recogni[tion] that certain objective characteristics of Government property and its customary use by the public may control the case."[116] And, herein lay the doctrinal problem. If the walkway was "more than a nonpublic forum," if it was also property with these "objective characteristics," into which of the Court's public forum categories did it fit? This was not a question that Kennedy openly addressed, but when his concurrence spoke of trying to ensure that the Court's "public forum jurisprudence . . . retain vitality," the concern about categorization was evident.[117]

Kennedy ultimately avoided this concern by concluding that he would prefer to see the case decided using a test for content neutral government action (which he felt the regulation was) rather than consideration of the public forum issues. Finding that postal property is used for "communicative purposes," of course, immediately opens up the possibility that the regulation could be construed as an example of content discrimination. For, if people use the property to engage in communication when they come to mail a letter or package, is there anything different about the communication that was Kokinda and Pearl's political advocacy? If the answer is yes, is it inevitably an answer that reflects a judgment about the content of the communication? Kennedy agreed that the walkway connecting the post office and the parking lot might be "an appropriate place for the exercise of *vital rights of expression*" because of the communicative nature of activities that take place at a post office. However, he was not led to conclude that the regulation discriminated against speech because of either its content or the views expressed by speakers. Instead, it was a narrowly written regulation that was content neutral. And, regardless of whether what we were dealing with was speech in a public forum, the regulation met the requirement that "restrictions on the time, place, or manner of protected speech" be "justified without reference to the content of the regulated speech, that they are narrowly tailored to serve a significant governmental interest, and that they leave open ample alternative channels for communication of the information"—a formulation of the *O'Brien* test.[118]

In the amicus brief that they jointly filed in *Kokinda*, the national committees of the Libertarian Party and the New Alliance Party encouraged the Court to rule that Kokinda and Pearl were engaging in constitutionally protected political advocacy. The brief made the important observation that any other ruling would deprive many individuals of the most effective opportunity to engage in speech about the policies of the federal government. This is because it is the rare American town that has a "federal presence" that extends beyond the existence of a postal facility. To be sure, it was a stretch to say that upholding the regulation would take the Court toward a First Amendment jurisprudence that "protects only the right to engage in political advocacy on the Village Green."[119] However, the fact remains that there are legitimate libertarian concerns about the implications of a ruling that did not find the postal regulation unconstitutional. In this respect, when analyzing Justice Kennedy's concurrence in *Kokinda*, there are two important things to remember. First, he was unwilling to decide the case by applying the public forum doctrine. Second, he was willing to uphold the regulation only after concluding that it was not an example of content discrimination. Together, these two elements of his opinion demonstrate that his vote in *Kokinda* is not inconsistent with the universal element of his jurisprudence. As we will see in the next section of this chapter, this evaluation is strengthened by the fact that two years later Kennedy demonstrated the same basic opposition to public forum categories.

ISKCON v. Lee and *Lee v. ISKCON*: "What's Next, Bus Stations?"

Most of the justices customarily have their laws clerks pool their resources for evaluating the thousands of petitions for certiorari received by the Court every year. On a copy of the cert pool memo for *ISKCON v. Lee* and *Lee v. ISKCON*, Stephanie Dangel, one of Justice Blackmun's clerks, noted that she was only reluctantly recommending that Blackmun vote to hear this pair of public forum cases during the October 1991 term. The Court was already scheduled to decide two other public forum cases involving polling places and shopping centers, and these two cases simply represented more of the same. "What's next," asked Dangel, "bus stations?"[120] The two *ISKCON* cases, which the Court did agree to hear, were decided on the same day in 1992. They addressed regulations banning the "solicitation and receipt of funds" in the terminals of the three main airports serving the New York and New Jersey metropolitan area. In two fractured decisions prompting numerous opinions, the Court upheld the solicitation ban, but struck down the ban on materials distribution—as applied in cases such as that before the Court. The cases involved the International Society for Krishna Consciousness (ISKCON). This is a religious organization whose sole ritual—sankirtan—involves soliciting funds and distributing materials in public places.

While the decisions were fractured, what we saw in Justice Kennedy's concurrence in these cases was, to that point, his "most fully developed and individual-centered interpretation of the First Amendment."[121] First, as Kennedy explained, "The First Amendment is a limitation on government, not a grant of power. *Its design is to prevent the government from controlling speech.*"[122] In Kennedy's view, the *ISKCON* decisions contained public forum analysis that upset the balance between the individual and the government (and disregarded "the values underlying the Speech and Press Clauses of the First Amendment"). This is because the analysis gave too much power to the government—power to determine when its property was a public forum.[123] Second, Kennedy's concurrence reflected his hostility to a judicial methodology that finds answers to constitutional interpretive questions by referring to tradition. Both Chief Justice Rehnquist (writing for the Court) and Justice O'Connor (concurring) heavily relied on tradition to reach the conclusion that airport terminals were not public forums.[124] Historically, they argued, terminals were places neither *designated* nor *identified* as locations for engaging in speech. Wrote Rehnquist: "The tradition of airport activity does not demonstrate that airports have historically been made available for speech activity."[125] Justice Kennedy could not accept that this automatically led to the conclusion that terminals were not public forums. He vehemently rejected the conclusion that the public forum doctrine was determined by the identification of "categories" of places, their designation as public forums contingent upon "their historical pedigree."[126]

One might reasonably assume that Justice Kennedy would look favorably on *Perry Ed. Assn. v. Perry Local Educators' Assn.* (1983).[127] This is because in this case the Court moved the public forum doctrine toward a "negative" liberty understanding of speech. Previously, the Court oscillated between a "positive" belief that "the purpose of the First Amendment is to promote the democratic process by enhancing the quantity and quality of speech," and the much more limited government "negative" conception that understands "the essential task of the First Amendment as 'restraining government from deliberately manipulating the content or outcome of public debate.'"[128] However, while *Perry Ed. Assn.* took the latter approach, the manner in which it did so was widely criticized.[129] In *ISKCON*, Justice Kennedy castigated what he perceived to be the primary flaw of the precedent—its categorical approach to the public forum doctrine. This was, he explained, antithetical to the First Amendment. "Our public forum doctrine," he wrote, "ought not to be a jurisprudence of categories, *rather than ideas*."[130] Why? Such an approach "convert[ed] what was once an analysis protective of expression into one which grants the government authority to restrict speech by fiat" because whether or not speech in a public forum was protected was ultimately "depend[ant] on the government's defined purpose for the property, or on an explicit decision by the government to dedicate the property to expressive activity."[131]

In *ISKCON*, Kennedy recognized that because:

> Certain government-owned property is a public forum [it] provides open notice to citizens that their freedoms may be exercised there without fear of a censorial government, adding tangible reinforcement to the idea that we are a free people.[132]

What he objected to was that under the majority's reasoning the determination of the boundaries of these freedoms could, to a large extent, be placed in the hands of the government. This, Kennedy explained, was contradicted by both the Court's jurisprudence and, far more important, the Constitution. Kennedy wrote:

> A fundamental tenet of our Constitution is that the government is subject to constraints which private persons are not. The public forum doctrine vindicates that principle by recognizing limits on the government's control over speech activities on property suitable for free expression. The doctrine focuses on the physical characteristics of the property, because government ownership is the source of its purported authority to regulate speech. *The right of speech protected by the doctrine, however, comes not from a Supreme Court dictum, but from the constitutional recognition that the government cannot impose silence on a free people.*[133]

To be sure, one could argue that permitting the Supreme Court to determine the boundaries is no different from giving that power to the government. However, under Justice Kennedy's libertarian vision of judicial power the public forum doctrine must be formulated to *respect* the freedom of speech that the Constitution *protects.* As he warned: "A grant of plenary power allows the government to tilt the dialog heard by the public, to exclude many, more marginal, voices."[134] Were the government to be given such authoritarian power, it would be able to act in a manner that betrays the founding, libertarian principles written into the First Amendment, especially the principle of tolerating a diverse range of views—which is at the heart of the universal element of Kennedy's jurisprudence.

"The Limitations of Labeling"

In a law review article published in 1993, Lawrence Friedman concluded that it was extremely difficult to try and apply any kind of consistent ideological label to the free speech opinions that Justice Kennedy had written since joining the Supreme Court in February 1988. As this chapter has shown, with the benefit of another fifteen years of opinions, it is now possible to see that there are some distinctly libertarian strands woven into the cloth from which Kennedy's expressive freedom jurisprudence is cut. This tendency is particularly noticeable from analysis of the justice's writings about content discrimination, a government practice to which Kennedy is clearly opposed. Analysis of the justice's public forum doctrine has shown, however, that this is not always an area of the law where the correct decision is automatically obvious to Kennedy. Generally, however, we have seen that in these cases Kennedy's free speech libertarianism triumphed. It is tougher to make this argument about *Burson v. Freeman* (decided in 1992, one year after *Simon & Schuster*).

Burson v. Freeman: A "Flower . . . Born to Blush Unseen"

On occasion, when reviewing the Supreme Court's decisions of the past year at the Fourth Circuit's Judicial Conference, Chief Justice Rehnquist liked to focus on the cases that flew under the media's radar. He described these cases using words from Thomas Gray's "Elegy Written in a Country Churchyard." The cases, Rehnquist said, were "flowers which are born to blush unseen and waste their sweetness on the desert air."[135] In terms of the lack of scholarly attention that has been paid to it, one might describe *Freeman* as such a flower. *Freeman* was decided during a term that produced a number of landmark decisions. In terms of freedom of speech, it was vastly overshadowed by *R.A.V. v. City of St. Paul, Minnesota* (striking down a hate speech ordinance)[136] and, to a lesser extent, the two *ISKCON* decisions.

Freeman involved Mary Rebecca Freeman's challenge to a Tennessee law that imposed a 100-foot campaign-free zone around polling places on election days. Within this zone all forms of vote solicitation, and the display or distribution of campaign materials, were prohibited. This was a governmental effort to protect those of its citizens who wished to exercise their voting rights. However, this method of ensuring unimpeded access to polling places came at the expense of what Freeman, who was active in state and local politics (both as a candidate and campaigner), argued was her equally important, and constitutionally protected, right to engage in free speech. The significance of this clash of rights was compounded by the fact that the speech being restricted was political speech. The difficulties of the case were not lost on Justice Blackmun who, in his opinion for a plurality of the Court, conceded that the case presented the Court "with a particularly difficult reconciliation: the accommodation of the right to engage in political discourse with the right to vote—a right at the heart of our democracy."[137]

As will become particularly clear in the next chapter, strict scrutiny review traditionally means "'strict' in theory and fatal in fact."[138] When applied to laws that discriminate against certain speech because of its content, the result is no different. Figure 2.2 helps to show why. It demonstrates that such laws are presumptively unconstitutional and that for the government to prevail it must overcome a formidable doctrinal obstacle, in the form of the compelling interest test. This is usually very difficult for the government to do; *Freeman* demonstrated, however, that it is not impossible. The Tennessee law withstood the Court's application of strict scrutiny review. This was even though, as Justice Blackmun explained, it was an example of content discrimination because "whether individuals may exercise their free speech rights near polling places depends entirely on whether their speech is related to a political campaign."[139] In other words, the law was directed at restricting one particular category of speech. Despite this, Mary Freeman's challenge to the law failed because, as

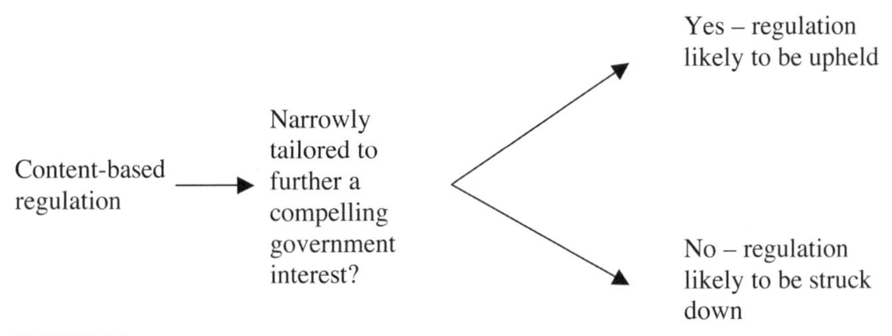

FIGURE 2.2
Traditional use of the compelling interest test in content-based speech cases.

Blackmun explained, the plurality was satisfied that Tennessee was indeed addressing a compelling state interest. Engaging in a lengthy historical discussion of election reform and voting rights, Blackmun concluded that this particular abridgement of free speech was justified as part of the nation's "persistent battle against two evils: voter intimidation and election fraud."[140]

Both the plurality and the dissenters referred to the 1966 decision in *Mills v. Alabama*, in which the Court struck down a law that prohibited newspaper editors from publishing election-day editorials in support of particular candidates for political office. Blackmun said that *Freeman* was a ruling on "the issue carefully left open in *Mills*"—"the extent of a State's power to regulate conduct in and around the polls in order to maintain peace, order and decorum there."[141] While Justice Stevens, who wrote for the three dissenters, agreed that the maintenance of order around, and access to, polling places was a compelling state interest, he did not believe that the Tennessee law could survive strict scrutiny. He emphasized the fact that *Mills* also clearly stood for the conclusion that the prevention of "last-minute campaigning" was not such an interest.[142] The reach of the Tennessee law extended beyond achieving the orderly access goal and into the territory of restricting even "the simple 'display of campaign posters, signs, or other campaign materials'"—speech that it was absurd to assume needed to be prohibited in order "to maintain the freedom to vote and the integrity of the ballot box."[143]

"Offer AMK a Way Out of the Corner He's Painted Himself Into"[144]

As we have seen, Justice Kennedy has never been comfortable with the compelling interest or strict scrutiny test for First Amendment free speech cases. After *Simon & Schuster* it was difficult to see how Kennedy could tolerate any content discrimination. Therefore, *Freeman* was a particularly difficult case for the justice, only complicated by the opinion—with its heavy emphasis on "exacting scrutiny"—that Blackmun was drafting.[145] Kennedy had second thoughts about writing separately in *Freeman*. Dangel, Blackmun's clerk, sent her boss two memos on the subject. The information provided in the first one—"AMK has decided to withdraw his concurrence and is now teetering btw our opinion and JPS"—was repeated in the second one, and accompanied by a suggestion. "Regardless of which way he goes," observed Dangel, "he's going to need to reconcile his approach in *Simon & Schuster* with his approach in this case. We'd all be a lot better off if he . . . could extricate himself from the *per se* language in his *Simon & Schuster* concurrence."[146] With the help of Justice Blackmun's chambers, Kennedy was able to disentangle himself from the absolutist approach he advocated in the "Son of Sam" case. However, he did so without relinquishing his libertarian commitment to casting a stern judicial eye over any governmental attempts to discriminate against expression because of disagreement with the speaker's views.

Recall that, in *Simon & Schuster*, Kennedy was concerned that use of the compelling interest test might open the door to governments deciding to "censor speech whenever *they* believe there is a compelling justification for doing so."[147] On March 24, 1992, two months before the announcement of the decision in *Freeman*, Justice Kennedy received a letter from Justice Blackmun. At this time, Kennedy was considering whether or not he really wanted to write separately in *Freeman*. Justice Blackmun suggested that it might be "possible to distinguish between a statute that is *facially* content-based and one that regulates speech *because of a concern about its content*."[148] This was specifically designed to appeal to the aforementioned concern, because the governmental abuse of the compelling interest that Kennedy feared was definitely more likely to occur when a law was not, on its face, an obvious content-based restriction of speech (unlike the "Son of Sam" statute in *Simon & Schuster*).

Blackmun's appeal to Kennedy's libertarian free speech sensibilities was successful. Later that day, Dangel reported that Kennedy's clerk "called to say that AMK . . . is in the process of working out a short concurrence in line with the letter that you just sent to him."[149] In a letter that he wrote to Blackmun on the day he circulated his second *Freeman* draft, Justice Kennedy expressed his gratitude for his colleague's help in crafting the concurrence: "Harry: Thanks so much for the careful memo on *Simon & Schuster*. As you can see, it was what I needed to guide me in preparing the separate concurrence."[150] What Kennedy concluded was: "In some cases, a censorial justification will not be apparent from the face of a regulation which draws distinctions based on content." This might lead "the government [to] tender a plausible justification unrelated to the suppression of speech or ideas." On such occasions, "the compelling-interest test may be one analytical device to detect, in an objective way, whether the asserted justification is in fact an accurate description of the purpose and effect of the law."[151] So, the inquiry becomes not whether a compelling government interest exists to justify a speech restriction (which is the traditional test, as shown in figure 2.2), but rather whether the government has identified a compelling interest consistent with the purpose of the law (as illustrated in figure 2.3).

Of course, Justice Kennedy's willingness to vote to uphold the law and to sign on to Blackmun's opinion definitely casts a shadow over the libertarianism of his free speech jurisprudence that this chapter has analyzed. However, it is important to understand that Kennedy's opinions in *Simon & Schuster* and *Freeman* do actually offer a consistent understanding of the First Amendment. Additionally, even in his *Freeman* concurrence there is evidence of Kennedy's libertarianism. He has not abandoned his commitment to placing considerable limitations on

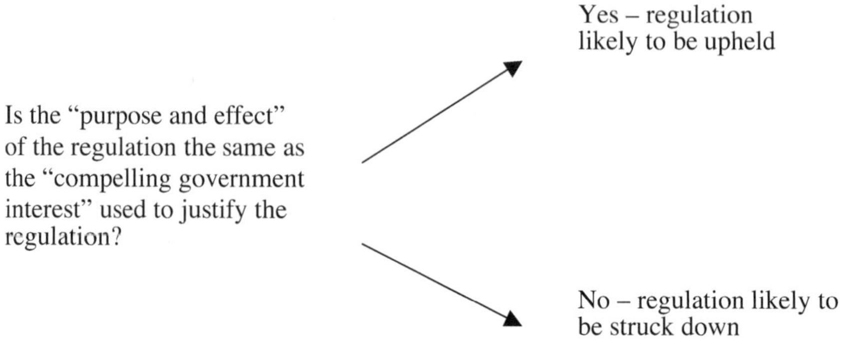

Yes – regulation likely to be upheld

Is the "purpose and effect" of the regulation the same as the "compelling government interest" used to justify the regulation?

No – regulation likely to be struck down

Figure 2.3. *Freeman* reformulation of the compelling interest test in content-based speech cases.

the use of the compelling interest test for strict judicial scrutiny. In both of these cases, we must not forget that the justice wrote separately to condemn the test as an accidental judicial contrivance that "produces a misunderstanding" about the true meaning of the First Amendment. We would do well to remember that Kennedy said that this misunderstanding is extremely dangerous for freedom of speech, because uncertainty "has the potential to encourage attempts to suppress legitimate expression."[152] In cases such as *Simon & Schuster*, where the Court is confronted with a law that is, on its face, a content-based restriction of speech, Kennedy concludes that the presumptive unconstitutionality is so strong that there is very little, if any, judicial need to bother applying the strict scrutiny test. The test may be necessary and proper, however, if a law ends up discriminating based on content, but for nonspeech reasons.

Conclusions

In its first significant statement about laws that discriminate against speech based on its content, the Court said that "above all else," what "the First Amendment means" is that "government has no power to restrict expression because of its message, its ideas, its subject matter, or its content."[153] Even though they have not been able to agree about what makes a law content- and/or viewpoint-based, the justices have, for the most part, adhered to this conclusion that governments should not be in the business of trying to tell their citizens what they may listen to; it cannot dictate what they are permitted to read and write; and it must not tell them what thoughts they may express—whether verbally or nonverbally (using symbols). The data show us that Justice Kennedy is definitely a free speech libertarian, and the opinions analyzed in this chapter demonstrate that an important part of this libertarianism is the justice's strong opposition to content discrimination.

However, even in this area of the law, where his resistance to government intrusions on individual liberty is well defined, we have seen that Justice Kennedy has sometimes struggled to remain faithful to the universal element of his modestly libertarian jurisprudence, an element at whose intellectual heart is an emphasis on preserving and protecting constitutionally guaranteed viewpoint diversity. There have been occasions when his desire to tolerate all views has been tempered by the realities of the different cases he has confronted. It is equally clear, however, as analysis of the opinions in these cases has shown, that overall these examples of judicial agonizing have never led him to stray far from his belief that "governments are most dangerous when they try to tell people what to think." This is because the "right to think is the beginning of freedom," a freedom embodied by the speech clause of the First Amendment.[154]

3

If Rational Basis Means Anything . . .

> I think it strikes him [Justice Kennedy] as terribly unfair that anyone's individual potential should be in any way limited by their being classed as a member of a group, and treated in accordance with their group membership, rather than what they deserve to receive as individuals.[1]
>
> —Pete Wilson, former Governor of California, and U.S. Senator

IN SIX DAYS TIME, JUSTICE BLACKMUN WOULD TURN HIS ATTENTION to the public announcement of his decision to retire at the end of the Supreme Court's October 1993 term. On this last day in March 1994, however, he was otherwise occupied with the ongoing deliberation of one of the as-yet-undecided cases on the Court's docket—*J.E.B. v. Alabama.*[2] Blackmun had just received the first draft of Justice Kennedy's opinion concurring in the judgment, and he wanted to know what had prompted his colleague to write separately—a decision that Kennedy made five months after the case was argued. It was a decision that particularly concerned Blackmun because it signaled Justice Kennedy's departure from Blackmun's majority opinion.[3] In this case, the Court concluded that the Constitution prohibits the exclusion of jurors based on their sex, because such action represents a violation of the Fourteenth Amendment's guarantee that "No State shall . . . deny to any person within its jurisdiction the equal protection of the laws." Alabama had sought to remove all but one of the ten men in a jury pool for a case in which it was seeking, on behalf of the mother of a minor, to recover unpaid child support from the child's father.

Michelle Alexander, one of Blackmun's clerks, sought an explanation for Kennedy's decision from one of her counterparts in Kennedy's chambers. As

Alexander explained in a memo to Blackmun, she was told that Kennedy had decided to write a concurrence because he:

> wanted to emphasize his "individual rights" theory. Apparently, Kennedy thought there were a few things in your opinion that were slightly inconsistent with his approach; rather than ask you to change your opinion, he decided to concur in the judgment since you already had five votes.[4]

What was this "individual rights" theory? Kennedy agreed with Blackmun's analysis of the relationship between the promise of the Equal Protection Clause and the government's actions in the case; he agreed that Alabama had violated this provision of the Fourteenth Amendment. Nevertheless, wrote Kennedy, "The importance of individual rights to our analysis prompts a further observation concerning what I conceive to be the intended effect of today's decision."[5] What Kennedy was worried about was not future prejudicial and/or discriminatory actions by *governments*, but rather the possibility that the members of a jury would fail to check their own, individual "racial or gender bias" at the courtroom doors. Individuals had a duty—if they were to ensure that their ability to responsibly exercise their liberty was preserved and their dignity maintained and protected—to treat other individuals as individuals. In other words, "a juror sits *not as a representative of a racial or sexual group but as an individual citizen*."[6] And the government needed to set a good example for the country's citizens, the people for whom it existed to serve. Time and again, Kennedy has written this theme into equal protection opinions. In chapter 4, we will see that this approach shines brightly in his writings about government policies that classify individuals (either in beneficial or negative ways) based on their race. In this chapter, we find the same libertarian principles driving Kennedy to take a dim view of government discrimination based on a person's sexual orientation. However, from the outset it is important to provide a brief overview of the important differences that we will see, in this chapter and the next, in the administration of, and conservative reaction to, these principles.

The protection of individual dignity and the associated right to pursue one's own constitutional visions dominates the Kennedy-authored opinions examined below. When Kennedy uses this libertarian theory to limit race-conscious government measures, he enjoys a lot of support from his more conservative colleagues. When the individuals being afforded this constitutional protection bring their claims based on their sexual orientation, however, this support vanishes. The standard conservative argument is that the protection of the "liberty" of which the Constitution speaks does not extend its coverage to intimate sexual conduct. Therefore, individuals seeking legal protection for this behavior must instead look to legislatures—federal and/or state—for passage of the desired laws. The problem with this deference to majoritarian institutions is the tendency of such bodies to make decisions that discriminate against minorities for morals- rather than law-based reasons. Kennedy has no doubt that the freedom of individuals to engage in harmless sexual intimacy is protected by the Constitution, regardless of a person's sexual orientation. Denying this liberty because a legislative majority makes an animus-based decision that real harm is occurring—harm to people's moral sensibilities—represents a fundamental failure to preserve the dignity of all.

Of course, it needs to be acknowledged that addressing majoritarian prejudice has always been a central component of the Court's equal protection jurisprudence.[7] Therefore, it is important to understand what sets Justice Kennedy apart from other justices, past and present. What we find is that Kennedy has adopted a controversial approach to protecting the rights of individuals from government action based on opposition to sexual orientation. The Court has long struggled to arrive at the appropriate test for its equal protection cases. Should the greatest constitutional protection—strict judicial scrutiny—only be afforded those who possess the characteristics that make them, *in the eyes of the justices*, members of certain "suspect" classes? Many members of the gay community argue that they will only be able to enjoy the full protection of the laws when the Court answers this question affirmatively. This is because for those who do not meet the "suspect classification" label, there is the realization that the government will often only have to demonstrate that there is an identifiable and legitimate reason, with a rational basis, for its action. In other words, while strict scrutiny traditionally means "'strict' in theory and fatal in fact," rational basis review tends to mean that a law is presumptively constitutional—"'rational' in theory and 'permissive' in fact."[8] In cases involving discrimination based on sexual orientation, Kennedy has wholeheartedly rejected the need to employ strict judicial scrutiny (which, as chapter 4 shows, defines the Court's analysis of race-based classifications). Instead, he argues that animus-driven discrimination can have no "rational basis." As we will see, in establishing his own formulation of this standard of review, Kennedy has drawn on the opinions of his colleagues, past and present. In the process, however, he has put his own modestly libertarian stamp on it—a stamp that identifies antigay legislation as fundamentally at odds with the Constitution that preserves and protects the dignity of every person, regardless of his or her sexual orientation.

Justice Kennedy: Equal Dignity for All

On June 24, 1992, the U.S. Supreme Court announced its decision in *Lee v. Weisman*.[9] This case involved a challenge to the constitutionality of the practice, employed by the principals of public middle and high schools in Rhode Island, of inviting members of the clergy to deliver nondenominational prayers at graduation ceremonies. The father of a girl who had to listen to one such invocation and benediction that was delivered at her high school graduation by a rabbi, whom the school principal had invited to speak, brought the challenge. The principal provided the rabbi with a booklet of guidelines for what would be a suitable nondenominational prayer. The question before the justices was whether this practice was a violation of the Establishment Clause of the First Amendment, which prohibits the government from enacting laws "respecting an establishment of religion." In his opinion that spoke for a five-member majority of the Court, Justice Kennedy decided that this inquiry needed to be answered affirmatively in large part because the intense presence of peer pressure at a high school graduation coerced individuals into participating. There was, he contended, little reason to believe that the average student would feel comfortable about opting out of the ceremony even if it meant involvement in a ceremony that was inconsistent with his or her religious beliefs.

While this coercion aspect of *Weisman* has since generated much discussion, absent from the scholarly dissection of Kennedy's opinion are references to his inclusion of the phrase "constitutional vision."[10] Admittedly, this is not a major academic oversight. However, Kennedy's inclusion of the phrase remains significant for two reasons. First, it is the only time a Supreme Court justice has ever used the phrase in an opinion.[11] It is likely that judicial hesitancy to invoke the term reflects, in large part, a fear that to talk of a "constitutional vision" is to enter dangerous territory that exposes a judge to the accusation that he or she is confusing political philosophy (or policy preferences) with the law. If jurists are described in terms of their constitutional visions, this is usually just another way of talking about their jurisprudence.[12] It is easy to understand why judges might be fearful of using the phrase, because it might direct attention away from the case and toward their own legal philosophy.

However, the second reason for the significance of Kennedy's vision reference in *Weisman* helps to explain why in this case Kennedy was not talking about his own constitutional vision, but rather that of a "free society."[13] Given academia's use of the term, a societal understanding of "constitutional vision" is completely appropriate. Possession of a constitutional vision is not confined to the judiciary. It has been used to refer to members of every branch of the government;[14] it can describe the work of international organizations,[15] labor unions,[16] and political parties;[17] it has been put to work in discussions of political[18] and/or ideological[19] coalitions, political institutions,[20] constitutional amendments;[21] and oftentimes it is invoked to describe the characteristics of a particular period in time. Most important, though, people possess their own constitutional visions, divorced from any understandings and/or definitions determined by either the government or its commentators. It may be true, as Mark Graber has written, that "constitutions settle political conflicts successfully in the short run by providing preexisting answers to contested political questions."[22] However, as Walter Murphy, another political scientist, observes, the boundaries of "governmental structures, procedures, and basic rights" that a document such as the U.S. Constitution establishes are both preceded and defined by the constitutional "goals, ideals, and the *moral* standards by which . . . [Americans] want others, including their own posterity, to judge the community."[23] And, as Justice Kennedy once observed in a commencement address at McGeorge Law School, it is this "moral and ethical code" that "the law is designed to vindicate."[24]

In Justice Kennedy's equal protection jurisprudence, a key part of this process of vindication is the preservation of the ability of each individual to pursue his or her own constitutional vision. Responding to this argument, one might be tempted (not unreasonably) to say, for example, "Well, I don't think my father has a constitutional vision."[25] What I am not suggesting here is that Justice Kennedy believes that either you (or your father) do, or should, have constitutional visions that you wish to pursue. What Kennedy seeks to ensure is that you have the opportunity, unencumbered by the government, to pursue freely a constitutional vision either now or at some point in the future. This freedom—your liberty—is in tension with policies that seek to categorize you, in the name of equality, as a member of a group rather than as an individual. This libertarian approach seeks to minimize the ability of the government to affect the equal status of persons (positively or negatively) by treating them in a particular way because they "belong" to a specific class of individuals. In other words, the belief that Kennedy expressed in *Metro Broadcasting v. FCC* (discussed in chapter 4)—that it is demeaning to assume that certain "minority views" are inevitably held by those individuals who happen to possess a certain "minority characteristic"—is just as applicable to cases involving homosexuals or women as it is to racial minorities, with whom that case was concerned.[26] This is a libertarian conception of equality to which we can apply the label "individual-regarding" equality—an approach that argues that "there is one class of equals, and one relation of equality holds among all its members"; and it makes "a claim of equality for one class of equals, each to be the equal of every other."[27] It is an understanding of equality at whose heart are the same key libertarian principles that we find in Justice Kennedy's jurisprudence.

A Jurist Who "Took the Issue of Gay Rights Seriously"?[28]

The argument that there is only "one class of equals"—human beings—does not sit well with those who, for quite justifiable reasons, wish to define themselves by the groups of which they are members. Many minorities are proud to associate themselves with those with whom they share certain characteristics. The actions and beliefs of these individuals are often defined by the views held by, and the norms associated with, that group. This is true of many members of the gay community, who make the argument that gay pride is hurt and/or diminished by the attitude that every individual, regardless of their sexual orientation, deserves to be treated in the same way. Justice Kennedy's modest libertarianism does not require him to deny the importance, in a pluralistic society, of allowing diverse groups to flourish. As he emphasized in his 1990 Gauer Distinguished Lecture in Law and Public Policy: "Groups and institutions in the private realm must have a real part in shaping society." What he proceeded to explain was that denying this role threatens to create a situation wherein groups "will be seen as irrelevant, as indistinguishable from the allurements of the state, a state always ready to co-opt private initiatives and talents for its own perpetuation."[29] And such a situation would pose a grave threat to the liberty and dignity of every individual member of the group. This observation, however, does not permit us to leave the following question unanswered. Justice Kennedy has written opinions that outline an expansive understanding of individual liberty and treat homosexuals with considerable dignity, but does his philosophical approach to this subject make him "a jurist potentially open to gay rights claims"?[30]

Although there were many indications that he was a less conservative nominee than Judge Bork, when then-Judge Kennedy was announced as the latest presidential choice to fill Justice Powell's vacated seat on the Supreme Court, President Reagan's decision was met with little enthusiasm by the gay community. Representative of the concerns expressed was an article written by law professor Arthur S. Leonard, a prominent voice on legal issues relating to sexual orientation. In that article, which appeared in the *New York Native* one week before the Kennedy hearings began, Leonard focused on the Judge's Ninth Circuit opinions and concluded that "Kennedy seems rather obtuse on important gay issues, and indeed must be counted a likely vote against us on most matters likely to come before the Supreme Court."[31] With the benefit of reading Justice Kennedy's opinions for the Court in *Romer v. Evans* (1996) and *Lawrence v. Texas* (2003)—the two main cases examined in this chapter—it is easy to argue that this was an overly pessimistic evaluation of the nominee's likely attitude toward claims of discrimination based on sexual orientation. In *Romer*, Kennedy wrote a passionate opinion striking down an amendment to the Colorado Constitution that prohibited the state from enacting any laws preventing discrimination based on sexual orientation. Said Kennedy: "It is not within our constitutional tradition to enact laws of this sort."[32] Seven years later, in *Lawrence*, Kennedy extended the Court's commitment to an expansive and individualized understanding of the Fourteenth Amendment's protection of liberty, striking down a Texas statute that made it a crime to engage in sexual relations with a person of the same sex. This was an opinion that Kennedy found no need to agonize over.[33] Even absent these opinions it would be possible to argue that a fairer evaluation of Kennedy's circuit court opinions leads one to the conclusion that prior to his Supreme Court nomination his work demonstrated that he did indeed take "gay rights claims seriously." In order to understand why this should be the case, we need to look at the opinion penned by Judge Kennedy in *Beller v. Middendorf* (1980), an opinion that lay at the center of what the conservative *National Review* described as "the skepticism on the Right, and the premature rejoicing on the Left" that greeted the Sacramentan's Supreme Court nomination.[34]

The litigation that culminated in the opinion that Judge Kennedy wrote for a two-member majority of a three-judge panel of the Ninth Circuit in *Beller* began when three individuals were discharged from the Navy. Their service records were not the sources of the justifications for the termination of their military service. Rather, they were found to have engaged in homosexual behavior, which violated the following Navy regulation:

> Members involved in homosexuality are military liabilities who cannot be tolerated in a military organization. In developing and documenting cases involving homosexual conduct, commanding officers should be keenly aware that members involved in homosexual acts are security and reliability risks who discredit themselves and the naval service by their homosexual conduct. Their prompt separation is essential.[35]

The discharged individuals challenged the constitutionality of this regulation, contending that it violated the due process clause of the Fourteenth Amendment, which guarantees that "no State shall . . . deprive any person of life, liberty, or property, without due process of law."

There is no doubt that the Navy's policy is entirely inconsistent with the principles of libertarianism that value the preservation of individual liberty through the protection of individual dignity and the toleration of harmless differences. It may therefore come as a surprise to learn that Judge Kennedy rejected the claim that the Navy's regulation violated constitutionally protected liberty. Certainly, this decision troubled the gay community when Kennedy was nominated to replace Justice Powell. There was some justification for this concern, but a close reading of Kennedy's *Beller* opinion shows that he really did care about (1) the stigmatizing effects of the Navy's policy, and (2) the irrationality of the government's action—both strong elements of his Supreme Court opinions in *Romer* and *Lawrence*.

Although troubled by the fact that the Navy only had a *mandatory* discharge policy for persons engaging in "homosexual acts, various sexual offenses, and sale or trafficking in drugs,"[36] Kennedy concluded that the court's hands were tied by a lengthy line of precedent and, given the traditional judicial deference to the military, the "nature of the employer—the Navy."[37] He took pains to emphasize that his opinion was not passing judgment over the wisdom of the policy—such a "judgment is neither implicit in our decision nor within our province to make"—and that its conclusion about "the constitutionality of the regulations stems from the needs of the military, the Navy in particular, and from the unique accommodation between military demands and what might be constitutionally protected activity in some other contexts."[38] Indeed, despite his above reference to maintaining a proper stance of judicial restraint, Kennedy made a point of expressing his misgivings about the stigma attached to the Navy's policy. He held that a finding that the Navy's policy created stigma for persons subject to its mandatory discharge would indeed be a deprivation of the individuals' constitutionally protected liberty. He concluded that the stigma was not present in the particular case before the court because the plaintiffs did not dispute the charge that they had engaged in homosexuality. Consequently, the circumstances did not exist under which the stigma would arise (if the charges were "false, made public, and followed by discharge").[39] But he reached this conclusion reluctantly, with full recognition that it ignored, or at the very least paid nothing more than lip service to, the argument that the mere existence of the policy was stigmatizing.

One of the ways in which Kennedy tried to acknowledge that he was sensitive to the stigmatizing nature of the Navy's policy was to make reference to the "substantial academic comment which argues that the choice to engage in homosexual action is a personal decision entitled, at least in some instances, to recognition as a fundamental right and to full protection as an aspect of the individual's right of privacy."[40] Citing an example of one such piece of commentary—an article by law professor Laurence Tribe—Kennedy observed:

> The real stigma imposed by the Navy's action, moreover, is the charge of homosexuality, not the fact of discharge or some implied statement that the individual is not sufficiently needed to be retained. This is especially true since the regulations do not make fitness of the particular individual a factor in the decision to discharge.[41]

During his confirmation hearings, the plentiful citations to academic commentary included in Kennedy's *Beller* opinion raised the eyebrows of some of the senators. Senator Gordon Humphrey (R-NH) expressed concern about the opinion's inclusion of a list of ten citations to constitutional law treatises and law-review articles.[42] When Senator Humphrey questioned Kennedy's use of these sources, the nominee responded that he "had read extensively in preparing for this opinion, in order to understand the right approach." He expressed the belief that, whether or not they formed the basis for the decision, "it is [only] fair to the parties to set forth the things that I have read." Unsatisfied, Senator Humphrey wanted to know whether Kennedy found "something commanding about academic opinion versus societal mores, when they differ?" Perhaps seeking to present a reassuring answer, Kennedy concluded that ultimately "I am not overly persuaded by academic comment. I frankly do not have time to read very much of it."[43]

To a certain extent, Kennedy's efforts to show that in *Beller* he did not *rely* on views from the academy are supported by the reference that he made to the articles' advocacy of the recognition that "the choice to engage in homosexual action" is "a fundamental right" protected by a constitutional "right of privacy."[44] As we will see in chapter 5, in non-economic liberty cases Kennedy has made a very conscious, and successful, effort to move the Court away from a jurisprudence of unenumerated "privacy" to reliance on the textually grounded "liberty." In the analysis that follows in this chapter, we will also see that in equal protection cases involving sexual orientation–based discrimination Kennedy has shied away from any endorsement of the argument that such discrimination should be treated in terms of fundamental rights.[45] As Kennedy pointed out in *Beller*:

> Plaintiffs' ultimate contention is that the Navy's regulations violate substantive guarantees inherent in the due process clause. We decide at the outset that this case does not require us to address the question whether consensual private homosexual conduct is a fundamental right, as that term is used in equal protection and some due process cases. *If we were to answer in the affirmative, it would follow that the conduct in question is subject to prohibition only to further compelling state interests and that the category used or burden imposed by the regulation must be a necessary, or the least restrictive, way to promote those interests. To formulate the issue in those terms would reflect, we think, a misunderstanding of proper substantive due process analysis.*[46]

This observation demonstrates Kennedy's libertarian sensitivity for the issues at stake, because it indicates his concern about trying to use the Court's current frames of doctrinal reference to define the boundaries of this particular aspect of liberty. The freedom of all, regardless of their sexual orientation, to engage in the intimate conduct of their choice, Kennedy implies, will actually receive inadequate protection if there needs to be proof that there is a "fundamental right" to engage in such behavior—in this case, homosexual behavior. Concluding that *Beller* "involve[d] neither" of the traditional judicial tests used in equal protection cases, Kennedy reached out to an approach that some members of the Supreme Court had begun to advocate in opinions during the

1970s. This is a stronger formulation of rational basis review that involves less deference to government actions, an approach that came to define the opinion in *Romer* and play an important role in *Lawrence*.[47]

If "Equal Protection of the Laws" Means Anything, It Means . . .

On the eve of the bicentennial of the U.S. Constitution in 1987, a national survey asked people to identify whether or not five different phrases could be found in the document. Eighty percent of respondents said that, yes, two hundred years ago when the Framers met in Philadelphia they did indeed write into the nation's supreme law the recognition that "all men are created equal" (for the other results see figure 3.1).[48] This phrase is normatively attractive, therefore it is unsurprising that those questioned assumed that its words, (actually from the Declaration of Independence), could be found in the Constitution, which is a revered part of the fabric of American society.[49] The fact remains, however, that prior to the addition of the Fourteenth Amendment in 1868 the Constitution did not explicitly speak about the fundamental subject of equality. And even after it was amended to require that "no State shall . . . deny to any person within its jurisdiction the equal protection of the laws,"

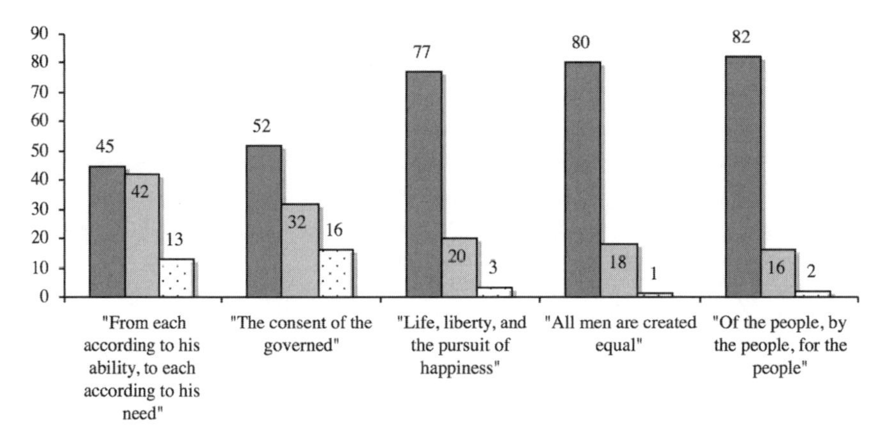

FIGURE 3.1
Responses to the statement "The following phrases are found in the Constitution" (Hearst Corporation-sponsored survey, 1986)
Source: Memo from Trait Trussell and Colleagues at the Commission on the Bicentennial of the United States Constitution to Everett C. Ladd, 10 April 1987; Decision Memos (March–April 1987) file; Office of the Chairman, Correspondence of the Chairman, 1985–1991, Correspondence thru Equal Justice Under Law, Box 1 NN3-220-92-004 H.M. 1992; Records of Temporary Committees, Commissions & Boards: Commission on the Bicentennial of the U.S. Constitution, Record Group 220; National Archives and Records Administration at College Park, MD.

these chosen words made "the concept of equality a test of legislation, but . . . [did] not stipulate any particular conception of that concept."[50]

It was the "privileges or immunities" clause of the Fourteenth Amendment ("No State shall make or enforce any law which shall abridge the privileges or immunities of citizens of the United States") that was originally meant to provide legal equality. This is because its language was considered as referring to the fundamental, natural rights that "belong, of right, to citizens of all free governments"; protection from discriminatory legislation was a part of this package of rights.[51] However, this clause was judicially eviscerated in the *Slaughterhouse Cases* (1873). Consequently, the task of providing substantive rights protections fell instead to the due process and equal protection clauses.[52] The "original emphasis" of the latter was solely "to impose a duty on the executive and judicial branches of state governments to *apply and enforce*, in an evenhanded manner, nondiscriminatory legislation."[53] Even absent the words "All men are created equal," a phrase that has been described as the Declaration of Independence's "glittering generalit[y]"[54] on equality, the spirit of Thomas Jefferson's words was certainly evident in the amendment language drafted by the 39th Congress during Reconstruction. Neither text denies the existence of the natural differences that exist between human beings; however, both speak of legal equality.[55] Of course, just what that means, and how the courts enforce it, is what we must now concern ourselves with.

Desperately Seeking a Standard

If a decisive majority of the justices on the Burger and Rehnquist Courts agreed about anything, it was that using the two-tier approach (strict scrutiny or rational basis) to decide equal protection cases was woefully inadequate. Although the Warren Court had only rather modestly extended the application of this dichotomous framework to cases involving non race–based "suspect classifications" and "fundamental interests," its use of the either-or approach nevertheless attracted considerable attention, both on and off the bench.[56] With the transition from the Warren Court to the Burger Court in the 1970s, the justices' expressions of doctrinal dissatisfaction became more obvious. However, as law professor Gerald Gunther noted in a prominent article published in 1972 in the *Harvard Law Review*, one thing remained constant—this judicial frustration cut across ideological lines.[57] This was clear in a memo that the conservative Justice Rehnquist wrote to his liberal colleague Justice Brennan in January 1976. "I presume," said Rehnquist, that "there will always be differences among us as to what sort of a classification demands 'strict scrutiny,' and perhaps unresolved questions as to whether there may be an intermediate level of scrutiny between 'strict' and 'rational basis.'"[58] During the next quarter century (through the decision in *Romer*), time and again the justices lined up to write equal protection opinions that demonstrated the continuing validity of this observation.[59]

In response to the definitional difficulties associated with "suspect classes," and the belief that these difficulties could best be resolved by exercising judicial restraint, a number of justices began to move toward an alternate understanding of the rational basis standard, a more sophisticated formulation of which ultimately prevailed in *Romer*. Accurately described as "rational basis with teeth," this reformulation began to gain attention as early as the Court's October 1971 term. In his evaluation of that term's decisions, Professor Gunther concluded that one result of the aforementioned doctrinal dissatisfaction was that even under rational basis review the government could no longer rely on the justices to undertake a hands-off, deferential analysis of the relationship between legislative means and ends. This was potentially of great significance because it showed that the Court could "use the [equal protection] clause as an interventionist tool without resorting to the strict scrutiny language."[60] Leading this jurisprudential revolution (albeit in a minority position for many years) was Justice Stevens.

Stevens: "There Is Only One Equal Protection Clause"

The justices' frustration with a framework that consisted of two polar opposite standards of review for equal protection cases was both empirical and normative. Citing several different decisions as supporting evidence, in 1985 Justice Stevens explained the empirical argument: "Our cases reflect a continuum of judgmental responses to differing classifications."[61] The "two standards fit all" description of the Court's equal protection jurisprudence simply did not, he noted, comport with the reality of what the Court was actually doing. Nowhere was this clearer than in *Massachusetts Board of Retirement v. Murgia*.[62] When Justice Stevens took his seat on the Court in 1975, he joined a bench of justices embroiled in a messy, internal dispute over the opinion writing in this case that involved a Massachusetts statute mandating retirement of state police officers when they reached the age of fifty.

Murgia was finally decided through a relatively short per curiam (unsigned) opinion, which its author, Justice Powell, described as "about as blandly written as one can write to dispose of the equal protection arguments advanced in this case." The opinion, he noted in a memo to his colleagues, left to "another day" the jurisprudential debate that was underpinned by deep divisions among the justices.[63] These divisions were only evident if one strained to read between the lines of Powell's "bland" opinion in which he said that the Court "need state only briefly" why rational basis was being used instead of strict scrutiny. The Court's precedents did not suggest an easy resolution of *Murgia.* However, the Court—speaking through Powell—nevertheless determined that past cases "reaffirmed that equal protection analysis requires strict scrutiny of a legislative classification *only when the classification impermissibly interferes with the exercise of a fundamental right or operates to the peculiar disadvantage of a suspect class.*" The fact was, Powell concluded, that "mandatory retirement at age 50 under the Massachusetts statute involves neither situation."[64] There does not appear to have been anything particularly special about *Murgia* that can account for the battle that was waged over the appropriate standard of judicial review to apply to the equal protection question before the Court. Rather, it came up to the justices during a time when any case would be contentious if it asked whether either (1) the list of characteristics constituting "suspect classifications" should be expanded, or (2) the Court should actively seek to determine the purpose of discriminatory legislation.

In *Murgia,* it was Powell's stated "objective . . . to frame E/P analysis ("rational basis") fairly broadly or flexibly without creating a *third* tier of analysis." This was an approach that many of his colleagues were willing to accept.[65] However, there was disagreement over just how flexible the test could be before it either resembled a third tier or committed the Court to excessive second-guessing of legislative purposes. Justice Brennan originally wrote an opinion that was slated to speak for the Court. On several occasions, Brennan sought to defend his views by saying that they did not represent a radical departure from the accepted standard of rational basis review. This standard, he said, was articulated in *Williamson v. Lee Optical,* a 1955 decision that made a major contribution to making "the presumption of constitutionality virtually irrebuttable"[66] because of its sweeping deference to what "the legislature *might* have concluded."[67] To be sure, his draft opinion on *Murgia* stated a "more flexible rule," but Brennan was adamant that this test had been both developed by and evolved through the Court's previous decisions.[68]

Commenting on an early draft of Powell's "compromise/peace treaty" in *Murgia,* William H. Block, one of Justice Blackmun's law clerks, wrote: "The price of the compromise . . . is ambiguity in the exact meaning of the terms used to deal with the 'rational relation' tier of analysis." To be sure, it would "end a number of the distracting skirmishes," but "the war" would probably continue.[69] Within a matter of months that prediction came true when, at the beginning of its October 1976 term, the Court took up *Craig v. Boren*[70]—the year's headline-grabbing equal protection decision. In *Craig,* Justice Stevens was the only member of the Court unencumbered by *Murgia* baggage. However, this did not mean that he came to the Supreme Court with an entirely open mind about the direction he hoped to see the Court's equal protection doctrine take. He held opinions that were just as strong as any of those of his new colleagues who did bear the battle scars of *Murgia*, and he wasted no time laying these out in what became the first of many separate concurrences on the subject.[71]

In *Craig*, the Court struck down a 1972 Oklahoma law that set the minimum ages for purchasing 3.2 percent beer at twenty-one years for men and eighteen for women. The law was challenged by Curtis Craig, a twenty-year-old who wanted to purchase beer, and a beer vendor who wanted to sell it to men between the ages of eighteen and twenty. As political scientists Lee Epstein and Jack Knight show in their excellent study of *Craig*, from the very beginning the case involved a disagreement about the level of judicial review that the Court should employ to resolve sex-based equal protection disputes. Craig sought review under the standard of strict scrutiny, the adoption of which would be a rather radical step for the Court to take. Oklahoma, by contrast, took a position that was more consistent with the Court's precedents. It encouraged the Court to engage in a far more deferential level of review in order to determine whether the law had a rational basis. In what amounted to a triumph for the strategic decision-making skills of Justice Brennan, the Court finally settled on a new, intermediate standard of scrutiny for sex discrimination, requiring "classifications by gender . . . [to] serve important governmental objectives and . . . be substantially related to achievement of those objectives."[72] The Oklahoma law was not deemed able to withstand this level of review and was struck down by the Court as a violation of the Fourteenth Amendment.

Justice Stevens's concurring opinion in *Craig* is famous for the following declaration. "There is only one Equal Protection Clause. It requires every State to govern impartially. It does not direct the courts to apply one standard of review in some cases and a different standard in other cases."[73] Stevens was willing to put more faith in the ability of the judiciary to apply rational basis review in a way that did not simply result in presumptive constitutionality through deference to legislative determinations. In *Craig*, this jurisprudential approach led him to conclude that responsible rational basis review was perfectly appropriate because the classification in the case was "not totally irrational"; there was "evidence . . . [to] indicate that there are more males than females in this age bracket who drive and also more who drink." Stevens concluded, however, that the law was unconstitutional because it was not rationally related to the overall stated goal of improving "traffic safety."[74]

While *Murgia* demonstrated that a majority of the Court held strong concerns about the appropriate standards for equal protection cases, when Stevens joined the Court his reservations about the state of the existing doctrine appear to have been stronger than those of any of his colleagues. Justice Powell also felt strongly about the "state of the doctrine," but was more easily accommodated than Stevens. For example, in *United States Railroad Retirement Board v. Fritz* (1980) (upholding the 1974 Railroad Retirement Act's distinctions between different classes of employees),[75] after intense negotiations between himself and Justices Stevens and Powell, Justice Rehnquist finally wrote Justice Stevens on November 24, informing him: "Since Lewis has now joined, and I seem to have a Court opinion, I am loath to try to make any additional changes that would embroil us still further in the *Murgia* . . . discussions. . . . Therefore, I believe I will let the matter rest as is."[76] Justice Stevens's solo concurrence, the first draft of which was circulated the next day, was a small price to pay after Rehnquist secured Powell's vote.[77] Five years later, the Court decided *City of Cleburne v. Cleburne Living Center*, which in many respects laid the doctrinal framework for the decision in *Romer* because it also involved governmental action that a majority of the Court deemed to be unconstitutional because it was motivated by "irrational fears."

City of Cleburne: Let's Give Them "Something to Think About"[78]

In 1980, after purchasing 201 Featherston Street in the city of Cleburne, Texas, Jan Hannah intended to lease the building to Cleburne Living Center Inc. (CLC), which would use it as a group home for mentally retarded adults. The building's location in an Apartment House District (zoning area R-3) meant that the potential lessees needed to apply for a special permit. The city's zoning regulations permitted a number of different properties in an R-3 area, including the following: "apartment houses, or multiple dwellings"; "fraternity or sorority houses and dormitories"; "private clubs or fraternal orders, except those whose chief activity is carried on as a business." It was also permissible to construct new buildings or use existing structures as "hospitals, sanitariums, nursing homes or homes for convalescents or aged." However, if a property was to house "the insane or feebleminded, or alcoholics or drug addicts," or if it was to be used as a "penal or correctional institution," it was singled out for special treatment—its operators were required to apply for a special permit.[79] When the Cleburne City Council denied this permit to CLC, it defended its decision by citing several concerns about permitting the home to be used as a facility for mentally retarded adults. First, it felt that allowing the property to be used in this way would generate negative attitudes in the immediate residential community. Second, there was the concern that students at the local junior high school would harass the home's residents. The council also expressed concern about (1) the home's location in the "500-year flood plain," (2) its size and number of intended occupants, and (3) the potential for congestion in the surrounding streets. Upon denial of the permit, CLC challenged the constitutionality of the zoning ordinance, arguing that it was an equal protection violation of the Fourteenth Amendment.

From the outset, a central question in the case, as it moved through the federal courts, was whether the proper level of judicial review was closest to rational basis or strict scrutiny, or perhaps an intermediate level such as that employed in *Craig*. The district court found that (1) under the terms of the ordinance the property could have been used for identical purposes, involving adults who were not retarded, without even the need to apply for a permit; and (2) the permit denial "was motivated primarily by the fact that the residents of the home would be persons who are mentally retarded." It reached the conclusion, however, that mental retardation was neither a suspect nor quasi-suspect classification, therefore the ordinance need only pass the lowest level of judicial scrutiny—which it easily did.[80] The Court of Appeals for the Fifth Circuit, by contrast, concluded that mental retardation was a quasi-suspect classification and that the ordinance failed an intermediate level of review.

When the Supreme Court announced its affirmation of the Fifth Circuit's decision, the justices' disagreements about standards of review for equal protection cases were evident in the opinion that Justice White penned for the Court. The justices did not find it particularly difficult to reach their conclusion that as applied to the CLC the ordinance was unconstitutional. Justice White concluded that only "irrational prejudice" against the mentally retarded could explain the Council's concerns, particularly given that they could just as easily apply to "apartment houses, multiple dwellings, and the like."[81] For example, White explained that the vague and undifferentiated nature of the Council's fear was particularly clear when one examined the concern about the home's proximity to a school—this was because of the fact that thirty students at the school were, themselves, mentally retarded.[82] What proved to be the greatest challenge for the justices was to reach the conclusion that the application of the ordinance be held to no higher standard of review than one whose "general rule is that legislation is presumed to be valid and will be sustained if the classification drawn by the statute is rationally related to a legitimate state interest."[83] However, White's subsequent discussion of the types of classifications that were suspect and therefore not afforded such judicial deference suggested that there was little that was general about the rules used by the Court in equal protection cases.[84]

Reflecting upon *Murgia*, Justice White concluded that that decision's "lesson . . . is that where individuals in the group affected by a law have distinguishing characteristics relevant to interests the State *has the authority to implement*, the courts have been very reluctant . . . to closely scrutinize legislative choices."[85] Justice Stevens (joined by Chief Justice Burger[86]) agreed with White that the city of Cleburne lacked this authority because its actions were the result of "irrational prejudice against the mentally retarded."[87] It was for this reason that Stevens joined White's opinion. However, he also felt compelled to write separately to express his displeasure at the state of the Court's equal protection jurisprudence. Reiterating the position that he staked out in *Craig*, Stevens argued that the Court was fooling both itself and its audiences by maintaining the appearance that its decisions used either strict scrutiny or rational basis review. The reality was far more complex:

> In fact, our cases have not delineated three—or even one or two—such well-defined standards. Rather, our cases reflect a *continuum of judgmental responses* to differing classifications which have been explained in opinions by terms ranging from "strict scrutiny" at one extreme to "rational basis" at the other.[88]

Given this situation, concluded Stevens, the most prudent judicial approach was to apply a more rigorous rational basis test rather than to simply defer to those classifications designated as "suspect." After all, what could be more unconstitutional than a classification that "an impartial lawmaker could [not] logically believe . . . would serve a legitimate public purpose that transcends the harm to the members of the disadvantaged class."[89]

Moreno: "Politically Unpopular Group[s]"

There can be little doubt that in *City of Cleburne* the Court employed "rational basis with teeth." To further understand some of the ways in which Justice Kennedy's *Romer* opinion draws on the doctrinal views from the 1985 decision—especially those expressed in concurrence by Justice Stevens—it is helpful to look back at one more decision made by the Burger Court. In *United States Department of Agriculture v. Moreno* (1973), the Court decided that a 1971 amendment to the 1964 Food Stamp Act failed rational basis review. It found that the two stated purposes of the Act (to prevent hippy communes from obtaining food stamps and to minimize food stamp program fraud) were not served by the amendment's requirement that any household that wished to participate in the food stamp program be comprised of only individuals who were related to each other. Concluding that passage of the amendment had most likely been fueled by antihippy sentiment, Justice Brennan emphatically stated that such an approach was unconstitutional. "If the constitutional conception of 'equal protection of the laws' means anything," he wrote, "it must at the very least mean that a bare congressional desire to harm a politically unpopular group cannot constitute a *legitimate* governmental interest."[90] The justices saw neither a desire nor a need to identify the group of affected individuals (unrelated, cohabiting food stamp recipients) as a classification of persons against whom government action was presumptively suspect and in need of being strictly scrutinized.

Interestingly, Justice Brennan's papers reveal that it was to his dismay that the government withdrew its original defense of the statute. It first argued that the law was a legitimate way to undertake government regulation of societal morality. When Brennan began to consider the case, his thoughts were directed at formulating a rejection of this justification. He proceeded on the assumption that the case could be decided through an opinion directed at exploring and explaining the illegitimacy of the morality defense.[91] However, in the brief that it submitted on January 31, 1973, three months before oral argument in the case, the government stated that this was no longer considered a purpose of the law and that "impact of the statutory classification on private morality, if any, is purely incidental." This change probably reflected the government's recognition that the morality argument would receive a very cool reaction from the justices in light of the decision, nine days earlier, in *Roe v. Wade*.[92] This did not stop Brennan from noting in his opinion, however, that policing morality was the government's original justification. Although he did not say so explicitly, he clearly had much respect for the district court's conclusion that "interpreting the amendment as an attempt to regulate morality would raise serious constitutional questions" that implicated "the rights to privacy and freedom of association *in the home*."[93]

"As it turned out," concluded Brennan, the government's contention that the law was a means to achieving the end of minimizing food stamp program fraud "was even less convincing than the 'morality' argument" because "in practical operation, the statute was not in any sense rationally designed to serve this goal."[94] However, as we will see, for the purposes of understanding Kennedy's opinion in *Romer*, *Moreno* remains important not only because of its place in the Court's line of precedents that find it unnecessary to apply anything stronger than rational basis review to laws borne of animus, but also because of Justice Brennan's behind-the-scenes remarks about the original justification for the 1971 statutory amendment.

Romer v. Evans: "I've Never Seen a Case Like This"[95]

In the late 1980s, Colorado Springs began to witness an influx of socially conservative, evangelical Christian groups. Some commentators have since described the city—and the surrounding area—as the "Vatican of evangelical Christianity."[96] One of the issues that united these groups was opposition to the legal and political gains that were being made by homosexuals. Some of these advances were extensive:

> Three home rule cities enacted ordinances prohibiting discrimination based on sexual orientation in jobs, housing, and public accommodations; the Colorado Civil Rights Commission voted to recommend that the General Assembly extend the State's civil rights act to ban discrimination based upon sexual orientation; the Governor issued an executive order prohibiting job discrimination for state classified employees based on sexual orientation; at least two state colleges adopted policies prohibiting discrimination based on sexual orientation; and the Colorado General Assembly enacted a statute prohibiting health insurance companies from determining insurability based on sexual orientation.[97]

Among the antigay groups, there was a perception that homosexuals were being afforded "special rights or protections" at the expense of the city's heterosexual residents.[98] And many felt "that those local gains would be used by homosexual activists as 'leverage to approach state legislators on larger scale measures.'"[99] *Romer v. Evans* involved a constitutional challenge to one of the responses to these gains.

Amendment 2, an addition to the Colorado State Constitution, was adopted in 1992 in a statewide referendum. Receiving 53 percent of the vote, it read as follows:

> No Protected Status Based on Homosexual, Lesbian or Bisexual Orientation. Neither the State of Colorado, through any of its branches or departments, nor any of its agencies, political subdivisions, municipalities or school districts, shall enact, adopt or enforce any statute, regulation, ordinance or policy whereby homosexual, lesbian or bisexual orientation, conduct, practices or relationships shall constitute or otherwise be the basis of or entitle any person or class of persons to have or claim any minority status, quota preferences, protected status or claim of discrimination. This Section of the Constitution shall be in all respects self-executing.[100]

This amendment had the effect of voiding ordinances, enacted by several state and local governments, that prohibited discrimination based on sexual orientation. The challenge to its constitutionality was led by Richard Evans, an administrator for the city and county of Denver—one of the municipalities whose nondiscrimination ordinance was repealed by Amendment 2. Reacting to the electoral endorsement of this change to the Colorado Constitution, Evans remarked that "it was as if 800,000 people had said [to homosexuals] 'You're not equal to us.'"[101] In his opinion that struck down Amendment 2 in the spring of 1996, Justice Kennedy agreed with Evans.

Romer and the Rule of Law

During the oral argument in *Romer*, Justice Kennedy exhibited noticeable opposition to Amendment 2. This hostility was not immediately apparent when he delivered the decision in the case on May 20, a fine early summer morning in Washington, D.C. This is because the justice omitted from his oral delivery the powerful statement with which he opened his opinion that spoke for himself and five of his colleagues:

> One century ago, the first Justice Harlan admonished this Court that the Constitution "neither knows nor tolerates classes among citizens." Unheeded then, those words now are understood to state a commitment to the law's neutrality where the rights of persons are at stake.[102]

This inclusion of a quotation from the famous Harlan dissent in *Plessy v. Ferguson*—about which we will hear much more in the following chapter—set the tone for an opinion that said to every individual, regardless of their sexual orientation, "You are equal to us." It demonstrated, as political scientist Artemus Ward has remarked, that "Kennedy likened the gay rights movement to the civil rights movement."[103] This is an astute observation because it suggests, quite correctly, that Kennedy's concern about the inequality sanctioned by Amendment 2 was neither confined to nor solely driven by the fact that the individuals being discriminated against were homosexuals. The arguments that he made could be applied to any "politically unpopular group" that is discriminated against because of a bare majoritarian "desire to harm" it. As Justice Brennan observed in *Moreno* (an opinion from which Kennedy admiringly quoted in *Romer*), "the constitutional conception of 'equal protection of the laws'" unequivocally tells us this "cannot constitute a *legitimate* governmental interest."[104]

Perhaps the most prominent aspect of Amendment 2 to catch the attention of Justice Kennedy was the breadth of its impact. He considered this to be particularly egregious because (in his opinion) the language precluded homosexuals from seeking *any* political or judicial recourse to state action that discriminated against them because of their sexual orientation. The amendment, he wrote, was an example of a state action that represented, for gays, a "sweeping and comprehensive . . . change in [their] legal status." They were "by state decree," he observed, "put in a solitary class with respect to *transactions and relations* in both the private and governmental spheres."[105] It is important to note that in *Romer* both the parties and the justices were sharply divided over the extent to which Amendment 2, if left standing, would have impacted the administration of generally applicable antidiscrimination laws (as opposed to laws specifically directed at banning discrimination based on sexual orientation, laws it clearly voided). This subject consumed much of the hour of oral argument and the pages of the opinions penned by Kennedy and Scalia (who, in dissent, lashed out at his colleague's arguments). What is interesting is that while Kennedy did not think it strictly necessary, he nevertheless thought it fair to "infer . . . from the broad language of the amendment that it deprives gays and lesbians even of the protection of general laws and policies that prohibit arbitrary discrimination in governmental and private settings." He was clearly unwilling to trust that somewhere down the road an official would not share this interpretation of the amendment.[106] Therefore, it was impossible to reach anything but the following conclusion: Amendment 2 deprives gays and lesbians, *and no one else*, of "specific legal protection from the injuries caused by discrimination, and it forbids reinstatement of these laws and policies." This was something that Kennedy said defied the country's "constitutional tradition" and threatened the rule of law, at whose heart is the "principle that government and each of its parts remain open on impartial terms to all who seek its assistance."[107] Denial of access to the political (and/or judicial) process would be the ultimate example of leaving a minority at the mercy of the majority, representing a fundamental challenge to the rule of law.

His focus on these aspects of the impact of Amendment 2 shows that to a certain extent Kennedy shared the concerns expressed by the Colorado Supreme Court, whose decision to strike down Amendment 2 was what prompted Colorado's appeal to the nine justices in Washington. The state court concluded that the Equal Protection Clause of the Fourteenth Amendment demanded strict judicial scrutiny of governmental actions that infringed on the fundamental interest (or right) of political participation—the element of liberty it considered abridged by Amendment 2.[108] In reaching this decision, it concluded that the lessons of an earlier U.S. Supreme Court decision, involving Colorado, were of relevance. In that decision, *Lucas v. Colorado General Assembly* (1964), Chief Justice Earl Warren made the following observation. "A citizen's constitutional rights," wrote Warren, "can hardly be infringed simply because a majority of the people choose that it be."[109] *Lucas* was one of the legislative reapportionment cases decided as a companion to *Reynolds v. Sims*, in which the Court reached the landmark conclusion that there were very few "constitutionally cognizable principles which would justify departures from the basic standard of equality among voters in the apportionment of seats in state legislatures."[110] In these cases, the Court expanded the definition of "fundamental interests" to include electoral representation. *Lucas* involved a challenge to an amendment to the Colorado State Constitution, an amendment that provided for per capita apportionment in the State House and not the State Senate. Under the revised standard, the Court found that this amendment violated the Equal Protection Clause.[111]

While Justice Kennedy's discussion of the rule of law impact of Amendment 2 shows his recognition that it did indeed place an obstacle in the path of the "fundamental right of gays and lesbians to participate in the political process," he chose to explore this issue in a different manner and to affirm the state court's decision using a different jurisprudential focus.[112] And in so doing, he demonstrated that even a more narrowly written amendment—whose impact on the legal status of homosexuals was neither sweeping nor comprehensive—could not pass constitutional muster as long as it was underpinned by the same majoritarian, and morality-driven animus that Kennedy concluded was the only way to explain the existence of Amendment 2.[113]

All About the Animus

Writing in a concurring opinion in a case decided five years after *Romer*, Justice Kennedy made the following observation:

> Prejudice, we are beginning to understand, rises not from malice or hostile animus alone. It may result as well from insensitivity caused by simple want of careful, rational reflection or from some instinctive mechanism to guard against people who appear to be different in some respects from ourselves.[114]

In *Romer*, the Court could easily have struck down Amendment 2 using what Kennedy described as the "conventional ['suspect class'] inquiry." This is because the provision had "the peculiar property of imposing a broad and undifferentiated disability on a single named group," thereby making it "an exceptional and . . . invalid form of legislation."[115] Instead, however, Kennedy followed the doctrinal path laid out by previous decisions, most prominently *City of Cleburne.* This is because, as we have seen, the Court's precedents teach us: "If the adverse impact on the disfavored class is an apparent aim of the legislature, its impartiality would be suspect."[116] In *Romer*, the foundations of animus and majoritarian conceptions of morality upon which Amendment 2 is constructed fall into this category of inherently suspicious actions.

Kennedy had no doubt that Amendment 2 was the product of "hostile animus." "Its sheer breadth," he wrote, "is so discontinuous with the reasons offered for it that *the amendment seems inexplicable by anything but animus toward the class it affects.*" Looking back to *City of Cleburne*, it was therefore appropriate to employ rational basis review and to find that Amendment 2 defied even this low standard of review.[117] But just what were the "reasons offered" by Colorado? The state defended Amendment 2 as a means for achieving the end of *remedying inequality*. This meant that, if anything, it was the antidiscrimination ordinances adopted by municipalities that were the source of the constitutionally objectionable unequal treatment, because they afforded homosexuals "special rights" by identifying sexual orientation as a characteristic that could not form the basis of discrimination. During the oral argument in *Romer*, Kennedy made it clear that he was troubled by this argument. In his opinion, this concern translated into his conclusion that this justification was best described as implausible.[118]

In the brief on the merits, and during oral argument, respondents' attorney in *Romer*, Jean Dubofsky, was careful to emphasize that her clients could prevail even if the justices chose not to use the case as a vehicle to decide some of the most politically charged and controversial issues associated with the case. "The Court need not decide whether preservation of traditional sexual morality can be a legitimate purpose for a legislative classification," and it certainly did not need to touch *Bowers v. Hardwick*, the Court's 1986 decision sustaining a law criminalizing homosexual sodomy (discussed below).[119] That Justice Kennedy subsequently wrote the opinion in *Romer* without including any references to *Bowers* was something that Justice Scalia criticized in detail in his dissenting opinion. Scalia took his colleague to task for writing what in Scalia's mind was an opinion that contradicted but left unchallenged the 1986 precedent.[120] One month later, in a speech to an audience at Gregorian University in Italy, Scalia expressed his views on democratic theory and repeatedly emphasized points that he had made in his *Romer* dissent. He made a sum of the parts argument. Society, as a whole, can only ever be as good, virtuous, or judicious in its decision making as the parts (the individuals) of which it is composed. He explained that he did not believe "that any state can provide for its people a society that is any better than the virtue of its people. And if the people do not have that virtue, the state cannot impose it. At least in a democratic system."[121]

In his dissenting opinion in *Romer*, Justice Scalia applied this argument to his critical analysis of Justice Kennedy's majority opinion. Scalia wrote that, like *Bowers*, *Romer* involved a majoritarian expression of "moral disapproval" of homosexuality. This, said Scalia, was the "only sort of 'animus'" involved; and the rationality of such a decision could not be legitimately challenged by the judiciary. Amendment 2 was a "modest attempt by seemingly tolerant Coloradans to preserve traditional sexual mores," and it was "unimpeachable under any constitutional doctrine hitherto pronounced. . . ." And, if the change to the Colorado Constitution demonstrated any "degree of hostility," it was surely "the smallest conceivable."[122] From Justice Kennedy's perspective, permitting this approach to prevail would threaten American society's quest to be good, virtuous, or judicious. This is because morality-based decisions fail to protect the dignity of all, and they threaten the ability of individuals to pursue their own equal constitutional visions. And, society is a whole that is composed of these individuals.

Lawrence: A "Libertarian Revolution"?

Three days after the decision in *Romer*, retired Justice Blackmun sent a short note to Justice Kennedy. "Monday's decision," he told his friend, "took courage." Reflecting on his own experience following his authorship of *Roe v. Wade*, Blackmun told Kennedy to expect "a lot of critical and even hateful mail." Blackmun's advice—"Hang in there." A few days later Kennedy expressed his gratitude in a short note of reply in which he made the astute observation: "No one told us it was an easy job when we signed on."[123] When Kennedy "signed on" to the position of associate justice of the U.S. Supreme Court, he surely knew that part of his job, in the years to come, would be to confront an issue, and a decision, upon which he had made his views quite clear in the 1986 Stanford University speech (discussed in chapter 1) that attracted the attention of many senators during Kennedy's 1987 nomination hearing. The issue was the constitutional status of laws that criminalized sodomy (whether just that engaged in by homosexuals or as applied to every individual regardless of sexual orientation). The decision was *Bowers v. Hardwick* (1986), which sustained just such a law.

Bowers v. Hardwick

The litigation that ended up at the Supreme Court in the form of *Bowers v. Hardwick* began when Officer K. R. Torick "saw a bedroom door partially open," and then through that door saw two men engaging in sodomy, which was a violation of Georgia state law. Torick was at the house of Michael Hardwick, one of the two men, to serve an outstanding arrest warrant. Although the warrant was no longer valid, and the prosecution of the two men for violation of the Georgia sodomy statute was not pursued, the American Civil Liberties Union (ACLU) encouraged Hardwick to challenge the constitutionality of the law as it was applied to consensual homosexual sodomy.[124]

The law, which carried a maximum penalty of twenty years imprisonment, said: "A person commits the offense of sodomy when he performs or submits to any sexual act involving the sex organs of one person and the mouth or anus of another."[125] Writing for the bare majority of the Court that upheld the law, Justice White offered a very narrow understanding of the issue before the Court. The justices were only asked, he said, to consider "whether the Federal Constitution confers a fundamental right upon homosexuals to engage in sodomy." From this starting point, White found it very easy to conclude that this right was neither present in the text of the Constitution nor "deeply rooted in this Nation's history and tradition," the two sources that the Court normally consulted when determining whether a stated "fundamental right" was one of the liberties afforded constitutional protection. White dismissed the claim that homosexual sodomy either had such an historical basis or was "implicit in the concept of ordered liberty," one of the Court's other ways of thinking about the boundaries of constitutionally protected liberty. Demonstrating a lack of sensitivity toward the gay community, White proclaimed that any argument to the contrary was "at best, facetious."[126]

Justice White brought his opinion to a close with a short paragraph that considered the argument that even under rational basis review the Georgia law could not pass constitutional muster. The basis for this argument was the conclusion that "there must be a rational basis for the law and that there is none in this case other than the presumed belief of a majority of the electorate in Georgia that homosexual sodomy is immoral and unacceptable." As easily as Justice Kennedy would later find that Amendment 2 was driven by such morality-driven animus, White dismissed this conclusion as unpersuasive. Why? It was a fact of life, he explained, that "the law . . . is constantly based on notions of morality, and if all laws representing essentially moral choices are to be invalidated under the Due Process Clause, the courts will be very busy indeed."[127]

In April 1986, when the justices met in conference to vote on *Bowers*, Justices Brennan and Marshall both reached back to *Stanley v. Georgia*, a case that is traditionally read for the First Amendment holding that it is unconstitutional to criminalize the "mere private possession of obscene matter."[128] Justice Brennan's papers show that in the late 1960s and early 1970s *Stanley* played an important role in the Court's expansion of an understanding of the types of individual decision making protected by constitutionally stated liberty (as discussed in chapter 5).[129] In *Bowers*, the two most liberal members of the Court were now recalling this decision because its observations about individual activities in the privacy of one's home were as relevant in *Bowers* as they had been in deciding the plaintiff's fate in 1969. By contrast, as Justice Blackmun's notes reveal, Justice Stevens did not find relevance in *Stanley*, because he did not view *Bowers* as involving a right to privacy. He believed that for both himself, and homosexuals, it was nothing less than a "*liberty* case."[130]

Michael Hardwick's personal account of the case suggests that this was not the case, as do the amicus briefs that were filed by gay rights groups.[131] However, perhaps aware of the strategic value of offering the Court two different doctrinal directions to take, Laurence Tribe, Hardwick's attorney, highlighted the importance of liberty *and* privacy. He closed his brief with the observation that it "is simply a feature of our system of ordered *liberty*" that a government's action must be subjected to strict judicial scrutiny "when it would reach deeply into our homes and *private* lives."[132] And, during oral argument, it is notable that he borrowed, but rephrased, the most famous passage from Brennan's opinion in *Eisenstadt v. Baird* that held that "whatever the rights of the individual to access to contraceptives may be, the rights must be the same for the unmarried and the married alike."[133] Ostensibly an equal protection decision, *Eisenstadt* is best remembered for Brennan's libertarian statement that "if the right of privacy means anything, it is the right of the *individual*, married or single, to be free from unwarranted governmental intrusion into matters so fundamentally affecting a person as the decision whether to bear or beget a child."[134] As Professor Tribe wrote in an article published after the decision in *Lawrence*, Brennan's opinion in *Eisenstadt* stood for the principle that individuals should be able "to govern for themselves and to choose the contours, sexual and otherwise, of their personal association rather than be treated as little more than footsoldiers, directed by the state."[135] In *Bowers*, Tribe made the following argument:

> Now, if *liberty* means anything in our Constitution, especially given the Ninth Amendment's proposition that it is not all expressly enumerated, if *liberty* means anything it means that the power of government is limited in a way that requires an articulated rationale by government for an intrusion on freedom as personal as this.[136]

Even when he rejected the constitutional validity of arguments favoring "the unquestioned authority of big brother [to] dictate every detail of intimate life in the home," Tribe did not speak in the language of privacy. Rather, he emphasized that such arguments could not be made about any governments that were "devoted to *liberty*."[137] When *Bowers* was decided three months later, Justice Stevens's eloquent and passionate dissenting opinion made it clear that he agreed that (as he had said at conference) this was indeed a "*liberty* case."

In an opinion that underwent only minor changes between the distribution of the first draft and the announcement of the decision, for the first time since he joined the Court ten years earlier Stevens quoted from *Fitzgerald v. Porter Memorial Hospital*, one of the last opinions he wrote as a member of the Seventh Circuit Court of Appeals:

> The Court has referred to such decisions as implicating "basic values," as being "fundamental," and as being dignified by history and tradition. The character of the Court's language in these cases brings to mind the origins of the American heritage of freedom—the abiding interest in individual liberty that makes certain state intrusions on the citizen's right to decide how he will live his own life intolerable. Guided by history, our tradition of respect for the dignity of individual choice in matters of conscience and the restraints implicit in the federal system, federal judges have accepted the responsibility for recognition and protection of these rights in appropriate cases.[138]

As we will see below, in *Lawrence* it was the reasoning in Justice Stevens's *Bowers* dissent, rather than that employed by Justice White, which Kennedy said should have prevailed. Stevens believes that the *Bowers* dissent that "later became law" in *Lawrence* was not his, but rather the eloquent one authored by Justice Blackmun. While the spirit of Blackmun's work can certainly be found in *Lawrence*, the fact remains that it is the opinion of Stevens to which Justice Kennedy turned in 2003.[139]

"An Exceptional Opinion"[140]

In July 1986, one month after the Supreme Court's decision in *Bowers*, then-Judge Kennedy stood before a gathering of Canadian jurists at Stanford University and spoke of "Unenumerated Rights and the Dictates of Judicial Restraint." He devoted part of the speech to a discussion of *Bowers*. Although he was careful not to endorse the conclusion that the case was wrongly decided, it was clear that he was sympathetic to this argument. He made favorable references to *Dudgeon v. United Kingdom* (1981), a European Court of Human Rights decision at odds with *Bowers* (in 2003 Kennedy mentioned *Dudgeon* in his *Lawrence* opinion that overruled *Bowers*).[141] He also noted:

> Many argue that a just society grants a right to engage in homosexual conduct. If that view is accepted, the *Bowers* decision in effect says the State of Georgia has the right to make a wrong decision—wrong in the sense that it violates some people's views of rights in a just society.[142]

This observation was consistent with the principal theme of the speech, which cautioned against a jurisprudence that too heavily emphasizes "unenumerated rights." Drawing on the speech's concurrent theme—judicial restraint, Kennedy remarked that it was important to remember that within the American constitutional scheme there existed checks on majoritarian impulses, checks that preserved and protected liberty in such a way as to reduce the need to rely on uneumerated rights. This was important because:

> In discussions of unenumerated rights, there seems to be an undercurrent that judicial power to declare them is a necessary antidote to the potential excesses of a democratic majority. That formulation tends to distract us from the fact that there are other protections in the American system.[143]

There is little doubt that Kennedy strongly believes one of the primary (and principled) protections is the Fourteenth Amendment. It is equally clear that it was this belief that he wrote into the opinion that overruled *Bowers.*

Kennedy's Stanford speech was just one of the things that led many, within the confines of the Court, to believe that for a long time the justice had sought an opportunity to remedy what he perceived to be the egregious legal wrong committed in 1986.[144] That opportunity came on December 2, 2002, when the justices voted to grant certiorari in 02–102, *John Geddes Lawrence and Tyron Garner v. Texas.* It was realized almost eight months later when Kennedy announced the decision in this case, declaring: "*Bowers* was not correct when it was decided, and it is not correct today."[145] What ended in Washington, D.C., with the Supreme Court's 2003 decision, began five years earlier—ironically, on September 17, Constitution Day—in Houston, Texas, under circumstances remarkably similar to those that prompted the litigation in *Bowers.* After lawfully entering an apartment in response to a falsely filed report of a weapons disturbance, police officers arrested John Lawrence and Tyron Garner after they found them having sex in Lawrence's room.[146] The two men were found to have violated a Texas state law that made it a crime to engage in "deviate sexual intercourse with another individual of the same sex." This activity was further defined as:

1. any contact between any part of the genitals of one person and the mouth or anus of another person; or
2. the penetration of the genitals or the anus of another person with an object.[147]

It was Lawrence and Garner's constitutional challenge to this law that a six-justice majority of the Supreme Court sustained in 2003.

As the senior associate justice voting in the majority in *Lawrence,* Justice Stevens assigned to Justice Kennedy the responsibility for crafting the Court's opinion (just as he did in *Romer*). This was likely not a difficult decision for Stevens to make; as law Professor Michael Dorf (a former clerk for Kennedy) observed in a 2003 article, following his authorship of *Romer* the choice of Kennedy to write in *Lawrence* was predictable: "The writing was, if not on the wall, at least in the vicinity of the wall."[148] And once assigned this task, it was not one that Kennedy agonized over. As he "later told Thurgood Marshall's wife," he was convinced that "the right result [in *Lawrence*] was so obvious"; therefore, he wrote the majority opinion striking down the Texas law "over the course of one weekend."[149] Like the opinion in *Romer*, *Lawrence* did not sit well with some commentators because it did not afford sexual orientation the protections that accompany the label "suspect classification." Nevertheless, such was the extent to which *Lawrence* preserved and protected an expansive understanding of individual liberty—as applied to all, regardless of one's sexual orientation—that the opinion was very well received by the gay community who saw in it another indication of the Sacramentan's concern for protecting individual freedom from majoritarian animus. It is indeed accurate to say that after *Lawrence*, Justice Kennedy became "the Rehnquist Court's de facto spokesperson for gay rights."[150]

Liberty, Not Equality

Justice Kennedy's opinion for the Court only spoke for himself and four of his colleagues. Justice O'Connor accepted that the Texas statute violated the Constitution, but instead of looking to the due process clause, she chose to focus her attention on the Fourteenth Amendment's equal protection component. The law could not pass constitutional muster, she concluded, because it criminalized "deviate sexual intercourse" only when engaged in by persons of the same sex. Repeating many of the anti-animus and anti-stigma arguments that were made by Justice Kennedy in *Romer*, she concluded that such discriminatory treatment denied homosexuals the equal protection of the laws that the Fourteenth Amendment guaranteed to them.[151] She therefore declined to join Kennedy's opinion because she felt it unnecessary to overrule *Bowers*. This conclusion stemmed, in part, from the fact that she was confident the equal protection clause could represent a constitutional deterrent strong enough to ensure that legislators would not react by passing laws banning all sodomy. Had the Court stated that the Constitution "requires a sodomy law to apply equally to the private consensual conduct of homosexuals and heterosexuals alike," then it was unlikely that "such a law would . . . long stand in our democratic society."[152] Although his response to this argument did not specifically refer to his colleague's separate opinion, it is clear that the last few pages of Justice Kennedy's opinion were directed at explaining why, in the name of individual liberty, it would be entirely wrong for the Court to take this "trust the legislators" approach.[153] Unsurprisingly, in rejection of the proposal that the Court decide the case on equal protection grounds, Kennedy referred to his opinion in *Romer*. When the decision in *Lawrence* was announced, much was made of the "Justice Kennedy and gay rights" precedent that *Romer* had seemed to set for the 2003 case.[154] *Romer* was indeed an important precursor, but not as a gay rights case; rather, it should be read as a significant exposition of Kennedy's understanding of liberty. Justice Kennedy's *Lawrence* discussion of *Romer* confirmed this; what really underpinned that 1996 decision was the preservation of the dignified *liberty* of all, regardless of sexual orientation.

In *Liberty for All*, law professor Elizabeth Price Foley analyzes the controversial and often uncomfortable relationship between concepts of morality and American law. Foley advocates a libertarian reading of law that is "based on a secular morality designed to maximize individual liberty." In her analysis of O'Connor's *Lawrence* concurrence, she makes the very astute observation that this is an opinion that "posits an interesting constitutional conundrum," because it says "a state may legitimately restrict the liberty of everyone solely because of moral offense, yet it may not restrict the liberty of a certain class of citizens because of moral offense." This, says Foley, leads to the conclusion that "moral condemnation can be the basis of law only if it is applied universally. Thus, if the Texas law had prohibited sodomy for all—not just homosexuals—O'Connor presumably would have viewed this as a valid exercise of government power." The implications of this are grim if one values individual liberty, because O'Connor is sending a message that does not demonstrate "respect for residual individual liberty, but [rather] a respect for equal application of the law."[155]

Generally, Foley is pessimistic about the possibility that her preferred, libertarian understanding of the law–morality relationship can successfully compete with (let alone triumph over) what she perceives to be the prevailing belief that what is legal is defined by reference to the "public morality" as determined by a legislative majority. In this respect, she has only tepid praise for Kennedy's *Lawrence* opinion.[156] However, what is interesting about her critique of O'Connor's opinion is that its substance is similar to that offered by Kennedy. "Equality of treatment and the due process right to demand respect for conduct protected by the substantive guarantee of liberty are linked in important respects," wrote Kennedy, and "a decision on the latter point advances both interests."[157] Had the Court held otherwise and decided the case using the equal protection clause, liberty would not have been advanced. The resulting freedom for legislators to pass laws banning all sodomy would inevitably ensure that the "lives of homosexual persons" would continue to be demeaned:

> If protected conduct is made criminal and the law which does so remains unexamined for its substantive validity, its stigma might remain even if it were not en-

> forceable as drawn for equal protection reasons. When homosexual conduct is made criminal by the law of the State, that declaration in and of itself is an invitation to subject homosexual persons to discrimination both in the public and in the private spheres.[158]

To substantiate this conclusion, and the related decision to overrule *Bowers*, Kennedy turned to the words of Justice Stevens writing in dissent in the 1986 case. In his opinion in *Lawrence*, Kennedy quoted admiringly from that dissent:

> Our prior cases make two propositions abundantly clear. First, the fact that the governing majority in a State has traditionally viewed a particular practice as immoral is not a sufficient reason for upholding a law prohibiting the practice; neither history nor tradition could save a law prohibiting miscegenation from constitutional attack. Second, individual decisions by married persons, concerning the intimacies of their physical relationship, even when not intended to produce offspring, *are a form of "liberty" protected by the Due Process Clause of the Fourteenth Amendment.*[159]

This analysis, concluded Kennedy, "should have been controlling . . . and should control here."[160] What we see in his decision to use this quotation to repudiate the majority's analysis in *Bowers* is Kennedy's belief that in 1986 that Court "fail[ed] to appreciate the extent of the *liberty* at stake." This is because it reduced a challenge to an undignified and degrading abrogation of individual freedom to the narrow question of "whether the Federal Constitution confers a fundamental right upon homosexuals to engage in sodomy."[161]

Liberty, Not Morality

"But how could this be?" This was the question posed by Justice Scalia who penned a scathing dissent attacking the majority opinion in *Lawrence.* In essence, Scalia's dissent was round 2 in the dialogue on liberty that he began with Kennedy in *Romer.*[162] Just as in 1996, Scalia took Kennedy to task for providing what in his mind amounted to a wholly inadequate attempt to discuss the jurisprudential relationship between *Lawrence* and *Bowers.* This time, he centered his concern on Kennedy's "apparent" use of rational basis review to evaluate the challenge to the Texas law. Although it was what he considered an "unheard-of form," there was no doubt in his mind that this was the standard of judicial scrutiny employed by his colleague. The proof lay in Kennedy's conclusion that "the Texas statute furthers no legitimate state interest which can justify its intrusion into the personal and private life of the individual."[163] There is scholarly disagreement as to just what type of review Kennedy used in *Lawrence*, and whether it was actually a proper and/or legitimate approach (after all, if it really was rational basis review, then why were the words "rational basis" conspicuous by their absence?).[164] However, as this chapter demonstrates, Kennedy did employ rational basis, and his formulation is entirely consistent with its use in other comparable Kennedy opinions (such as *Romer*), and its use is strongly representative of the libertarian components of the justice's jurisprudence. This, therefore, does not make it unheard of, even if, in Justice Scalia's mind, its dubious application in *Lawrence* was entirely "out of accord with [the Court's equal protection] jurisprudence."[165]

What, then, are we to make of Kennedy's use of rational basis review to overrule *Bowers*? There are two main components of Scalia's argument—and Kennedy's response—that we need to look at in order to answer this question. First, what of Kennedy's failure to talk the talk of "fundamental rights"? Scalia says that this omission means *Lawrence* only partially replaces *Bowers*, leaving intact that decision's holding that there is no such right to engage in homosexual sodomy. Kennedy's answer is clear. Consistent with *Romer*, and demonstrative of the humane element of his libertarian jurisprudence, he says that *Lawrence* involves personal, private, and harmless conduct—"the most private human conduct, sexual behavior . . . in the most private of places, the home"—that cannot be criminalized, because it is entirely "within the liberty of persons to choose" to engage in it without fear of arrest and/or prosecution. That this is true, he says, means that such persons should not be required to show that their preferred behavior reaches the "fundamental rights" threshold. This is an aspect of liberty that the government cannot abrogate regardless of "whether or not [such behavior is] entitled to formal recognition in the law."[166] And it is a conclusion that is supported by the Constitution. At his nomination hearing, Kennedy said: "The framers of the Constitution originally, in 1789, knew that they did not live in a perfect society, but they promulgated the Constitution anyway."[167] As understood by Kennedy, in writing the Constitution James Madison was not working on the assumption that he and the other Framers were either intelligent enough or possessed sufficient foresight to be able to, or even want to bind the country to a document unable to recognize changing circumstances. This recognition of human fallibility is explicitly written into the Constitution—in the Ninth Amendment—and Kennedy acknowledged this, not only during the confirmation hearings[168] but, more importantly, in *Lawrence*:

> Had those who drew and ratified the Due Process Clause of the Fifth Amendment or the Fourteenth Amendment known the components of liberty in its manifold possibilities, they might have been more specific. They did not pre-

> sume to have this insight. They knew times can blind us to certain truths and later generations can see that laws once thought necessary and proper in fact serve only to oppress. As the Constitution endures, persons in every generation can invoke its principles in their own search for greater freedom.[169]

Kennedy's response to the second of Scalia's two main dissenting concerns was equally libertarian. Echoing Justice White's *Bowers* observation that judges could expect their workload to dramatically increase were "all laws representing essentially moral choices" to be considered constitutionally suspect, Scalia complained that the decision to strike down the Texas law using rational basis review imperiled all morals legislation. Using this rationale to prevent majoritarian disapproval of homosexual sodomy threatened to condemn other bans on "certain forms of sexual behavior"—bans that Scalia was certain were underpinned by "the same interest." The parade of horribles he listed included laws prohibiting "fornication, bigamy, adultery, adult incest, bestiality, and obscenity."[170] This criticism completely ignores Justice Kennedy's invocation of the harm principle when identifying the boundaries of the liberty that *Lawrence* protects.

To be sure, *Lawrence* opens with a bold statement about the scope of liberty that is being afforded constitutional protection:

> Liberty protects the person from unwarranted government intrusions into a dwelling or other private places. In our tradition the State is not omnipresent in the home. And there are *other spheres of our lives and existence, outside the home*, where the State should not be a dominant presence. *Freedom extends beyond spatial bounds.* Liberty presumes an autonomy of self that includes freedom of thought, belief, expression, and certain intimate conduct. The instant case involves *liberty of the person both in its spatial and in its more transcendent dimensions.*[171]

While this is a clear statement that liberty means something more than simply freedom within a particular area (in this respect, in *Lawrence*, Kennedy's liberty certainly should not be characterized as domesticated[172]), Kennedy is not identifying an unbounded "realm of *personal* liberty."[173] For, as he goes on to explain, the state should not try "to define the meaning of the [personal] relationship or to set its boundaries *absent injury to a person or abuse of an institution the law protects*."[174] *Lawrence* involved such harmless behavior, therefore it is entirely distinguishable from the other examples stated by Scalia. That is, of course, unless an "injury" occurs when one engages in behavior that causes morals-based offense to the sensibilities of a majority.

In both of his dissents in *Romer* and *Lawrence*, Justice Scalia picked up on the point upon which Senator Humphrey had focused during Kennedy's

Supreme Court nomination hearing—the jurist's penchant for making plentiful references to legal academia's arguments. As these arguments pertain to gay rights and individual sexual relations or decisional autonomy, Kennedy has been no less keen to cite them in Supreme Court opinions as he was to use them in his writings while sitting on the Ninth Circuit. In *Lawrence*, in particular, Scalia was critical of his colleague for permitting these outside views to influence a decision that should have been made solely based on the Constitution's text and the country's history and traditions. While law professor Earl Maltz is correct that "Kennedy's opinion in *Romer* . . . stood at the confluence of two strands of elite public opinion in the early 1990s"—equal treatment for homosexual relationships and protection for unenumerated and nonfundamental rights (encompassed by the textually anchored "liberty")—not until *Lawrence* do we really see Kennedy make a concerted effort to demonstrate the importance and judicial relevance of this elite perspective.[175]

Entirely consistent with the elements of his modestly libertarian jurisprudence, and his belief in the importance of education, Kennedy used the views expressed by legal academia in order to identify flaws in the interpretation that was given to history by the majority in *Bowers*. He was willing to concede that "the Court in *Bowers* was making the broader point that for centuries there have been powerful voices to condemn homosexual conduct as immoral" and that the views of those who raised their voices, or who shared the beliefs of those who did, were deeply and sincerely held.[176] The judiciary does not exist, however, to answer legal questions using the moral and ethical views of the populace. Quoting one of the most famous phrases from his contribution to the joint opinion in the 1992 landmark abortion case *Planned Parenthood v. Casey* (discussed in chapter 5), Kennedy stated unequivocally: "Our obligation is to define the liberty of all, not to mandate our own moral code."[177] Only when the boundaries of liberty are defined may the people then craft laws, as will inevitably happen, reflecting their moral views, and only then by concurrently respecting the aforementioned boundaries. Once the Court has initiated the dialogue, society is free to continue it—thereby preserving individual dignity and the ability of all to pursue their own constitutional visions.[178]

Limited Constitutional Vision(s)?

Before bringing this chapter to a close, it is important to consider one case that might be held up as containing a Kennedy-authored opinion that challenges this chapter's conclusion that the justice is deeply committed to preserving individual dignity. Decided in 1993, *Heller v. Doe* concerned the constitutionality of Kentucky's statutory provisions relating to the legal and judicial procedures for civil commitment.[179] While for the most part the system treated the mentally ill and the mentally retarded the same way, under some circumstances the state was permitted to apply different procedures for the two categories. Kennedy's majority opinion spoke for five justices when it upheld a "clear and convincing evidence" burden of proof standard for the mentally retarded, as opposed to "beyond reasonable doubt" for the mentally ill. He gained Justice O'Connor's vote for a 6–3 decision upholding the provision permitting the guardians and family members of retarded persons to participate in proceedings as though they were legal parties to the case.

After the justices' conference on March 24, there existed a five-justice coalition (albeit a very fragile one) willing to *strike down* both provisions as violations of the Equal Protection Clause. Almost three months later, as the Court's term was coming to an end, Justice Kennedy circulated the first draft of his dissent. In doing so, he immediately secured the vote of Justice White (who had originally joined the opinion of Justice Souter, the member of the Court assigned to write the majority's opinion). At conference, White only hesitantly voted to affirm the lower court's rejection of the Kentucky provisions.[180] At the end of the draft dissent, Kennedy rejected the respondents' request that the Court consider applying heightened scrutiny, because at every stage below they had instead contended that the relevant standard, one that the provisions could not meet, was rational basis. He then wrote: "Even if respondents were correct that strict scrutiny applies, it would be inappropriate for us to apply that standard here." With the wording almost unchanged, these observations were given a far more prominent place when Kennedy's opinion finally spoke for the Court.[181]

While there is reason to believe that this sensitivity to the absence of a previously presented strict scrutiny argument was included by Kennedy in part to gain Justice White's vote,[182] there is solid evidence that a sentence that found its way into Kennedy's second draft (upon the suggestion of Justice Scalia) was removed from the fourth and final drafts in order to retain White's commitment to the Court's main opinion. The language that White found objectionable was intended to follow Kennedy's discussion about not addressing the respondent's argument. Upon Scalia's suggestion, the second draft made the following observation: "Nor does our case law establish that rational basis is not the proper standard of review for the equal protection claim raised by respondents." Justice Scalia suggested citing five pages of arguments from Justice White's opinion in *City of Cleburne*, pages that he believed would embolden the judicial restraint thrust of this sentence by declining to label the mentally retarded as a suspect class. As quickly as Kennedy accepted this recommendation, White wrote that he was issuing a separate opinion explaining why he could no longer join the part of Kennedy's opinion that took this approach.

The logical response for Kennedy was to remove the passage, because he did not need to secure Scalia's vote.[183]

In *Heller*, Justice Scalia wanted the Court to commit itself to the *restrained* position that it was a foregone conclusion that rational basis review was the legitimate standard to apply in this case. Kennedy clearly resisted this approach. Even though he did so in part because of the need to retain White's vote, his objection to Scalia's preferred judicial deference still has important implications for this book's examination of his generally libertarian equal protection jurisprudence. To be sure, in *Heller* Kennedy did find a rational basis for the government's actions. What Kennedy was not willing to do, however, was to apply rational basis review in the deferential, "the government obviously wins, so let's move on" kind of way that some of his conservative colleagues have advocated. The adoption of such an approach would not result in the tie going to freedom, because only in the most remote circumstances would one actually get to the situation wherein a tie was possible.

In Kennedy's opinion, in *Heller*, Kentucky did not commit the cardinal sin of equal protection law—irrationally labeling persons in such a way as to negatively affect their individual dignity. One could make the case, in fact, that individual dignity would be threatened by not permitting Kentucky to treat the mentally retarded and the mentally ill in different ways. Differences in detection ability and treatment methods made it possible to envision an undignified situation in which the mentally ill would suffer greatly were the legal system to treat them in the same way as the mentally retarded.[184] If *Heller* means anything, then, it means that by 1993 Kennedy had placed himself in a central and key jurisprudential position on the Rehnquist Court. He had distanced himself from Chief Justice Rehnquist and Justice Scalia because he was unwilling to subscribe to their hands-off reading of rational basis review. Kennedy found equally objectionable, however, the assumption that the Constitution could only afford individuals adequate equal protection of the law if the Fourteenth Amendment was read to require strict judicial scrutiny that condemned laws for using suspect classifications. Three years later, the full meaning of this reluctance to embrace one of the two polar opposite standards of review became clear in *Romer*, a case that, in Kennedy's opinion, clearly involved an undignified, demeaning, and, above all, irrational government action.

Conclusion

In the fall of 1987, when President Reagan announced the Supreme Court nomination of then-Judge Kennedy, the gay community was not impressed with this choice to replace Justice Powell. By this time, it was already well known that Powell had vacillated during the Court's deliberation of *Bowers*; any hopes that his replacement would bring to the Court the possibility of righting the wrong of this decision faded with the appointment of the author of the opinion in *Beller v. Middendorf*. In this respect, there could be little consolation in finding out, in 1990, that Powell considered his *Bowers* vote mistaken.[185] As we have seen, a close reading of *Beller* and Judge Kennedy's Stanford speech shows that Powell's replacement possessed both a sympathetic recognition of the social stigma suffered by homosexuals and an understanding of individual liberty broad enough to find unconstitutional laws that criminalized sodomy. What we have seen in this chapter, though, is that the realization of this change in the law has been achieved without either a focus on protecting gays as a specific group—a suspect classification—or a finding that there is a fundamental right to engage in homosexual intimacy.

When the Court decided *Lawrence* in 2003, many people pointed to *Romer* and *Beller* as justification for the conclusion that Kennedy's writings in these later cases were predictable. After all, *Beller* was a gay rights case and then-Judge Kennedy did express sympathy for the rights claims made and the discrimination suffered by homosexuals. This conclusion that *Beller* was an indication of Kennedy's future votes in gay rights cases is correct. However, there is more that unites *Beller*, *Romer*, and *Lawrence* than simply the gay rights common link. This chapter has shown that there is an additional and very significant commonality between the three opinions. This is Kennedy's belief that the proper "dimensions"[186] of constitutional liberty involve considerable respect for and deference to the *private* actions of the *individual*, a respect that ensures that the fundamental dignity held by every human being is not demeaned. Without such respect, no individual, regardless of their sexual orientation, is free to pursue their own constitutional vision. Without this freedom, says Kennedy, the Constitution's text may remain, but the principles of constitutionalism upon which it is founded will be threatened.

4

When Only Strict Scrutiny Will Do

> Until the Court is candid about the existence of stigma imposed by racial preferences on both affected classes, candid about the "animosity and discontent" they create . . . and open about defending a theory that explains why the cost of this stigma is worth bearing and why it can consist with the Constitution, no basis can be shown for today's casual abandonment of strict scrutiny.[1]
>
> —Justice Kennedy, dissenting in *Metro Broadcasting v. FCC*

It was March 30, 1990, and Justice Kennedy had been a member of the U.S. Supreme Court for just over two years. In the justices' conference room, the presence of eight senior colleagues meant that Kennedy would be the last to speak and the last to vote. In case number 89-453, however, this did not position him to cast the decisive vote. At this stage Justice White tentatively joined the four more liberal members of the Court (Brennan, Marshall, Blackmun, and Stevens) in affirming the decision of the lower court (he never changed his vote).[2] So Kennedy knew that, as the current Court was constituted, he was about to express views that were unlikely to find their way into a majority opinion. If Kennedy had a habit, during these closed-door meetings, of referring to the Sacramento community in which he was raised, Justice Blackmun's notes provide no indication that he did so on a regular basis. Today would be different. Exhibiting a degree of emotion that Justice Blackmun found significant enough to mention in the notes he took during the conference, Justice Kennedy lashed out at the Federal Communications Commission's policy of making race-preferential broadcast licensing decisions, the constitutionality of which was at issue in the case under discussion—*Metro Broadcasting v. FCC* (analyzed below). It was an indefensible policy, said Justice Kennedy, which, in short, contradicted the most basic values for which the Constitution stood.[3]

As Kennedy would later say in a passion-filled and biting dissent, it was quite simply demeaning to assume that a person held certain views—or would, in this particular case, broadcast television programs containing these views—just because they were of a particular race or particular ethnic origin.[4] In the privacy of the justices' conference, when Kennedy discussed these views in the context of *Metro Broadcasting*, he spoke of "Sacramento['s] racial animosity."[5] Since then, time and again, Kennedy's opinions have proven that in this area of the law he came to the Court with an egalitarian and fundamentally color-blind understanding of the Constitution etched into his mind. And, as the opinions analyzed below demonstrate, this is an understanding that leads him to the conclusion that the Constitution only permits the Court to employ one particular standard of review in cases dealing with race—government actions must be reviewed with strict judicial scrutiny.

Confronting the "Suspect Classification"

Whether viewed from a sociological, historical, economic, or political perspective, in American constitutional law race is the quintessential "suspect classification." When this term first entered the Court's legal lexicon in *Korematsu v. United States* (1944) (upholding the federal government's policy of interning Japanese Americans during World War II), it was employed by Justice Black to describe "racial group[s]." These were groups of individuals against whom the government could not act (with the consequence of abrogating civil rights) when its motive was "racial antagonism." Such action could not withstand the strictest judicial scrutiny.[6] As we will see in the cases analyzed below, when the government singles out racial groups for *preferential* treatment, it is no longer possible to describe legal doctrine in such neat terms. In "race-dependent" cases ("decisions and conduct . . . that would have been different but for the race of those benefited or disadvantaged by them"[7]), doctrinal dissatisfaction is just as prevalent in the Court's equal protection jurisprudence as it was in the non race-related cases examined in the previous chapter. Deliberating the "far from 'plain'" Equal Protection Clause becomes even more complicated, and mired in a web of emotions and controversy, when cases involve race.[8] Plurality opinions abound, and pointed concurrences and heated dissents are the norm in this area of the law. Justices have been accused, by their opposing colleagues, of arriving at racial classifications for which historical precedents can be found in the regimes of Nazi Germany or South Africa under apartheid. Dissenting from the bench, justices in the minority have excoriated the Court for taking the opportunity to eviscerate a landmark precedent as soon as there were five amenable justices, and this area of the law is home to what has been described as "one of the angriest dissenting opinions in recent times."[9] Behind the scenes, the discussions have been no smoother. The justices' search for answers to the legal cases and controversies within the realm of the intractable problem of race has led them into a decidedly thorny political thicket.

Why Kennedy's Modest Libertarianism Is Not "Race Absolutist"

There is nothing complex about the position taken by Justices Scalia and Thomas in race-dependent cases. They argue that only under an exceptionally small number of circumstances may race be a factor in governmental decisions. As Edward Lazarus observed in a 1988 memorandum to Justice Blackmun, for whom he was clerking, "Justice Scalia, in the interest of an absolutely color blind society, would essentially prohibit race-conscious remedies on the state or local level."[10] Given libertarianism's commitment to a belief that the individual is the primary political unit in society, one might reasonably conclude that this race absolutism position is consistent with strong libertarian theory. After all, libertarians have not been shy about taking extreme individualist positions when addressing the question of race. In a prominent volume of libertarian essays published in the 1970s, one writer provocatively titled her contribution "Individualism Versus Racism." She lashed out at the civil rights movement's quest to improve the social and political standing of individuals by treating them as members of groups—rather than as individuals. In this respect, she argued, the landmark Civil Rights Act of 1964 was just as much to blame because it "elevated the dubious principles of altruism, collectivism, and racism above life, liberty, and the pursuit of happiness."[11] This is a position that can also be found in some libertarian commentaries about affirmative action. For example, David Boaz opposes this particular policy because he says its "denial of the humanity and individuality of African Americans" is comparable, in its effects, to the enslavement of human beings and the system of Jim Crow laws.[12] Libertarians, however, do not universally accept these positions. Indeed, as chapter 1 made clear, there are too many variants of the theory for us to even expect this to be so. However, it is easy to see why, when it comes to such a sensitive subject as race, the reputation of libertarianism might be tarnished by such radical views.

To be sure, as we will see below—particularly when we examine his opinion in *Metro Broadcasting*—on occasion the views Kennedy expresses in race-dependent cases do sound as though they have much in common with an absolutist approach. From the beginning of his Supreme Court tenure, Justice Kennedy has not been shy about expressing his opposition to government actions that treat individuals differently because of the color of their skin. However, he generally has not shared his conservative colleagues' endorsement of an absolutist approach—particularly in cases addressing affirmative action policies employed by educational establishments. He has consistently penned separate opinions that embrace the theoretical foundations of the equal protection jurisprudence set forth in the first Justice Harlan's famous color-blind dissent in *Plessy v. Ferguson* and argues that what that opinion said in 1896 remains valid over a century later.[13] His praise for, and retention and use of, Harlan's maxim demonstrates the humane element of Kennedy's libertarian jurisprudence, because his commitment to it is grounded in his belief that the Constitution does not permit the government to treat people differently, either positively or negatively, based on their race. However, unlike some of his more conservative colleagues, Kennedy does acknowledge that encouraging racial diversity in society—particularly in establishments of learning—is a constitutionally legitimate goal for a government. This is because living in a diverse environment enriches the lives of every individual. What the government cannot do is to try and force this diversity upon a person by, for the purposes of its policies, "reducing" them "to an assigned racial identity for differential treatment." This, says Kennedy, "is among the most pernicious actions our government can undertake" because it deprives individuals of the opportunity to pursue their own constitutional visions. To argue otherwise, says Kennedy, is to lend one's support to an approach that "is inconsistent with the dignity of individuals in our society."[14] In order to avoid this situation, the Court must faithfully and consistently apply the standard of strict judicial scrutiny.

Plessy v. Ferguson and the Color-Blind Constitution

In a memorandum that he wrote to his colleagues during the deliberation of *Regents of the University of California v. Bakke*, the Supreme Court's landmark 1978 affirmative action decision (discussed below), Justice Blackmun concluded that whether the policy would pass constitutional scrutiny "will depend, I suspect, in large part upon our respective personal conceptions of the kind of America that was contemplated by Title VI and by the Fourteenth Amendment."[15] In preparation for the 2006 celebration of Constitution Day (September 17), Lawrence Douglas and Alexander George, two professors at Amherst College, composed a mock, comical quiz about the nation's supreme legal document. The following was one of their multiple-choice questions:

The 14th Amendment guarantees equal protection under the law. This means:

1. States are empowered to adopt a broad range of affirmative-action programs in order to deliver on the Constitution's promise of equality.
2. States are forbidden from adopting affirmative-action programs because these make hash of the Constitution's promise of equality.
3. Both A and B.
4. It all depends on Justice Kennedy.[16]

Although the quiz was compiled in jest, this observation about the role of Justice Kennedy in equal protection law rings true, making it all the more important to understand the "kind of America" that Justice Kennedy envisions when he reads the Constitution's equality provisions. Before we seek to achieve this understanding by looking at some of his opinions in race-dependent cases, we need to take a close look at the first Justice John Marshall Harlan's dissent in *Plessy v. Ferguson* (1896).

In this opinion, Harlan predicted that *Plessy* would "in time, prove to be quite as pernicious" as the infamous decision in *Dred Scott v. Sanford* (1857).[17] Harlan was dissenting from a judgment that upheld a Louisiana state public accommodations law that, among other things, required blacks and whites to ride in racially segregated railroad cars. The Supreme Court chose to ignore the reality of the considerable difference in quality between the far superior whites-only accommodations and those provided for black railway passengers. It famously concluded that by providing for "equal but separate accommodations," the law did not violate the equal protection clause of the Fourteenth Amendment.[18] Justice Kennedy has never hidden the fact that he places both the first and second Justices Harlan high on his list of "favorite" individuals who have preceded him as members of the Supreme Court; he praises the two men for "their understanding of the Constitution."[19] In race-dependent cases, he is fond of referring to the most famous passage from Harlan's *Plessy* dissent, the statement: "Our Constitution is color-blind, and neither knows nor tolerates classes among citizens." To be sure, Harlan recognized the *political* and *social* reality that, at the time, "the white race deems itself to be the dominant race. And so it is, in prestige, in achievements, in education, in wealth and in power." However, he was equally sensitive to, and as a justice of the Supreme Court considered it of far greater importance, that the only reality that should matter was that which was written into the law, in whose "eye . . . there is in this country no superior, dominant, ruling class of citizens."[20]

As legal historian Andrew Kull observes in his seminal book about the origins of reading the Constitution as color-blind, it is a concept that "is notably the work of lawyers."[21] The first lawyer to give it life, however, was not Justice

Harlan; the concept has a pedigree that stretches much further back than the litigation in *Plessy*. Harlan most likely crafted his famous sentences out of material from the brief filed by Albion W. Tourgée, lead counsel for Plessy, who wrote: "Justice is pictured blind, and her daughter, the Law, ought at least to be color-blind."[22] The first use of the color-blind concept, as we know it today, however, can be found in an 1846 document addressing racial segregation in the schools of Boston, Massachusetts—a report that "inaugurated a line of argument running straight . . . to Justice Harlan's dissent in *Plessy*." The document contained an argument that was subsequently adopted and put to legal and political use by Wendell Phillips, the prominent Garrisonian abolitionist, and Charles Sumner, the future U.S. senator with whom Phillips graduated from Harvard Law School.[23] At his Supreme Court nomination hearing, Justice Kennedy said: "In my view . . . the abolitionist writings are critical to an understanding of the 14th amendment. It was in response to their concerns that that amendment was enacted."[24] Did he specifically mean the Equal Protection Clause? Kennedy's observation is certainly consistent with the history and theory behind that particular clause.[25] However, providing a conclusive resolution of this inquiry is unnecessary for the purpose of extending the line of adherence to a color-blindness concept from Phillips, through Harlan, to Kennedy. This was particularly clear in a case decided by the Court early in Kennedy's tenure as a member of that institution.

Metro Broadcasting: Approaching the Apocalypse?

At the heart of this case, *Metro Broadcasting v. Federal Communications Commission*, was the importance of an individual's viewpoint. The case involved a challenge to a Federal Communications Commission (FCC) policy that gave preferential treatment to minority-owned broadcasting stations that were competing for FCC licenses.[26] It was a remedial policy intended to remedy an historical disparity. Over the years, as the percentage of the population classified as "minority" had risen, the number of minority-owned and/or operated broadcast stations had not. In the early 1970s, the FCC made the decision to confront this situation not through preferential treatment for minorities seeking broadcast licenses, but rather through a policy of denying licenses to entities that engaged in racially discriminatory employment practices. Reflecting changes in national attitudes toward affirmative action, in May 1978 (just one month before the Supreme Court's decision in *Bakke*) the FCC adopted a new policy that now considered race as a plus factor in decisions about the assignment of licenses.[27] This was justified as a means to achieving the goal of fostering "broadcast diversity," something that would benefit every American because minorities would have greater access to the airwaves, and hence the material that people received from the broadcast media would be more representative of the ethnic and racial makeup of America. As the FCC explained in a 1978 policy statement:

> We are compelled to observe that the views of racial minorities continue to be inadequately represented in the broadcast media. This situation is detrimental not only to the minority audience, but to all of the viewing and listening public. Adequate representation of minority viewpoints in programming serves not only the needs and interests of the minority community but also enriches and educates the non-minority audience. It enhances the diversified programming which is a key objective not only of the Communications Act of 1934 but also of the First Amendment.[28]

The litigation that concluded with the Supreme Court's decision in *Metro Broadcasting* resulted from the awarding of a license to Rainbow Broadcasting, which was 90 percent minority owned, over Metro Broadcasting, which could claim important ties to the local community but was only 19.8 percent minority owned.[29] Metro Broadcasting challenged the FCC policy, under which this licensing decision was made, arguing that it was a violation of the Fifth Amendment's due process clause, which has long been held to afford individuals the same level of protection from unequal treatment as the Fourteenth Amendment's equal protection clause provides them when the government action is that which is undertaken by a state.[30]

On his last day on the Court—he retired three weeks later—Justice Brennan announced the decision in the case. The significance of his opinion was immediately obvious. Not only did he write for a five-justice majority willing to uphold the FCC policy, but he also reached this constitutional conclusion by applying a standard of judicial review that was more deferential to the wishes of Congress than strict scrutiny. Justice Brennan agreed that the federal government's goal of opening up the airwaves to minority points of view that might otherwise not be heard was "at the very least, an important governmental objective" that accurately addressed both the history of exclusion of minorities from the media and the need to expose all Americans to more diverse views. Brennan said:

> Just as a "diverse student body" contributing to a "robust exchange of ideas" is a "constitutionally permissible goal" on which a race-conscious university admissions program may be predicated, the diversity of views and information on the airwaves serves important First Amendment values. The benefits of such

> diversity are not limited to the members of minority groups who gain access to the broadcasting industry by virtue of the ownership policies; rather, the benefits redound to all members of the viewing and listening audience.[31]

Having found that the FCC policy served "the important governmental objective of broadcast diversity," Brennan proceeded to conclude that it was "substantially related to the achievement of that objective." He identified two key factors that—as the Court had explained in several previous decisions—made the use of this deferential standard of review (which is clearly far lower than strict scrutiny) constitutionally permissible: (1) the policy was mandated by Congress, and (2) the policy used what could accurately be described as "benign racial classifications." Finally, in a departure from precedent, Brennan concluded that this standard of review was applicable regardless of whether the "benign race conscious measures" were "'remedial' in the sense of being designed to compensate victims of past governmental or societal discrimination."[32] In his dissenting opinion, Kennedy found fault with every aspect of this new judicial standard.

Justice Kennedy's Dissent: "History Suggests Much Peril in This Enterprise"[33]

At 10:02 A.M., on March 28, 1990, a crisp spring morning in Washington, D.C., inside the Supreme Court, Chief Justice Rehnquist called for Gregory Guillot to open the oral argument in *Metro Broadcasting*. Very quickly Justice Scalia made no secret of his deep-seated belief that Guillot's client had every reason to lodge a constitutional objection to the FCC's policies. These were, as Scalia described them, policies that assumed that "white people think and express themselves one way and Aleutians another way and Asians another way."[34] By contrast, Justice Kennedy asked only a few questions, inquiries that did not in any perceptible manner tip his hand. Two days later, however, when all of the justices sat down in conference, Kennedy left absolutely no doubt about his opposition to race-based classifications. Kennedy could not even find a rational basis for awarding enhancement credits to a minority group in the name of programming diversity. Justice Blackmun noted the emotional way in which his colleague predicted that upholding this indefensible policy would have unlimited negative effects that would make a mockery of the values embodied in the Constitution.[35] Three months later, on the final day of the Court's term, when the decision was announced and the opinions released, Kennedy made these views known to the public in what political scientist Thomas Keck has described as an apocalyptic dissenting opinion.

Kennedy compared the standard of review employed by Brennan to both *Plessy* and *Korematsu*.[36]

Underpinning the FCC's policy was a belief that (1) minority broadcasters would choose to put out programs that espoused minority viewpoints, and (2) such minority viewpoints did actually exist. For example, black Americans were assumed to automatically think about the world in a way that differed perceptibly from that of whites. This is not an unreasonable position to adopt. People who are of the same race do often think about issues in a common manner. This is not to say that *every* individual of a particular race thinks or feels the same way about a particular issue. Nor is it to suggest that these individuals *should* think or feel as one. Rather, it is a far more modest conclusion that many people either instinctively, or through choice, adopt certain positions because of their membership of a particular race or ethnic minority.[37] The FCC policy reflected this conclusion and the accompanying reality that majoritarian discrimination inherent in the political system oftentimes makes the adequate expression of these minority positions difficult to achieve. Justice Kennedy does appear to be sensitive to the existence of these institutional obstacles, and to the preference of many individuals to act and express themselves in ways that reflect group identity. However, he believes that it is constitutionally impermissible for a government to adopt policies that account for these group tendencies by limiting the behavior of people based on their membership in such a group. For, as he wrote in his dissent in *Metro Broadcasting*:

> Once the Government takes the step, which itself should be forbidden, of enacting into law the stereotypical assumption that the race of owners is linked to broadcast content, it follows a path that becomes ever more tortuous.

Why does it become more tortuous? Using language that, as shown in table 4.1, he inserted into the second and final draft of the dissent, Kennedy wrote: "It must decide which races to favor."[38] Placing such choices in the hands of the government, rather than individuals, strips those individuals of their dignity and their ability freely to pursue their own unique constitutional visions.

Interestingly, Kennedy did not circulate the first draft of his dissent until June 25, only two days before the decision was announced; and, thereafter, it underwent only a few small changes. Kennedy was writing in response to at least four circulated drafts of Justice Brennan's opinion for a tenuous five-justice majority (Justice White's vote was not guaranteed) and several drafts of Justice Stevens's concurrence and Justice O'Connor's dissent.[39] From the outset, Kennedy's anger and frustration at the Court's decision was obvious. He made the decision to open his opinion by invoking what he considered to be the doctrinal lessons that should have been learned from *Plessy*.[40] The horrors of the Court's opinion in that case, said Kennedy, "have disturbing parallels to today's majority opinion"—parallels "that should warn us something is amiss here."[41] Why? Kennedy objected to the Court's conclusion, in *Metro Broadcasting*, that the race consciousness FCC program was only benign. Wrote Kennedy: "A fundamental error of the *Plessy* Court was its similar confidence in its ability to identify 'benign' discrimination." As we can see in table 4.1, this chastisement of Brennan's rejection of the judicial restraint called for by Harlan (in dissent) in *Plessy* was articulated in even stronger language in the second and final draft of Kennedy's dissent. Unlike the first, this version contained the additional conclusion that while "the majority is 'confident' that it can determine when racial discrimination is benign, it offers no explanation

TABLE 4.1
Passages from the First and Final Versions of Justice Kennedy's Dissent in *Metro Broadcasting v. FCC* (the changes are indicated in bold).

First draft	*Final version (joined by Justice Scalia)*
"The fundamental errors in *Plessy*, its standard of review and its shameful result, distorted the law for six decades before the Court announced its apparent demise in *Brown v. Board of Education*, 347 U.S. 483 (1954)."	"The fundamental errors in *Plessy*, its standard of review and **its validation of rank racial insult by the State**, distorted the law for six decades before the Court announced its apparent demise in *Brown v. Board of Education*, 347 U.S. 483 (1954)."
"Once the Government takes the step, which itself should be forbidden, of enacting into law the stereotypical assumption that the race of owners is linked to broadcast content, it follows a path that becomes ever more tortuous."	"Once the Government takes the step, which itself should be forbidden, of enacting into law the stereotypical assumption that the race of owners is linked to broadcast content, it follows a path that becomes ever more tortuous. **It must decide which races to favor**."
"The Court insists that the programs under review are 'benign.' . . . A fundamental error of the *Plessy* Court was its similar confidence in its ability to identify 'benign' discrimination."	"The Court insists that the programs under review are 'benign.' . . . A fundamental error of the *Plessy* Court was its similar confidence in its ability to identify 'benign' discrimination. . . . **Although the majority is 'confident' that it can determine when racial discrimination is benign, it offers no explanation as to how it will do so**."

Justice Kennedy's dissent in *Metro Broadcasting*, first and second (final) drafts, 25 and 26 June 1990; Box 558, Harry A. Blackmun Papers (first draft); Box 508, Papers of Thurgood Marshall (final draft), Manuscript Division, Library of Congress, Washington, DC.

as to how it will do so."[42] In this respect, said Kennedy, the Court was repeating *Plessy*'s "validation of rank racial insult" (which, in the first draft of his opinion, Kennedy had simply described as a "shameful result"). Additionally, it was oblivious to the all-too-recent history of governments enacting "racial policies defended as benign" but which "often are not seen that way by the individuals affected by them." The South African policy of apartheid was, in Kennedy's opinion, exhibit number one in justification of this conclusion.[43]

Kennedy returned to the subject of *Plessy* in order to close his opinion. In the final paragraph of his dissent, he recognized that the *social* and *political* realities of America's racial composition had changed dramatically from the time when Harlan wrote of white primacy. There was far more racial diversity in America in 1990 than there had been in 1896. This, however, did not weaken the *legal* and *constitutional* warning issued by Harlan. Today, wrote Kennedy, that warning "is now all the more apposite." In a passage that clearly illustrates the importance to his race-based equal protection jurisprudence of preserving the dignity of every person, Kennedy said:

> Perhaps the Court can succeed in its assumed role of case-by-case arbiter of when it is desirable and benign for the Government to disfavor some citizens and favor others based on the color of their skin. Perhaps the tolerance and decency to which our people aspire will let the disfavored rise above hostility and the favored escape condescension. But history suggests much peril in this enterprise, and so the Constitution forbids us to undertake it. I regret that after a century of judicial opinions we interpret the Constitution to do no more than move us from "separate but equal" to "unequal but benign."[44]

When this passage appeared in the final version of Justice Kennedy's dissent in *Metro Broadcasting*, it was unchanged from the language that was used in the first draft of that opinion.

On October 7, 1988, at the end of the first week of Justice Kennedy's first full term as a member of the Supreme Court, the justices met in conference to discuss *Richmond v. Croson*, a case involving a challenge to the constitutionality of an ordinance enacted by the City of Richmond, Virginia. The ordinance required any non minority-owned business that was awarded a city construction contract to allocate at least 30 percent of the work to minority subcontractors. Minorities were defined as "Blacks, Spanish-speaking, Orientals, Indians, Eskimos, or Aleuts." The case generated several different opinions from the justices, and the one that Justice O'Connor penned for the Court did not secure a majority vote for every part of its holding. However, each section that Kennedy did join is entirely consistent with the libertarian themes of his race-dependent jurisprudence and with the comments he made during the conference (he circulated his short partial concurrence only six days before the announcement of the decision, and almost three months after he and his colleagues received Justice O'Connor's first draft).[45]

Justice Blackmun's conference notes tell us several interesting things about Justice Kennedy's reaction to the ordinance. There is no doubt that Kennedy considered the ordinance "unconstitutional in its racial preferences." He was unsure, however, as to how the Court should react to Richmond's argument that this set-aside provision was required to remedy the effects of past discrimination. His uncertainty stemmed from the city's "definition of minority," which, he concluded, "is too broad." Both concerns were ultimately addressed in the section of O'Connor's opinion that found there was insufficient evidence of this past discrimination of the minorities as defined by the city. The absence of this discrimination meant that the ordinance could not survive strict scrutiny. This "searching judicial inquiry into the justification for such race-based measures," wrote O'Connor, is necessary because it is the only "way of determining what classifications are 'benign' or 'remedial' and what classifications are in fact motivated by illegitimate notions of racial inferiority or simple racial politics." And it was essential to ensure that race-based classifications are "*strictly reserved for remedial settings*" because of this "danger of stigmatic harm." It was precisely this danger that Justice Kennedy envisioned occurring when, the following term, he wrote his passionate dissent from Justice Brennan's *Metro Broadcasting* abandonment of this "only as a remedy" holding.[46]

Rice v. Cayetano: "A Principled Vote"[47]

It was the second case argued on the second day of the Supreme Court's October 1999 term; at counsel table sat a current assistant to the U.S. solicitor general, a future solicitor general, and a future chief justice of the United States. Even though race-dependent cases often attract a high-powered array of advocates, it was nevertheless a mark of the legal significance of the case that on this occasion the three men awaiting the opportunity to argue their clients' positions in *Rice v. Cayetano* were Edwin Kneedler, Ted Olson, and John Roberts. A very experienced oral advocate before the Court that he would later lead, Roberts won twenty-five of the thirty-nine cases that he argued (64 percent).[48] On this particular fall day in 1999, however, he fought an uphill battle against the justices, a majority of whom clearly seemed inclined to disagree with the position Roberts took in defense of the actions of the respondent, the state of Hawaii. From the outset, Olson (also a well-known face before the Court), arguing on behalf of petitioner Harold Rice, adopted a position that he was both familiar with and comfortable defending. In this case, it was the position that prevailed during the oral argument and also in the opinion that Justice Kennedy wrote for the Court.

Rice addressed issues that related to both of the "two bedrock constitutional provisions that commit our Nation to racial equality"[49]—the Equal Protection Clause of the Fourteenth Amendment and the Fifteenth Amendment. The ultimate focus of the decision, however, was only on the latter, which reads as follows:

> SECTION. 1. The right of citizens of the United States to vote shall not be denied or abridged by the United States or by any State on account of race, color, or previous condition of servitude.
>
> SECTION. 2. The Congress shall have power to enforce this article by appropriate legislation.

This Amendment represented a profound change to the text of the nation's supreme law, because for the first time the document now included an explicit reference to race. Even though race was a central component of the snake of slavery coiled under the table at the constitutional convention, like slavery it was a word missing from the final document that was sent to the states by the framers in Philadelphia. In *Rice*, the Fifteenth Amendment challenge was to certain rules set forth in the Hawaii Constitution.

When Hawaii became a state in 1959, the federal government granted it title to all public lands within the state, on the understanding that these lands would be held in public trust and be used to achieve a number of goals—one of which was "the betterment of the conditions of native Hawaiians." Two decades later, in furtherance of this goal, the state constitution was amended to establish the Office of Hawaiian Affairs (OHA). The OHA was empowered to administer several different programs and funds that were to be used for "the betterment of conditions of native Hawaiians . . . *[and] Hawaiians*."[50] As Justice Kennedy explained in his opinion for the Court in *Rice*, the intention was "to treat the early Hawaiians as a distinct people, commanding their own recognition and respect."[51] This was reflected in the voting rules established for the selection of the nine-member board of trustees that was charged with overseeing the operations of the OHA. These rules precluded groups of individuals from voting in the statewide election for trustees of the OHA even if they were composed of what were, as Kennedy observed in his opinion, "in a well-accepted sense of the term" citizens of Hawaii and endowed with all the traditional privileges and rights attached to citizenship (one of the most important being the right to vote).[52] The rules at issue made only two groups eligible to vote in this election. The first group, labeled as "Hawaiians," was defined as:

> any descendant of the aboriginal peoples inhabiting the Hawaiian Islands which exercised sovereignty and subsisted in the Hawaiian Islands in 1778, and which peoples thereafter have continued to reside in Hawaii.

"Native Hawaiians," who comprised the second eligible group, were described as:

> any descendant of not less than one-half part of the races inhabiting the Hawaiian Islands previous to 1778, as defined by the Hawaiian Homes Commission Act, 1920, as amended; provided that the term identically refers to the descendants of such blood quantum of such aboriginal peoples which exercised sovereignty and subsisted in the Hawaiian Islands in 1778 and which peoples thereafter continued to reside in Hawaii.[53]

The voting restrictions, therefore, reflected the overall goal of ensuring that those who voted for the members of the OHA were those who would benefit from the OHA's work—and, therefore, best understand the qualifications required of the candidates. The Ninth Circuit ruling upholding the rules succinctly stated the state's justification. Hawaii had permissibly and "rationally conclude[d] that Hawaiians, being the group to whom trust obligations run and to whom OHA trustees owe a duty of loyalty, should be the group to decide who the trustees ought to be."[54] The challenge to the constitutionality of the rules was brought by Harold Rice, a citizen of Hawaii. Rice and his ancestors had resided in Hawaii since before its annexation in 1898, but under these above provisions of the state constitution he was ineligible to vote in elections to determine the membership of the OHA because he was not a descendant of either of these two groups. This, he argued, violated the Fifteenth Amendment because it was a race-based denial of voting rights.

Justice Kennedy's Opinion for the Court: "Committed to Protecting Human Freedom"[55]

One of the prominent themes of then-Judge Kennedy's testimony at his Supreme Court confirmation hearing was his belief that future generations—particularly those who will become the keepers of the Constitution's flame—should maintain that document's imposition of strict limitations on the power of the government. As he explained to the members of the Senate Judiciary Committee:

> The whole lesson of our constitutional experience has been that a people can rise above its own injustice, that a people can rise above the inequities that prevail at a particular time. The framers of the Constitution originally, in 1789, knew that they did not live in a perfect society, but they promulgated the Constitution anyway. They were willing to be bound by its consequences.[56]

This theme was much in evidence in Justice Kennedy's opinion in *Rice.* Kennedy found little that was either ambiguous or complex about the text of the Fifteenth Amendment, whose "purpose and command . . . are set forth in language both explicit and comprehensive. The National Government and the States may not violate a fundamental principle: They may not deny or abridge the right to vote on account of race."[57] Extending his confirmation hearing comments about the original Constitution to the Fifteenth Amendment, Kennedy emphasized that even though a child of the tumultuous post–Civil War period, the amendment's language, principles, and application were timeless: "Vital as its objective remains," the terms of the Amendment "transcend . . . the particular controversy which was the immediate impetus for its enactment." And the fact that these terms were fundamental made *Rice* a fairly easy twenty-first-century decision.[58]

As we saw in chapter 2 in *Burson v. Freeman*, Kennedy considered voting rights (in that case, unimpeded access to polling places) of such importance—we might call them "super-duper" rights—that their protection could even be ensured by placing a normally constitutionally dubious limitation on free speech.[59] Although *Rice* did not involve a clash of fundamental rights, there can be no doubt that the importance of preserving the ultimate right of citizenship was just as important to Kennedy here as it was in *Freeman.* The "exercise of the voting franchise," he observed, is "the most basic level of the democratic process." Why is the ability to vote so cherished? As Chief Justice Earl Warren observed in 1964, in *Reynolds v. Sims*, the landmark legislative apportionment case: "Legislators represent people, not trees or acres."[60] Even if one is inclined to view the political process far more skeptically, focusing on the role that special interests play in policymaking, it is impossible to deny the basic point that Warren made—elected officials are, well, elected. They make decisions affecting every aspect of our lives. Therefore, the right to vote is a right to say "no more" or "we demand change." Without the ability to vote, and the ability of the people to act as the gatekeepers of their governors, the concept of limited government breaks down. It is for precisely this reason that the voting franchise cannot be limited to individuals of a particular race—"all citizens have an interest in selecting officials who make policies on their behalf, even if those policies will affect some groups more than others." Once again invoking the theme of dignity, Kennedy observed that this precious link between the governed and the governors is broken by policies such as the one enacted by Hawaii. Why? "The State's position rests, in the end, on the demeaning premise that citizens of a particular race are somehow more qualified than others to vote on certain matters."[61]

It is in his discussion of these aspects of the case that we see the humane (dignity) element of Justice Kennedy's libertarian jurisprudence playing a very important role. As he explained at some length, there was much in the history of Hawaii that justified the state's efforts to afford the early residents of the islands special treatment. "When the culture and way of life of a people are all but engulfed by a history beyond their control," he wrote, "their sense of loss may extend down through generations; and their dismay may be shared by many members of the larger community." These were realities that the state, quite understandably, believed it needed to confront. According to Kennedy, it was the method that it sought to use to achieve this goal that was constitutionally flawed. As much as it sought to afford *one group* its "own recognition and respect," ultimately the state ignored all the other *individuals* who were just as much its citizens as those who could trace their ancestors back to a certain point in time. The result was that these other Hawaiians were denied *their* "own recognition and respect."[62] And, as Kennedy reminded us:

> One of the principal reasons race is treated as a forbidden classification is that it *demeans the dignity and worth of a person* to be judged by ancestry instead of by his or her own merit and essential qualities. An inquiry into ancestral lines is not consistent with respect based on the unique personality each of us possesses, a respect the Constitution itself secures in its concern for persons and citizens.[63]

This is why Kennedy concluded that the OHA voting restrictions ended up demeaning every single citizen of Hawaii, thereby "giv[ing] rise to the same indignities, and the same resulting tensions and animosities, the [Fifteenth] Amendment was designed to eliminate."[64]

Affirmative Action: A "Sensitive, Difficult Question"[65]

America had to wait until after a bloody Civil War for its supreme law explicitly to recognize race. That word only became part of the Constitution when the Fifteenth Amendment was ratified in 1870. However, what the document has never done is to "condemn racial classification directly, as it does condemn censorship or the establishment of a state religion."[66] There is no provision stipulating that neither Congress nor the states shall make any law treating individuals differently because of their race. What the document does include, of course, is the Fourteenth Amendment's promise "to any person within its jurisdiction" that they will receive "the equal protection of the laws." What happens to this promise, however, when, in the famous words of President Lyndon Johnson, one throws into the equation the "scars of centuries" of racial animosity and discriminatory treatment of racial minorities?[67]

In the early 1960s, liberal Democratic politicians generally said that race-conscious government actions should account for these scars, but the recommended policy was not one of engaging in preferential treatment for minorities, but rather ensuring that no groups were treated in a discriminatory fashion. This was the "Liberal of 1960" approach taken by the administration of President Kennedy.[68] The ascendancy to the presidency of Lyndon Johnson; the passage of the 1964 Civil Rights Act; and Executive Order 11246 (issued by Johnson in 1965, and mandating equal employment opportunity—including requiring contractors to use affirmative action in their personnel practices) began to set the stage for a more progressive approach that considered it both sociopolitically desirable and constitutional for the government to engage in the preferential treatment approach that would become known as affirmative action.[69]

President Johnson gave a passionate defense and explanation of this approach in the commencement address that he delivered at the historically black Howard University in 1965. This speech, which drew, in large part, on material in the recently released Moynihan Report (*The Negro Family: The Case for National Action*), is of particular significance here because of its many references to individual, human dignity.[70] For example, freedom, said Johnson, "is the right to be treated in every part of our national life as a person equal in dignity and promise to all others." This seems entirely consistent with both the humane element of Justice Kennedy's libertarian jurisprudence and the concept of constitutional visions. However, what Johnson went on to say demonstrates a marked difference between his understanding of dignity and that held by Kennedy. It was insufficient, noted Johnson, to simply speak of freedom.

> You do not wipe away the scars of centuries by saying: Now you are free to go where you want, and do as you desire, and choose the leaders you please. You do not take a person who, for years, has been hobbled by chains and liberate him, bring him up to the starting line of a race and then say, "You are free to compete with all the others," and still justly believe that you have been completely fair.[71]

Johnson later equated "dignity" with the "justice" he believed would result from affording minorities preferential treatment because of past discrimination.[72] This is inconsistent with Justice Kennedy's understanding of what it means to respect individual dignity.

As I explained in chapter 1, disagreement with Justice Kennedy's interpretation of human dignity does not make one inhumane. Rather, what the

Justice emphasizes is enabling people to be benevolent and compassionate individuals through the pursuit of their own constitutional visions. This is something that he believes cannot be achieved when the government imposes either benefits or burdens upon individuals because they possess characteristics that make them de facto members of specific groups.

"We Are Stuck With This Case"[73]

It was not until the early 1970s that solid liberal Democratic support began to be placed behind affirmative action. Inevitably, given the fact that the language of the Fourteenth Amendment can be read as requiring color blindness, lawsuits were initiated fairly quickly thereafter.[74] *Regents of the University of California v. Bakke* was one such case and, when decided by the Supreme Court in 1978, it became an instant landmark in the Court's race-dependent jurisprudence.[75]

Writing in the *Washington Post*, William Greider described the atmosphere in the courtroom when *Bakke* was finally decided:

> The justices' wives gathered in summery dresses in the family gallery, as they often do at historic moments. Law clerks crowded in the alcoves. The press and tourists await a milestone, a watershed of some sort. But there was no thunderclap. Instead, the nine justices spoke in many voices, a chorus of competing viewpoints adding up to a well-modulated counterpoint. The court delivered, collectively, a middle outcome that may ricochet through many corridors of American society, but will not revolutionize the issue of "affirmative action" for blacks and other minorities.[76]

The fact that the Court was about to deliver a complicated set of opinions in the case was not lost on Justice Powell who, a week earlier, sent a confidential memorandum to his colleagues; he attached a draft of the statement that he intended to read announcing the decision in *Bakke*. He told the other justices that he had written the statement in such a way as "to assist the representatives of the media present in understanding 'what in the world' the Court has done!"[77]

Bakke was the Supreme Court's resolution of a case that began when, on two occasions, Allan Bakke, who is white, unsuccessfully applied for admission to the medical school at the University of California at Davis. His application was processed as part of the general admissions program, which filled eighty-four places each year. There were one hundred seats available for new students, but the remaining sixteen were filled using a special admissions program, which only considered applications from "disadvantaged" members of the following minorities: "Blacks, Chicanos, Asians, and

American Indians."[78] The case decided by the Supreme Court in 1978 was the result of Bakke's equal protection clause challenge to this program that he labeled a racial quota because his race automatically prevented him from competing for a specified number of places in the incoming classes of the medical school at Davis. Although the California courts agreed with this characterization, in his opinion for the Supreme Court Justice Powell felt it unnecessary to decide whether the program could be properly "described as a quota or a goal." This is because there was no escaping the fact that "it is a line drawn on the basis of race and ethnic status." Powell concluded that this could mean only one thing in terms of the "crucial battle over the scope of judicial review." Strict scrutiny had to be applied, because "racial and ethnic distinctions of any sort are inherently suspect."[79] The Constitution, wrote Powell, demanded nothing less:

> It is settled beyond question that the "rights created by the first section of the Fourteenth Amendment are, by its terms, guaranteed to the individual. The rights established are personal rights." . . . The guarantee of equal protection cannot mean one thing when applied to one individual and something else when applied to a person of another color. If both are not accorded the same protection, then it is not equal.[80]

As Professor Keck has shown, it is this clearly color-blind language of Powell's opinion to which conservative interest groups and jurists have looked for support of their own absolutist opposition to race-based classifications. For all their lower court success in pushing this position, however, on the Supreme Court they have run into problems because of the other part of the pragmatic compromise that is Powell's opinion.[81] Justice O'Connor has consistently adhered to Powell's conclusion that the educational benefits that accrue from a diverse classroom (which includes, but is not limited to, racial and ethnic diversity) justify judicial deference to college admissions policies that are race conscious but do not employ quotas. This is because such approaches are sufficiently individualized as to fulfill the strict scrutiny requirement that they be narrowly tailored to meet the compelling government interest of having a diverse student population.[82]

In 1987, when Kennedy was nominated for a seat on the Supreme Court, there was no escaping the fact that affirmative action was, at the time, the highest profile aspect of the Court's race relations jurisprudence. Unsurprisingly, the Senate Judiciary Committee was eager to know how the vote of Justice Kennedy would impact this issue. After all, if confirmed, Kennedy would replace Justice Powell, whose *Bakke* opinion was, at the time, still the Court's definitive statement on affirmative action. Writing in the *New York Times* on the eve of the hearings, Linda Greenhouse observed that affirmative action was one of the controversial issues about which Kennedy had "no clear position"—"despite 12 years on the Federal bench and nearly 500 opinions."[83] After the hearings were completed, she concluded that Kennedy's views remained just as unclear, because the future justice shied away from expressing views on issues that he might confront on the Supreme Court.[84] The hearings did, however, tell us some important things about Kennedy's views on laws that classified individuals based on their race. Some of his comments about the subject were very revealing. Take, for example, an exchange between Kennedy and Senator Joseph Biden (D-DE). In order to answer Biden's questions about affirmative action, Kennedy drew on his experience teaching at McGeorge School of Law in Sacramento. Kennedy noted, "In the law schools, in 1965," which was the year he started teaching evening classes at McGeorge, "one percent of the nation's law school student body was black." Continuing, Kennedy recalled that:

> After 10 years of effort by the law schools, including the one where I was privileged to teach, to encourage applicants from the black community, that had risen to 8 percent, an 800 percent increase. I know of no professor in legal education that does not think that it is highly important that we have a representative group of black law students in law schools. It has apparently stayed about that rate, at 8 percent. I will notice in some of my classes there are not as many blacks as the year before, and then I will notice it picks up again. So, it is an area that the law schools, and I am sure other professional schools, are continuing to pay attention to, and I think it is a very important objective on the part of the schools.[85]

Kennedy explained that teaching at McGeorge educated him about "the arguments in favor of affirmative action." He noted, though, that it was "by no means certain" (in terms of the Supreme Court's jurisprudence) "whether or not they would prevail *in a court of law on a constitutional basis*. . . ."[86] Why would Kennedy think this? The answer lies in his commitment to ensuring that, consistent with the promise of the Fourteenth Amendment's equal protection clause, the dignity of an individual is preserved by prohibiting the government from treating that person in a particular way (negatively or positively) because of his or her race. In *Grutter v. Bollinger* and *Parents Involved*, we see this commitment explained using several references to the Harlan dissent in *Plessy*. However, despite his admiration for the concept of constitutional color blindness, we also see that Justice Kennedy is more willing than some of his conservative colleagues (but not as willing as Justice O'Connor) to express his support for this concept while recognizing that diversity is a compelling government interest.

Grutter: "A Broad Social and Political Concern"[87]

Speaking during an interview with Tom Brokaw for an NBC documentary about her pending Supreme Court case, Jennifer Gratz recalled her reaction to the letter that she received from the admissions office at the flagship Ann Arbor campus of the University of Michigan. Upon the news that she had not been offered the opportunity to become part of that college's class of 1999, she immediately turned to her father and asked: "Can we sue them?"[88] Gratz, who is white, was reacting to the university's affirmative action admissions policy—to which she attributed her failure to gain admission. It was Gratz's subsequent constitutional challenge to this policy that was at the center of *Gratz v. Bollinger*, decided by the Supreme Court in 2003.[89] Writing for a six-justice majority, Chief Justice Rehnquist struck down the plan because its automatic awarding of twenty points to applicants who were "underrepresented minorities" could not survive strict scrutiny.[90]

Justice O'Connor's Opinion for the Court in *Grutter*: Strict Scrutiny Is Not "Strict in Theory, but Fatal in Fact"

Justice O'Connor was a part of that majority. Therefore, when, on the same day, she voted to *uphold* the affirmative action policy of the University of Michigan Law School, Justice Scalia wrote a separate dissent accusing her of creating a "*Grutter-Gratz* split double header."[91] In her opinion for the five-justice majority in *Grutter v. Bollinger*, the law school case, O'Connor explained that the admissions plan passed constitutional muster—including strict scrutiny review, as she understood it—primarily because it did not use specific race-based quotas. Instead, its review of applications was undertaken by considering race as one of several factors that were important for meeting the stated goal of achieving a "'critical mass' of [under-represented] minority students."[92] In that respect, she concluded, "the Law School's admissions program bears the hallmarks of a narrowly tailored plan" that served the compelling interest in achieving a diverse student body.[93]

Grutter was the end result of the lawsuit that Barbara Grutter decided to bring after she was denied admission to the University of Michigan Law School in 1996. Like Gratz, Grutter, a white in-state applicant, alleged that her failure to gain acceptance was the result of unconstitutional racial discrimination because the law school had a policy of taking the race of applicants into consideration when making its decisions. Just as it was for the undergraduate admissions staff, bringing diversity—including racial and ethnic diversity—to the classroom was considered crucial for the establishment of a learning environment that produced well-rounded students who were exposed to many points of view of which they might hitherto have been unaware. In her opinion upholding the law school's policy, Justice O'Connor relied heavily on Justice Powell's *Bakke* opinion. She echoed his approach of deferring to the "educational judgment" of the law school that had concluded that a diverse learning environment was, as O'Connor described it, "essential to its educational mission." This conclusion, she observed, was particularly valid for an institution such as the University of Michigan Law School. This was because it could be considered a "training ground for a large number of the Nation's leaders" who, upon graduation, would enrich society and future generations with the knowledge and appreciation of diversity their education had provided them.[94]

Having established that the law school's approach to admissions was designed to achieve this compelling interest, O'Connor identified the crucial reason why the plan survived the narrowly tailored requirement of strict judicial scrutiny. As noted above, unlike the undergraduate admissions plan, the law school could not be accused of employing quotas. Rather, O'Connor explained, it:

> engages in a highly individualized, holistic review of each applicant's file, giving serious consideration to all the ways an applicant might contribute to a diverse educational environment. The Law School affords this individualized consideration to applicants of all races. There is no policy, either *de jure* or *de facto*, of automatic acceptance or rejection based on any single "soft" variable.[95]

In an opinion in an earlier affirmative action case, O'Connor wrote, "We wish to dispel the notion that strict scrutiny is 'strict in theory, but fatal in fact.'"[98] In *Grutter* she confirmed that applying strict scrutiny did not automatically condemn a policy of affirmative action; it remained entirely possible for the Court to find that a policy met the narrowly tailored requirement.[99] Her conclusion that the law school's plan was such a policy met with sharp resistance from Kennedy.

Justice Kennedy's Dissent: Will the Real Strict Scrutiny Please Stand Up

On June 5, 1980, as part of the deliberations in another race-dependent case decided two years after *Bakke*, Justice Powell sent a letter to Chief Justice Burger, in which he restated the position he had taken in the 1978 case:

> The first step in equal protection analysis is identification of the proper standard of review. . . . Prior to *Bakke*, I had understood—and I read all of the prior deci-

sions to say—that the appropriate standard for a racial classification is strict scrutiny. In *Bakke*, of the five of us who reached the constitutional question, *I was the only Justice who adhered to strict scrutiny analysis.*[100]

A quarter century later, dissenting in *Grutter*, Justice Kennedy made no attempt to hide his frustration with the majority of justices that prevailed in the case. They had, he vociferously stated, betrayed the strict scrutiny legacy of Justice Powell's opinion in *Bakke*, an opinion that, "in my view," wrote Kennedy, "states the correct rule for resolving this case. The Court, however, does not apply strict scrutiny. By trying to say otherwise, it undermines both the test and its own controlling precedents."[101] Powell became an instant mentor to Justice O'Connor when she joined the Court, and during their six terms as colleagues the two assumed very similar, moderate conservative positions on, among other things, the constitutionality of affirmative action. After Powell left the Court in 1987, O'Connor remained committed to her friend's famous *Bakke* arguments and formulation of strict scrutiny. And, in *Grutter* she believed that the standard of review employed by her opinion was entirely consistent with that laid out by Powell a quarter century earlier.[102] Justice Kennedy could not have disagreed more.

During oral arguments in *Grutter*, most of Justice Kennedy's questions were directed toward the subject of diversity. The dialogue in which he engaged with all three advocates—Kirk O. Kolbo (Barbara Grutter's attorney), Maureen Mahoney (representing the law school), and Ted Olson (who was now the solicitor general and was arguing on behalf of the federal government as amicus supporting petitioner Grutter)—presaged the efforts that he would make in his dissenting opinion (and later in his concurrence in *Parents Involved*) to reach a compromise between the need for strict scrutiny and his rejection of the absolutist conservative position on diversity. Seeking to determine whether it could be reconciled with strict judicial scrutiny, he asked Olson whether diversity was "a permissible governmental goal." To this question, Olson responded:

> Well, the only way to answer that, Justice Kennedy, is that the word diversity means so many things to so many different people. It means both a means to get experience and a diversity of experience. It also means, I think what the law school has done, it's an end in and of itself. If it's an end in and of itself, obviously it's constitutionally objectionable.[103]

Kennedy was somewhat sympathetic to this position. This was reflected in the concerns that he expressed about diversity during the argument of Mahoney. Kennedy was skeptical that the law school's choice of diversity was anything more than a convenient choice—a major factor in his rejection of the conclusion that it met the compelling interest requirement of strict scrutiny.[104] His comments about diversity were not, however, all negative.

Justice Kennedy's support for the goal of diversity within the educational setting is unsurprising given his fondness for teaching and his deep commitment to imparting knowledge to future generations. Kennedy has always considered it important that law schools be concerned about the underrepresentation of minorities in their classrooms. When Kolbo, Grutter's attorney, argued otherwise, Kennedy exhibited just as much skepticism as he had toward Mahoney's position. As the Justice observed, "It's a broad social and political concern that there are not adequate members of—of the profession which is designed to protect our rights and to—and to promote progress." This, he emphasized, was something "I should think that's a very legitimate concern on the part of the State."[105] Kennedy does not believe, however, that the Constitution permits this concern to be addressed by a policy that treats persons as de facto members of racial groups rather than as individuals. As he wrote in his *Grutter* dissent, "An educational institution must ensure, through sufficient procedures, that each applicant receives individual consideration."[106] He could not accept the argument that "the concept of a critical mass" was anything more than "a delusion by the Law School to mask its attempt to make race an automatic factor in most instances and to achieve numerical goals indistinguishable from quotas."[107] This was constitutionally problematic, because by ignoring the importance of "*individual* consideration" of applications, the law school was ignoring what lies at the heart of the relationship between education and diversity: "A school admits students, in large part, so that they will be teachers to other students."[108]

"At Least for Now"

In the spring of 2003, at the same time as the Court was preparing to hear oral arguments in *Grutter*, Archibald Cox received a phone call from Ken Gormley. The aging lawyer's answer to the question that his biographer called to ask was exactly the same as it had been about fifteen years earlier when Gormley made the identical inquiry of the person who argued before the Court, on behalf of the regents of the University of California, in *Bakke*. How long, Gormley wanted to know, will affirmative action be necessary? Cox's answer was short and simple: "At least for now."[109] The long-term timetable for the phasing out of affirmative action—because it would no longer be a tool that society found it necessary to use in order to bring about racial equality (however one determines that)—was something that troubled the justices in *Bakke*. For all their differences, many of them agreed that their endeavors in this one case would certainly not constitute the definitive text on affirmative action. Perhaps it would be a small chapter, but certainly not the conclusion. Indeed, two weeks after the oral argument Chief Justice Burger indicated to his colleagues that it was probably best to predicate their deliberation of the case on a conscious understanding that all they could hope to achieve was to bring to a close this particular chapter of this particular legal dispute. As the Chief wrote:

> With all deference to the distinguished array of counsel who have been plunged into a very difficult case on a record any good lawyer would shun, I see no reason why we should let them (aided by the mildly hysterical media) rush us to judgment. The notion of putting this sensitive, difficult question to rest in one "hard" case is about as sound [as] trying to put all First Amendment issues to rest in one case. . . . If it is to take years to work out a rational solution of the current problem, so be it. That is what we are paid for.[110]

Justice Powell later expressed the same sentiment, bolstering his argument by directing the other justices' attention to the fact that "even the petitioner estimates that 'minority conscious programs' will be necessary for some 25 to 50 years." In short, concluded Powell, "There is no reason to believe that in so short a span of time the socio-economic position of racial and ethnic minorities will have changed so drastically as to end the demand for some types of preferential admission programs."[111]

Six months after the oral argument in *Bakke*, Justice Blackmun summarized the feelings of many of his colleagues who were frustrated at both the progress of the case and the media speculation about their deliberations. "I yield to no one in my earnest hope that the time soon will come when an 'affirmative action' program is unnecessary and only a relic of the past," he wrote. As the author of *Roe v. Wade*, however, he was painfully aware that such decisions had a tendency to generate more questions than they answered. He wistfully, but realistically, observed: "I would hope that we could reach this stage within a decade, but history strongly suggests that that hope is a forlorn one."[112]

In *Grutter*, Justice O'Connor was considerably more optimistic and found the subject of "the future of affirmative action" compelling enough that she was willing, publicly, to address it in her opinion for the Court. A quarter century had passed since Powell's landmark compromise in *Bakke*. One of the important positive legacies of that decision, she concluded, was its perpetuation of a program that could claim an increase in the academic achievement of minorities (as judged by rising grades and scores). Anticipating the positive impact of her own opinion, O'Connor wrote: "We expect that 25 years from now, the use of racial preferences will no longer be necessary to further the interest approved today."[113]

Twenty-five years was a convenient figure that had the added advantage of being the period of time that had elapsed since *Bakke.* Yet, its pragmatic ring did not sit well with a majority of O'Connor's colleagues. Although she joined O'Connor's opinion, Justice Ginsburg wrote separately to indicate that she and Justice Breyer (who joined her concurrence) did not share their colleague's optimism. The ability of the next generation to "sunset affirmative action" without sacrificing "progress toward nondiscrimination and genuinely equal opportunity" was only a "hope," she wrote. It could not be a reliable "forecast."[114]

The four members of the Court who dissented from the decision in *Grutter* all wrote their own opinions in which they also expressed objections to O'Connor's prediction. Chief Justice Rehnquist believed that the twenty-five-year remark provided "the vaguest of assurances" that educational institutions would not read the Court's opinion as an open invitation to continue to use affirmative action programs. He was concerned that they would think that the Court had given the policy a status close to presumptive constitutionality. This threat existed, Rehnquist said, because "discussions of a time limit . . . permit the Law School's use of racial preferences on a seemingly permanent basis. Thus, an important component of strict scrutiny—that a program be limited in time—is casually subverted."[115] In his brief dissenting opinion, Justice Scalia expressed concern that the Court had created a doctrinal and jurisprudential mess that was very unlikely to bring the country any closer to a situation wherein the existence of sufficient racial harmony would negate the need for affirmative action.[116] Justice Thomas, the Court's solitary black member, also penned his own, far longer rejection of the Court's decision. He shared his colleagues' concern about O'Connor's twenty-five-year optimism. However, the first sentence of his reference to this aspect of her opinion *almost* led one to think otherwise. "I agree with the Court's holding that racial discrimination in higher education admissions will be illegal in 25 years," wrote Thomas. I emphasize that this is *almost* suggestive of an unlikely agreement between O'Connor and Thomas. This is because what Thomas wrote in the next sentence completely disabuses us of any feeling of judicial harmony. Continuing, Thomas chided his colleague: "I believe that the Law School's *current* use of race violates the Equal Protection Clause and that the Constitution means the same thing today as it will in 300 months."[117]

Justice Kennedy was perplexed by O'Connor's prediction. Consistent with the overall theme of his opinion, he wrote:

> It is difficult to assess the Court's pronouncement that race-conscious admissions programs will be unnecessary 25 years from now. If it is intended to mitigate the damage the Court does to the concept of strict scrutiny, neither peti-

> tioners nor other rejected law school applicants will find solace in knowing the basic protection put in place by Justice Powell will be suspended for a full quarter of a century. *Deference is antithetical to strict scrutiny, not consistent with it.*[118]

In other words, Justice Kennedy was deeply concerned at the possibility that the traditional standard of review to which the Court held the government in race-dependent cases, and the individual dignity that it was designed to protect, would be sacrificed at the altar of pragmatism.

Parents Involved: Emerging Inconsistencies?

In the mid 1950s, when Kennedy was an undergraduate majoring in political science, he had the opportunity to escort around the campus of Stanford University the man who, very recently, had argued and prevailed before the Court in the most famous of the school segregation cases—*Brown v. Board of Education* (1954).[119] The student and the advocate later became colleagues on the Supreme Court. After that Court decided *Parents Involved* in 2007, a case in which both the majority and the dissenters frequently referred to the legacy of *Brown*, Justice Kennedy recalled his time, half a century earlier, with the great Thurgood Marshall. Kennedy said that at the time he "thought that we had solved the race problem."[120] In *The Hollow Hope*, *Brown* was one of the two Supreme Court decisions (the other being *Roe v. Wade*) that Gerald Rosenberg argued sustained the myth that the judicial branch could facilitate social change through its resolution of cases involving questions about important public-policy issues. He concluded that *Brown*, like other civil rights decisions, failed to bring about substantive social change *on its own*; only when accompanied by compliance and meaningful action by the other two branches of the government was such change forthcoming.[121] Such was the belief in the power of the law held by the young Tony Kennedy, a feeling that was fostered throughout his early years and one that remains with him to this day, he could not imagine that the decision in *Brown* would be held up as the paradigmatic negative answer to the main question that Rosenberg asked—"Can Courts bring about social change?" As Kennedy said in 2007, in an interview shortly after the decision in *Parents Involved*, "How naïve many of us were."[122]

In *Parents Involved*, we do not see an indication of a sudden shift to the conservative right in race-based cases brought about by new judicial appointments. It was not, as Justice Breyer concluded in his "hand-down statement" announcing the details of his dissent (a statement that he read from the bench), one of those rare examples when, as Winston Churchill might have said, "so few have so quickly undone so much" of a particular body of law.[123]

This was, in part, because of the concurring opinion authored by Kennedy. As we will see, this is not a concurrence that signifies a "concrete doctrinal reversal" by the Justice;[124] it does not contain an abandonment of his previous adherence to strict scrutiny in race-dependent cases. Rather, it takes very seriously the need for adherence to this level of judicial review. But in so doing it does not reject—as does the Chief Justice's plurality opinion that Kennedy declined to join—the conclusion that "diversity, depending on its meaning and definition, is a compelling educational goal a school district may pursue."[125]

What Is "the Promise of *Brown*"?[126]

The decision was the culmination of litigation in two cases—which the Court decided together—that involved constitutional challenges to plans adopted by school districts in Seattle, Washington, and Louisville, Kentucky. Both plans provided for the use of race as a factor in the assignment of students to public high schools. The plan enacted in 1998 by Seattle School District No. 1 was viewed as a means to achieving the goal of having schools with student populations that reflected the racial makeup of the district. Students could ask to be assigned to any of the high schools in the district, but because they were not guaranteed admission to any particular school—many of the more popular schools were oversubscribed—they had to rank their choices so as to indicate their preferences. Their race (the district classified students as either "white" or "non-white") was used as one of a number of tiebreakers for making final allocation decisions. The challenge to this race-conscious plan was brought by a nonprofit organization composed of parents whose children were not offered a place at their chosen schools because of their race. The plan adopted by the Jefferson County Public Schools in Louisville was similarly directed at ensuring racial balance; it required that, in order to reflect the diverse makeup of the district, between 15 and 50 percent of each school's population be composed of black students. For assignment purposes, it labeled students as either "black" or "other." The challenge to this plan resulted from the race-based denial of admission, to a kindergarten, of a white student whose choice to attend one of the local schools was rejected in favor of attendance at a school ten miles from his house. In his opinion announcing the judgment of the Court, but in a section that spoke for only a plurality of the Court (because Kennedy refused to join it), Roberts concluded that this classification of children was "directed only to racial balance . . . an objective this Court has repeatedly condemned as illegitimate," and not a compelling government interest as is required by the strict scrutiny level of judicial review.[127]

Taking "Social 'Facts'" Seriously?

In an essay examining the ability of the law and the legal system to "shape . . . society from the inside out, by providing the principal categories that make social life seem natural, normal, cohesive, and coherent," Austin Sarat and Thomas R. Kearns, professors of political science and philosophy at Amherst College, make the following argument:

> The image of self-sufficiency is one that pervades our legal system, yet it powerfully inhibits injured persons from availing themselves of legal remedies in response to racial discrimination. Indeed, one might see here a perfect example of law's constitutive powers, of its capacity to induce in legal subjects self-images that are then projected back onto law, masquerading as an independent kind of moral evaluation and acceptance.[128]

This, one might justifiably argue, offers a powerful reason for a policy of affirmative action, because it suggests that the promise of the Equal Protection Clause cannot be realized unless such policies are utilized. This is because of the ability of the legal system to reinforce white, majoritarian, and primarily negative stereotypes about racial minorities. The positions he takes in race-dependent cases, and his insistence that affirmative action policies be strictly scrutinized by the Court, have subjected Justice Kennedy to the criticism that he either fails to recognize or chooses to ignore this reality.

Although the language he employed was harsher than that of most commentators, in a 2007 article law professor Jeffrey Rosen expressed a commonly held view when he criticized this aspect of Kennedy's decision making. Rosen discussed what he perceived to be the Justice's arrogant propensity for lecturing to the American public about morality, and he was sharply critical of the utopian nature of some of the justice's arguments. Kennedy, "like many sweeping visionaries," wrote Rosen, "is unwilling to accept the radical implications of his own abstractions." Rosen was writing shortly after the Court's decision in *Parents Involved*, a case with whose outcome he clearly disagreed. Kennedy's decision to join the majority in striking down the two school district policies prompted Rosen to conclude that Kennedy's "moral arrogance" was positively frightening when it led to his color-blind reading of the Constitution.[129] Rosen speculated that "Kennedy's sunny vision of color-blind harmony may have come from the racially peaceful memories of his Sacramento upbringing, where the best man at his parents' wedding was Roger Traynor, the California Supreme Court justice who struck down anti-miscegenation laws in 1948."[130] The histories of Sacramento and the surrounding region of northern California demonstrate that this speculation ignores the different indignities suffered by, and the racial struggles of, the numerous different ethnic groups that have been part of the social fabric of that area.[131] And, as we have seen, comments made during his Supreme Court confirmation hearing, and the arguments that have appeared in his judicial opinions, demonstrate that Justice Kennedy is neither ignorant of, nor chooses to close his eyes to, these indignities.

In *A Theory of Liberty*, his important book about the relationship between considerations of social reality and the power of judicial review, H. N. Hirsch, a political scientist, outlines and defends a theory that "understands liberty to require the absence of governmental arbitrariness, and, further, relates this question of arbitrariness to social 'facts.'" He argues that when the law (and, by extension, the courts) ignores these facts—that constitute social reality—there exists a real danger that liberty will be abridged, and the Constitution violated.[132] It is clearly very difficult to reconcile this theory with the modest libertarianism of Justice Kennedy's race-dependent jurisprudence. In fact, it is easy to read the justice's opinions in this area of the law and jump to the conclusion, as Rosen did, that Kennedy is blissfully unaware of the social reality that is the pervasive existence in America of problematic relationships between the races and the many political obstacles in the path of minorities seeking social advancement. However, *Parents Involved* is perhaps the best example of a Kennedy-authored opinion, in a race-dependent case, which does take social facts seriously.

A Cautious Concurrence?

Consistent with the jurisprudential patterns that he created in the race-dependent cases discussed above, Justice Kennedy declined to join the absolutist sections of Chief Justice Roberts's opinion. He could not accept the resulting "postulate that 'the way to stop discrimination on the basis of race is to stop discriminating on the basis of race.'"[133] Showing that he was no longer the naïve undergraduate, Kennedy wrote: "Fifty years of experience since *Brown v. Board of Education* should teach us that the problem before us defies so easy a solution."[134] To be sure, he penned a concurrence that remained faithful to the concept of a color-blind Constitution—which, echoing what he said at his nomination hearing, he described as "most certainly justified in the context of his [Harlan's] dissent in *Plessy*."[135] Indeed, his invocations of that opinion in his previous writings are no different from his references to it in the *Parents Involved* concurrence. They serve the purpose of emphasizing the humane element of his jurisprudence—which insists on strict scrutiny in race-dependent cases in order to preserve and protect individual dignity. However, Kennedy was also quick to recognize—in his concurrence—that "as an aspiration, Justice Harlan's axiom must command our assent" even though "in the real world, it is regrettable to say, it cannot be a universal constitutional principle." As Kennedy proceeded to explain, "This Nation has a moral and ethical obligation to fulfill its historic commitment to creating an integrated society that ensures equal opportunity for all of its children." Governments must not be told that the Constitution permits only absolute color blindness (or, in the language used by the Chief Justice, an end to "discriminating on the basis of race"). Instead, what the Constitution permits, Kennedy said, is "race-conscious measures" that survive strict judicial scrutiny—that are narrowly tailored to meet a compelling government interest and, therefore, do not end up "treating each student in different fashion solely on the basis of a systematic, individual typing by race."[136]

The plurality's conclusion that neither of the school districts had crafted plans that addressed a compelling interest was another reason why Kennedy declined to join Roberts's opinion. "Depending on its meaning and definition," wrote Kennedy, this interest—diversity—is "a compelling educational goal a school district may pursue."[137] Why, then, did Kennedy conclude that the Louisville and Seattle plans were unconstitutional? For Kennedy, this case turned on the narrowly tailoring component of strict scrutiny. First, he expressed his clear disapproval of the particular way in which both school districts had classified students—he emphasized that he objected to "the state-mandated racial classifications . . . *as the cases now come to us*." This was because, in classifying their students, both districts increased the "sense of stigma" that often "become[s] the fate of those separated out by circumstances beyond their immediate control." Why? The answer lay in the districts' use of "blunt distinction[s]"—he pointed to Seattle's choice between "white" and "non-white." Kennedy was at a loss to understand how this could possibly further the districts' stated goal of student body diversity.[138] He further concluded that both of the school districts had also failed to narrowly tailor their plans because they had not demonstrated that the means they employed to achieve this goal were administered in a fair manner that afforded every student the individualized treatment that Powell emphasized in *Bakke*. Neither school district had offered any indication as to how their race-based allocation decisions were made. This, said Kennedy, made it impossible for the justices to apply strict scrutiny because they could not tell if diversity was the ultimate goal. To rule otherwise would be to ignore the requirements of strict scrutiny. As Kennedy explained, "When a court subjects governmental action" to such a high level of judicial review, "it cannot construe ambiguities in favor of the State." Were it to do so, the tie would not go to freedom. Therefore, it was impossible for the Court to decide whether or not the plans were the most narrowly tailored way of achieving the compelling interest of "avoiding racial isolation" of students by fostering racial diversity in the classroom.[139]

In *Parents Involved*, every member of the Court agreed that the constitutional fate of the Seattle and Louisville plans should be decided by applying strict judicial scrutiny. And, as a result, there is much to be said for concluding that it is now as difficult to identify the meaning and definition of this standard of judicial review, as it is to try and reach a consensus about what constitutes diversity. Writing in dissent, Justice Breyer accurately portrayed the quest of the Roberts-led plurality when he said it was seeking to "rewrite this Court's prior jurisprudence, at least in practical application, transforming the 'strict scrutiny' test into a rule that is *fatal in fact across the board*." In a perfect world, Breyer would have preferred to adopt a more "contextual approach to scrutiny" which was "not 'strict' in the traditional sense of that word." He concluded, however, that this was not necessary in order to enable the Seattle and Louisville plans to survive. The Court's opinion in *Grutter* and Justice Powell's seminal opinion in *Bakke* provided a perfectly adequate alternative "version of strict scrutiny."[140] As we have seen in this chapter, Justice Kennedy would agree with Justice Breyer's condemnation of the absolutist approach adopted by Chief Justice Roberts. He would be unwilling, however, to accept that the version of strict scrutiny that he believes was adopted in *Bakke* is consistent with either that which was employed in Justice O'Connor's opinion for the Court in *Grutter* or that which was advocated by Breyer's *Parents Involved* dissent. In his concurrence in the 2007 case, Justice Kennedy described Breyer's approach as "permissive strict scrutiny (which bears more than a passing resemblance to rational-basis review)."[141] Kennedy's jurisprudential preference is for an approach that is faithful to Powell's *Bakke* opinion *as he understands it*. What are the implications of this for the fate of future race-dependent cases—especially those involving education and diversity—heard by a Supreme Court that includes Kennedy? As this chapter has shown, Kennedy has been consistent in his opposition to race-based classifications and his belief that they should be strictly scrutinized. Nevertheless, it is probably fairest to say that answer D on the Douglas-George multiple-choice quiz accurately describes the future. In other words: "It all depends on Justice Kennedy."

Conclusions

Between June 5 and June 22, 1989, the Court handed down closely divided decisions in five cases that all involved race. Collectively, *Wards Cove Packing Co. v. Atonio, Martin v. Wilks, Lorance v. AT&T Technologies, Jett v. Dallas Independent School District*, and *Patterson v. McLean Credit Union* are described by political scientists Henry Abraham and Barbara Perry as the "June 1989 Quintet."[142] Abraham and Perry suggest that these five decisions were, collectively, a good indication of the impact that Kennedy, the Court's newest member, could have in this area of the law. In one of her articles summarizing the Court's October 1988 term, Linda Greenhouse concurred in this conclusion that the new vote of Justice Kennedy had been both crucial and determinative in these race cases.[143]

Justice Kennedy has recently said that the public unpopularity of some of these decisions caught him by surprise.[144] However, over the course of the past two decades, Kennedy has not allowed this reaction to guide his jurisprudence in race-dependent cases. Instead, his overriding concern has been to ensure that, through the use of strict judicial scrutiny, the Court has preserved and protected the dignity of individuals. He has repeatedly rejected an absolutist, zero-tolerance approach to race-based regulations, in no small part because such a strategy would relegate to the sidelines the relevance, to American society, of the concept of diversity. Instead, Kennedy has asked that this diversity not be created, fostered, or protected by programs based on the assumption that individuals will think or act in a certain way because of their race or ethnicity. Out of this belief comes Kennedy's commitment to the use of strict judicial scrutiny in race-dependent cases, because government agencies (including courts) cannot be trusted to say what a *reasonable* race-based law is. The only political unit in society who is entitled to say that race matters is the most important political unit in society—the individual.

5

Liberty, Exercised Responsibly

> I do not think that there is a choice between order and liberty. We can have both. Without ordered liberty, there is no liberty at all.[1]
>
> —Justice Kennedy

ON WEDNESDAY APRIL 22, 1992, the justices of the U.S. Supreme Court heard arguments in a case whose outcome they knew would deeply divide them. *Planned Parenthood v. Casey* had the potential to remake the landscape of American abortion law if a quartet of the Court's members—Chief Justice Rehnquist and Justices Byron White, Antonin Scalia, and Clarence Thomas—could persuade Justice Kennedy to provide the fifth vote necessary for overturning *Roe v. Wade*.[2] One month later, Rehnquist distributed to his colleagues the first printed draft of his opinion in *Casey*. It was an opinion that spoke for a majority that included Kennedy. This suggested that the Chief Justice had a reasonably good idea of the jurisprudential approach that Kennedy wanted the Court to take when deciding the case. In the margin of his copy of the draft opinion, Justice Blackmun—the author of *Roe*—indicated his hostile reaction to Rehnquist's arguments. "Pretty extreme!" wrote Blackmun.[3] Although he may not have felt the same way, Justice Kennedy also had a negative response to Rehnquist's *Casey* draft opinion. In a now famous about-turn, two days after distribution of the opinion Kennedy indicated to some of his colleagues that he was having second thoughts about the Court's intended resolution of the case—which involved a constitutional challenge to the provisions of a Pennsylvania state law that imposed numerous restrictions on women's access to abortions.

The memoranda that flowed between the justices during their deliberation of *Casey* seem to indicate that the chief was not kept informed of many of these developments.[4] Consequently, Rehnquist continued to believe that *Casey* was finally the opportunity he had been looking for. It would enable him to forge a *majority* opinion around two beliefs. First, he would be able to explain why women had an "*interest* in having an abortion"—not a *right.* Second, he would be able to emphasize that this "interest" was limited by the fact that "States may regulate abortion procedures in ways rationally related to a legitimate state interest."[5] When Justice Kennedy joined with Justices O'Connor and Souter to coauthor a landmark opinion that preserved the "essential holding" of *Roe*, Rehnquist was forced to accept that his arguments would appear in a dissenting opinion—and that *Roe* would not be overturned.

In the three justice-authored joint opinion in *Casey*, it was explained that the holding in *Roe* had three components:

1. A recognition of the right of the woman to choose to have an abortion before viability and to obtain it without undue interference from the State;
2. Confirmation of the State's power to restrict abortions after fetal viability, if the law contains exceptions for pregnancies which endanger the woman's life or health; and
3. The principle that the State has legitimate interests from the outset of the pregnancy in protecting the health of the woman and the life of the fetus that may become a child.[6]

To be sure, the standard of review employed by O'Connor, Kennedy, and Souter did not call for the strict scrutiny of *Roe.* There can be no doubt that the scope of individual liberty was reduced by the *Casey* substitution of an undue burden test—finding laws invalid if they have "the purpose or effect of placing a substantial obstacle in the path of a woman seeking an abortion of a nonviable fetus"[7]—for the *Roe* requirement that the government justify an abortion regulation by demonstrating that it was designed to meet a compelling state interest. However, it is equally clear that this trio of justices wrote into the Court's abortion law a level of review that was far more protective of individual liberty than the "rationally related to a legitimate state interest" standard envisioned by Rehnquist.

After *Casey*, abortion disappeared from the Court's radar screen for most of the rest of the twentieth century. When it did return it came before the justices in the form of laws with clearly antiabortion subtexts. However, instead of imposing outright bans on any form of the procedure, these laws contained provisions designed to place significant restrictions on abortions—even during the first trimester. In the adjudication of the constitutional challenges to these laws, Justice Kennedy played the lead role in defining the state interest whose importance he helped to elevate in *Casey*. In so doing, he employed a controversial abortion jurisprudence that challenges the modestly libertarian principles that were certainly evident in *Casey*. Kennedy's efforts to define the "real meaning" of *Casey* are underpinned by his belief that the woman who seeks to terminate her pregnancy has the constitutionally protected liberty to do so. However, this is a liberty that is bounded by important state interests—particularly the preservation of fetal life—that permit the state to require the woman to exercise her liberty in an informed and responsible manner.

Pleasing All of the People Some of the Time

Justice Kennedy's jurisprudential approach to abortion law has enabled him to please all of the people some of the time. The justice, himself, believes that he has steered a consistent course through the law; any changes people perceive, he says, can be attributed to the fact that "the cases swing"—not the justices or the law.[8] Yet the reality is that his positions in abortion cases do not always attract support from the same groups of people. Support for his expansive reading of the Constitution's protections of liberty has disappointed the conservatives who applauded his appointment in 1988. The decision in *Casey* is held up as one reason why Kennedy vies, with Justice Souter, for what conservative commentator Jonah Goldberg has described as the distinction of being "the most disappointing Republican appointee."[9] Fifteen years later, when Kennedy authored the opinion in *Gonzales v. Carhart*, upholding a federal ban on so-called partial-birth abortion, it was the liberal commentators who assailed his jurisprudence. He was castigated for his role in permitting the Court to arrive at what a *New York Times* editorial described as an "atrocious result."[10]

Libertarian scholars have also had mixed reactions to Justice Kennedy's abortion jurisprudence. In so doing, they have taken positions reflective of the numerous different approaches to, and formulations of, the basic principles of libertarianism. As we have seen, there is no single definitive libertarian answer to the question "When and how is it permissible to restrict an individual's liberty?" This is because, to a large extent, there is no single definitive answer to the question "Where do the boundaries of individual liberty lie?" Consequently, it is unsurprising that under this political theory's umbrella we find a mixture of opinions about the relationships between (1) libertarianism and abortion and (2) libertarianism and personal responsibility.

One of the most obvious principles that we might expect libertarians to invoke in opposition to abortion is the harm principle. For an example of what this argument might look like, we can turn to the quasi-utilitarian libertarianism of law professor Richard Epstein. Although Epstein has written relatively little about abortion law, he has consistently supported giving very little constitutional protection to a woman's access to this practice. Ever since 1973 when, in the months immediately following the decision in *Roe v. Wade*, he published an article critical of the decision, Epstein has maintained the position that abortion is "in manifest conflict with the basic libertarian theory" because of the harm that the procedure causes to the fetus.[11] This, says Epstein, means "*Roe* [and its progeny] . . . gets matters upside down by protecting the very kinds of external harms that states are in the business to prevent."[12] This is a radical argument (Epstein has long since admitted that on many issues he is "'way off the scale' of modern constitutional doctrine"[13]) for two important reasons—one normative, the other empirical. Normatively, as Epstein has recognized, there is a fundamental difficulty with reconciling fidelity to a libertarian harm principle with abortion bans that do not include maternal life exceptions. This is because of the possibility that the ban would result in women either seeking illegal and potentially unsafe abortions, or continuing with a pregnancy against medical advice. Both scenarios would generate harm for the pregnant woman—something that the harm principle cannot tolerate.[14] From an empirical perspective, Epstein is also fully aware of the practical irrelevance—with regard to American constitutional law—of the line of argument that values the fetus over the woman. For the purposes of the Fifth and Fourteenth Amendments, the fetus is not considered a person. Consequently, there can be no legitimate claim that it has a constitutionally guaranteed right to the life that an abortion would abridge.

Even if Professor Epstein did not acknowledge the libertarian limitations of his argument against abortion, given what we learned in chapter 1 about his particular brand of libertarianism, we would not expect him to see eye to eye with Justice Kennedy about the scope of the decision-making liberty of a woman who seeks to terminate her pregnancy. Epstein adheres to the view that abortion rights should never have been viewed as one of the "new rights to self-rule" that evolved out of a line of personal liberty cases decided by the Court in the 1960s. By contrast, Kennedy is of the opinion that this is precisely the type of right involved. The adoption of this view positions him to agree with many libertarians who do not share Epstein's view about abortion and individual liberty. However, it is important to note that the bonds of this agreement are weak. This is because of the justice's emphasis on responsibly exercised liberty. Some libertarians believe that rights do not, per se, entail responsibilities. Responsibilities, they argue, attach to "other people"—who have "duties and responsibilities" not to engage in behavior that violates the rights of others. Justice Kennedy's jurisprudence suggests he does not agree that "so far as a right is a right, and no more, it does not entail responsibilities, but rather, freedom on the part of the right-holder and responsibilities and duties on the part of other people."[15]

In order to understand Kennedy's objection to a separation of rights and responsibilities, and how it impacts his opinions in abortion cases, it is instructive to consult the following statement from *Libertarianism: A Primer*. In this book, one of the policies that David Boaz (of the Cato Institute) criticizes is affirmative action. Boaz believes that this is a policy that "white elites . . . implemented" because they "assumed that blacks couldn't get admitted to college or get hired for jobs on their individual merits but would need the paternalistic help of the federal government."[16] Toward the end of this chapter, we will encounter the opinion that Justice Kennedy penned for the five-justice majority in *Carhart* (2007). This controversial opinion suggests that the state can, with constitutional legitimacy, regulate abortion in order to protect a woman from the life of suffering and regret that it is unexceptionable to conclude she will experience after the termination of her pregnancy.[17] Using the same sort of paternalistic reasoning that Boaz attributes to affirmative action, Kennedy goes on to suggest that state intervention in these intimate and very individual decisions is needed because doctors are performing partial-birth abortions without providing women with adequate knowledge of the procedure. The state, so the reasoning goes, is therefore justified in stepping in to educate—and therefore protect—these women. One might assume that the ability to identify these parallels between paternalism-based affirmative action (as Boaz understands it) and paternalism-based abortion restrictions (as one might interpret Justice Kennedy's opinion in *Carhart* as endorsing) would lead us to conclude that *Carhart* is entirely inconsistent with libertarianism. However, as we will see, this would be an erroneous reading of the Justice's use of the responsible element of his modestly libertarian jurisprudence.

Before we can proceed to an analysis of *Carhart*, and a discussion of the tensions that it causes within the legal philosophical principles of Kennedy's judicial decision making, we need to spend time evaluating the justice's jurisprudential contributions to the opinion in *Casey*. In order to understand *Casey*, it is necessary to review the opinions, written by his Supreme Court predecessors, that constitute the vein into which Kennedy tapped for help in constructing his own abortion jurisprudence. In so doing, the most important opinions we will encounter are those penned by the second Justice Harlan, one of the Supreme Court justices most respected by Kennedy.[18]

From a Value to a Right

During their discussions about whether or not to nominate him for a seat on the Supreme Court, members of the Reagan administration solicited then-Judge Kennedy's views on the right to privacy.[19] William Bradford Reynolds, who was an assistant attorney general who helped to review files on the nominee, recalls that Kennedy "was quite emphatic that that sort of discovered right was not something that he found embedded in the Constitution, but something that came from the Court."[20] We do not know whether, through this response, Kennedy intended to convey support or opposition for such a product. Nevertheless, we do know that his belief that a right to privacy is not "embedded in the Constitution" in no way means that he thinks it cannot be found within the document's statements about individual liberty. Rather, he believes in the existence of a privacy *value* that is part of the liberty *right* explicitly protected by the Due Process Clause of the Fourteenth Amendment. This, he explained at his Supreme Court nomination hearings, was not a novel position for a justice to take.

From *Poe* to *Bowers*—Privacy Triumphant?

The dawning of the 1960s brought to the Supreme Court challenges to provisions of a Connecticut law that criminalized both the use of contraception and the giving of advice about its use. Although, as Justice Potter Stewart would write, this was an "uncommonly silly law," there was no escaping the fact that it posed a threat to the liberty of both those who wished to use contraception and those who desired to distribute information about this form of family planning.[21] Was this an unconstitutional threat? This was the primary question confronting the Court in *Griswold v. Connecticut* (1965). Four years earlier, the Court granted certiorari in *Poe v. Ullman*, a constitutional challenge to the Connecticut law. However, in that case the Court eventually dismissed the appeal. The justices were deeply divided as to why, but five of them agreed that the case, as it was presented to them, did not involve a "justiciable controversy." Absent such a controversy, the Court, they concluded, was not authorized to reach a decision on the merits of the case.[22] This view changed four years later, when *Griswold*, a very similar challenge to the Connecticut statute, came to the Court. The challenge was successful because six justices agreed that the state statute was an unconstitutional abridgment of individual liberty.

This result is only the starting point for this chapter's discussion of *Griswold*, because the vote disguises the difficulties that all of the justices had when they attempted to answer the following question: Where in the Constitution does it say that individuals enjoy legally protected freedom to use contraception? In an infamous opinion that spoke for himself and four of his colleagues, Justice Douglas struck down the Connecticut law and answered this question in a manner that left both his colleagues and Court commentators wondering whether his dubious doctrinal explanation would stand the test of time. This is because Douglas concluded that the law violated the "zones of privacy" that could be found in the shadows—the "emanations" and "penumbras"—of the First, Third, Fourth, Fifth, and Ninth Amendments.[23] This did not impress the two dissenters, Justice Stewart and Justice Hugo Black, who had no doubt that the answer to the above question was "Nowhere." Struggling to comprehend the idea that a privacy right could be found in the emanations of parts of the Constitution, without any trace of equivocation Black famously declared: "I like my privacy as well as the next one, but I am nevertheless compelled to admit that government has a right to invade it unless prohibited by some specific constitutional provision."[24]

Similarly unimpressed by Douglas's interpretation of the Constitution was Justice Harlan, who was primarily concerned that his colleague had ignored what to Harlan was the obvious constitutional source of the protection of an individual's right to choose to use contraception—the Fourteenth Amendment's Due Process Clause. In *Poe*, Harlan had penned a lengthy opinion dissenting from the dismissal of the appeal in that case. He argued that when it came to decisions about activities involving "the privacy of the home in its most basic sense," the Court could not sit idly by and watch the other branches of the government violate "the fundamental aspect of 'liberty'" that the Fourteenth Amendment expressly protected.[25] He began the constitutionality section of his dissent by saying that the Connecticut statute violated the Fourteenth Amendment. Using language that Justice Kennedy would later employ in *Casey*, Harlan wrote:

> Due process has not been reduced to any formula; its content cannot be determined by reference to any code. The best that can be said is that through the course of this Court's decisions it has represented the balance which our Nation, built upon postulates of respect for the liberty of the individual, has struck between that liberty and the demands of organized society.[26]

Harlan reaffirmed this position in *Griswold*. Emphasizing that what mattered was the protection afforded individuals by the libertarian *principles* of the Due Process Clause, Harlan wrote:

> In my view, the proper constitutional inquiry in this case is whether this Connecticut statute infringes the Due Process Clause of the Fourteenth Amendment

> because the enactment violates basic values "implicit in the concept of ordered liberty." . . . For reasons stated at length in my dissenting opinion in *Poe v. Ullman*, I believe that it does. While the relevant inquiry may be aided by resort to one or more of the provisions of the Bill of Rights, it is not dependent on them or any of their radiations. The Due Process Clause of the Fourteenth Amendment stands, in my opinion, on its own bottom.[27]

Although no other justice joined Harlan's *Griswold* concurrence, the other opinions in the case do indicate that there was significant support for emphasizing liberty rather than privacy. Justice Goldberg concurred, finding the statute to be a violation of the "concept of liberty" as "supported" by precedents and "the language and history of the Ninth Amendment."[28] And Justice White wrote to say, "This Connecticut law as applied to married couples deprives them of 'liberty' without due process of law, as that concept is used in the Fourteenth Amendment."[29]

In 1972, in *Eisenstadt v. Baird*,[30] the Court extended *Griswold* to apply to unmarried individuals when it overturned the conviction of a person who provided a single woman[31] with a packet of contraceptive vaginal foam (after he gave a lecture at Boston University), in violation of a Massachusetts law prohibiting the distribution of contraception. *Eisenstadt* was an equal protection decision, holding that "whatever the rights of the individual to access to contraceptives may be, the rights must be the same for the unmarried and the married alike."[32] As we saw in chapter 3, Brennan's opinion in the case is most remembered for the following statement: "If the right to privacy means anything, it is the right of the *individual*, married or single, to be free from unwarranted governmental intrusion into matters so fundamentally affecting a person as the decision whether to bear or beget a child."[33] However, the justice's papers confirm that this opinion was "crafted to apply in the abortion context."[34]

The files also tell us that while Brennan had one eye turned toward *Roe*, he believed that the significance of his opinion lay not in its application to a particular issue, but in its expansive understanding of the individual's place in society. In a letter to Justice Douglas on December 30, 1971, Brennan recommended a number of improvements to his colleague's concurrence in *Doe v. Bolton*, a companion case to *Roe* that was argued earlier that month.[35] Brennan suggested that Douglas "identify three groups of fundamental freedoms that, 'liberty' encompasses." These, he said, were as follows:

> First, freedom from bodily restraint or inspection, freedom to do with one's body as one likes, and freedom to care for one's health and person;
>
> second, freedom of choice in the basic decisions of life, such as marriage, divorce, procreation, contraception, and the education of children;
>
> third, autonomous control over the development and expression of one's intellect and personality.[36]

Doe was finally decided (after a reargument) with *Roe v. Wade* in January 1973.[37] In both cases the Court held that the right to privacy that protects abortion rights was located in the Due Process Clause of the Fourteenth Amendment. This was the first time that the Court had looked to this provision to protect substantive privacy rights. As such, their focus on privacy notwithstanding, *Roe* and *Doe* served to elevate the jurisprudential stature of the Fourteenth Amendment's protection of individual liberty. Interestingly, although his solo concurring opinion (that applied to both cases) shared the Court's commitment to the Fourteenth Amendment, Justice Douglas was more inclined than the majority to argue that it was *liberty* that was at stake in these cases. The concurrence eased itself away from the "penumbras" and "emanations" approach of *Griswold* and instead embraced the idea that many of the rights and privileges the Constitution protects "come within the meaning of the term 'liberty' as used in the Fourteenth Amendment."[38] Directly applying Brennan's suggested "fundamental freedoms" approach, Douglas argued that this liberty included:

> First . . . the autonomous control over the development and expression of one's intellect, interests, tastes, and personality.
>
> Second . . . the freedom of choice in the basic decisions of one's life respecting marriage, divorce, procreation, contraception, and the education and upbringing of children.
>
> Third . . . the freedom to care for one's health and person, freedom from bodily restraint or compulsion, freedom to walk, stroll, or loaf.[39]

Roe and *Doe* are remembered for their effusive embrace of a right to privacy, a right that afforded a woman constitutional protection to seek an abortion. The seeds had been planted, however, for future judicial use of and reliance upon the expansive and individualist liberty provisions of the Constitution.

As we saw in chapter 3, in *Bowers v. Hardwick* the Court refused to apply this understanding of liberty—or a formulation of it as privacy—to homosexual relations. In July 1986, just a few weeks after the decision in that case, then-Judge Kennedy gave his Stanford Lecture on Unenumerated Rights and the Dictates of Judicial Restraint. When he turned to the subject of enumerated liberty versus unenumerated privacy, Kennedy's comments demonstrated that he agreed with Justice Stevens's emphasis on liberty (recall that Stevens interpreted *Bowers* as nothing less than a "*liberty* case.")[40] In his speech, Kennedy used a line from Keats' *Ode on a Grecian Urn* to make the following point:

> The mystic attraction of the untested and undefined word catches all of us now and then. As Keats wrote: "Heard melodies are sweet, but those unheard are

> sweeter." This is good inspiration for poets, but promises considerable understanding for judges charged with enforcing a written constitution.[41]

This demonstrates that Kennedy considers it important to draw the boundaries of constitutionally protected liberty by actually focusing on the interest, concept, or, most important, the *right* of "*liberty*," a word which does appear in the Constitution. Justice Kennedy believes that this is preferable to an approach that places the emphasis on unenumerated privacy, which is nothing more than a part, or constituent value, of the liberty right.

He made this clear during his Supreme Court nomination hearings, when he repeatedly responded to the question "Is there a right to privacy?" by explaining that privacy is a value, rather than a right, and that it is (1) part of liberty, and (2) protected by liberty.[42] He rejected the argument that distinguishing between privacy as a value and liberty as a right was purely a matter of semantics. Rather, he saw a very important relationship between the two:

> I think that the concept of liberty in the due process clause is quite expansive, quite sufficient, to protect the values of privacy that Americans legitimately think are part of their constitutional heritage. It seems to me that sometimes by using some word that is not in the Constitution, we almost create more uncertainties than we solve. It is very clear that privacy is a most helpful noun, in that it seems to sum up rather quickly values that we hold very deeply.[43]

So, in Justice Kennedy's opinion, privacy is afforded constitutional protection, but only insofar as it is one of the *values* covered by the *right* to liberty.

Of course, one might argue that liberty is just as susceptible to expansive and subjective interpretations as privacy. Implicit in this argument is the belief that jurists should exercise judicial self-restraint when called upon to give meaning to the Constitution's ambiguous phrases. Justice Kennedy has created an interesting jurisprudential response to this. Part of his response has been the aforementioned rejection of a reliance on privacy. However, he has also said that it would be wrong to accompany a switch from "privacy" to "liberty" with a very narrow reading of "liberty." This is because, as we saw in chapter 1, Justice Kennedy is strongly committed to a belief that the liberty protected by the Fifth and Fourteenth Amendments is a "spacious phrase" that can only be understood by taking account of both the Constitution and the small "c" unwritten constitution—"our ethical culture, our shared beliefs, our common vision." Drawing on this "small 'c'" constitution to understand the "the big 'C'" Constitution improves society, and provides a protection for individual liberty envisioned by the Framers.[44]

History and Tradition

In *Poe*, Justice Harlan expressed his belief that in its decisions the Court strove to achieve a due process balance between "liberty of the individual . . . and the demands of organized society." He explained that in order to perform this judicial task the justices used several different tools. One was a consideration of "what history teaches are the traditions from which" the balance "developed as well as the traditions from which it broke."[45] By this, Harlan did not mean a stilted use of constitutional traditions; he was not about to determine whether Amendment Y grants constitutional protection to alleged right X by asking whether alleged right X involves an activity that existed and was considered legal when Amendment Y was written. This is because the Court constantly works to "perceive distinctions in the imperative character of Constitutional provisions," and this character comes "from a provision's larger context," which is to a large extent defined by its "history and purposes." In other words, the liberty of which the Constitution—in particular, the Fourteenth Amendment—speaks cannot be either defined by or confined to a narrow and/or subject-specific interpretation.[46]

In *American Constitutionalism*, the political scientist Stephen Griffin provides an excellent discussion of the role that this "rational continuum" argument played in the post-*Poe* development of the Supreme Court's Fourteenth Amendment due process jurisprudence. Says Griffin, in many cases the more conservative members of the Court have sought to bring new meaning to "Harlan's method of history and tradition" by turning it "into a barrier to the recognition of new fundamental rights." These justices have done this by confining themselves to interpreting rights claims at a very narrow level of generality. This has enabled them to deny the claims on the basis that the right at stake does not have the requisite American constitutional pedigree to justify labeling it as "fundamental."[47] This is clearly not what Harlan had in mind when he wrote of the role of history and tradition in constitutional interpretation. Nor is it Justice Kennedy's understanding of his predecessor's judicial methodology.

Unlike *Bowers*, *Michael H. v. Gerald D.* (1989) was a case decided by a Supreme Court that did include Justice Kennedy; oral arguments were heard on October 11, 1988, the second week of the first full term of Kennedy's tenure on the high court. Nowhere is the conservative commitment to a narrow understanding of the role of history and tradition in constitutional interpretation more obvious and stronger than in the sixth footnote of Justice Scalia's plurality opinion in *Michael H.*[48] In this case, five members of the Court upheld a state law that presumed a woman's husband to be the father of his wife's children even if he was not the biological father. The law survived a constitutional challenge alleging that it violated the Due Process Clause of the Fourteenth Amendment. Although a majority of the Court reached this judgment, the justices—in particular the Republican appointments—were deeply divided over the method of interpretation to apply, as Scalia's sixth footnote (which was joined only by Chief Justice Rehnquist) demonstrated. There, Scalia concluded that constitutionally protected liberty should be interpreted in accordance with "the most specific level at which a relevant tradition protecting, or denying protection to, the asserted right can be identified." Applied to the case at hand, such a narrow reading of liberty led Scalia to conclude that the Court was dealing with a conflict involving the "rights of an adulterous natural father," for which a tradition of protection did not exist in American legal history.[49]

Scalia wrote this footnote in response to Justice Brennan's dissenting opinion that would have read the rights involved at the broader level of parenthood. In dissent, Justice Brennan, joined by Justice Blackmun (Eisenhower and Nixon appointees respectively, but most definitely not conservative members of the Court), wrote scathingly of Scalia's focus on tradition. "Apparently oblivious to the fact that this concept can be as malleable and as elusive as 'liberty' itself," wrote Brennan, "the plurality pretends that tradition places a discernible border around the Constitution. The pretense is seductive," continued Brennan. Of course, "it would be comforting to believe that a search for 'tradition' involves nothing more idiosyncratic or complicated than poring through dusty volumes on American history." This simply was not the case, he concluded, quoting from one of the opinions of his colleague, Justice White: "What the deeply rooted traditions of the country are is arguable." Even "reasonable people," Brennan observed, "can disagree about the content of particular traditions, and because they can disagree even about which traditions are relevant to the definition of 'liberty,' the plurality has not found the objective boundary that it seeks."[50]

What is perhaps most interesting about the *Michael H.* footnote 6 is the reaction that it elicited from Justices O'Connor and Kennedy. Joined by her centrist colleague, O'Connor penned a pointed concurrence whose brevity merits reprinting it here in its entirety:

> I concur in all but footnote 6 of Justice Scalia's opinion. This footnote sketches a mode of historical analysis to be used when identifying liberty interests protected by the Due Process Clause of the Fourteenth Amendment that may be somewhat inconsistent with our past decisions in this area. On occasion the Court has characterized relevant traditions protecting asserted rights at levels of generality that might not be "the most specific level" available. I would not foreclose the unanticipated by the prior imposition of a single mode of historical analysis.[51]

Kennedy joined this concurrence only at a very late stage in the justices' deliberations.[52] Nevertheless, his Supreme Court nomination hearings discussion (which took place less than a year before oral arguments in *Michael H.*) about the role of history in constitutional interpretation tells us that from the outset he probably had serious reservations regarding Justice Scalia's absolutist approach.

At those hearings, in response to questioning from Senator Robert Byrd (D-WV), Kennedy exhibited considerable skepticism about the at-the-time high profile belief that failure to read the Constitution by referring to the original intent of the Framers (assuming, for the sake of argument, that the intent could be determined) made a judge a friend of a "living Constitution"—a document whose meaning was based upon the subjective and ever-changing interpretations of unelected judges. This was obviously a useful point to make at a confirmation hearing coming just one year after the Senate's rejection of Robert Bork, a major supporter of the "original intent originalism" approach. However, Kennedy was also making this argument in order to emphasize one of the important elements of his judicial philosophy. Justice Kennedy cares deeply about the role that new generations can (and indeed must) play in interpreting the Constitution. In his opinion, these future keepers of the document's flame are important because they will "yield new insights" into and bring to bear "new perspectives" on the document's meaning. What this "does not mean [is that] the Constitution changes," says Kennedy. "It just means that our understanding of it changes."[53] The Framers, he says, expected nothing less, because they "well understood that it [the Constitution] was to apply to exigencies and circumstances and perhaps even crises that they could never foresee. *So any theory which is predicated on the intent the framers had what they actually thought about, is just not helpful.*"[54]

As Professor Griffin observes, conservative members of the Rehnquist Court such as "Justices White and Scalia . . . argued that the Court should rarely exercise the power of judicial review to create new fundamental rights." This was an argument they felt able to win because of their belief that "history and tradition could be construed as limits on the recognition of new rights." This stands in contrast to Justice Harlan's far greater willingness to use judicial review "to remedy the violation of fundamental rights by the states"—a willingness constructed upon the same sort of expansive interpretation of liberty that we see employed by Justice Kennedy.[55]

It was April 24, 1992. Six months had elapsed since oral arguments in *Burson v. Freeman*, and still a decision had not been announced. As we saw in chapter 2, Justice Blackmun's assignment to write the majority opinion in *Freeman* was complicated, in part, by Kennedy's decision to pen a concurrence. The separate opinion was necessary, said Kennedy, because he viewed his "essential First Amendment analysis" as "somewhat different" from his colleague's.[56] And so it was that on this Friday morning before the justices met in conference to discuss *Planned Parenthood v. Casey*, Stephanie Dangel sent a memorandum to Justice Blackmun, for whom she was clerking. It is worth reprinting a lengthy extract from this document:

> I can't help but be concerned that this case, as you put it, may come back to haunt us—perhaps even in *Casey*, although we should know better after the vote today. In short, AS [Antonin Scalia] & Co. may try to argue that we have held that history can be used to determine whether there exists a fundamental liberty under the Constitution . . . they will go on to say that historically, there is no fundamental right to an abortion. We have three answers to this challenge. First, we can point out that we did not hold that history determines the contours of fundamental liberty—we held that history could be used in deciding whether the State's regulation was *necessary* to serve a recognized compelling State interest. In *Casey*, there is no recognized compelling State interest in protecting fetal life during the first trimester (or however else PA chooses to characterize its interest). Second, we can attack the SG's [solicitor general's] distorted view of history. Third, there is always AMK's [Justice Kennedy's] confusing *Burson* concurrence, which his clerk says translates into "I don't really think the majority was applying strict scrutiny in *Burson*." Nonetheless, AS is pretty good at blurring distinctions, and he will thus superficially look like he's got a point.[57]

These concerns related to Blackmun's lengthy discussion in *Freeman* of the *history* and *traditions* surrounding the fundamental right to vote—factors that helped to account for the Court's willingness to uphold the Tennessee law that placed a "campaign-free zone" around polling places.[58] Kennedy's *Freeman* concurrence did not discuss his colleague's references to history; and, as we have seen, time and again Kennedy has resisted deciding cases by examining the historical pedigree of the rights involved. Dangel had every reason to be cautious, however, because even absent a willingness to sign on to the history-based argument of "AS & Co." it was unclear whether, and to what extent, Kennedy believed in a "fundamental right to an abortion"—the type of right that the government could only abridge by demonstrating that its regulatory effort served a compelling state interest. *Casey* would not be the Sacramentan's first Supreme Court encounter with an abortion case, but between February 1988 (when he joined the Court) and April 1992, Kennedy did not give his new colleagues much indication as to the nature of his views on the subject.

Life before *Casey*

In 1989, Dane Cameron, a political scientist, expressed concern about the ideological direction that many observers expected the Rehnquist Court to take after the appointment of Justice Kennedy. Writing in the months leading up to the oral argument and decision in the first Supreme Court abortion case upon which Kennedy would vote, Cameron concluded that whatever the outcome of *Webster v. Reproductive Health Services* (discussed below), "It does not look good for the 'pro-choice' side" because:

> one can only look to a generally conservative ideology, his willingness to impose that ideology judicially, and the influence other conservative members of the Court assert over him, in an effort to determine Kennedy's impact in this area. Insofar as it is the point of this paper to indicate that Justice Kennedy is a conservative activist jurist who consistently votes with his conservative colleagues, to this observer, Kennedy appears ready to join them in paring back *Roe*.[59]

As we will see, Cameron's concerns about the impact of Kennedy on the Court's abortion law were, to a large extent, misplaced. However, through the end of June 1990—after Kennedy had spent two full terms with his new colleagues—Cameron, and those who shared his views, appeared to have been vindicated. At first glance, it was difficult to reconcile the Justice's opinions in *Ohio v. Akron Center* (1990) and *Hodgson v. Minnesota* (1990) with his pre-confirmation statements about expansive liberty. Upon closer inspection, however, it is clear that Kennedy's opinions in these cases provide us with important indications that his understanding of responsibly exercised liberty did not suddenly emerge in *Casey* during the "three weeks in May, [when] he holed up in his Virginia home" writing his contributions to the joint opinion in that case.[60]

"Abortion after *Webster*"[61]

In order to understand *Akron Center*, *Hodgson*, and the justices' deliberations about these two cases, we must begin with a brief discussion of *Webster*, a 1989 abortion decision in which Kennedy did not write an opinion.[62] In this case the Court was asked to consider a constitutional challenge to provisions of a Missouri law that prohibited the use of (1) public employees and facilities to perform abortions, and (2) public monies to fund abortion counseling. Exceptions were made in instances when the termination of a pregnancy was required to save the life of the mother. Chief Justice Rehnquist was able to muster a majority of the Court in support of the conclusion that the provisions were constitutional. However, this case deeply divided the justices. Rehnquist's opinion spoke only for himself and four colleagues (including Kennedy)—a quintet of justices who agreed that the law did not place impermissible obstacles in the paths of women seeking abortions.

In the weeks following oral argument in *Hodgson* and *Akron Center*, Anne Dupre, one of his law clerks, wrote a memo to Justice Blackmun, précising and analyzing a recently published law review article about *Webster*.[63] Interestingly, in "Abortion after *Webster*" law professor Daniel A. Farber reaches conclusions that appear to paint an extremely insightful picture of what might have happened behind the scenes in *Webster*—particularly with regard to Justice Kennedy's involvement. Although he did not pen an opinion in *Webster*, when the justices met in conference to vote on the case there is an indication that one of things concerning Kennedy was the test used by the Court in its abortion jurisprudence.[64] By this Kennedy surely meant the strict judicial scrutiny that was triggered by the *Roe* declaration that abortion was a "fundamental" right. This language was absent from the final *Webster* opinion, as was a willingness to overrule *Roe*. Professor Farber pointed to these aspects of the opinion as evidence in support of his conclusion that *Webster* should rightly be remembered for doing very little to change the legal status quo. In particular, Farber highlighted the following passage from Rehnquist's opinion (the italics are Farber's):

> The experience of the Court in applying *Roe v. Wade* in later cases suggests to us that there is a wisdom in not necessarily attempting to elaborate the abstract differences between a "fundamental right" to abortion . . . a "limited fundamental constitutional right" . . . or *a liberty interest protected by the Due Process Clause, which we believe it to be.*[65]

To be sure, at the time Farber was right that this passage was remarkable because of its strong implication that a woman had a constitutionally protected right to terminate her pregnancy.[66] What subsequently seems far more significant, however, is that this portion of the Chief's opinion appears to speak directly to Justice Kennedy.

When the justices met in conference to discuss *Webster*, the Court's newest member expressed concern about *Roe*'s continuing ability to hurt the Court and to present the justices with a forceful challenge to the traditional and proper conception of the judicial role. Additionally, Kennedy was worried about the wisdom of that decision's fundamental rights rationale. Nevertheless, reminiscing about his fifteen years spent teaching *Roe*, he concluded that the pull of the principle of stare decisis was too strong to ignore.[67] In his mind, *Roe* was secure, because it protected the individual liberty that Kennedy emphasized in his preconfirmation speeches and his nomination hearings testimony. The aforementioned passage from the Chief Justice's opinion in *Webster* demonstrated sympathy toward, and respect for, all these facets of Kennedy's abortion jurisprudence. Indeed, it is almost as though it was written by Kennedy.

June 25, 1990

What we *do* know is that Justice Kennedy authored opinions in two abortion cases decided the following year. These opinions in *Hodgson* and *Akron Center* laid much of the jurisprudential groundwork for what was to come two years later in *Casey*. The two 1990 decisions addressed state laws that placed sharp restrictions on the ability of a minor to obtain an abortion without providing proof that she had notified one or both of her parents. Both produced opinions that exposed sharp divisions among the justices and demonstrated that the definitive "swing" justice in abortion cases was Justice O'Connor. In *Hodgson*, O'Connor was the key vote for deciding the fate of both of the provisions of the Minnesota law whose constitutionality the case questioned.[68] She joined a five-justice majority to strike down the state's requirement that no abortions be performed on women under the age of eighteen without notification of *both* of the pregnant woman's parents forty-eight hours prior to the procedure (with some exceptions). She voted to uphold the notification provision when it was accompanied by a judicial bypass procedure—which provides a way for the minor to ask a judge for an exemption from the parental notification requirement.

Kennedy dissented from the holding that the two-parent-plus-bypass requirement was unconstitutional. He opened with a quotation from an opinion in a 1976 abortion case, in which Justice Stewart captured the essence of what Kennedy wanted to say:

> There can be little doubt that the State furthers a constitutionally permissible end by encouraging an unmarried pregnant minor to seek the help and advice of her parents in making the very important decision whether or not to bear a child. That is a grave decision, and a girl of tender years, under emotional stress, may be ill-equipped to make it without mature advice and emotional support.[69]

The importance of pursuing this goal of ensuring that a child has (or at least seeks) parental assistance when deciding whether to have an abortion led Kennedy to write that it would "no doubt come as a surprise to most parents" to find that this state interest could not be furthered by a two-parent notification statute.[70] Fourteen years earlier, in a letter to Chief Justice Burger, Justice Thurgood Marshall was sharply critical of the Chief's argument, made in a dissenting opinion, that the nuclear family is "the basic building block of our society." To Justice Marshall, this was "a middle class norm that government has no business foisting on those to whom economic or psychological necessity dictates otherwise." Their colleague, Justice Brennan, supplemented Marshall's letter with his own memorandum that accused Burger of employing a "concept . . . completely out of touch with the reality of a vast number of relationships in our society, including my own as a youngster growing up."[71] To be sure, in *Akron Center* and *Hodgson* Kennedy did not ignore the fact that abusive and incestuous family relationships could seriously threaten a pregnant minor's ability to seek the loving paternal support that the Justice's notion of family responsibility seemed to require. However, he did not agree that the Court should "command . . . its own solution to the cruel consequences of individual misconduct, parental failure, and social ills."[72]

Akron Center, decided on the same day as *Hodgson*, upheld an Ohio law that made it a criminal offense to perform an abortion on a minor unless the physician notified *one* of the minor's parents twenty-four hours in advance, or the minor obtained a judicial bypass of these requirements. The first four sections of Justice Kennedy's opinion for the Court in *Akron Center* were unremarkable. They won the support of five of his colleagues—including O'Connor and Stevens—in holding that this *one-parent* notification-plus-bypass provision (1) was constitutional and (2) was not actually required by the Fourteenth Amendment—because "unlike parental consent laws, a law requiring parental notice does not give any third party the legal right to make the minor's decision for her, or to prevent her from obtaining an abortion should she choose to have one performed."[73]

In *Akron Center*, Stevens and O'Connor both switched their votes after the justices met in conference to discuss the case. At this meeting they had expressed support (albeit tentatively) for striking down the Ohio law. Although it appears that the first draft of his opinion encouraged Justice Stevens to join the majority (O'Connor had already switched her vote), neither justice was willing to join Part V of Kennedy's arguments, the final language of which was unchanged from the opinion's first draft.[74] This is significant because it is in Part V that we see the clearest expression, in this case, of the responsible element of Justice Kennedy's modestly libertarian jurisprudence. Joined by only three of his colleagues, Kennedy wrote:

> A free and enlightened society may decide that each of its members should attain a clearer, more tolerant understanding of the profound philosophic choices confronted by a woman who is considering whether to seek an abortion. Her decision will embrace her own destiny and personal dignity, and the origins of the other human life that lie within the embryo. The State is entitled to assume that, for most of its people, the beginnings of that understanding will be within the family, society's most intimate association. It is both rational and fair for the State to conclude that, in most instances, the family will strive to give a lonely or even terrified minor advice that is both compassionate and mature. The statute in issue is a rational way to further those ends. It would deny all dignity to the family to say that the State cannot take this reasonable step in regulating its

> health professions to ensure that, in most cases, a young woman will receive guidance and understanding from a parent.[75]

Part III of Kennedy's opinion underwent significant revisions during the decision-making process. With each new draft he gradually removed any discussion of possible liberty interests or rights that might be held by women, under the age of eighteen, who sought abortions.[76] The language of Part V went unchanged from start to finish.

During the months that passed between the oral arguments and decision announcement in *Akron Center* and *Hodgson*, one of the memos about these cases that Anne Dupre sent to Justice Blackmun conveyed "some last minute grapevine news." This included the following information:

> SOC is back to being "troubled" again. Perahaps [*sic*] after reading the recent article in the Post, she is concerned that her abortion jurisprudence looks "murky" and that to strike down the Minnesota statute would somehow add to the murkiness. She is receiving a lot of pressure from her conservative clerks . . . to uphold the statute and to abandon even the "undue burden" test.[77]

Ultimately, this was not a scenario that materialized. What did happen was, in fact, quite the opposite. After she joined the Supreme Court in 1981, Justice O'Connor began to use separate opinions in abortion cases as vehicles for expressing her discontent with the strict scrutiny approach of *Roe*. In so doing, she employed her own formulation of a standard that the Court in the 1970s had begun to use in cases addressing government funding of abortions and minors' access to abortion.[78]

Following the approach of the earlier cases, O'Connor created a test that was designed to establish whether a government action constituted an obstacle that blocked or unduly obstructed a woman's path to an abortion. In a 1983 dissenting opinion, she emphasized the ways in which the Court had already moved away from *Roe*'s holding that, under heightened judicial scrutiny, a law restricting abortion was only constitutional if the government could show that it was in furtherance of a compelling state interest. Instead, she explained, "The Court and its individual Justices have repeatedly utilized the 'unduly burdensome' standard" under which laws will not be subjected to strict scrutiny unless they "'infringe substantially' or 'heavily burden'" the abortion right. Three years later, again in dissent, she reinforced her belief that this standard was preferable to that used in *Roe*, but at the same time consistent with the 1973 decision.[79] In 1992, when *Casey* was decided, it was impossible to reach any conclusion other than that this was (1) a doctrinal move that Justice O'Connor cared about deeply and (2) could accommodate Justice Kennedy's jurisprudential views about abortion.

Casey at the Court

On November 1, 2005, one day after President George W. Bush announced that he was nominating Samuel Alito, a judge on the U.S. Court of Appeals for the Third Circuit, to be his next appointment to the Supreme Court, many of the nation's newspapers ran articles that had one very important thing in common. The articles made references to *Planned Parenthood v. Casey.* One might think that this is unsurprising. After all, Alito was being nominated to replace Justice O'Connor, one of the pivotal players in the Supreme Court's decision in that 1992 case. However, the articles primarily referred to the 1991 decision reached by the Third Circuit, the decision later appealed to the Supreme Court. This decision, journalists agreed, would play an important role in the Alito nomination hearings because of the fact that President Bush's nominee had penned a separate opinion in that case, an opinion that evinced conservative views about abortion.[80]

Casey involved a challenge to six different provisions of a Pennsylvania law. Three provisions were directed at abortion providers and imposed different reporting requirements; the other three were designed to make it difficult for women to seek abortions. They stated that: (1) the woman's consent to have an abortion needs to be informed, so she must be provided with certain information about the procedure and then wait twenty-four hours before having her pregnancy terminated; (2) any minor seeking an abortion must have either the informed consent of one of her parents or secure a judicial bypass; and (3) a married woman can only have an abortion upon producing a statement indicating that she had notified her husband of the impending procedure. The law also included a provision that excluded compliance with these requirements in the event of a "medical emergency," which was defined as:

> that condition which, on the basis of the physician's good faith clinical judgment, so complicates the medical condition of a pregnant woman as to necessitate the immediate abortion of her pregnancy to avert her death or for which a delay will create serious risk of substantial and irreversible impairment of a major bodily function.[81]

In evaluating their constitutionality, the Third Circuit three-judge panel concluded that it was necessary to apply the undue burden standard, as articulated by Justice O'Connor in *Webster* and *Hodgson.* In so doing, it found only the spousal notification provision unconstitutional (Judge Alito dissented from this part of the decision, because his interpretation of O'Connor's test led him to conclude that the law, in its entirety, passed constitutional muster).[82]

When the Supreme Court reviewed *Casey*, it affirmed much of the Third Circuit's ruling and reasoning. The joint opinion, coauthored by Justices O'Connor, Kennedy, and Souter, became the defining judicial statement. Only these three members of the Court agreed with every part of the judgment: (1) to strike down the spousal notification provision; (2) to uphold the informed consent/twenty-four hour waiting period (but with the recognition that in some specific instances, down the line, this might be unconstitutional); (3) to uphold the parental notification provision (because it contained a judicial bypass option), the "medical emergency" definition, and the abortion provider reporting and recordkeeping requirements. The joint opinion became Justice O'Connor's definitive statement of the undue burden standard. As the opinion carefully explained, a state regulation would constitute an undue burden if it "has the purpose or effect of placing a substantial obstacle in the path of a woman seeking an abortion of a nonviable fetus." It went on to say that "a statute with this purpose is invalid because the means chosen by the State to further the interest in potential life must be calculated to inform the woman's free choice, not hinder it."[83]

The Joint Opinion, Part 2

From the outset, the joint opinion in *Casey* made the jurisprudential focus of its authors abundantly clear. This was not an opinion about privacy rights. It opened with what has become a much-quoted observation: "*Liberty* finds no refuge in a jurisprudence of doubt." It closed with: "We invoke it [the Constitution] once again to define the freedom guaranteed by the Constitution's own promise, the promise of *liberty*."[84] The papers of Justice Blackmun do not tell us whether this was a conscious linguistic approach. However, it is important to remember that (1) it was Justice Kennedy who crafted these first and last sentences, and (2) their liberty references were unchanged from those that appeared in the first draft of the opinion.[85] Such was Kennedy's involvement in the crafting of the most libertarian portions of the *Casey* joint opinion, there is every reason to believe that the opinion deliberately opened and closed with this important word.

Many prominent commentaries applaud the decision in *Casey*, but agree with Justice Scalia's dissenting, belittling description of the opening liberty statement as an "august and sonorous phrase."[86] This should come as no surprise, because as this book has made clear, Justice Kennedy's opinions frequently contain rhetoric that is susceptible to being labeled as either "elitist" or "pompous." Similarly, in terms of both their jurisprudential content and their literary style, it should not be a shock to learn that Kennedy's contributions to *Casey* raised the ire of his conservative colleagues. As the journalist

Jan Crawford Greenburg writes: "Conservatives had long believed that landmark cases brought out the worst in Kennedy." *Casey* was definitely such a case, and Part II contained precisely the type of "grand phrases and philosophical musings" that Kennedy is apt to employ when talking about individual liberty—the sort of rhetoric "that drives conservatives bananas."[87]

In an article published the year after the decision, the political scientist Nancy Kassop said that Part II of the *Casey* joint opinion "may be the most direct and expansive exposition to date" of "the central question of the interpretation of protected liberty in the Due Process Clause."[88] Even if this "expansive exposition" was innovative for the Court, it was not for its author. This becomes clear when one examines its discussion of the scope of constitutionally protected individual "liberty," the word that, at the beginning of Part II, Kennedy stated was controlling in the case.[89] Kennedy reiterated the objection to a narrow, historically determined interpretive method that he and Justice O'Connor voiced in *Michael H.* "Tempting" as it might be, wrote Kennedy, "to suppose that the Due Process Clause protects only those practices, defined at the most specific level, that were protected against government interference by other rules of law when the Fourteenth Amendment was ratified," it was essential to understand that "such a view would be inconsistent" with the nation's law.[90] What was consistent with the Constitution, wrote Kennedy, was the "promise . . . that there is a realm of personal liberty which the government may not enter."[91]

This is exactly what then-Judge Kennedy explained to the members of the Senate Judiciary Committee during his Supreme Court nomination hearings. In *Casey*, the Justice repeated the sentiment of his testimony that "there is a zone of liberty, a zone of protection, a line that is drawn where the individual can tell the Government: Beyond this line you may not go."[92] In doing so, he also stayed true to the modestly libertarian argument that we have seen him make in his opinions in many different areas of the law. This is the argument that there is an important and crucial distinction between "liberty" and "license." In order to fulfill the promise of the Constitution's Preamble—to "secure the Blessings of [this] Liberty to ourselves and our Posterity"—this distinction needs to be articulated in the form of an explanation of the nature and location of the line that separates the individual from the government. When Justice Kennedy sought to identify and analyze the boundaries of liberty in *Casey*, he turned to Justice Harlan's dissent in *Poe*.

Quoting extensively from that opinion, Kennedy expressed his admiration and respect for Harlan's conclusion that the liberty protected by the Fourteenth Amendment protects many different aspects of our lives. Kennedy agreed that it was best understood as a "rational continuum which, broadly speaking, includes a freedom from all substantial arbitrary impositions and purposeless restraints."[93] Just like Harlan, though, Kennedy is careful not to permit this interpretation to descend into something that would more closely resemble license than liberty. In *Poe*, Harlan counseled judicial use of "judgment and restraint" when "supplying . . . content" to the "Constitutional concept" of balancing individual and societal needs. Kennedy explained that this "capacity" for "reasoned judgment" was one that "courts always have exercised."[94] In *Poe*, Harlan said that "Due Process has not been reduced to any formula; its content cannot be determined by reference to any code." Again this was a lead that Kennedy followed. "Some of us as individuals," he wrote, "find abortion offensive to our most basic principles of morality . . . that cannot control our decision." However: "Our obligation is to define the liberty of all, not to mandate our own moral code."[95]

"Fraught With Consequences"

The nature of some of Kennedy's rhetoric in Part II of the joint opinion in *Casey* makes it easy to overlook the passages that actually serve to qualify the effusive embrace of individual liberty that has come to define the opinion. *Casey* is well known for its "sweet-mystery-of-life" passage, as Justice Scalia has disparagingly described it, in which Kennedy wrote:

> At the heart of liberty is the right to define one's own concept of existence, of meaning, of the universe, and of the mystery of human life. Beliefs about these matters could not define the attributes of personhood were they formed under compulsion of the State.[96]

Far less attention is paid to *Casey*'s reminder that the Supreme Court's abortion jurisprudence is not about to close its eyes to the fact that "abortion is a unique act."[97] This is unfortunate because, as Justice Kennedy's opinions in subsequent abortion cases have shown, this fact is of crucial importance to him.

In *Casey*, Kennedy engaged in a lengthy explanation regarding just what made the termination of a pregnancy an action that the Court could not, in good conscience, simply treat as just another example of individual decision making. In the paragraph immediately following the "mystery of human life" statement, Kennedy made it clear that the Court's "analysis of the woman's *interest*"—following the lead of *Webster*, Kennedy does not say "right"—"in terminating her pregnancy cannot end" with a sweeping declaration of individual liberty, dignity, and autonomy.[98] Continuing along the path that he began to lay in *Akron Center*, Kennedy explained that this was because the decision to have an abortion was not one that a woman should believe that she had the freedom to make on her own, without consideration of the "consequences for others."[99] To be sure, Justice Kennedy was sensitive to the fact that, ultimately, the emotional anxieties and physical constraints of a pregnancy were experienced by only one person—the mother-to-be. He had great admiration for the woman who "from the beginning of the human race," endured these sacrifices "with a pride that ennobles her in the eyes of others." Yet, he could not permit either himself, or the Constitution as he read it, to extend this admiration to the woman who chose to have an abortion. The opinion made this clear, because Kennedy only spoke of these "anxieties" and "constraints" as attaching to "the mother who carries a child to full term."[100] This did not mean that women no longer had a constitutionally protected right to end a pregnancy. However, what Kennedy said in *Casey* was that although a woman's "destiny . . . must be shaped to a large extent on her own conception of her spiritual imperatives," she was not free to arrive at this conception without taking responsibility for "her place in society." And while it is the very essence of individual liberty that she be free to determine what this place is, a "pregnant woman cannot" "be isolated in her privacy."[101] Why? As Justice Blackmun observed in *Roe*:

> She carries an embryo and, later, a fetus, if one accepts the medical definitions of the developing young in the human uterus. . . . The situation therefore is inherently different from marital intimacy, or bedroom possession of obscene material, or marriage, or procreation, or education, with which *Eisenstadt* and *Griswold, Stanley, Loving, Skinner*, and *Pierce* and *Meyer* were respectively concerned.[102]

These cases involved intimate decisions which, said Kennedy in *Casey*, are "in *some* critical respects . . . of the same character" as the choice whether to have an abortion. However, it must never be forgotten that "they support the reasoning in *Roe* relating to the woman's liberty because they involve personal decisions concerning not only the meaning of procreation *but also human responsibility and respect for it.*"[103]

This was elaborated upon in Parts IV and V of the joint opinion in *Casey*, suggesting that here, as in Part II, Justice Kennedy played an important role in crafting the content. Building on the reasoning adopted in previous cases, the opinion was critical of the rigid trimester-based analysis employed in *Roe*. This, said the joint opinion's authors, was a framework that "sometimes contradicted the State's permissible objectives" by ignoring the fact that the previability right to an abortion was a right that the Constitution permitted the state to ensure was exercised in a "thoughtful and informed" manner.[104] As we will see below, commentators have rightly identified the presence of decidedly paternalistic language in Justice Kennedy's 2007 *Carhart* discussion of his belief that liberty needs to be informed and responsibly exercised. However, this commitment was not without overtones of paternalism (albeit a kinder, gentler version than that which appeared in *Carhart*) in either its first Kennedy-authored Supreme Court iteration in Part V of *Akron Center*, or in *Casey*. Even in the 1992 joint opinion, which is heralded for its expansive understanding of liberty, we can see strong evidence of Justice Kennedy's belief that women will benefit from laws that "provide a reasonable framework . . . to make a decision," such as abortion, "that has such profound and lasting meaning." This is because the joint opinion does not simply say that these regulations may be enacted. It offers a justification for their existence—they are "aimed at ensuring that a woman's choice contemplates the consequences for the fetus" because "the woman's right to make the ultimate decision" is "not a right to be insulated from all others in doing so."[105] As we have seen, this emphasis on the consequences of abortions is a prominent theme of the responsible element of Justice Kennedy's modestly libertarian jurisprudence.

The Partial-Birth Cases

In a 1992 interview with journalist David Savage, one member of the Court (who remained anonymous) expressed their belief that *Casey* signaled that "the battle is over. It [*Roe*] will never be overturned now."[106] Justice Blackmun did not share his colleague's confidence. In his separate opinion in *Webster*, Blackmun famously accused the plurality of "discard[ing] a landmark case of the last generation, and cast[ing] into darkness the hopes and visions of every woman in this country who had come to believe that the Constitution guaranteed her the right to exercise some control over her unique ability to bear children."[107] In his separate opinion in *Casey*, he conceded that this prediction had been mercifully premature. However, Blackmun considered it important to emphasize that premature was a long way from incorrect. After *Casey*, the author of *Roe* was still worried that "four Justices [were] anxiously await[ing] the single vote necessary to extinguish the light" that was the right to choose.[108] President Clinton's decisions to appoint Ruth Bader Ginsburg and Stephen Breyer to replace Justices White and Blackmun in 1993 and 1994 suggested that these fears had been allayed. However, predicting the course of Supreme Court decision making is a perilous exercise. Therefore, on January 14, 2000, the Court's announcement that it had granted certiorari in *Stenberg v. Carhart* was met with considerable anticipation.[109]

Stenberg v. Carhart: What *Casey* Really Meant (According to Justice Breyer)

Stenberg involved a constitutional challenge to Nebraska's ban on so-called partial-birth abortions. As the Court moved into the twenty-first century, did the votes exist to uphold the law and place further restrictions on abortions? The answer came on June 28, 2000. Applying *Casey*'s formulation of the undue burden standard, a five-justice majority of the Court found the law to be unconstitutional.[110]

According to the Nebraska law, the banned procedure involved "deliberately and intentionally delivering into the vagina a living unborn child, or a substantial portion thereof, for the purpose of performing a procedure that the person performing such procedure knows will kill the unborn child and does kill the unborn child." Violation of this law was punishable by imprisonment; the only exception to the ban was in circumstances when the abortion was "necessary to save the life of the mother whose life is endangered by a physical disorder, physical illness, or physical injury, including a life-endangering physical condition caused by or arising from the pregnancy itself."[111]

This statutory language played a crucial role in the Court's decision to strike down the law. There were two main reasons for this. First, it was difficult to tell whether Nebraska had intended to ban only the dilation and extraction (D&X) form of late-term abortions, or to also include the more frequently used dilation and evacuation (D&E) procedure—which is "the most commonly used method for previability second trimester abortions."[112] Nebraska conceded that a law banning the D&E procedure would indeed fail to pass constitutional muster because it would represent the "substantial obstacle" to abortions that *Casey* said amounted to an "undue burden."[113] The Court rejected the state's accompanying argument that its ban only extended to D&X abortions.

The second flaw in the language of the Nebraska law was the absence of an exception for instances when the procedure would be needed to preserve maternal health. It is this aspect of the law that was the most controversial, and created the deepest divisions among the justices. The decision in *Casey* seemed to suggest that the following standard set forth in *Roe* was settled law:

> Subsequent to viability, the State in promoting its interest in the potentiality of human life may, if it chooses, regulate, and even proscribe, abortion except where it is necessary, in appropriate medical judgment, for the preservation of the *life or health* of the mother.[114]

As Justice Breyer explained, this did not simply mean that the state could impose abortion regulations as long as health and life exceptions were included.

There was a concomitant requirement that the law further the "potentiality of human life" interest. This the Nebraska law did not do, said Breyer, because instead of preventing all abortions (thereby "saving the fetus in question from destruction") it "regulates only a *method* of performing abortion." Nebraska argued that the law "shows concern for the life of the unborn," "prevents cruelty to partially born children," and "preserves the integrity of the medical profession." Perhaps this was true but, as Breyer explained, a law with a health exception could easily meet these interests.[115]

In a short concurring opinion, Justice Stevens confirmed that what *Roe* stood for was the liberty that protected "a woman's right to make this difficult and extremely personal decision" to terminate a pregnancy. Consequently, he wrote that he could not:

> understand how a State has any legitimate interest in requiring a doctor to follow any procedure other than the one that he or she reasonably believes will best protect the woman in her exercise of this constitutional liberty.[116]

Stevens's concurrence is entirely consistent with the positions that we have seen him take in earlier individual decision-making cases. The liberty about which he wrote in *Stenberg* is the same species of freedom and is marked by the same boundaries as that which he forcefully championed in dissent in *Bowers*. It is an expansive understanding of individual autonomy based on analysis which, as we saw in chapter 3, in *Lawrence* Kennedy concluded "should have been controlling [in *Bowers*] . . . and should control here."[117] Consequently, when the Court announced its decision in *Stenberg*, Justice Kennedy's dissent attracted a considerable amount of attention. Commentators interpreted both the vote and Kennedy's passion-filled opinion as sure signs that he had defected from the understanding of liberty about which he had so eloquently written in *Casey*. Surely, they concluded, Kennedy was now "ruing and rethinking" that joint opinion; it was clear, they said, that its position on abortion rights was causing him personal, "deep unease."[118]

Justice Kennedy's *Stenberg* Dissent: "This Is Not What I Signed onto in 1992"[119]

The majority in *Stenberg* believed that its holding in the case was completely consistent with the decision in *Casey*. Justice Breyer clearly believed that the Constitution the majority found to be violated by the Nebraska law was the Constitution "as interpreted in" *Casey* and *Roe*.[120] By contrast, "Kennedy felt had"; this was not the interpretation of the document that "he thought the three of them [himself and Justices O'Connor and Souter] had agreed to in the *Casey* decision."[121] In *Casey*, Kennedy had opened the joint opinion with an observation about the state of the Court's abortion jurisprudence since 1973, when *Roe v. Wade* was decided. The right of women to choose had been preserved, but the scope and nature of the constitutional liberty protecting that right had been in doubt. In *Stenberg*, Kennedy scolded the Court for, among other things, producing a decision that was a "misinterpretation of *Casey*."[122] He again chose to begin with a remark about the two-decade time period between *Roe* and *Casey*, and again he saw no problem in either the existence or preservation "of a woman's right to elect an abortion in defined circumstances."[123] What changed, however, was that from the outset, in *Stenberg*, Kennedy now placed the emphasis of his concern on the importance of state interests:

> For close to two decades after *Roe v. Wade* the Court gave but slight weight to the interests of the separate States when their legislatures sought to address persisting concerns raised by the existence of a woman's right to elect an abortion in defined circumstances.[124]

Kennedy proceeded to make it very clear that this twenty-year trend rightfully came to an end with *Casey*, for it was the "central premise" of that decision "that the States retain a critical and legitimate role in legislating on the subject of abortion, as limited by the woman's right" to choose to terminate her pregnancy.[125] To be sure, the joint opinion had opened with a reference to the threat to individual *liberty* that the nineteen years of post-*Roe* abortion jurisprudence posed. Yet, it had also taken care—as we have seen above—to remind the woman contemplating an abortion that this was not a decision that she should be able to make in splendid isolation.

In his *Stenberg* dissent, Justice Kennedy lashed out at Justice Breyer's majority opinion because of its use of clinical language to describe the D&E and D&X procedures. Breyer accepted that the very fact that these procedures "seek to terminate a potential human life" might make the use of such language objectionable and inadequate, but saw "no alternative way." This did not satisfy his colleague.[126] Justice Kennedy spent quite some time discussing the legitimacy and importance of enabling states to make themselves heard and have their positions represented in the abortion debate—again something upon which "*Casey* is premised." This, he said, was betrayed by an opinion that prided itself on the factual accuracy of its words rather than on making itself understandable to "citizens who seek to know why laws on this subject have been enacted across the Nation,"[127] citizens who should be afforded the opportunity to inform themselves about the diverse views that the subject inevitably generates. This dialogue on liberty, Kennedy concluded, could be legitimately maintained by laws, such as that enacted by Nebraska, that the Court now found to be offensive to the Constitution.

Gonzales v. Carhart: What *Casey* Really Meant (According to Kennedy)

After the decision in *Stenberg*, Court commentators were quick to conclude that Justice Kennedy was no longer committed to (or, at the very least, was doing some serious soul searching about) the understanding of liberty that he wrote into the joint opinion in *Casey*. Seven years later, many scholars of the Court were convinced that this commitment was dead. This conclusion was prompted by Justice Kennedy's opinion for the Court in *Gonzales v. Carhart*, an opinion that law professor Steven Calabresi concluded "fail[ed] . . . to in any way reaffirm the abortion right derived from *Roe* and *Casey*."[128] As the member of the five-justice majority assigned to write this opinion upholding a federal ban on partial-birth abortion, Justice Kennedy had the opportunity to correct what he perceived to be the interpretive errors of *Stenberg* and to provide the (for now, anyway) final answer to the question, "What was the real meaning of *Casey*?" In her dissenting opinion, which spoke for herself and Justices Stevens, Souter, and Breyer, Justice Ginsburg did not hesitate to provide her understanding of Justice Kennedy's apparent answer to this question. She opened with a reminder of the *Casey* joint opinion's declaration "that 'liberty finds no refuge in a jurisprudence of doubt.'" She then proceeded to observe that in its reaffirmation of *Roe*, the *Casey* opinion "described the centrality of 'the decision whether to bear . . . a child' . . . to a woman's 'dignity and autonomy,' her 'personhood' and 'destiny.'" These were all important and valued principles betrayed by Kennedy's *Carhart* opinion that, said Ginsburg, "refuses to take *Casey* and *Stenberg* seriously."[129] "Today's decision," she wrote, was nothing short of "alarming" for both individual liberty and women's rights.[130]

Carhart involved a constitutional challenge to the Partial-Birth Abortion Ban Act of 2003 (PBABA). In 1996, President Clinton vetoed H.R. 1833, the Partial-Birth Abortion Ban Act of 1995. In his message to Congress, Clinton focused on what he described as the bill's "indifference to women's health." The law only provided a life-of-the-mother exception from its prohibition of this type of abortion. It did not include an exception covering "serious health consequences." Therefore, said Clinton, it put women at risk and exhibited significant congressional distrust of the medical profession.[131] The House of Representatives overrode the veto, but the equivalent effort in the Senate fell eight votes short. In 2003, Republican control of the White House and both chambers of Congress enabled passage of the PBABA (again, without a maternal health exception), which was signed into law by President George W. Bush.

As we have seen from the very beginning of this book, the liberty, rights, dignity, and autonomy of every individual are highly valued by Justice Kennedy. On numerous occasions he has been willing to defend constitutional protection of them for all persons, regardless of sex (or race or sexual orientation). This is why, in their commentary for Slate.com, law professor Garret Epps and journalist Dahlia Lithwick described Kennedy's *Carhart* opinion as "truly baffling." "Somehow," they wrote, "the one sitting justice who has written most eloquently about moral autonomy and dignity and choice in one context has now, in another, endorsed a view of women that would be at home in the awful world of Margaret Atwood's *The Handmaid's Tale*."[132] Do these criticisms accurately portray Kennedy's opinion? Are Ginsburg, Epps, and Lithwick right to conclude that the 2007 opinion is jurisprudentially inconsistent with the joint opinion in *Casey*? It is this book's conclusion that the answer to this question is "maybe."

One might argue that in *Carhart* Kennedy made a disingenuous attempt to reconcile the decision with that in *Stenberg*. Similarly, a possible criticism of his approach to the decision might be that he was really trying to achieve the impossible and that he really should not have undertaken this effort. These observations notwithstanding, the end result of Justice Kennedy's effort to decide *Carhart* in a way that did not require him to say *Stenberg* was wrong was actually one of the least controversial aspects of his opinion. Kennedy distinguished between the vague language of the Nebraska law challenged in *Stenberg* and the PBABA passed by Congress in response to *Stenberg*. The vagueness of the Nebraska law left open the possibility of hindering the rights of more women than just the relatively small number seeking an "intact D&E abortion" (this is the term that Kennedy chose to use to describe the procedure that he interpreted the PBABA as covering). This vagueness was gone from the federal law. To understand the significance of Kennedy's conclusion that the PBABA is "more specific concerning the instances to which it applies and in this respect more precise in its coverage," it is necessary to examine the law's definition of a "partial-birth abortion."[133] For an abortion to be classified as such, there must be a deliberate and intentional act to terminate fetal life, and this must take place after vaginal delivery has brought "the entire fetal head" (for head-first deliveries) or "any part of the fetal trunk past the navel" (for breech deliveries) outside of the mother. These requirements, said Kennedy, excluded an extremely large number of abortions, and they protected from prosecution medical professionals who, while in the process of either attempting a successful live birth or a nonintact D&E abortion, ultimately performed a procedure that could be described, under the law, as a "partial-birth abortion." A "straightforward reading of the Act's text" led to this conclusion about the narrowness of its coverage.[134]

Wherefore Art Thou "Liberty"?

In comparison to his reading of the PBABA's language, Justice Kennedy's treatment of liberty in *Carhart* is far more controversial. In his article about the opinion, Professor Calabresi argues that "Kennedy's writing style is dramatically different and more restrained . . . than it was in the prior cases."[135] If the precedents to which Calabresi referred were *Stenberg* and *Hill v. Colorado* (discussed in chapter 2), then here it would be appropriate to recall that in those two cases Justice Kennedy wrote in dissent. He was not restricted in the use of his reasoning and rhetoric—as he was in *Carhart*—by the forces and norms of collegiality that require a majority opinion author to take into account the views of his or her colleagues. In *Carhart*, Kennedy was assigned to write from "the institutional approach," which "depends upon suppressing" the individuality that is present in separate opinions, individuality that is expressed using a "different voice."[136] However, Calabresi's references were to *Casey* and *Lawrence*. In other words, he was arguing that, in Justice Kennedy's opinion upholding the PBABA, conspicuous by its absence was a discussion and defense of an expansive understanding of individual liberty, dignity, and autonomy (amazingly, the opinion did not use the word "liberty"). There is no doubt that this is the most striking characteristic of the opinion. However, it is important to understand that this linguistic absence of "liberty" does not mean that it was *thematically* missing from the opinion in *Carhart*. To the contrary, what we find is that Justice Kennedy engaged in prominent discussion of two of the main elements of his understanding of individual freedom—dignity and responsibility. The *Carhart* formulations of these elements are not, however, quite what we might have come to expect from Kennedy's modestly libertarian jurisprudence. Indeed, their usage is cloaked in what might best be described as modest paternalism.

In *Stenberg*, Kennedy made no secret of his personal objection to the partial-birth method of abortion.[137] In *Carhart*, this opposition continued as he wrote of the PBABA's expression of "respect for the dignity of human life."[138] What he meant to convey through this use of the word "dignity" is not entirely clear, but the opinion strongly suggests a moral hostility to what Kennedy considers an undignified practice. This is because his reference to the law's respect for human dignity came at the end of the following passage:

> A description of the prohibited abortion procedure demonstrates the rationale for the congressional enactment. The Act proscribes a method of abortion in which a fetus is killed just inches before completion of the birth process. Congress stated as follows: "Implicitly approving such a brutal and inhumane procedure by choosing not to prohibit it will further coarsen society to the humanity of not only newborns, but all vulnerable and innocent human life, making it increasingly difficult to protect such life."[139]

For help in interpreting Kennedy's reference to dignity in *Carhart*, one might be tempted to look at other statements, by conservative supporters of the PBABA, that feature the idea of human dignity—particularly the dignity of the unborn child.[140] For example, President George W. Bush described the decision in *Carhart* as "an affirmation of the progress we have made over the past six years in protecting human dignity and upholding the sanctity of life." Continuing, he promised: "We will continue to work for the day when every child is welcomed in life and protected in law."[141] This is *not* what Justice Kennedy meant when *he* spoke of the "dignity of human life" that the PBABA respected (and protected). Why? Consistent with his modestly libertarian opinions involving other areas of the law, Kennedy thinks that dignity is something possessed equally (and therefore entitled to equal constitutional protection) by *every* human form. He does not distinguish between the pregnant woman and the fetus that she carries; nor does he consciously emphasize the dignity of the latter at the expense of the former. The problem in *Carhart*, however, is that Justice Kennedy expresses his commitment to responsibly exercised liberty in such a way as to threaten this evenhanded protection of dignity.

The joint opinion in *Casey* partially overruled two of the Court's abortion decisions from the 1980s. Emphasizing that a woman's right to terminate her pregnancy was one that must be exercised with "apprehen[sion] [of] the full consequences of her decision," *Casey* concluded that the Court had been wrong to strike down requirements that a woman contemplating an abortion be provided with "truthful, nonmisleading information about the nature of the procedure, the attendant health risks and those of childbirth, and the 'probable gestational age' of the fetus."[142] What the opinion made clear, however, was that its acceptance of this requirement was contingent upon the existence—in this case, in the Pennsylvania statute—of an exemption for instances when a physician decided that the provision of this information would likely have "a severely adverse effect on the physical or mental health of the patient." To rule otherwise, Justices O'Connor, Kennedy, and Souter said, would represent an unconstitutional intrusion into the relationship between doctor and patient.[143]

As we have seen in his dissenting opinions in *Stenberg* and *Hill*, Justice Kennedy presented a formulation of the informed responsibility requirement that is far less respectful of individual liberty. *Carhart* took this one step further. "The State's interest in respect for life," wrote Kennedy, "is advanced by the dialogue that better informs the political and legal systems, the medical profession, expectant mothers, and society as a whole of the consequences that follow from a decision to elect a late-term abortion."[144] However, it does not appear that Kennedy expected women to be either willing or able to adequately represent their interests in this dialogue. Although he conceded that the Court found "no reliable data" to support it, he nevertheless considered it "unexceptionable" to conclude "some women come to regret their choice to abort the infant life they once created and sustained." The state, therefore, is justified in protecting women from this emotional suffering by requiring that physicians performing abortions ensure their patients are fully informed about the details of the procedure to be used. Doctors were less likely, Kennedy concluded, to make a genuine contribution to the dialogue when the information they were supposed to provide related to intact D&E abortions; this "lack of information concerning the way in which the fetus will be killed . . . is of legitimate concern to the State."[145]

Conclusions

In a constitutional democracy, there is something inherently disconcerting and disquieting about a conclusion that the final, and authoritative, judicial interpretation of the scope of government restrictions on abortion rights comes from the mind and pen of one individual. There is no escaping the fact, however, that on the morning of April 18, 2007, it was to Justice Kennedy that Chief Justice John Roberts turned for the reading of the majority's opinion in *Gonzales v. Carhart*. As he did in every case decided by a 5–4 vote during the October 2006 term (a remarkable and historical feat), Kennedy found himself in the majority in this decision upholding a federal ban on so-called partial-birth abortions. This is one of the many important and highly divisive topics whose constitutional boundaries have been and will continue to be drawn by this mild-mannered Californian. Such opinion-writing opportunities certainly suggest that the Constitution has become "what Anthony Kennedy says it is."[146]

What, then, did that Constitution look like? As this chapter demonstrates, Kennedy's decision to omit *direct* references to that document's protections of liberty in *Carhart* should not lead us to conclude that the Constitution, according to Kennedy, now offers a paternalistic understanding of women's abortion rights that is a jurisprudential betrayal of *Casey*. This is because Kennedy's opinion in the 2007 decision was simply the latest formulation of what he believed the 1992 opinion stood for. The Constitution did indeed provide libertarian protection for abortion rights, but it did so by establishing boundaries of liberty identified by the twin principles of personal responsibility and informed decision making. Does this threaten the essential holding of *Roe*? If Kennedy holds the key to the future of the Roberts Court in this area of the law, should those who support a woman's right to choose be unduly concerned about the Justice's opinion in *Carhart*? I would suggest that the answer to this question is no.

Every summer, the *Harvard Law Review* invites a (usually senior) scholar of the Supreme Court's jurisprudence to write the foreword article for its fall volume. The article provides an evaluation of the Supreme Court's just-ended term. In her study of the October 1989 term—which included the decisions in *Hodgson* and *Akron Center*—law professor Robin West pondered the following. "There is one change on the Court," she wrote, "that might emerge should liberalism embrace responsibility as well as rights as the hallmark of liberty." As this chapter has shown, this embrace has been modestly libertarian, rather than liberal, and has been for the most part championed by Justice Kennedy alone, rather than by the Court in its entirety. Nevertheless, the change that Professor West contemplated has indeed taken place. The Court's opinions—at least, those authored by Kennedy—have adopted an educative role. They have informed Americans that there is much more to their constitutionally protected liberty than simply rights (whether enumerated or not). Liberty, these opinions have reminded us, is composed of dignity, "tolerance, plurality, and diversity"—and without responsible respect for these core elements of humanity, the tie cannot, in any shape or form, be sent to freedom.[147]

Conclusion: "It All Depends on Justice Kennedy"

> We tend to think the case has been made that a free society is a stable society, that a free society is the birthright of all people. We do not know why we must make the case all over again when judgment has been given in our favor. History, however, does not acknowledge res judicata. History teaches that freedom must make its case, again and again, from one generation to the next. The work of freedom is never done.[1]
>
> —Justice Anthony M. Kennedy

IN OCTOBER 1987, JUST ONE MONTH BEFORE HIS NOMINATION to the U.S. Supreme Court, then-Judge Anthony M. Kennedy addressed the Historical Society for the United States District Court for the Northern District of California. In his speech, Kennedy observed that it was because the Framers were "marvelous and astute students of human behavior" that "they knew that no matter how precise the compact they drew for future generations, only a continued commitment to constitutional rule would keep it alive. They knew that no people of strength or vision want to live in a world without a challenge."[2] Meeting this challenge is not easy. This is in large part because the U.S. Constitution, which plays a major role in limiting the government, and therefore "Secur[ing] the Blessings of Liberty to ourselves and our Posterity," does not tell us where the boundaries of that liberty lie. The responsibility for mapping many of those legal limits has fallen on the shoulders of the men and women appointed to the Supreme Court—including Justice Kennedy. It has been the contention of this book that this mild-mannered Californian jurist rose to this challenge by employing a judicial philosophy that can, for several areas of the law, be characterized as (1) modestly libertarian and (2) consistent. I have challenged the belief (that has prevailed for most of his twenty years on the Court) that Kennedy takes his jurisprudential cues from the editorial pages of either the *New York Times* (when courting political liberals) or the *Wall Street Journal* (when seeking to placate conservatives). To be sure, as Justice Kennedy has said on numerous occasions, he does not have an all-encompassing judicial philosophy; he frequently agonizes over his votes and opinions; and, in some of his public extrajudicial endeavors and speeches, Justice Kennedy gives the impression of being "innocent[ly]" pompous.[3] However, these characteristics do not translate into a process of judicial decision making that sacrifices commitments to the Constitution and the rule of law at the altar of political partisanship and divisive ideologies.

Justice Kennedy, the Principled Justice

After receiving the American Bar Association's highest award, the ABA Medal, Justice Kennedy gave an emotion-laden speech at that organization's annual meeting in San Francisco in August 2007. He invoked themes that have been present in many of his speeches, themes that have also found their way into his Supreme Court opinions. Kennedy spoke of the need for current and future generations of lawyers to remember that they belong to a profession whose duties include maintaining awareness of the injustices that exist around the world—injustices that paint a very depressing picture of the global state of the rule of law. Members of the ABA, he said, need to step up to the plate and address this situation. They need to do so not in an arrogant, American-exceptionalist manner—because, as Kennedy said: "We've learned that we cannot say to some foreign country, 'Here's a red-white-and-blue package, the rule of law.'" Rather, they should act out of the recognition that these injustices threaten "universal moral precepts that all free people share."[4] In his Supreme Court opinions in the areas of the law studied in this book, Justice Kennedy has pursued this goal using a jurisprudence that emphasizes what he considers to be three of the most important of these principles.

The Elements of Justice Kennedy's Modestly Libertarian Jurisprudence

I have argued that Justice Kennedy's formulation of these principles is modestly libertarian. Although the meaning of this thesis was explored in detail in chapter 1, here it is important briefly to revisit it. Recall that the dictionary defines "modest" as "moderate or restrained in amount, extent, severity, etc.; not excessive or exaggerated."[5] All too often, neither the supporters nor opponents of libertarianism appear to be aware that it is a political philosophy that can speak, and be spoken about, using tones of moderation. It is easy for those who are hostile to (or at the very least wary of) libertarian principles to make one of several erroneous assumptions. For example, they might argue that there is a very short, slippery slope connecting libertarianism and anarchism. Or they might contend that it leaves individuals to their own devices by making them participate in a Darwinian contest to find the fittest survivor. Justice Kennedy's jurisprudence suggests that he is an adherent of libertarian principles, but only insofar as he has constructed an approach to judicial decision making that places a premium on several of the political theory's most fundamental precepts—as they are modestly, rather than radically, stated.

The nature of much of the power that Justice Kennedy holds find its expression in the opinions that he writes—whether for a majority of the Court or for himself in concurrence or dissent. This book has taken this reality seriously. The Supreme Court, says Kennedy, "is based on the reasons that we give in our opinions"; therefore, given the justice's strong belief that his role is to a large extent educational—he "think[s] of judges as teachers"—an opinion-based approach offers the most appropriate type of insight into Kennedy's thought processes.[6]

In the opinions examined in chapter 2, we saw the justice educate us about the nature of our First Amendment freedom to express ourselves. More than in any other area of the law, here we see Kennedy striving to defend liberty by drawing its boundaries to give the government very few opportunities to interfere with individual diversity and autonomy. Why? Chapter 2 demonstrated that the strongest formulation of Kennedy's answer to this question comes in cases involving government efforts to restrict expression of certain viewpoints that it finds disagreeable, dangerous, or offensive. When the government "tr[ies] to tell people what to think," it acts dangerously, and almost always—says Kennedy—unconstitutionally.[7] I opened my analysis of Justice Kennedy's opinions by focusing on this universal element of his jurisprudence for two reasons. First, it is the area of constitutional law in which he has penned the greatest number of opinions. Second, and more important, it is the natural starting point for examining any other topic because, as Kennedy has said, "Speech is the beginning of thought."[8]

Chapters 3 and 4 build on this by providing analyses of opinions in which we see strong formulations of the humane element of Justice Kennedy's jurisprudence, which protects an individual's "right to search for" the dignity that is central to his or her liberty.[9] On its own, the concept of human dignity is something that receives respect from across the political and jurisprudential spectrums. Justice Kennedy's use of it, however, is certainly not without its critics. This is because he is firmly committed to the decidedly libertarian belief that an individual's dignity is violated (or at the very least, threatened) by government actions that treat that person in a particular way because of their possession of a certain characteristic. Justice Kennedy champions individualized equality, rather than group-based equality, regardless of whether the characteristic at issue is race or sexual orientation. In chapter 3, we saw him passionately object to treating gays and lesbians differently because of their sexual orientation. He could find no rational basis for such discrimination—because there can be nothing constitutionally rational about simple, majoritarian-based discrimination that is furthered by animus toward "different" individuals. Chapter 4 provides analyses of equal protection cases in which Kennedy has penned opinions advocating the standard of judicial review at the other end of the spectrum—strict scrutiny. Taking his lead from (but without proclaiming wholesale fidelity to) a color-blind reading of the Constitution, Kennedy believes that an individual is stripped of his or her dignity by government treatment—positive or negative—that is driven by the race of that individual.

This book's analysis of Justice Kennedy's opinions was brought to a close in chapter 5, with an examination of undoubtedly the most controversial element of his jurisprudence. How can a jurist who is committed to principles of libertarianism that pursue the goal of limiting the government and championing the liberty of the individual, the most important political unit in society, justify intruding upon a woman's decision whether or not to terminate her pregnancy because it feels that she is not making that decision responsibly? The answer that we have seen Kennedy give hinges on the word "responsibility." This is because the woman must realize that this is not a decision that she should be permitted to make without informed and responsible recognition that her choice will have consequences (of sufficient import to justify state regulation) that affect the liberty of others.

By design, the majority of Justice Kennedy's opinions analyzed in this book were penned during the tenure of the Rehnquist Court. By necessity, I have supplemented this study with examinations of several of the most recent, relevant opinions that he wrote during the first years of the Roberts Court. This book must, however, stop somewhere, even though Kennedy remains a Justice of the U.S. Supreme Court. Consequently, here it is appropriate to ask . . .

What Next?

On January 31, 2006, almost exactly eighteen years after Anthony Kennedy was sworn in as an Associate Justice of the U.S. Supreme Court, the same honor was bestowed upon Samuel Alito, President George W. Bush's appointment to replace the retiring Justice Sandra Day O'Connor. Just as was the case at the beginning of 1988, this change in Court personnel ushered in a period of judicial-ideological uncertainty. Although its future direction is not clear, what we do know is that the Roberts Court, like its predecessor, is evenly divided between four reliably conservative and four dependably moderate justices. Depending upon one's point of view, replacing O'Connor with Alito signaled the beginning of a period during which either (1) Justice Kennedy's ability to dash conservatives' hopes of a judicial revolution would grow immeasurably or (2) liberals' hopes that this would be the case would decrease significantly. On the Rehnquist Court, "The struggle over Kennedy's vote was a familiar one over the eleven-year period the Rehnquist Court was intact. Both he and O'Connor came to wield the most power—not because of their influence on the law or on the other justices, but because their votes were so frequently in play. They weren't the most influential justices; they had the most power."[10] This was not expected to change as the Rehnquist Court gave way to one led by Chief Justice Roberts.

It may be unfair to suggest that, of all the Justices, Kennedy is "the only interesting one" and that "the definition of an insignificant case is one where Justice Kennedy is in the minority."[11] However, there is no escaping the fact that data from the Court's October 2006 term (the first full term of a Court that included Roberts and Alito) demonstrate that Kennedy initially became the *decisive* vote in the closest cases (Kennedy does not like the label "swing vote" because, as he has said, it inaccurately suggests "that you elect to swing for the purpose of accommodating one side or the other").[12] Between October 2006 and June 2007, Justice Kennedy batted an extraordinary 1.000 in cases decided by a 5–4 vote. He was the only member of the Court in the majority in every one of these cases. As shown in figure C.1, the Court's two newest members, Chief Justice Roberts and Associate Justice Alito, also enjoyed excellent averages, because they were respectively members of the prevailing quintet in seventeen and sixteen of the twenty-four closely divided cases. This gained considerable attention because many believed that Roberts and Alito held the keys to unlocking a potentially monumental ideological shift of the Court. However, in July 2007, when the justices departed Washington, D.C. for speaking engagements, traveling, lecturing, and vacations, the consensus of opinion was that if any such key existed, it was currently, and would for the foreseeable future, be held by Justice Kennedy.[13]

In July 2008, commentators continued to contemplate Kennedy's decisive role. They still asked whether it was the Roberts Court in name only. Perhaps, they argued, it was still more realistic to describe the current nine justices as members of the *Kennedy* Court.[14] Compared to its immediate predecessor, however, the October 2007 term generated far fewer 5–4 decisions. For the October 2006 term that ended in June 2007, twenty-four of the Court's cases were decided by this narrowest of margins; only twelve were resolved this way the following year (overall, the number of cases decided on the merits was almost identical across these two terms).[15] And, as shown in figure C.2, between October 2007 and June 2008, Justice Kennedy batted *only* .667 in these cases. What has not changed with these data, however, is the realization that Justice Kennedy still holds much of the power that political scientists attribute to "super median" justices: the ability "to exercise significant control over the outcome and content of the Court's decisions."[16]

Who Will Be "Driven Bananas"?

In December 1987, the *Harvard Law Review* published a tribute to Justice Powell, who had announced his retirement from the Supreme Court earlier that year. Contributing to the article, J. Harvie Wilkinson III (a judge on the U.S. Court of Appeals for the Fourth Circuit and a former Powell clerk) an-

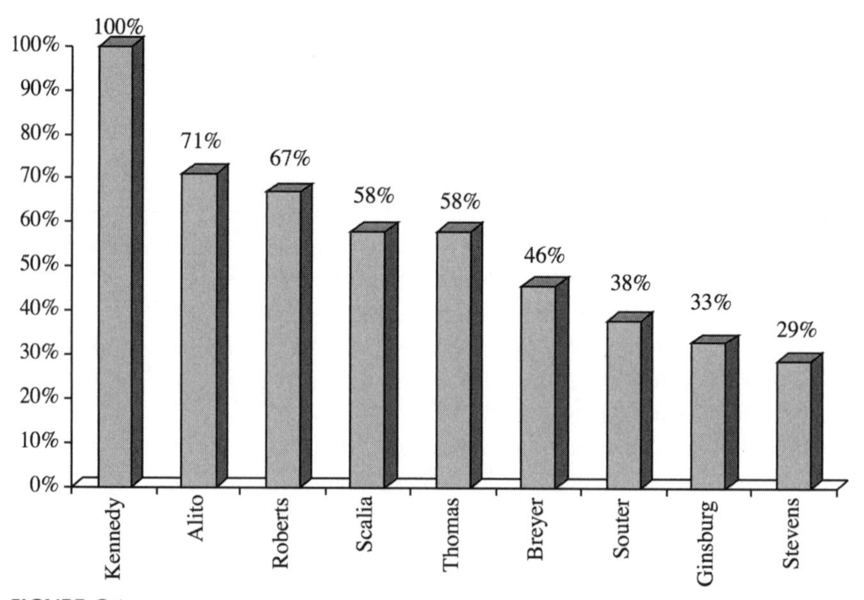

FIGURE C.1
Percentage of majority votes, for members of the Roberts Court, in cases decided by a 5–4 vote during the October 2006 term.
Source: Compiled with data from SCOTUSblog Super StatPack–OT07 Term Recap. www.scotusblog.com/wp/wp-content/uploads/2008/06/superstatpack07.pdf (accessed 10 July 2008).

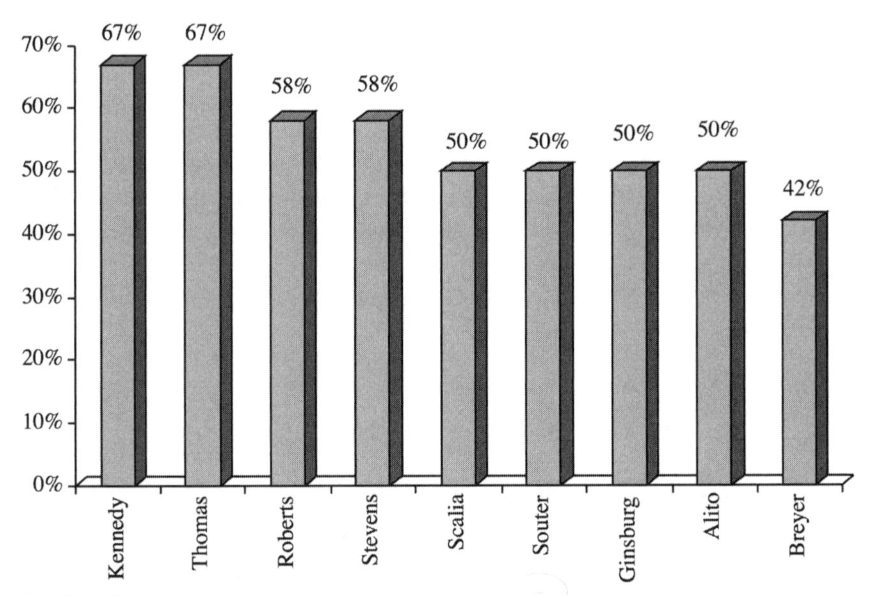

FIGURE C.2
Percentage of majority votes, for members of the Roberts Court, in cases decided by a 5–4 vote during the October 2007 term.
Source: Compiled with data from SCOTUSblog Super StatPack–OT07 Term Recap.

ticipated that Powell would be criticized because "some of his votes are not easy to reconcile. Some of his theory is not seamlessly consistent." The "debate about what the nation wanted from its highest court," which Wilkinson observed was already under way, was a debate that in no shape or form ended when Kennedy was confirmed that month.[17] It is a debate that continues to this day, perhaps because Kennedy's opinions elicit responses from his colleagues who do not find his "votes . . . easy to reconcile" or "his theory . . . seamlessly consistent." This prompts the question: As the Rehnquist Court gives way to the Roberts Court, who will now be "driven bananas" by the rhetoric of Kennedy's judicial opinions?[18]

Had I first started to ask this question in the early 1990s, I might have initially been tempted to view Kennedy as an "essentially rudderless and unpredictable" jurist who had only temporarily "strayed off the [conservative] reservation."[19] After all, while early on in his Supreme Court tenure, his votes and opinions in cases such as *Texas v. Johnson* (1989) and *Planned Parenthood v. Casey* (1992) raised the ire of many conservatives, at that end of the ideological spectrum there was little discontent with his judicial behavior in *Metro Broadcasting v. FCC*, *Ohio v. Akron Center*, and *Hodgson v. Minnesota*, all decided in 1990. However, it was not until the fall of 2003 that I first started to ponder the identity of those individuals—both on and off the Court—who would be frustrated by the content of Justice Kennedy's opinions. In the wake of the landmark decision in *Lawrence v. Texas*, there seemed to be very little doubt that Justice Kennedy's opinion for the Court in *Lawrence* was exhibit number one in "the case that might be titled Conservatism v. Kennedy."[20] It was also clear that this was a case that did not begin in 2003. As we have seen, Kennedy's authorship of the majority opinion in *Romer v. Evans* (1996) led many conservatives—both on and off the Court—to believe that his jurisprudence was driven by a commitment to individual liberty that suggested he should never really have been considered "on" the "conservative reservation."

In 2007, however, the revolt that was prompted by the Justice's opinions in *Gonzales v. Carhart* and *Parents Involved* was of a decidedly liberal nature. Writing in the *New York Times* in July 2007, Linda Greenhouse summed up this reaction when she concluded that the October 2006 term had brought forth "the Supreme Court that conservatives had long yearned for and that liberals feared. By the time the Roberts court ended its first full term," she wrote, "the picture was clear. This was a more conservative court, sometimes muscularly so, sometimes more tentatively, its majority sometimes differing on methodology but agreeing on the outcome in cases big and small."[21] All of this was, seemingly, because of the ability of the Court's conservatives to woo the vote of the centrist Kennedy. In other words, conservatives could take comfort in the fact that while he "may not be Robert Bork," Kennedy "is not William Brennan or Harry Blackmun either."[22] Can we expect these vacillating ideological reactions to Kennedy's judicial writings—and the diverse jurisprudential responses that his colleagues write into their opinions—to continue? To quote Henry Fonda's character in *12 Angry Men*, "It's *possible*."[23] This is the most appropriate conclusion for this book to reach, because it has not attempted to explain others' perceptions of Kennedy. It has drawn on the opinions of his colleagues; it has consulted the papers of former members of the Court; and it has surveyed the views of a diverse contingent of Supreme Court scholars—from both the media and the academy. Ultimately, however, it has sought to inform you, the reader, about just one person—Justice Kennedy. Hopefully it has left you better equipped to understand his future writings, an informed understanding that will then enable you to form your own individual responses to some of his arguments and, in doing so, to continue the dialogue on liberty.

When John Roberts became the seventeenth Chief Justice, he publicly expressed a desire to bring greater unanimity to the Court's decisions. Roberts acknowledged that "division should not be artificially suppressed," but concluded that "the rule of law benefits from a broader agreement."[24] As we have seen, Justice Kennedy is no stranger to writing separate concurring opinions.

When asked whether this tendency could peacefully coexist with the Chief's call for greater consensus, during a 2007 *Newsweek* interview "Kennedy laughed and interjected, 'I guess I haven't helped much. My initial reaction was going to be, 'Just let me write all the opinions.'"[25] Of course, Kennedy never has done nor ever will do this. What we can expect him to do, however, is to continue authoring opinions into which he writes expressions of the three main elements of the modestly libertarian jurisprudence that defines his adjudication of cases involving (1) the toleration of diverse viewpoints, (2) the equal dignity of every individual, and (3) the responsibility that attaches to making decisions about abortion.

We can expect him to consistently assert this approach, an approach that highly values individual liberty. This is because, as Justice Kennedy reminds us, "History teaches that freedom must make its case, again and again, from one generation to the next. The work of freedom is never done." As he explained in his 2007 address to the American Bar Association, "The work of freedom has just begun." Therefore, he says, "We have devised a system for the formal transmission of our legal culture from one generation to the next, and we have a national commitment to maintaining this system."[26] Justice Kennedy does not believe that this commitment can be achieved unless the tie goes to freedom.

Notes

Preface

1. Marc Galanter, "Why The 'Haves' Come out Ahead: Speculations on the Limits of Legal Change," *Law and Society* 9 (1974): 95–160.

2. Lest any individuals who have argued, or will have occasion to argue, before the Supreme Court think that this scene from an imaginary oral argument either insults them or belittles the arduous nature of the task, I would draw their attention to comments made by Chief Justice John Roberts at Northwestern University School of Law in February 2007. Robert Barnes, "Chief Justice Counsels Humility; Roberts Says Lawyers Must Put Themselves in Judges' Shoes," *Washington Post*, 6 February 2007, 15(A).

3. Mark Tushnet, quoted in Carl M. Cannon, "Anthony Kennedy," *California Journal*, 1 November 1997.

4. Through the 2005 term, Kennedy participated in 1,700 cases, writing 381 opinions. Lee Epstein, Thomas G. Walker, Nancy Staudt, Scott Hendrickson, and Jason Roberts, *The U.S. Supreme Court Justices Database* (2007). <http://epstein.law.northwestern.edu/research/justicesdata.html> (accessed 7 September 2007).

Acknowledgments

1. Jonathan Swift, *Gulliver's Travels* (West Berlin, NJ : Townsend Press, 2004).

Introduction

1. Jeffrey Rosen, "The Agonizer," *The New Yorker*, 11 November 1996, 85.

2. Quotations taken from Dana Milbank, "And the Verdict on Justice Kennedy Is: Guilty," *Washington Post*, 9 April 2005, 3(A); Jason DeParle, "In Battle to Pick Next Justice, Right Says, Avoid a Kennedy," *New York Times*, 27 June 2005, 1(A).

3. Richard Brust, "The Man in the Middle," *ABA Journal* 89 (October 2003): 24–25.

4. Akhil Reed Amar, "Justice Kennedy and the Ideal of Equality," *Pacific Law Journal* 28 (Spring 1997): 516.

5. Alex Kozinski, quoted in Carl M. Cannon, "Anthony Kennedy," *California Journal* 28 (1997).

6. DeParle, "Avoid a Kennedy."

7. United States Senate, Committee on the Judiciary, *Hearings on the Nomination of Anthony M. Kennedy to be Associate Justice of the Supreme Court of the United States*, 100th Cong., 1st sess., 14–16 December 1987, 154 [hereafter Kennedy Sup. Ct. Nomination Hearings]; Terry Carter, "Crossing the Rubicon," *California Lawyer*, October 1992, 104.

8. Kennedy Sup. Ct. Nomination Hearings, 154.

9. Anthony M. Kennedy, Judge, Rotary Speech, Sacramento Chapter of the Rotary Club, Sacramento, CA, February 1984, *Committee on the Judiciary*, Judiciary Nominations files, A. Kennedy, Sup. Court, 100th Congress, Records of the Senate, Record Group 46, National Archives, Washington, DC [hereafter Sen. RG46–NAB].

10. Della Thompson, ed., *The Concise Oxford Dictionary of Current English*, 9th ed. (Oxford: Clarendon Press, 1995), 875.

11. Justice Kennedy quoted in DeParle, "Avoid a Kennedy."

12. 529 U.S. 803, 819 (2000).

13. Arriving at precise numbers is very difficult. Tom Keck has concluded that the Rehnquist Court struck down, on constitutional grounds, 42 federal and 132 state and local laws. Thomas M. Keck, *The Most Activist Supreme Court in History: The Road to Modern Judicial Conservatism* (Chicago: University of Chicago Press, 2004), 40–41. Updated at "Research Updates for the Most Activist Supreme Court in History," http://faculty.maxwell.syr.edu/tmkeck/Book_1/Research_Updates.htm (accessed 16 June 2008).

14. Mark Tushnet, *A Court Divided: The Rehnquist Court and the Future of Constitutional Law* (New York: W. W. Norton, 2005); Nancy Maveety, "The Rehnquist Era and the Court's Commentators" (paper presented at the annual meeting of the American Political Science Association, Washington, DC, 1–4 September 2005), 14.

15. Justice Kennedy quoted in Jan Crawford Greenburg, *Supreme Conflict: The Inside Story of the Struggle for Control of the United States Supreme Court* (New York: Penguin, 2007), 177.

16. Andrew D. Martin, Kevin Quinn, and Lee Epstein, "The Median Justice on the United States Supreme Court," *North Carolina Law Review* 83 (June 2005): 1277.

17. Lee Epstein and Tonja Jacobi, "Super Medians," *Stanford Law Review* 61(2008): 41.

18. Michael Dorf quoted in Brust, "Middle," 25.

19. Keck, *Most Activist Supreme Court*, 251.

20. Michael C. Dorf, *No Litmus Test: Law versus Politics in the Twenty-first Century* (Lanham, MD: Rowman & Littlefield, 2006), 5.

21. Like his late father, one of the activities in which Kennedy engaged in Sacramento was legislative lobbying. For the younger Kennedy, though, this was only a sidelight to the lawyering. "Records Spotlight Kennedy Lobbying," *New York Times*, 15 November 1987, 31.

22. For an excellent overview of the influence on the Kennedy nomination of Meese and Reagan and their reservations about appointing the Sacramentan, see David Alistair Yalof, *Pursuit of Justices: Presidential Politics and the Selection of Supreme Court Nominees* (Chicago: University of Chicago Press, 1999), chapter 6.

23. Robert Reinhold, "Restrained Pragmatist Anthony M. Kennedy," *New York Times*, 12 November 1987, 1(A) (quoting R. Dobie Langenkamp, Kennedy's roommate at Harvard Law School); "Academy of Achievement Interview, Anthony Kennedy, 23 June, 2005," http://www.achievement.org/autodoc/printmember/ken0int-1 (accessed 13 June 2007).

24. "Academy of Achievement Interview: Anthony Kennedy."

25. Judge Ginsburg, quoted in Al Kamen, "Ginsburg Acknowledges He Smoked Marijuana; Judge Says Use Was Occasional in '60s, '70s, " *Washington Post*, 6 November 1987, 1(A).

26. Letter from Justice Blackmun to Justice Kennedy, 12 November 1987, Box 1405, Harry A. Blackmun Papers, Manuscript Division, Library of Congress, Washington, D.C. [hereafter HAB-LOC]; Stuart Taylor Jr., "Which Way Will Kennedy Tilt the Bench?," *New York Times*, 7 February 1988, 4(4). For an interesting discussion of whether Kennedy really was actually only a member of the "#2 club" and Blackmun a member of the "#4 club," see Artemus Ward, "The 'Good Old #3 Club' Gets a New Member," *Journal of Supreme Court History* 33, no. 1 (March 2008): 110–19.

27. Mark Silverstein and William Haltom, "You Can't Always Get What You Want: Reflections on the Ginsburg and Breyer Nominations," *Journal of Law and Politics* 3 (Summer 1996): 459–79.

28. "Remarks by the President upon Nomination of Judge Anthony Kennedy as Supreme Court Justice," 11 November 1987, 2; "White House Talking Points: Judge Anthony M. Kennedy, The President's Nominee to the Supreme Court," 12 and 20 November 1987, Box 1405, HAB-LOC.

29. The jurisprudential concerns that the White House had about the Kennedy nomination primarily related to individual privacy, not criminal justice. Yalof, *Pursuit of Justices*, 145–46.

30. Tushnet, *A Court Divided*, 10. For an excellent firsthand account of O'Connor's western, Republican upbringing, see Sandra Day O'Connor and H. Alan Day, *Lazy B: Growing Up on a Cattle Ranch in the American Southwest* (New York: Random House, 2002).

31. "Academy of Achievement Interview: Anthony Kennedy"; Reinhold, "Restrained Pragmatist."

32. Jeffrey Rosen, "Supreme Leader: The Arrogance of Justice Anthony Kennedy," *New Republic* 236, no. 18 (June 2007): 16–22.

33. Reinhold, "Restrained Pragmatist."

34. Terence Moran, "Kennedy's Constitutional Journey," *Legal Times*, 6 July 1992, 20; Earl M. Maltz, "Anthony Kennedy and the Jurisprudence of Respectable Conservatism," in *Rehnquist Justice: Understanding the Court Dynamic*, ed. Earl M. Maltz (Lawrence: University Press of Kansas, 2003), 140–56; Richard C. Reuben, "Man in the Middle," *California Lawyer*, October 1992, 36; Tushnet, *A Court Divided*, 70; Brust, "Middle," 25 (quoting Earl M. Maltz).

35. Kenneth M. Cosgrove, *Branded Conservatives: How the Brand Brought the Right from the Fringes to the Center of American Politics* (New York: Peter Lang, 2007); Joseph Bottum, "Social Conservatism and the New Fusionism," in *Varieties of Conservatism in America*, ed. Peter Berkowitz (Stanford, CA: Hoover Institution Press, 2004), 37.

36. Bottum, "Social Conservatism," 39.

37. Mark C. Henrie, "Understanding Traditionalist Conservatism," in *Varieties of Conservatism in America*, ed. Peter Berkowitz (Stanford, CA: Hoover Institution Press, 2004), 7 (quotation), and in general 3–30.

38. Ibid., 17–19.

39. "The Role of the Judiciary in Promoting the Rule of Law," (C-SPAN, 2005).

40. Wayne V. McIntosh et al., "Textualism v. Active Liberty: Testing the Doctrinal Approaches of Justice Scalia and Breyer" (paper presented at the UK American Politics Group annual conference, Institute for the Study of the Americas, University of London, 3–5 January 2008), 1.

41. C. Herman Pritchett, "The Development of Judicial Research," in Joel Grossman and Joseph Tanenhaus, eds., *Frontiers of Judicial Research* (New York: Wiley, 1969), 42.

42. The classic work in this field is undeniably Jeffrey A. Segal and Harold J. Spaeth, *The Supreme Court and the Attitudinal Model* (New York: Cambridge University Press, 2002). This work has been revised and updated for the twenty-first century, although the authors' main conclusions remain unchanged. For an equally important classic, earlier behavioral examination of the justices' work, see C. Herman Pritchett, *The Roosevelt Court: A Study in Judicial Politics and Values, 1937–1947* (New York: Macmillan, 1948).

43. The classic strategic model writings are Walter F. Murphy, *Elements of Judicial Strategy* (Chicago: University of Chicago Press, 1964); Lee Epstein and Jack Knight, *The Choices Justices Make* (Washington, DC: CQ Press, 1997); Forrest Maltzman, James F. Spriggs, and Paul J. Wahlbeck, *Crafting Law on the Supreme Court: The Collegial Game* (New York: Cambridge University Press, 2000). In recent years, the new institutional and American political development schools of Supreme Court scholarship have only served to further deepen our understanding of the Court. See Cornell W. Clayton and Howard Gillman, eds., *Supreme Court Decision-Making: New Institutionalist Approaches* (Chicago: University of Chicago Press, 1999); Howard Gillman and Cornell Clayton, eds., *The Supreme Court in American Politics: New Institutionalist Interpretations* (Lawrence: University Press of Kansas, 1999); Ronald Kahn and Ken I.

Kersch, eds., *The Supreme Court and American Political Development* (Lawrence: University Press of Kansas, 2006).

44. Justice Kennedy quoted in Charles Lane, "Justice Kennedy's Future Role Pondered; High-Profile Activities Spark Talk About Aims," *Washington Post*, 17 June 2002, 1(A).

45. Quoted in Fred R. Shapiro, *The Oxford Dictionary of American Legal Quotations* (New York: Oxford University Press, 1993), 243.

46. Louis H. Pollack, "Professional Attitude," *ABA Journal* 84 (1998): 68 (Kennedy quotation), 66 (italics added).

47. Justice Kennedy quoted in Lane, "Justice Kennedy's Future Role."

48. Quoted in Reinhold, "Restrained Pragmatist."

49. Jeffrey Toobin, "Swing Shift; How Anthony Kennedy's Passion for Foreign Law Could Change the Supreme Court," *New Yorker*, 12 September 2005, 42–51. Of course, this is not a very solid basis upon which to evaluate one's teaching skills. I am grateful to Mark Graber for reminding me of this.

50. Anthony M. Kennedy, Judge, McGeorge Commencement Speech, 6, McGeorge School of Law of the University of the Pacific Commencement, Sacramento, California, 30 May 1981, Sen. RG46-NAB.

51. Justice Kennedy quoted in Moran, "Kennedy's Constitutional Journey," 21.

52. Testimony of Justice Kennedy, March 13, 2008, "Fiscal Year 2009 Supreme Court Budget–House Appropriations Committee Meeting," (C-SPAN, 2008).

53. Anthony M. Kennedy, Judge, Rotary Speech, 1, Sacramento Chapter of the Rotary Club, Sacramento, CA, 15 October 1987, Sen. RG46-NAB.

54. Kennedy Sup. Ct. Nomination Hearings, 230 (italics added).

55. Justice Kennedy quoted in Donald R. Murray, "The President's Message: A Call to Action: Please Join Us in This Vital 'Dialogue on Freedom,'" *Montana Lawyer* 27 (April 2002): 4.

56. Kennedy Appropriations Committee Testimony, March 2008.

57. Michael McConnell quoted in Reuben, "Man in the Middle," 36.

58. Handwritten note from Justice Kennedy to Justice Blackmun, 21 June 1990, Box 544, HAB-LOC; 497 U.S. 502 (1990).

59. For some analysis on this theme, see Frank J. Colucci, "Still Struggling: Anthony Kennedy and Abortion" (paper presented at the annual meeting of the Midwest Political Science Association, Chicago, 4–6 April 2008).

60. Justice Kennedy quoted in Greenburg, *Supreme Conflict*, 181.

61. Kennedy quoted in Carter, "Crossing the Rubicon," 39–40.

62. Comments by Justice Kennedy, "The Supreme Court of the United States," video produced by York Associates Television.

63. Michael Boudin, "Commentary," *New York University Law Review* 70 (June 1995): 773.

64. Lee Epstein et al., "Ideological Drift Among Supreme Court Justices: Who, When, and How Important?," *Northwestern University Law Review* 101 (March 2007): 127–31.

65. See McIntosh et al., "Textualism v. Active Liberty." For more information about the Digital Docket Project, see "University of Maryland: The Digital Docket," http://www.umiacs.umd.edu/~digidock/ (accessed 13 June 2008).

66. Ronald Dworkin, *Taking Rights Seriously* (Cambridge, MA: Harvard University Press, 1977), xiv.

67. Interestingly, with one exception, Justice Kennedy has refrained from providing copies of his speeches to the Court's Public Information Office—which are then posted on the Court's website. Between May 2000 and July 2008, six different members of the Court made sixty-two speeches available to the public in this manner. Almost half (twenty-nine) were authored by Chief Justice Rehnquist; Justices Ginsburg and Breyer have each provided copies of fifteen speeches; Justices Stevens, O'Connor, and Kennedy are each authors of only one speech. Kennedy's lone speech is the address he made to the 2003 annual meeting of the American Bar Association. For the speeches, see "Speeches," http://www.supremecourtus.gov/publicinfo/speeches/speeches.html (accessed 1 July 2008).

68. For a case study that sustains this conclusion, see Helen J. Knowles, "Clerkish Control of Recent Supreme Court Opinions? A Case Study of Justice Kennedy's Opinion in *Gonzales v. Carhart*," *Georgetown Journal of Gender and the Law* 10 (forthcoming, 2009).

69. This becomes particularly clear when one uses as the measure the ideological background of the federal judge for whom the clerk previously worked. This standard of measurement shows that, after his first full term on the Court, the percentage of Democratic clerks hired by Kennedy never rose above fifteen (through 2004). Corey Ditslear, "Building New Measures of Supreme Court Ideology: Clerk Selection as an Indicator of Preferences" (paper presented at the annual meeting of the American Political Science Association, Washington, DC, 2005), table 1. I am grateful to Ditslear for sharing with me his data on Justice Kennedy's clerks. For further information about ideological compatibility between justices and their clerks, see Corey Ditslear and Lawrence Baum, "Selection of Law Clerks and Polarization in the U.S. Supreme Court," *Journal of Politics* 63 (2001): 869–85; Artemus Ward and David L. Weiden, *Sorcerers' Apprentices: 100 Years of Law Clerks at the United States Supreme Court* (New York: New York University Press, 2006), 99–107.

70. Stuart Taylor Jr., "When High Court's Away, Clerks' Work Begins," *New York Times*, 23 September 1988 7(B).

71. Ward and Weiden, *Sorcerers' Apprentices*, 223.

72. Former Kennedy clerk Ward Farnsworth, quoted in Todd C. Peppers, *Courtiers of the Marble Palace: The Rise and Influence of the Supreme Court Law Clerk* (Stanford, CA: Stanford University Press, 2006), 202.

73. Linda Greenhouse's book about Justice Blackmun demonstrates, in rich detail, the immense value of the research resource that is the Blackmun papers. Linda Greenhouse, *Becoming Justice Blackmun: Harry Blackmun's Supreme Court Journey* (New York: Times Books, 2005).

74. Timothy R. Johnson, Paul J. Wahlbeck, and James F. Spriggs II, "The Influence of Oral Arguments on the U.S. Supreme Court," *American Political Science Review* 100 (February 2006), 99–113; Jack E. Rossotti, Laura Natelson, and Raymond Tatalovich, "Nonlegal Advice: The Amicus Briefs in *Webster v. Reproductive Health Services*," in *Judicial Politics: Readings From Judicature*, ed. Elliott E. Slotnick (Washington, DC: CQ Press, 2005), 193–96; John M. Harlan II, "The Role of Oral Argument," in *Judges on*

Judging: Views from the Bench, ed. David M. O'Brien (Washington, DC: CQ Press, 2004), 104–7.

75. *Ashcroft v. The Free Speech Coalition*, 535 U.S. 234, 253 (2002).

Chapter 1

1. United States Senate, Committee on the Judiciary, Hearings on the Nomination of Anthony M. Kennedy to be Associate Justice of the Supreme Court of the United States, 100th Cong., 1st sess., 14–16 December 1987, 86.

2. For a good discussion of this, see Friedrich A. Hayek, *The Constitution of Liberty* (Chicago: University of Chicago Press, 1960), postscript. I would like to thank my fellow 2006 Institute for Humane Studies Summer Graduate Research Fellows for contributing to my thoughts about this.

3. For example, see David Boaz, *Libertarianism: A Primer* (New York: Free Press, 1998), 23; Hayek, *The Constitution of Liberty*, postscript. Richard Epstein makes the following observation about his decision to include the word "modern" in the title of one of his books: "I included the words 'classical liberalism' in the title of this book in order to emphasize that I do not think that 'free markets,' let alone 'capitalism,' supply the answer to all the questions of social organization—a connotation that is sometimes attached to the terms 'laissez-faire' and 'libertarianism' by their most ardent defenders. I also have consciously inserted the word 'modern' in the title to indicate that methodological approaches that I use to defend this outcome are of recent origin. I use the word 'classical' to indicate that I use modern techniques to reaffirm traditional rules and outlooks, which were often—and still are—defended on very different grounds." Richard A. Epstein, *Skepticism and Freedom: A Modern Case for Classical Liberalism* (Chicago: University of Chicago Press, 2003), 1.

4. William Goodell, "Letter XXIII: All Theories of Government, Under All Forms, Preclude the Idea of Power to Legalize Slavery, but Imply the Obligation of Suppressing It.—Concluded," *National Era*, 7 December 1854.

5. Boaz, *Libertarianism*, 229.

6. For a discussion of this, see Wendy McElroy, *The Debates of Liberty: An Overview of Individualist Anarchism, 1881–1908* (Lanham, MD: Lexington, 2003), 51.

7. Robert Nozick, *Anarchy, State, and Utopia* (New York: Basic Books, 1974), 331.

8. Jan Narveson, *The Libertarian Idea* (Toronto: Broadview, 2001), 7.

9. Chris Brown, *Sovereignty, Rights and Justice: International Political Theory Today* (Cambridge: Polity, 2002), 8.

10. Robert H. Jackson, *The Global Covenant: Human Conduct in a World of States* (Oxford: Oxford University Press, 2000), 19.

11. Boaz, *Libertarianism*, 16.

12. Nozick, *Anarchy, State, and Utopia*, in particular, see chapter 7.

13. Brief of the Institute for Justice as Amicus Curiae in Support of Petitioners, *Lawrence v. Texas*, No. 02-102, 2002 U.S. Briefs 102, 28.

14. Narveson, *The Libertarian Idea*, 13; Randy E. Barnett, *The Structure of Liberty: Justice and the Rule of Law* (New York: Oxford University Press, 1998), 2 (italics added).

15. Richard A. Epstein, *Simple Rules for a Complex World* (Cambridge, MA: Harvard University Press, 1995), 59. As the political scientist Stephen Macedo has observed, it is important to correctly apply this to an understanding of the relationship between government and the individual. For example: "When conservatives like [Robert] Bork treat rights as islands surrounded by a sea of government powers, they precisely reverse the view of the Founders as enshrined in the Constitution, wherein government powers are limited and specified and rendered as islands surrounded by a sea of individual rights." Stephen Macedo, *The New Right v. The Constitution* (Washington, DC: CATO Institute, 1987), 32.

16. Michael P. Zuckert, *Natural Rights and the New Republicanism* (Princeton, NJ: Princeton University Press, 1994), 3, 14–15.

17. Barnett, *Structure of Liberty*, 21.

18. This is a paraphrase of Justice Stewart's observation about pornography. *Jacobellis v. Ohio*, 378 U.S. 184, 197 (1964) (Stewart, J., concurring).

19. Jeremy Bentham, "Anarchical Fallacies; Being an Examination of the Declaration of Rights Issued During the French Revolution," in *Nonsense Upon Stilts: Bentham, Burke and Marx on the Rights of Man*, ed. Jeremy Waldron (London: Methuen, 1987), 53.

20. Quoted in Fred R. Shapiro, *The Oxford Dictionary of American Legal Quotations* (New York: Oxford University Press, 1993), 361–62.

21. Boaz, *Libertarianism*, 89.

22. William Raymond Smith, "The Rhetoric of the Declaration of Independence," *College English* 26, no. 4 (January 1965): 306.

23. Boaz, *Libertarianism*, 65–66. Also see Narveson, *The Libertarian Idea*, 66–68.

24. Peter Laslett, ed., *John Locke, Two Treatises of Government* (Cambridge: Cambridge University Press, 1989).

25. Thomas Hobbes, *Leviathan*, ed. Richard Tuck (New York: Cambridge University Press, 1996).

26. Craig Duncan, "The Errors of Libertarianism," in *Libertarianism: For and Against*, ed. Craig Duncan and Tibor R. Machan (Lanham, MD: Rowman & Littlefield, 2005), 51.

27. Charles Fried, *Modern Liberty and the Limits of Government* (New York: W. W. Norton, 2006).

28. John Stuart Mill, "On Liberty," in Geraint Williams, ed., *John Stuart Mill, Utilitarianism, On Liberty, Considerations on Representative Government, Remarks on Bentham's Philosophy* (London: Everyman's Library, 1993), 78.

29. Richard A. Epstein, *Principles for a Free Society: Reconciling Individual Liberty with the Common Good* (Cambridge, MA: Perseus, 1998), 71.

30. Richard A. Epstein, "Skepticism and Freedom: The Intellectual Foundations of Our Constitutional Order," *University of Pennsylvania Journal of Constitutional Law* 6 (2004): 674; Institute for Justice Amicus Brief, 10 (italics added).

31. Hayek, *The Constitution of Liberty*, postscript.

32. Stephen L. Newman, *Liberalism at Wits' End: The Libertarian Revolt Against the Modern State* (Ithaca, NY: Cornell University Press, 1984), 10.

33. Boaz, *Libertarianism*, 104.

34. Representative works include Richard A. Epstein, *How Progressives Rewrote the Constitution* (Washington, DC: CATO Institute, 2007); Epstein, "Skepticism and Freedom," 657–83; Richard A. Epstein, "Of Same Sex Relationships and Affirmative Action: The Covert Libertarianism of the United States Supreme Court," *Supreme Court Economic Review* 12 (2004): 75–113; Epstein, *Principles for a Free Society*; Richard A. Epstein, *Takings: Private Property and the Power of Eminent Domain* (Cambridge, MA: Harvard University Press, 1985).

35. Although, as Ian Shapiro has detailed, we should be careful not to exaggerate the differences and tensions between utilitarianism and theories, such as libertarianism, that emphasize individual rights. Through history, Shapiro shows, these tensions have not been as strong as has often been suggested. Ian Shapiro, *The Evolution of Rights in Liberal Theory* (Cambridge: Cambridge University Press, 1986).

36. Will Kymlicka, *Contemporary Political Philosophy: An Introduction*, 2nd ed. (Oxford: Oxford University Press, 2002), 128–29.

37. David Gauthier, *Morals by Agreement* (New York: Oxford University Press, 1986), 2 (italics added); Narveson, *The Libertarian Idea*, 131.

38. Representative works include Randy E. Barnett, "The Moral Foundations of Modern Libertarianism," in *Varieties of Conservatism in America*, ed. Peter Berkowitz (Stanford, CA: Hoover Institution Press, 2004), 51–74; Randy E. Barnett, *Restoring the Lost Constitution: The Presumption of Liberty* (Princeton, NJ: Princeton University Press, 2004); Barnett, *Structure of Liberty*; Randy E. Barnett, "Getting Normative: The Role of Natural Rights in Constitutional Adjudication," *Constitutional Commentary* 12 (1995): 93–122; Randy E. Barnett, "Unenumerated Constitutional Rights and the Rule of Law," *Harvard Journal of Law and Public Policy* 14 (1991): 615–44.

39. Barnett, "Moral Foundations," 72.

40. Anthony M. Kennedy, Judge, McGeorge Commencement Speech, 4, McGeorge School of Law of the University of the Pacific Commencement, Sacramento, CA, 30 May 1981, *Committee on the Judiciary*, Judiciary Nominations files, A. Kennedy, Sup. Court, 100th Congress, Records of the Senate, Record Group 46, National Archives, Washington, DC [hereafter Sen. RG46-NAB]; *Planned Parenthood v. Casey*, 505 U.S. 833, 850 (1992).

41. Robert H. Bork, *The Tempting of America: The Political Seduction of the Law* (New York: Free Press, 1990), 139.

42. "Excerpts from the Bork Hearing: Pinning Down His Positions," *New York Times*, 17 September 1987.

43. It seems fairly clear that Senator Grassley (R-IA), to whom Kennedy was responding, was using this opportunity directly to compare and contrast the constitutional theories of Bork and Kennedy. When Grassley described the Madisonian Dilemma, he used language almost identical to that which later appeared in Bork's book. *Kennedy Sup. Ct. Nomination Hearings*, 207.

44. Ibid., 207, 113. Although Kennedy attributed this sentiment to Justice Stanley Reed, it is actually taken from one of Justice Robert Jackson's opinions: "The choice is

not between order and liberty. It is between liberty with order and anarchy without either." *Terminiello v. Chicago*, 337 U.S. 1, 37 (1949) (Jackson, J., dissenting).

45. Barnett, *Structure of Liberty*, chapter 1.

46. By combining personal responsibility and liberty, Hayek was mounting a challenge to the work of, for example, Clinton Rossiter, who five years earlier had professed a distinct desire for personal responsibility *over* liberty. See Clinton Rossiter, *Conservatism in America* (New York: 1955); Hayek, *The Constitution of Liberty*, 71.

47. Hayek, *The Constitution of Liberty*, postscript.

48. Macedo, *New Right*, 90.

49. For an excellent discussion of this characteristic of the rule of law, see Brian Z. Tamanaha, *On the Rule of Law: History, Politics, Theory* (Cambridge: Cambridge University Press, 2004).

50. A particularly good example is *United States v. Drayton*, 536 U.S. 194, 207 (2002) ("In a society based on law, the concept of agreement and consent should be given a weight and dignity of its own. Police officers act in full accord with the law when they ask citizens for consent. It reinforces the rule of law for the citizen to advise the police of his or her wishes and for the police to act in reliance on that understanding. When this exchange takes place, it dispels inferences of coercion.")

51. He also explored the subject of the components of the rule of law during an ABA symposium in 2005 (where he was joined by Justices O'Connor and Breyer). All of Kennedy's comments about these components are drawn from this event and the ABA 2006 speech. "The Role of the Judiciary in Promoting the Rule of Law" (C-SPAN, 2005); "Justice Kennedy Address" (C-SPAN, 2006).

52. Tamanaha, *On the Rule of Law*, 114.

53. Ibid., 114–15, 37.

54. In 2006, he added "equality" to this list. It is interesting to compare Edward Corwin's inclusion of "equal protection" in his summary of John Locke's definition of the rule of law. Locke described this concept in the following way: "*Freedom of Men under Government*, is, to have a standing Rule to live by, common to every one of that Society, and made by the Legislative Power erected in it; A Liberty to follow my own Will in all things, where the Rule prescribes not; and not to be subject to the inconstant, uncertain, unknown, Arbitrary Will of another Man." Locke, "Second Treatise," Chapter IV, Laslett, ed., *Locke*, 284. Corwin summarized this as meaning: "Law must be general: it must afford equal protection for all: it may not validly operate retroactively; it must be enforced through courts—legislative power does not include judicial power." Edward S. Corwin, "'The "Higher Law"' Background of American Constitutional Law," *Harvard Law Review* 42 (1928): 390.

55. "Justice Kennedy Address."

56. Tamanaha, *On the Rule of Law*, 95–96.

57. Joseph Raz, *The Authority of Law: Essays on Law and Morality* (Oxford: Clarendon Press, 1979), 212, 221, and generally chapter 11. The principles of the rule of law, according to Raz, are: (1) "All laws should be prospective, open, and clear"; (2) "Laws should be relatively stable"; (3) "The making of particular laws (particular legal orders) should be guided by open, stable, clear, and general rules"; (4) "The independence of the judiciary must be guaranteed"; (5) "The principles of natural justice must

be observed"; (6) "The courts should have review powers over the implementation of the other principles"; (7) "The courts should be easily accessible"; (8) "The discretion of the crime-preventing agencies should not be allowed to pervert the law," 214–18.

58. (1) "a system of legal rules"; (2) publication of the rules; (3) no "abuse of retroactive legislation"; (4) understandable rules; (5) no contradictory rules; (6) no "rules that require conduct beyond the powers of the affected party"; (7) no rules that undergo frequent changes; and (8) "congruence between the rules as announced and their actual administration." Lon L. Fuller, *The Morality of Law*, rev. ed. (New Haven, CT: Yale University Press, 1969), 38–39.

59. Ibid., 11–12.

60. Tamanaha, *On the Rule of Law*, 95–96.

61. Anthony M. Kennedy, "Speech at the American Bar Association Annual Meeting," 9 August 2003 (revised 14 August 2003) (paginated transcript on file at the Public Information Office, U.S. Supreme Court), 8.

62. Ibid., 9.

63. Jeffrey Toobin, *The Nine: Inside the Secret World of the Supreme Court* (New York: Doubleday, 2007).

64. Tony Mauro, "Visiting Justices Get an Earful in London," *Legal Times*, 31 July 2000, 10. Also see Tony Mauro, "Court Shows Interest in International Law," *New York Law Journal*, 14 July 2003, 1 (suggesting that the exchange between Lord Lester and Justice Kennedy contributed to the latter's subsequent display of interest in the relevance, to American judicial decision making, of international law). In her contributing essay to a 2002 volume about the Rehnquist Court, Claire L'Heureux-Dubé, a justice of the Canadian Supreme Court, also criticized the American justices for their failure "to take part in the international dialogue among the courts of the world." This, she argued, was "contributing to a growing isolation and diminished influence. This failure is a loss for American jurisprudence, and for the development of human rights around the world." Claire L'Heureux-Dube, "The Importance of Dialogue: Globalization, the Rehnquist Court, and Human Rights," in *The Rehnquist Court: A Retrospective*, ed. Martin H. Belsky (Oxford: Oxford University Press, 2002), 235.

65. Justice Kennedy, quoted in Bob Egelko, "Justice Kennedy Wins ABA's Highest Award," *San Francisco Chronicle*, 14 August 2007, 2(B); "Dialogue on Freedom Summary," http://www.abavideonews.org/ABA243D/DOF_summary.html (accessed 6 June 2008).

66. Justice Kennedy, quoted in Egelko, "Justice Kennedy Wins ABA's Highest Award."

67. 543 U.S. 551, 575 (2005).

68. "Symposium: To What Extent Should the Interpretation and Application of Provisions of the U.S. Constitution Be Informed by Rulings of Foreign and International Tribunals: University of Hawai'i Law Review Symposium: Comments of Justice Ruth Bader Ginsburg," *University of Hawai'i Law Review* 26 (2004): 335 (italics added).

69. 543 U.S. at 575, citing 356 U.S. 86, 102–103 (1958) (italics added).

70. 543 U.S. at 608 (Scalia, J., joined by Rehnquist, CJ., and Thomas, J., dissenting).

71. 543 U.S. at 605 (O'Connor, J., dissenting). Justice O'Connor dissented in part because she did not agree with the majority that the domestic consensus on the

unconstitutionality of executing juveniles existed. For an instructive discussion of this "confirmatory role," and the theory of an international "dialogue," see Melissa A. Waters, "Mediating Norms and Identity: The Role of Transnational Judicial Dialogue in Creating and Enforcing International Law," *Georgetown Law Journal* 93 (2005): 487–574.

72. 543 U.S. at 578.

73. I am indebted to the students in my Critical Thinking in Politics course for providing invaluable student feedback about the Dialogue on Freedom program.

74. "Academy of Achievement Interview, Anthony Kennedy, 23 June, 2005," http://www.achievement.org/autodoc/printmember/ken0int-1 (accessed 13 June 2007).

75. For example, see Mark Tushnet, *A Court Divided: The Rehnquist Court and the Future of Constitutional Law* (New York: W. W. Norton, 2005), 172–73.

76. Charles Lane, "Justice Kennedy's Future Role Pondered; High-Profile Activities Spark Talk About Aims," *Washington Post*, 17 June 2002, 1(A).

77. Quoted in ibid.

78. Tony Mauro, "A Lost Chance to Be the Chief," *Legal Times*, 7 March 2005, 1.

79. Jeffrey Rosen, "Supreme Leader: The Arrogance of Justice Anthony Kennedy," *The New Republic* 236, no. 18 (2007): 16–22.

80. Justice Kennedy quoted in *Dialogue on Freedom Summary*; Charles Lane, "Attacks Led to 'Dialogue' for Justice Kennedy," *Washington Post*, 26 January 2002, 11(A).

81. Justice Kennedy quoted in Donald R. Murray, "The President's Message: A Call to Action: Please Join Us in This Vital 'Dialogue on Freedom,'" *Montana Lawyer* 27 (2002): 4–5, 11.

82. "Dialogue on Freedom Summary."

83. Lane, "Attacks Led to 'Dialogue.'"

84. Excerpted from *Dialogue on Freedom*, 2002, by American Bar Association, published by the American Bar Association. Copyright © 2002 by the American Bar Association. Reprinted with permission. For the entire hypothetical, see "Dialogue on Freedom: What is a Dialogue on Freedom?" http://www.abanet.org/dialogue/whatis.html (accessed 25 February 2005). I would like to thank Hilary Glazer and Stephanie Ortbals-Tibbs at the American Bar Association for providing me with information about the "Dialogue on Freedom" program.

85. Amy Goldstein and Charles Lane, "At D.C. School, Justice Kennedy and Teens Explore U.S. Values," *Washington Post*, 29 January 2002, 17(A).

86. Tushnet, *A Court Divided*, 172–73; Rosen, "Supreme Leader," 16–22.

87. Quoted in Goldstein and Lane, "At D.C. School, Justice Kennedy and Teens," 17(A). Again, here I am grateful to the input from my fellow 2006 Institute for Humane Studies Summer Graduate Research Fellows.

88. Nozick, *Anarchy, State, and Utopia*, 334.

89. Anthony M. Kennedy, Judge, Unenumerated Rights and the Dictates of Judicial Restraint, Speech, Canadian Institute for Advanced Legal Studies, The Stanford Lectures, Palo Alto, CA, 24 July–1 August 1986, Sen. RG46-NAB; *Kennedy Sup. Ct. Nomination Hearings*, 170.

90. *Kennedy Sup. Ct. Nomination Hearings*, 170.

91. Ibid., 170–71.
92. Ibid., 180.
93. Ibid.
94. Remarks of Justice Anthony M. Kennedy, "The Role of the Judiciary in Promoting the Rule of Law." As Kennedy explained on another occasion, the dignity of every individual needs to be respected. Being a convicted and imprisoned criminal, for example, does not make someone that much less "a person . . . part of the family of humankind." It is true that criminal law is distinguished from civil law by the fact that it deals with offenses against *society*; in criminal cases the government pursues convictions on behalf of society. Society in no way benefits, however, if during the process it loses sight of the fact that the defendant is one of its own. A society can be "decent and free," says Kennedy, only if it is "founded in respect for the individual." Kennedy, "Speech at the American Bar Association," 3, 7. The Supreme Court has, in various contexts, repeatedly reminded us that people do not relinquish their constitutional rights at the prison gate. See, for example, *Kentucky Dept. of Corrections v. Thompson*, 490 U.S. 454, 459-461 (1989); *Bell v. Wolfish*, 441 U.S. 520, 545 (1979); *Johnson v. Avery*, 393 U.S. 483 (1969). In 2003, Kennedy reminded us that society cannot afford to "run a system with a sign at the entrance for inmates saying, 'Abandon Hope, All Ye Who Enter Here.'" This is significant because, as James Q. Whitman explains in *Harsh Justice*, degrading punishment (which Whitman argues is one of the signature characteristics of the American criminal justice system) affects both the offending individual *and* the general public—it influences society's views of the criminal, the system, and, more generally, human rights, responsibilities, and relations. When Kennedy referenced Professor Whitman's book during his ABA speech, he was careful to refrain from saying whether or not he agreed with its conclusion that "the goal of the American corrections system is to degrade and demean the prisoner." It was clear, however, that he agrees that Americans should be concerned about the existence of a criminal justice system that fails adequately to respect the dignity of those over whom it exerts authority. Kennedy, "Speech at the American Bar Association," 7; James Q. Whitman, *Harsh Justice: Criminal Punishment and the Widening Divide between America and Europe* (Oxford: Oxford University Press, 2003). It is also important with regard to criminal *process*: Margareth Etienne, "Parity, Disparity, and Adversariality: First Principles of Sentencing," *Stanford Law Review* 58 (2005): 310 ("The public's faith in the criminal justice system rests upon the belief that the victor in any adversarial process has triumphed over a capable opponent who had a fair opportunity to soundly test her adversary's case").
95. "Speech of Senator John F. Kennedy, Commodore Hotel, New York, NY, Acceptance of Party Nomination, September 14th, 1960," John T. Woolley and Gerhard Peters, *The American Presidency Project*, Santa Barbara: University of California (hosted), Gerhard Peters (database), http://www.presidency.ucsb.edu/ws/?pid=74012 (accessed 9 April 2008). Here, it is worth considering that Senator and later President John F. Kennedy can accurately be described as a "1960 liberal." See William E. Nelson, "Byron White: A Liberal of 1960," in *The Warren Court in Historical and Political Perspective*, ed. Mark Tushnet (Charlottesville: University Press of Virginia, 1993).
96. I am grateful to Mark Graber for making me consider this aspect of my arguments.

97. *The Oxford American Dictionary and Language Guide* (New York: Oxford University Press, 1999), 475.

98. Kennedy, "Speech at the American Bar Association," 10.

99. 497 U.S. 547, 636 (1990) (Kennedy, J., joined by Scalia, J., dissenting).

100. Kennedy, "Speech at the American Bar Association," 10.

101. Ibid., 2.

102. Nozick, *Anarchy, State, and Utopia*, 334.

103. Testimony of Justice Kennedy, 13 March 2008, "Fiscal Year 2009 Supreme Court Budget—House Appropriations Committee Meeting," (C-SPAN, 2008); Kennedy, "Speech at the American Bar Association," 10.

104. Discussions (and critiques) of the passivity of individuals can also be found in the work of John Stuart Mill, but his treatment of the subject has a very different emphasis than that of Justice Kennedy and is a good example of why Mill was a utilitarian who sometimes made libertarian arguments (rather than vice versa). See W. J. Ashley, ed., *John Stuart Mill, Principles of Political Economy with Some of Their Applications to Social Philosophy* (New York: A. M. Kelley, 1965).

105. 543 U.S. at 578.

106. Kennedy, "McGeorge Commencement Speech," 6.

107. Jan Narveson, "Liberty and Equality—A Question of Balance?" in *Liberty and Equality*, ed. Tibor R. Machan (Stanford, CA: Hoover Institution Press, 2002), 41.

108. Judge Kennedy's Comments at the Ninth Circuit Judicial Conference, Hawaii, 21 August 1987, 5, Sen. RG46-NAB.

109. Kennedy quoted in Jeffrey Toobin, "Swing Shift," *New Yorker*, 12 September 2005, 42–51. An important discussion of the relationship of the small "c" constitution and constitutionalism is provided by Stephen Griffin, who has observed: "Throughout American history, the values suggested by the document [the U.S. Constitution] have provided a succession of normative orderings, ideologies inspired by the text *and the constitutional tradition in which it is embedded*." Stephen M. Griffin, *American Constitutionalism: From Theory to Politics* (Princeton, NJ: Princeton University Press, 1996), 73 (italics added).

110. Kennedy, "Stanford Lectures," 1.

111. Ibid.

112. Kennedy Sup. Ct. Nomination Hearings, 170–71.

113. Quoted in Randy E. Barnett, "A Ninth Amendment for Today's Constitution," *Valparaiso University Law Review* 26 (1991): 419.

114. For example, see Randy E. Barnett, ed., *The Rights Retained by the People: The History and Meaning of the Ninth Amendment*, vol. 2 (Fairfax, VA: George Mason University Press, 1993); Randy E. Barnett, ed., *The Rights Retained by the People: The History and Meaning of the Ninth Amendment*, vol. 1 (Fairfax, VA: George Mason University Press, 1989).

115. Kennedy Sup. Ct. Nomination Hearings, 179.

116. 505 U.S. at 848. For commentary on this, see Randy E. Barnett, "Justice Kennedy's Libertarian Revolution: *Lawrence v. Texas*," *Cato Supreme Court Review* (2003): 33; Randy E. Barnett, "Scrutiny Land," *Michigan Law Review* 106, no. 8 (June 2008): 1493.

117. 505 U.S. at 999–1000 (Scalia, J., joined by Rehnquist, CJ., and White and Thomas, JJ., concurring in the judgment in part, and dissenting in part) (quoting 505 U.S. at 849).

118. Kennedy, "Stanford Lectures," 3. In an earlier speech he devoted much of his remarks to a discussion of the responsibility of the political branches. Anthony M. Kennedy, Judge, Patent Lawyers Speech, Los Angeles Patent Lawyers Association, Los Angeles, February 1982, Sen. RG46-NAB.

119. Justice Kennedy quoted in Lane, "Attacks Led to 'Dialogue,'" 11(A).

120. Nozick, *Anarchy, State, and Utopia*, ix (italics added).

121. Epstein, "Covert Libertarianism," 82.

122. John Gerring, "Ideology: A Definitional Analysis," *Political Research Quarterly* 50, no. 4 (1997): 980.

123. Richard Epstein has devoted much of his career to writing about takings of property. He remains famous for his argument that, properly interpreted, the Fifth Amendment Takings Clause places far greater limitations on government appropriations of private property than the Supreme Court has understood it to. Epstein, *Takings*. However, as he has acknowledged, rectifying the Supreme Court's interpretation of it would not make the Takings Clause a "strong libertarian" instrument. Epstein, "Covert Libertarianism," 82.

124. Rick Tilman, *Ideology and Utopia in the Social Philosophy of the Libertarian Economists* (Westport, CT: Greenwood, 2001), xiii.

125. For example, see Boaz, *Libertarianism*.

126. This certainly seems to be the argument that Rick Tilman makes. He implies that libertarians are not good defenders of civil liberties. To be sure, he does draw some distinctions between the different approaches and emphasis of libertarianism, but he still draws his conclusions from assumptions that libertarians are overwhelmingly concerned with economics. Tilman, *Ideology and Utopia*, chapter 2.

127. For an excellent analysis of the historical, political, and doctrinal context of these changes in the Court's jurisprudence, see Barry Cushman, *Rethinking the New Deal Court: The Structure of a Constitutional Revolution* (New York: Oxford University Press, 1998).

128. "There may be narrower scope for operation of the presumption of constitutionality when legislation appears on its face to be within a specific prohibition of the Constitution, such as those of the first ten amendments, which are deemed equally specific when held to be embraced within the Fourteenth.

"It is unnecessary to consider now whether legislation which restricts those political processes which can ordinarily be expected to bring about repeal of undesirable legislation, is to be subjected to more exacting judicial scrutiny under the general prohibitions of the Fourteenth Amendment than are most other types of legislation. On restrictions upon the right to vote; on restraints upon the dissemination of information; on interferences with political organizations; as to prohibition of peaceable assembly.

"Nor need we enquire whether similar considerations enter into the review of statutes directed at particular religious, or national, or racial minorities, whether prejudice against discrete and insular minorities may be a special condition, which tends seriously to curtail the operation of those political processes ordinarily to be relied upon to protect minorities, and which may call for a correspondingly more searching judicial inquiry." *U.S. v. Carolene Products Co.*, 304 U.S. 144, 153, n.4 (1938) (citations omitted).

129. Quoted in Stuart Taylor, "Newest Judicial Activists Come from the Right," *New York Times*, 8 February 1987, 24(A).

130. Barnett, *Restoring the Lost Constitution*, 243 (italics added).

131. Tushnet, *A Court Divided*, 177–78 (italics added).

132. Ibid, 132.

Chapter 2

1. *International Society for Krishna Consciousness, Inc. v. Lee*, 505 U.S. 672, 701 (1992) (Kennedy, J., joined by Blackmun, Stevens, and Souter, JJ., concurring in the judgment).

2. United States Senate, Committee on the Judiciary, *Hearings on the Nomination of Anthony M. Kennedy to be Associate Justice of the Supreme Court of the United States*, 100th Cong., 1st sess., 14–16 December 1987, 118.

3. *Smith v. California*, 361 U.S. 147, 157 (1959) (Black, J., concurring). It should be noted that even Black's absolutism was tempered by a firm distinction between speech and conduct. See Mark Silverstein, *Constitutional Faiths: Felix Frankfurter, Hugo Black, and the Process of Judicial Decision Making* (Ithaca, NY: Cornell University Press, 1984), chapter 5.

4. *Simon & Schuster v. Crime Victims Bd.*, 502 U.S. 105, 127 (1991) (Kennedy, J., concurring in the judgment).

5. Lawrence Friedman, "The Limitations of Labeling: Justice Anthony M. Kennedy and the First Amendment," *Ohio Northern University Law Review* 20 (1993): 225–62.

6. This is consistent with the findings of Albert P. Melone, because although Professor Melone concluded that Kennedy did not confirm the "freshman effect" hypothesis (that during his or her first few terms on the Court a justice is unlikely to desire to (and probably will not) write prominent and/or controversial opinions, especially dissents), it is clear that Kennedy's faith in using the power of the Court did accrue over time. Albert P. Melone, "Revisiting the Freshman Effect Hypothesis: The First Two Terms of Justice Anthony Kennedy," *Judicature* 74 (1990): 6–13; Richard Brust, "The Man in the Middle," *ABA Journal* 89 (2003), 24–25.

7. *Ashcroft v. Free Speech Coalition*, 535 U.S. 234, 253 (2002).

8. Friedman, "Limitations of Labeling." For examples of arguments that Kennedy's free speech jurisprudence is libertarian, see Steven G. Calabresi, "The Libertarian-Lite Constitutional Order and the Rehnquist Court: Reviewing the New Constitutional Order. By Mark Tushnet," *Georgetown Law Journal* 93 (2005): 1049 (describing Kennedy's free speech opinions as "strikingly libertarian"); Thomas W. Merrill, "The Constitution and the Cathedral: Prohibiting, Purchasing, and Possibly Condemning Tobacco Advertising," *Northwestern University Law Review* 93 (1999): 1169–204; Mark Tushnet, "Kormendy Lecture Series: Understanding the Rehnquist

Court," *Ohio Northern University Law Review* 31 (2005): 199 (discussing Kennedy's "libertarian inclinations" in First Amendment opinions); Eugene Volokh, "The Rehnquist Court: Pragmatism vs. Ideology in Free Speech Cases," *Northwestern University Law Review* 99 (2004): 41 (Kennedy is "broadly speech-libertarian").

9. Lee Epstein and Jeffrey A. Segal, "The Rehnquist Court and the First Amendment: Trumping the First Amendment?" *Washington University Journal of Law & Policy* 21 (2006): 81, 109, 93.

10. Suzanna Sherry, "Hard Cases Make Good Judges," *Northwestern University Law Review* 99 (2004): 3–31.

11. My use of this word is not meant to suggest that the majority of justices who usually took the speech-protective position in cases always consisted of the same individuals, because it clearly did not.

12. John Gerring, "Ideology: A Definitional Analysis," *Political Research Quarterly* 50, no. 4 (1997): 980.

13. Sherry, "Hard Cases"; Volokh, "The Rehnquist Court: Pragmatism vs. Ideology," 34.

14. Burt Neuborne, "First Amendment," *Touro Law Review* 6 (1989): 130.

15. Eric Foner, *The Story of American Freedom* (New York: W. W. Norton, 1998), xiv. Also see Daniel T. Rodgers, *Contested Truths: Keywords in American Politics Since Independence* (New York: Basic, 1987), 44 (The Framers "made out of their keywords, their axioms, their definitional wrangles not a political consensus but the tools of debate.")

16. Antonin Scalia, "The Judges Are Coming," printed in *Congressional Record*, 96th Cong., 2nd sess., 1980, vol. 126, pt 14: 18921.

17. 319 U.S. 624, 642 (1943).

18. Testimony of Michael C. Munger, Hearings on Political Parties in America, Committee on Rules and Administration, United States Senate, 5 April 2000, http://rules.senate.gov/hearings/2000/04500munger.htm (accessed 1 July 2008).

19. Richard A. Epstein, "Property, Speech, and the Politics of Distrust," *University of Chicago Law Review* 59 (1992): 46.

20. John Locke, *The Second Treatise of Government*, chapter 19, in Peter Laslett, ed., *John Locke, Two Treatises of Government* (Cambridge: Cambridge University Press, 1989), 406–28.

21. 535 U.S. at 253.

22. Neuborne, "First Amendment," 130.

23. 535 U.S. at 253. Justice Kennedy quoted in Amy Goldstein and Charles Lane, "At D.C. School, Justice Kennedy and Teens Explore U.S. Values," *Washington Post*, 29 January 2002, 17(A).

24. *Police Department of the City of Chicago v. Mosley*, 408 U.S. 92, 95 (1972). My discussion of the main arguments relating to viewpoint and content discrimination draws heavily on the following two excellent overviews of the subject: Daniel A. Farber, *The First Amendment*, 2nd ed. (New York: Foundation, 2003), chapter 2; Steven J. Heyman, *Free Speech and Human Dignity* (New Haven, CT: Yale University Press, 2008), chapter 6.

25. 502 U.S. at 125 (Kennedy, J., concurring in the judgment), citing *Texas v. Johnson*, 491 U.S. 397, 412 (1989).

26. *Rosenberger v. Rector and Visitors of University of Virginia* 515 U.S. 819, 829 (1995); Farber, *The First Amendment*, 31.

27. 408 U.S. at 92–93 (quoting Chicago Municipal Code, c. 193-1 (i)).

28. 408 U.S. at 95–96 (quoting *New York Times v. Sullivan*, 376 U.S. 254, 269–70 (1964)).

29. 319 U.S. at 637: "educating the young for citizenship is reason for scrupulous protection of Constitutional freedoms of the individual, if we are not to strangle the free mind at its source and teach youth to discount important principles of our government as mere platitudes."

30. Farber, *The First Amendment*, 34–35.

31. Geoffrey R. Stone, "Content Regulation and the First Amendment," *William & Mary Law Review* 25 (1983): 212–16.

32. Randy E. Barnett, *The Structure of Liberty: Justice and the Rule of Law* (New York: Oxford University Press, 1998), chapter 2.

33. Richard Epstein, "Property, Speech," 54.

34. *The Oxford American Dictionary and Language Guide* (New York: Oxford University Press, 1999), 262.

35. Friedrich A. Hayek, *The Constitution of Liberty* (Chicago: University of Chicago Press, 1960), 401–2.

36. Farber, *The First Amendment*, 34.

37. 274 U.S. 357, 377 (1927) (Brandeis, J., concurring).

38. David A. Strauss, "Persuasion, Autonomy, and Freedom of Expression," *Columbia Law Review* 91 (1991): 354.

39. Joseph Raz, "Free Expression and Personal Identification," in *Free Expression: Essays in Law and Philosophy*, ed. W. J. Waluchow (Oxford: Clarendon Press, 1994), 13.

40. *Kennedy Sup. Ct. Nomination Hearings*, 111.

41. *Texas v. Johnson*, 491 U.S. 397, 420 (1989) (Kennedy, J., concurring).

42. For an extensive treatment of the public and political reaction to the case, see Robert Justin Goldstein, *Flag Burning and Free Speech: The Case of Texas v. Johnson* (Lawrence: University Press of Kansas, 2000).

43. "The Role of the Judiciary in Promoting the Rule of Law," (C-SPAN, November 10, 2005); Justice Kennedy quoted in Tony Mauro, "Justice Kennedy to ABA: 'The Work of Freedom Has Just Begun,'" *Legal Times*, 14 August 2007.

44. Memo from Justice Blackmun to Justice Brennan, 19 June 1989, Thurgood Marshall Papers, Manuscript Division, Library of Congress, Washington, D.C. [hereinafter TM-LOC].

45. Texas Penal Code Ann. 42.09 (1989), quoted at 491 U.S. at 400, n1.

46. 491 U.S. at 404, quoting *Spence v. Washington*, 418 U.S. 405, 410–11 (1974).

47. Title 50, App. United States Code, Section 462(b), quoted at 391 U.S. at 370.

48. *United States v. O'Brien*, 391 U.S. 367, 377 (1968).

49. 491 U.S. at 410, 414.

50. Ibid. at 429 (Rehnquist, CJ., joined by White and O'Connor, JJ., dissenting).

51. Ibid. at 420 (Kennedy, J., concurring).

52. Ibid.

53. Justice Kennedy quoted in Jeffrey Rosen, "The Agonizer," *New Yorker*, 11 November 1996, 82; 491 U.S. at 420–21 (Kennedy, J., concurring).

54. As Justice Brennan wrote for the Court in *Johnson*: "We can imagine no more appropriate response to burning a flag than waving one's own." 491 U.S. at 420.

55. 491 U.S. at 421 (Kennedy, J., concurring).

56. *Texas v. Johnson*, Justice Kennedy concurrence, first and final drafts, Box 533, Harry A. Blackmun Papers, Manuscript Division, Library of Congress, Washington, D.C. [hereinafter HAB-LOC] (first draft); Box 478, TM-LOC (final draft).

57. Patricia M. Wald, "The Rhetoric of Results and the Results of Rhetoric: Judicial Writings," *University of Chicago Law Review* 62 (1995): 1415. Similarly, see R. Dean Moorhead, "Concurring and Dissenting Opinions," *American Bar Association Journal* 38 (1952): 822 (arguing that separate opinions can provide significant information about appellate judges). An excellent example of the "personal toll" analysis of Kennedy's opinion is Linda Greenhouse, "Justices, 5–4, Back Protesters' Right to Burn the Flag," *New York Times*, 22 June 1989, 1(A). A notable exception to this journalistic trend was Al Kamen, "Court Nullifies Flag-Desecration Laws; First Amendment is Held to Protect Burnings During Political Demonstrations," *Washington Post*, 22 June 1989, 1(A) (picking up on the key First Amendment sections in the opinion).

58. Ruth Bader Ginsburg, "Remarks on Writing Separately," *Washington Law Review* 65 (1990): 143.

59. Richard C. Reuben, "Man in the Middle," *California Lawyer*, October 1992, 38.

60. 502 U.S. 105 (1991). The vote was 8–0 because Justice Thomas did not participate in the case. At conference the vote was the same, and Justice Blackmun's notes indicate that none of the justices made many substantive comments about the issues involved. *Simon & Schuster* conference notes, 18 October 1991, Box 589, HAB-LOC.

61. Hill received immunity from prosecution in return for his testimony against former colleagues.

62. 502 U.S. at 118.

63. Ibid., 121.

64. 502 U.S. at 128 (Kennedy, J., concurring in the judgment).

65. Memo from Jeff Meyer to Justice Blackmun, 1 December 1991; First draft of Kennedy's concurrence in the judgment in *Simon & Schuster*, December 5, 1991; Box 589, HAB-LOC.

66. 502 U.S. at 124 (Kennedy, J., concurring in the judgment).

67. Ibid., 124–25 (italics added).

68. Ibid., 127.

69. Ibid., 125 (italics added).

70. Ibid.

71. Richard Delgado and David H. Yun, "Pressure Valves and Bloodied Chickens: An Analysis of Paternalistic Objections to Hate Speech Regulation," *California Law Review* 82 (1994): 891; Brendan P. Lynch, "Personal Injuries or Petty Complaints?: Evaluating the Case for Campus Hate Speech Codes: The Argument from Experience," *Suffolk University Law Review* 32 (1999): 655. For excellent discussions concerning this area of free speech, see Jon B. Gould, *Speak No Evil: The Triumph of Hate Speech*

Regulation (Chicago: University of Chicago Press, 2005); Donald Alexander Downs, *Restoring Free Speech and Liberty on Campus* (New York: Cambridge University Press, 2005); David E. Bernstein, *You Can't Say That!: The Growing Threat to Civil Liberties from Antidiscrimination Laws* (Washington, DC: CATO Institute, 2003).

72. 530 U.S. 703, 716 (2000); *Olmstead v. United States*, 277 U.S. 438, 478 (1928). This approach was advocated by the petitioner in *Hill*. Brief for the Petitioner at 8, *Hill v. Colorado*, 530 U.S. 703 (2000) (No. 98-1856), 1998 U.S. Briefs 1856.

73. Quoted at 530 U.S. at 707.

74. Ibid., 708.

75. 530 U.S. at 714.

76. Ibid., 716, quoting *Madsen v. Women's Health Center, Inc.*, 512 U.S. 753, 772–73 (1994).

77. 530 U.S. at 789 (Kennedy, J., dissenting).

78. Ibid., 776, 765.

79. 530 U.S. at 719.

80. Ibid, 720.

81. 530 U.S. at 769 (Kennedy, J., dissenting); 530 U.S. at 735.

82. Justice Scalia's dissent strongly suggests that Justice Kennedy distributed the first draft of his dissent after Justice Stevens had written most of his opinion. See 530 U.S. at 762 (Scalia, J., joined by Thomas, J., dissenting).

83. 530 U.S. at 769 (Kennedy, J., dissenting).

84. *Nixon v. Shrink Missouri Government PAC*, 528 U.S. 377, 410–11 (2000) (Thomas, J., joined by Scalia, J., dissenting); *McConnell v. Federal Election Commission*, 540 U.S. 93, 323 (2003) (Kennedy, J., concurring in the judgment in part and dissenting in part with respect to BCRA Titles I and II).

85. The recordings of the opinion announcements in the case are available at "*Hill v. Colorado*, 530 U.S. 703 (2000), U.S. Supreme Court Opinion Announcement," http://www.oyez.org/cases/1990-1999/1999/1999_98_1856/opinion/ (accessed 1 July 2008).

86. 530 U.S. at 767 (Kennedy, J., dissenting).

87. Ibid. Justice Stevens did respond to Kennedy's analogy, but only by drawing on his own civil rights analogy that hypothesized about a law that was very different from the Colorado law: "A statute making it a misdemeanor to sit at a lunch counter for an hour without ordering food would also not be 'content based' . . ." 530 U.S. at 724.

88. Frank J. Colucci, "The Jurisprudence of Justice Anthony Kennedy" (PhD Dissertation, University of Notre Dame, 2004), 150.

89. 530 U.S. at 715.

90. 530 U.S. at 762 (Scalia, J., joined by Thomas, J., dissenting).

91. 410 U.S. 113 (1973).

92. 530 U.S. at 762–63 (Scalia, J., joined by Thomas, J., dissenting).

93. Ibid., 763. This conclusion was supported by the absence of "evidence . . . that the 'sidewalk counseling' conducted by petitioners in this case was ever abusive or confrontational." 530 U.S. at 710.

94. Ibid.

95. 530 U.S. at 765 (Kennedy, J., dissenting).

96. Colucci, "Jurisprudence of Justice Anthony Kennedy," 150. Compare Linda Greenhouse, "Court Rules That Governments Can't Outlaw Type of Abortion," *New York Times*, 29 June 2000, 1(A) ("Justice Scalia and Justice Kennedy read their impassioned dissenting opinions in the courtroom . . . for more than half an hour, making clear that this First Amendment debate was in many respects a proxy for the court's ongoing abortion debate").

97. 530 U.S. 914 (2000).

98. 505 U.S. 833 (1992).

99. 530 U.S. at 791 (Kennedy, J., dissenting), quoting 505 U.S. at 852.

100. 530 U.S. at 789 (Kennedy, J., dissenting).

101. Ibid., 792.

102. Ibid., 790–91.

103. Ibid., 790 (italics added).

104. Robert C. Post, "Between Governance and Management: The History and Theory of the Public Forum," *UCLA Law Review* 34 (1987), 1713–835; Daniel A. Farber and John E. Nowak, "The Misleading Nature of Public Forum Analysis: Content and Context in First Amendment Adjudication," *Virginia Law Review* 70 (1984): 1219, 1221–222.

105. *Perry Ed. Assn. v. Perry Local Educators' Assn.*, 460 U.S. 37, 45 (1983).

106. Daniel A. Farber, "Free Speech without Romance: Public Choice and the First Amendment," *Harvard Law Review* 105 (1991): 574.

107. Dawn C. Nunziato, "The Death of the Public Forum in Cyberspace," *Berkeley Technology Law Journal* 20 (2005): 1143–44.

108. Brief for the National Committees of the Libertarian Party and the New Alliance Party as Amici Curiae Supporting Respondents, 3, *United States v. Kokinda*, 497 U.S. 720 (1990) (No. 88-2031) 1988 U.S. Briefs 2031.

109. 39 CFR 232.1(h)(1) (1989), quoted at 497 U.S. 720, 724 (1990).

110. 497 U.S. at 727.

111. 497 U.S. at 742, 745 (Brennan, J., joined by Marshall and Stevens, J J., and Blackmun, J. as to Part 1, dissenting).

112. Ibid., 759–62.

113. *Kokinda* conference notes, 28 February 1990, Box 552, HAB-LOC.

114. Ibid.

115. 497 U.S. at 737 (Kennedy, J., concurring in the judgment).

116. Ibid., 737–38.

117. Ibid., 737.

118. Ibid., 738, quoting *Ward v. Rock Against Racism*, 491 U.S. at 791 (1989) (quoting *Clark v. Community for Creative Non-Violence*, 468 U.S. 288, 293 (1984)).

119. Brief for the National Committees of the Libertarian Party and the New Alliance Party at 6, 3.

120. Marginalia on cert petition pool memo, Box 598, HAB-LOC.

121. Friedman, "Limitations of Labeling," 231–32.

122. 505 U.S. at 695 (Kennedy, J., joined by Blackmun and Stevens, J. J., and Souter, J. (in part), concurring in the judgments) (italics added).

123. Ibid., 693–94.

124. 505 U.S. at 678–83; 505 U.S. at 686–93 (O'Connor, J., concurring in No. 91-155 and concurring in the judgment in No. 91-339).

125. 505 U.S. at 680.

126. 505 U.S. at 693, 697 (Kennedy, J., joined by Blackmun and Stevens, J.J., and Souter, J. (in part), concurring in the judgments).

127. 460 U.S. 37 (1983).

128. Edward J. Neveril, "'Objective' Approaches to the Public Forum Doctrine: The First Amendment at the Mercy of Architectural Chicanery," *Northwestern University Law Review* 90 (1996): 1189, quoting Lillian R. BeVier, "Rehabilitating Public Forum Doctrine: In Defense of Categories," *Supreme Court Review* 1992 (1992): 103.

129. Neveril, "'Objective' Approaches," 1190 n32 (providing a bibliographical summary of the major critical works).

130. 505 U.S. at 693 (italics added) (Kennedy, J., joined by Blackmun and Stevens, J.J., and Souter, J. (in part), concurring in the judgments).

131. Ibid., 693–94, 695.

132. Ibid., 696.

133. Ibid., 696 (italics added).

134. Ibid., 702.

135. Richard W. Garnett, "William H. Rehnquist: A Life Lived Greatly, and Well," *Yale Law Journal* 115 (2006): 1849. I am grateful to Barbara Aronstein Black, Eric Freedman, Charles Hallinan, and Edward Jocque for all providing valuable responses to my H-Law listserv request for information about this quotation.

136. 505 U.S. 377 (1992).

137. 504 U.S. 191, 198 (1992).

138. Gerald Gunther, "Foreword: In Search of Evolving Doctrine on a Changing Court: A Model for a Newer Equal Protection," *Harvard Law Review* 86 (1972): 8.

139. 504 U.S. at 197.

140. Ibid., 206. Blackmun's opinion only spoke for a plurality because Justice Scalia concurred in the judgment only, separately concluding that the case did not involve either a public forum ("because restrictions on speech around polling places on election day are as venerable a part of the American tradition as the secret ballot") or a viewpoint-based restriction of speech. 504 U.S. at 214 (Scalia, J., concurring in the judgment).

141. 504 U.S. at 193, quoting 384 U.S. 214, 218 (1966).

142. 504 U.S. at 218 (Stevens, J., joined by O'Connor and Souter, JJ., dissenting).

143. Ibid., 218–19.

144. Memo from Stephanie Dangel to Justice Blackmun, 23 March 1992, Box 589, HAB-LOC.

145. See the first draft of Justice Blackmun's opinion in *Freeman*, 8 January 1992, Box 589, HAB-LOC.

146. Memos from Stephanie Dangel to Justice Blackmun, 18 and 20 March 1992, Box 589, HAB-LOC.

147. 502 U.S. at 124–25 (Kennedy, J., concurring in the judgment) (italics added).

148. Letter from Justice Blackmun to Justice Kennedy, 24 March 1992, Box 589, HAB-LOC.

149. Memo from Stephanie Dangel to Justice Blackmun, 24 March 1992, Box 589, HAB-LOC.

150. Memo from Justice Kennedy to Justice Blackmun, 26 March 1992, Box 589, HAB-LOC.

151. 504 U.S. at 213 (Kennedy, J., concurring).

152. Ibid.

153. 408 U.S. at 95.

154. 535 U.S. at 253; Justice Kennedy quoted in Goldstein and Lane, "At D.C. School," 17(A).

Chapter 3

1. Quoted in Jeffrey Rosen, "The Agonizer," *New Yorker*, 11 November 1996, 86.

2. 511 U.S. 127 (1994).

3. First draft of Justice Kennedy's concurrence in the judgment in *J.E.B.*, 31 March 1994, Box 636, Harry A. Blackmun Papers, Manuscript Division, Library of Congress, Washington, D.C. [hereafter HAB-LOC].

4. Memo from Michelle Alexander to Justice Blackmun, 31 March 1994, Box 636, HAB-LOC.

5. 511 U.S. at 153 (Kennedy, J., concurring in the judgment).

6. Ibid., 153–54 (italics added). Kennedy also observed: "We do not prohibit racial and gender bias in jury selection only to encourage it in jury deliberations." Ibid., 153. This statement raises an interesting question about whether it is really consistent with libertarianism. An objection that it is inconsistent would be grounded in the following argument. One of the key aims of libertarianism is to check (to place specific limits on) the influence of government on people's lives, in order, among other things, to preserve the liberty and decision making autonomy of individuals. Therefore, voting one's conscience during jury deliberations is surely preferable to the alternative—placing in the hands of government the power to determine the guilt or innocence of the accused. As stated in a classic text on the principles of trial by jury, "trial 'by the country,' or by the people, [is] in preference to a trial by the government." Why? The answer is simple: "to guard against every species of oppression by the government." Lysander Spooner, "An Essay on the Trial by Jury (1852)," in *The Collected Works of Lysander Spooner: Volume 2, Legal Writings (I)*, ed. Charles Shively (Weston, MA: M&S Press, 1971), 6. To be sure, this is a quintessentially libertarian argument. How, then, is Kennedy's concern about individual jurors' biased decision making consistent with this? After all, it has been suggested (albeit controversially), that ethnic minorities would actually benefit from race-based jury nullification (which is, essentially, the broad topic that we are discussing here—the power of a jury to find a person innocent not because of the facts of a case but because it considers the law unjust—it is the law that is put on trial). This, it is argued, is because their "fellow men" could

protect them from an otherwise discriminatory (white-dominated) criminal justice system. Paul Butler, "Racially Based Jury Nullification: Black Power in the Criminal Justice System," *Yale Law Journal* 105 (December 1995): 677–725. For an excellent reply to Butler's arguments and suggestions of alternative approaches, see Long X. Do, "Jury Nullification and Race-Conscious Reasonable Doubt: Overlapping Reifications of Commonsense Justice and the Potential Voir Dire Mistake," *UCLA Law Review* 47 (August 2000): 1843–83. However, it should be quite clear that such an approach really is not at all libertarian because it is not pursuing the empowerment of the individual for individual liberty's sake. Rather, it is based on the assumption that a group in society, whose judgment is simply being substituted for the government, is thinking for those that *it* perceives as its members. In *J.E.B.*, it was this kind of group paternalism that Kennedy hoped would not prevail.

7. For a detailed discussion of this, see H. N. Hirsch, *A Theory of Liberty: The Constitution and Minorities* (New York: Routledge, 1992), chapter 5.

8. Gerald Gunther, "Foreword: In Search of Evolving Doctrine on a Changing Court: A Model for a Newer Equal Protection," *Harvard Law Review* 86 (November 1972): 8; Richard A. Epstein, "A Rational Basis for Affirmative Action: A Shaky but Classical Liberal Defense," *Michigan Law Review* 100 (August 2002): 2044.

9. 505 U.S. 577 (1992).

10. Ibid., 591.

11. In fact, beyond the Supreme Court, federal judges have used the term extremely sparingly. It has only appeared in six other federal opinions (LexisNexis search, 24 June, 2008).

12. Numerous articles explicitly discussing a judge's "constitutional vision" simply use the term as a "jurisprudence" synonym. For example, on William Brennan's "constitutional vision," see Frank I. Michelman, "Symposium: Reason, Passion & the Progress of Law: Remembering and Advancing the Constitutional Vision of Justice William J. Brennan," *Harvard Civil Rights Civil–Liberties Law Review* 33 (Summer 1998): 325–32; Joshua E. Rosenkranz, "Remembering and Advancing the Constitutional Vision of Justice William J. Brennan Jr.: Foreword," *New York Law School Law Review* 43 (1999): 1–7. On Thurgood Marshall, see U. W. Clemon and Bryan K. Fair, "Lawyers, Civil Disobedience, and Equality in the Twenty-First Century: Lessons from Two American Heroes," *Alabama Law Review* 54 (Spring 2003): 966, 969, 979; Cass R. Sunstein, "On Marshall's Conception of Equality," *Stanford Law Review* 44 (Summer 1992): 1267–75. On William Rehnquist, see Nat Stern, "State Action, Establishment Clause, and Defamation: Blueprints for Civil Liberties in the Rehnquist Court," *University of Cincinnati Law Review* 57 (1989): 1231, 1241. On Byron White, see Richard Cordray, "Justice White and the Exercise of Judicial Power: Justice White and the Democratic-Republicans," *University of Colorado Law Review* 74 (Fall 2003): 1319–26; Rex E. Lee and Richard G. Wilkins, "On Greatness and Constitutional Vision: Justice Byron R. White," *Brigham Young University Law Review* 1994 (1994): 291–312.

13. 505 U.S. at 591.

14. On the executive branch, see Dawn E. Johnsen, "Ronald Reagan and the Rehnquist Court on Congressional Power: Presidential Influences on Constitutional Change," *Indiana Law Journal* 78 (Winter/Spring 2003): 363–412. On the legislative

branch, see David Barron, "Constitutionalism in the Shadow of Doctrine: The President's Non-Enforcement Power," *Law & Contemporary Problems* 63 (Winter/Spring 2000): 75, 89.

15. Peter M. Gerhart, "The Two Constitutional Visions of the World Trade Organization," *University of Pennsylvania Journal of International Economic Law* 24 (Spring 2003): 1–75.

16. James Gray Pope, "Labor's Constitution of Freedom," *Yale Law Journal* 106 (January 1997): 941–1031.

17. H. W. Perry Jr. and L. A. Powe Jr., "The Political Battle for the Constitution," *Constitutional Commentary* 21 (Winter 2004): 641–96.

18. Mark A. Graber, "Popular Constitutionalism, Judicial Supremacy, and the Complete Lincoln-Douglas Debates," *Chicago-Kent Law Review* 81 (2006): 923–51.

19. David J. Barron, "Fighting Federalism with Federalism: If It's Not Just a Battle between Federalists and Nationalists, What Is It?" *Fordham Law Review* 74 (March 2006): 2081–121.

20. Mark A. Graber, "Social Democracy and Constitutional Theory: An Institutional Perspective," *Fordham Law Review* 69 (April 2001): 1969–87.

21. Joel K. Goldstein, "The New Constitutional Vice Presidency," *Wake Forest Law Review* 30 (Fall 1995): 505–61.

22. Mark A. Graber, *Dred Scott and the Problem of Constitutional Evil* (New York: Cambridge University Press, 2006), 3.

23. Walter F. Murphy, "Constitutions, Constitutionalism, and Democracy," in *Constitutionalism and Democracy: Transitions in the Contemporary World*, ed. Douglas Greenberg et al. (New York: Oxford University Press, 1993), 10 (italics added). How much these constitutional visions are directed by the Constitution's text is, of course, an open question. See Sanford Levinson, *Constitutional Faith* (Princeton, NJ: Princeton University Press, 1988); Larry D. Kramer, *The People Themselves: Popular Constitutionalism and Judicial Review* (New York: Oxford University Press, 2004).

24. Anthony M. Kennedy, Judge, McGeorge Commencement Speech 4, McGeorge School of Law of the University of the Pacific Commencement, Sacramento, CA, 30 May 1981. Committee on the Judiciary, Judiciary Nominations files, A. Kennedy, Sup. Court, 100th Congress, Records of the Senate, Record Group 46, National Archives, Washington, D.C. [hereafter Sen. RG46, NAB].

25. I am grateful to Doug Edlin for drawing my attention to this potential response.

26. *Metro Broadcasting v. FCC*, 497 U.S. 547, 636 (1990) (Kennedy, J., joined by Scalia, J., dissenting).

27. Douglas Rae et al., *Equalities* (Cambridge, MA: Harvard University Press, 1981), 20, 43 (and generally, chapter 2).

28. Artemus Ward, "The Gay Rights Jurisprudence of Anthony Kennedy: An Institutional Analysis" (paper presented at the annual meeting of the Midwest Political Science Association, Chicago, 15–18 April 2004), 4.

29. *The Gauer Distinguished Lecture in Law and Public Policy, Vol. 1: The Constitution and the Spirit of Freedom by Anthony M. Kennedy Associate Justice Supreme Court of the United States of America* (Washington, DC.: National Legal Center for the Public Interest, 1990), 18.

30. Ward, "Gay Rights Jurisprudence," 4.

31. Arthur S. Leonard, "Kennedy and the Gays, Again," *New York Native*, 7 December 1987, 18. A copy of this article was filed in the Senate Judiciary Committee's materials pertaining to the Kennedy nomination.

32. 517 U.S. 620, 633 (1996).

33. 539 U.S. 558 (2003). Jan Crawford Greenburg, *Supreme Conflict: The Inside Story of the Struggle for Control of the United States Supreme Court* (New York: Penguin, 2007), 37.

34. *Beller v. Middendorf*, 632 F.2d 788 (9th Cir. 1980). Maggie Gallagher, "Here Comes the Judge," *National Review*, 18 December 1987, 33.

35. SECNAVINST 1900.9A., quoted at 632 F.2d at 803.

36. 632 F.2d at 803.

37. Ibid., 810 (quotation), and generally see 810–12. The high level of deference to the needs of the armed forces pervades all levels of the federal judiciary. See, for example, Mark Strasser, "Unconstitutional? Don't Ask; If It Is, Don't Tell: On Deference, Rationality, and the Constitution," *University of Colorado Law Review* 66 (1995): 375–460; Steven B. Lichtman, "The Justices and the Generals: A Critical Examination of the U.S. Supreme Court's Tradition of Deference to the Military, 1918–2004," *Maryland Law Review* 65 (2006): 907–64.

38. 632 F.2d at 812.

39. Ibid., 806.

40. Ibid., 809.

41. Ibid., 806, citation omitted. The citation was to Laurence H. Tribe, "Structural Due Process," *Harvard Civil Rights-Civil Liberties Law Review* 10 (1975): 282–83, n42.

42. The citations are at 632 F.2d at 809.

43. United States Senate, Committee on the Judiciary, *Hearings on the Nomination of Anthony M. Kennedy to be Associate Justice of the Supreme Court of the United States*, 100th Cong., 1st sess., 14–16 December 1987, 177.

44. 632 F.2d at 809.

45. Several scholars have concluded that in *Beller* Kennedy employed a standard of review somewhere between rational basis and strict scrutiny. For example, see Ward, "Gay Rights Jurisprudence," 6; Joyce Murdoch and Deb Price, *Courting Justice: Gay Men and Lesbians v. the Supreme Court* (New York: Basic Books, 2001), 210.

46. 632 F.2d at 807 (italics added).

47. Ibid., 808, n20.

48. Memo from Trait Trussell and Colleagues at the Commission on the Bicentennial of the United States Constitution to Everett C. Ladd, 10 April 1987; Decision Memos (March–April 1987) file; Office of the Chairman, Correspondence of the Chairman, 1985–1991, Correspondence thru Equal Justice Under Law, Box 1 NN3-220-92-004 H.M. 1992; Records of Temporary Committees, Commissions & Boards: Commission on the Bicentennial of the U.S. Constitution, Record Group 220; National Archives and Records Administration at College Park, MD [hereafter Trussell memo].

49. Sandy Levinson's book remains the best description of this role that the Constitution plays in American life. See Levinson, *Faith*.

50. Ronald Dworkin, "The *Defunis* Case: The Right to Go to Law School (1976)," in *Affirmative Action: Social Justice or Reverse Discrimination*, eds. Francis J. Beckwith and Todd E. Jones (Amherst, NY: Prometheus, 1997), 73.

51. *Corfield v. Coryell*, 6 Fed. Cas. 546, 551-52 (Cir. Ct. 1823) (No. 3,230) (Washington, J); Randy E. Barnett, *Restoring the Lost Constitution: The Presumption of Liberty* (Princeton, NJ: Princeton University Press, 2004), chapter 8. Also see Michael Kent Curtis, *No State Shall Abridge: The Fourteenth Amendment and the Bill of Rights* (Durham, NC: Duke University Press, 1986); Edward S. Corwin, "The Basic Doctrine of American Constitutional Law," *Michigan Law Review* 12 (1914): 275.

52. 83 U.S. 36 (1873). The *Slaughterhouse Cases* questioned the constitutionality of a Louisiana state law that gave a single slaughterhouse the exclusive rights to slaughter livestock in the city of New Orleans—the law was justified as an exercise of the state's police power (enabling the state to legislate for the health, safety, and welfare of its citizens). The constitutionality of the statute was contested on the grounds that it violated the Thirteenth and Fourteenth Amendments because it prohibited individuals from exercising their "common rights"—in this case the right to engage in the work of one's choice. The Court upheld the law, concluding that the Privileges or Immunities Clause of the Fourteenth Amendment only applies to U.S. citizens; therefore, it only protects a limited number of rights—those already expressly or implicitly stated in the Constitution.

53. Barnett, *Presumption of Liberty*, 208n51 (italics added).

54. William Raymond Smith, "The Rhetoric of the Declaration of Independence," *College English* 26, no. 4 (January 1965): 306.

55. Indeed, as Will Kymlicka reminds us, it would be profoundly inhumane (and therefore inconsistent with libertarian principles) to argue otherwise. Will Kymlicka, *Contemporary Political Philosophy: An Introduction*, 2nd ed. (Oxford: Oxford University Press, 2002), 156.

56. Gunther, "Evolving Doctrine," 8–10.

57. Ibid., 17.

58. Memo from Justice Rehnquist to Justice Brennan, 30 January 1976, Box 219, HAB-LOC.

59. There were notable exceptions. For example, Justice Thurgood Marshall insisted on a sliding scale of equal protection review based on "the constitutional and societal importance of the interest adversely affected and the recognized invidiousness of the basis upon which the particular classification is drawn." (*San Antonio Independent School District v. Rodriguez*, 411 U.S. 1, 99 (1973) (Marshall, J., dissenting), quoted in *City of Cleburne v. Cleburne Living Center*, 473 U.S. 432, 460 (1985) (Marshall, J., joined by Brennan and Blackmun, JJ., concurring in the judgment in part and dissenting in part).

60. Gunther, "Evolving Doctrine," 12.

61. 473 U.S. at 451 (Stevens, J., joined by Burger, CJ., concurring).

62. 427 U.S. 307 (1976).

63. Powell summarized the views of his colleagues when he wrote: "My zeal for writing has been so thoroughly dampened by this spring's experience." Memo to the conference from Justice Powell, 15 June 1976, Box 219, HAB-LOC.

64. 427 U.S. at 312–13 (italics added).

65. Handwritten note from Justice Powell to Justice Blackmun, 7 June 1976, Box 219, HAB-LOC.

66. Barnett, *Presumption of Liberty*, 230.

67. 348 U.S. 483, 487 (1955) (emphasis added). For a prominent example of Rehnquist's objections to Brennan's opinion, see memo from Justice Rehnquist to Justice Brennan, 30 January 1976, Box 219, HAB-LOC (arguing that rational basis review should be "simply stated and ought to virtually foreclose judicial invalidation except in the rare, rare case where the legislature has all but run amok and acted in a patently arbitrary manner").

68. Memo from Justice Brennan to Justice Rehnquist, 9 February 1976, Box 219, HAB-LOC.

69. Memo from William H. Block to Justice Blackmun, 19 May 1976, Box 219, HAB-LOC.

70. 429 U.S. 190 (1976).

71. Such was Stevens's influence on the post-*Murgia* case law, that while the memos in *Murgia* suggested that Justice Rehnquist might have maneuvered himself into a position from which he could direct the Court's equal protection jurisprudence (albeit, by toning down some of the rhetoric that would have constituted his ideal approach), in reality it was the (at the time lonely) position staked out by Stevens that would ultimately prevail. Rehnquist's objection to any attempt to give rational basis review some teeth was based on his belief that it was not the Court's place to second-guess legislative equality decisions unless a clear "suspect classification" was involved. With regard to *Murgia*, see the memos between Justices Rehnquist and Powell, 25 May and 9 June 1976, Box 219, HAB-LOC.

72. 429 U.S. at 197. Lee Epstein and Jack Knight, *The Choices Justices Make* (Washington, DC: CQ Press, 1997).

73. 429 U.S. at 211–12 (Stevens, J. concurring).

74. Ibid., 213.

75. 449 U.S. 166 (1980).

76. Memo from Justice Rehnquist to Justice Stevens, 24 November 1980; also see the memos between Justices Stevens, Rehnquist, and Powell, 10, 13, 17 November 1980; Box 322, HAB-LOC. Also useful is the memo from Justice Powell to Justice Rehnquist, 10 November 1980; and the memo from Justice Rehnquist to Justice Stevens, 24 November 1980; Box 268, Thurgood Marshall Papers, Manuscript Division, Library of Congress, Washington, D.C. [hereafter TM-LOC].

77. First draft, Justice Stevens's *Fritz* concurrence in the judgment, 25 November, 1980, Box 322, HAB-LOC.

78. Marginalia, Justice Blackmun's copy of the first draft of Justice Stevens's concurrence in *City of Cleburne*, 19 June, 1985, Box 428, HAB-LOC.

79. Quoted in 473 U.S. at 436n3.

80. Quoted in Ibid., 437.

81. Ibid., 448–50.

82. Ibid., 449.

83. Ibid., 440.

84. Ibid., 440–42.

85. Ibid., 441 (emphasis added).

86. After he circulated the second draft of the concurrence, in which he had made a small change to one footnote, Stevens almost lost Burger and needed to return to the footnote language in the first draft before the Chief was satisfied that the footnote did not undermine what he read to be Stevens's main point: "opposition to the *range* of tests." Letter from Chief Justice Burger to Justice Stevens, 24 June 1985, Box 428, HAB-LOC; first, second, and third drafts of Justice Stevens's *City of Cleburne* concurrence, 19, 21, and 26 June 1985, Box 428 HAB-LOC (first and third drafts); Box I: 684, Papers of William J. Brennan Jr., Manuscript Division, Library of Congress, Washington, DC, [hereafter WJB-LOC] (second draft).

87. 473 U.S. at 450.

88. Ibid., 451.

89. Ibid., 452.

90. 413 U.S. 528, 534 (1973) (italics added).

91. Summaries and history of opinions of Justice Brennan, October term, 1972, compiled by law clerks William J. Maledon, Gerald M. Rosberg, and Geoffrey R. Stone, case history of *Moreno*, lxxiii–lxxiv, Box II:6, WJB-LOC. Also see memo from Justice Brennan to Justice Douglas, 11 May 1973, Box I:302, WJB-LOC.

92. Brief for the Appellants 9, *United States Department of Agriculture v. Moreno*, No. 72-534, 1973 WL 173826 (U.S.); 410 U.S. 113 (1973).

93. 413 U.S. at 535n7 (quoting 345 F.Supp. 310, 314 (1972)) (italics added).

94. Brennan law clerks' case history of *Moreno*, lxxiii–lxxiv.

95. Comment of Justice Kennedy, in Transcript of Oral Argument, 4, *Romer v. Evans*, (No. 94-1039), WL 605822. Audio recording available at "Oyez: *Romer v. Evans*, 517 U.S. 620 (1996), U.S. Supreme Court Oral Argument," http://www.oyez.org/cases/1990-1999/1995/1995_94_1039/argument/ (accessed 24 June 2008).

96. Tom Kenworthy, "Colorado Springs Culture Wars; After Years of Conservatism, a March Toward Middle Ground Is Picking Up Speed in the 'Vatican of Evangelical Christianity,'" *Washington Post*, 18 November 1997, 3(A).

97. John Daniel Dailey and Paul Farley, "Colorado's Amendment 2: A Result in Search of a Reason," *Harvard Journal of Law and Public Policy* 20 (Fall 1996): 216–17.

98. Ibid., 216.

99. Ibid., 217 (quoting Kevin Tebedo, one of the main proponents of Amendment 2).

100. Quoted at 517 U.S. at 624.

101. Quoted in Joan Biskupic, "Gay Rights Case Closely Watched at High Court," *Washington Post*, 10 October 1995 1(A).

102. 517 U.S. at 623. For audio of the opinion announcement in *Romer*, see "Oyez: *Romer v. Evans*, 517 U.S. 620 (1996), U.S. Supreme Court Opinion Announcement," http://www.oyez.org/cases/1990-1999/1995/1995_94_1039/opinion/ (accessed 24 June 2008).

103. Ward, "Gay Rights Jurisprudence," 22. The announcement of the decision in *Romer* was profoundly symbolic because it came very close to the 100th anniversary

of the decision in *Plessy*. Mark Tushnet, *A Court Divided: The Rehnquist Court and the Future of Constitutional Law* (New York: W. W. Norton, 2005), 167.

104. 517 U.S. at 634, quoting 413 U.S. at 534 (Kennedy added the italics). In his dissenting opinion in *Romer*, Justice Scalia described Kennedy's use of Brennan's *Moreno* opinion as "nothing short of insulting" to the people of Colorado. 517 U.S. at 652 (Scalia, J., joined by Rehnquist, CJ., and Thomas, J., dissenting).

105. 517 U.S. at 627 (italics added).

106. Ibid., 630.

107. Ibid., 627, 633.

108. *Evans v. Romer*, 854 P.2d 1270 (Colo. 1993).

109. 377 U.S. 713, 736–37 (1964).

110. 377 U.S. 533, 561 (1964).

111. For a discussion of the significance of the strict scrutiny-fundamental rights equal protection holding in *Lucas*, see Helen J. Knowles, "May It Please the Court?: The Solicitor General's Not So 'Special' Relationship—Archibald Cox and the 1963–1964 Reapportionment Cases," *Journal of Supreme Court History* 31, no. 3 (July 2006): 289–91.

112. 517 U.S. at 625.

113. I am grateful to Mark Graber for encouraging me to think about this aspect of *Romer*.

114. *Board of Trustees of University of Alabama v. Garrett*, 531 U.S. 356, 374 (2001) (Kennedy, J., joined by O'Connor, J., concurring).

115. 517 U.S. at 632.

116. 449 U.S. at 181 (Stevens, J., concurring), quoted at 517 U.S. at 633.

117. 517 U.S. at 632 (italics added).

118. 517 U.S. at 626.

119. 478 U.S. 186 (1986). Dubofsky distinguished *Romer* from *Bowers* on the basis that while the 1986 precedent addressed homosexual *conduct*, Amendment 2 was directed at homosexual *orientation*. Discussion of this distinction consumed a considerable amount of the oral argument. Brief for the Respondents at 45n32, *Romer v. Evans*, 517 U.S. 620 (1996) (No. 94-1039), 1995 WL 17008447; *Romer* oral argument, 53–54. Justice Scalia mentioned this in his dissenting opinion. 517 U.S. at 641 (Scalia, J., joined by Rehnquist, CJ., and Thomas, J., dissenting).

120. 517 U.S. at 636 (Scalia, J., joined by Rehnquist, CJ., and Thomas, J., dissenting).

121. Antonin Scalia, "Of Democracy, Morality and the Majority (Rome Address Transcript)," *Origins* 26, no. 6 (1996): 87.

122. 517 U.S. at 644, 636 (Scalia, J., joined by Rehnquist, CJ., and Thomas, J., dissenting).

123. Letter from Justice Blackmun to Justice Kennedy, 23 May 1996; letter from Justice Kennedy to Justice Blackmun, 28 May 1996; Box 1405, HAB-LOC.

124. Peter Irons, *The Courage of Their Convictions: Sixteen Americans Who Fought Their Way to the Supreme Court* (New York: Penguin, 1990), 381–83.

125. Georgia Code Ann. § 16-6-2 (1984), quoted in 478 U.S. 186, 188n1 (1986).

126. 478 U.S. at 190, 191–92 (quoting *Moore v. East Cleveland*, 431 U.S. 494, 503 (1977) (opinion of Powell, J.)); 478 U.S. at 194 (quoting *Palko v. Connecticut*, 302 U.S. 319, 325 (1937)).

127. 478 U.S. at 196.

128. 394 U.S. 557, 559 (1969).

129. Letter from Justice Brennan to Justice Douglas, 30 December 1971; first draft of *Eisenstadt v. Baird*, Box I:258, WJB-LOC.

130. *Bowers* conference notes, Box 451, HAB-LOC.

131. Irons, *Courage of Their Convictions*, 392–403. Briefs of National Gay Rights Advocates et al.; Lambda Legal Defense and Education Fund Inc. et al.; Lesbian Rights Project et al. as Amici Curiae Supporting Respondents, *Bowers v. Hardwick*, 478 U.S. 186 (1986) (No. 85-140).

132. Brief for Respondent at 46 (italics added), *Bowers v. Hardwick*, 478 U.S. 186 (1986) (No. 85-140).

133. 405 U.S. 438, 453 (1972).

134. Ibid.

135. Laurence H. Tribe, "*Lawrence v. Texas*: The 'Fundamental Right' That Dare Not Speak Its Name," *Harvard Law Review* 117 (April 2004): 1939.

136. Transcript of oral argument at 34 (italics added), *Bowers v. Hardwick*, 478 U.S. 186 (1986) (No. 85-140) 1986 U.S. Trans Lexis 74.

137. Ibid.

138. 523 F.2d 716, 719–20 (CA7 1975) (footnotes omitted), *cert. denied*, 425 U.S. 916 (1976), quoted at 478 U.S. at 217 (1986) (Stevens, J., joined by Brennan and Marshall, JJ., dissenting). Since *Bowers*, Stevens has included this quotation, or significant parts of it, in the following opinions: *Thornburgh v. American College of Obstetricians and Gynecologists*, 476 U.S. 747, 781n11 (1986) (Stevens, J., concurring); *Washington v. Glucksberg*, 521 U.S. 702, 744–45 (1997) (Stevens, J., concurring in the judgments); *Vacco v. Quill*, 521 U.S. 793, 809 (1997), (Stevens, J., concurring in the judgments).

139. John Paul Stevens, "Learning on the Job," *Fordham Law Review* 74 (March 2006): 1563.

140. Justice Stevens quoted in Jeffrey Rosen, "The Dissenter," *New York Times Magazine*, 23 September 2007, 54.

141. 45 Eur. Ct. H. R. (1981) P 52, discussed in Anthony M. Kennedy, Judge, "Unenumerated Rights and the Dictates of Judicial Restraint," Speech, Canadian Institute for Advanced Legal Studies, The Stanford Lectures, Palo Alto, CA, 24 July–1 August 1986, 10–11 [Sen. RG46 NAB]. For the *Lawrence* reference, see 539 U.S. at 573.

142. Stanford Lecture, 13–14.

143. Ibid., 2.

144. Tushnet, *A Court Divided*, 169.

145. *Lawrence v. State*, 41 S.W.3d 349 (Tex. App. Houston 14th Dist., 2001), *cert. granted*, 537 U.S. 1044 (2002); 539 U.S. 558, 578 (2003).

146. Brief for the Petitioners, 2, *Lawrence v. Texas*, No. 02-102, 2002 U.S. Briefs 102; 539 U.S. at 562–63.

147. Tex. Penal Code Ann. §§ 21.06(a), 21.01(1) (2003), quoted in 539 U.S. at 563.

148. Michael Dorf, quoted in Richard Brust, "The Man in the Middle," *ABA Journal* 89 (October 2003): 24.

149. Greenburg, *Supreme Conflict*, 37.

150. Ward, "Gay Rights Jurisprudence," 1.

151. 539 U.S. at 579 (O'Connor, J., concurring in the judgment).

152. Ibid., 584–85.

153. Instead of referring to O'Connor's opinion, Kennedy wrote: "As an alternative argument in this case, counsel for the petitioners and some *amici* contend that *Romer* provides the basis for declaring the Texas statute invalid under the Equal Protection Clause." 539 U.S. at 574.

154. For example, see Tushnet, *A Court Divided*, chapter 6.

155. Elizabeth Price Foley, *Liberty for All: Reclaiming Individual Privacy in a New Era of Public Morality* (New Haven, CT: Yale University Press, 2006), xiii, 62.

156. Ibid., 63–64.

157. 539 U.S. at 575.

158. Ibid.

159. 478 U.S. at 216 (Stevens, J., joined by Brennan and Marshall, JJ., dissenting) (italics added), quoted at 539 U.S. at 577–78.

160. 539 U.S. at 578.

161. 539 U.S. at 567, 566 (italics added), quoting 478 U.S. at 190.

162. Michael Greve offers an interesting and very plausible defense of the argument that *Romer* was a defining moment in Scalia's gradual realization that through the 1990s he was experiencing a diminishment in the power of his own role on the Court. In 2004, Greve suggested that we were beginning to witness the emergence of a "new Scalia positivism" as the justice turned to legal positivism, a move that is part of a quest to restrain the federal judiciary in a way that structuralism and formalism cannot. Michael S. Greve, "New Scalia Positivism" (panel presentation at the annual meeting of the American Political Science Association, Chicago, 2–5 September 2004). Greve argued that the extent of this shift in the justice's jurisprudence became clear in 2004 in *Sosa v. Alvarez-Machain*, 542 U.S. 692 (2004), where in a concurrence Scalia did not acknowledge the existence of federal common law in the way he did when he wrote for the Court in 1988 in *Boyle v. United Technologies*, 487 U.S. 500 (1988). Interestingly, *Boyle* was one of the cases of the October 1987 term that was set down for reargument before the full Court (including the newly appointed Justice Kennedy) because the initial vote was 4–4. David G. Savage, *Turning Right: The Making of the Rehnquist Supreme Court* (New York: John Wiley & Sons, 1992), 192–94. Disillusionment following the decision in *Planned Parenthood v. Casey*, 505 U.S. 833 (1992) might be a strong candidate for explaining why Scalia felt the need to fashion a new, decidedly positivist approach to judicial restraint and rules-based adjudication. As Greve pointed out, however, in terms of chronology this decision is too close to *Boyle* and too far from *Alvarez* for it to have been the deciding factor. It is more likely that we saw the early indications of this jurisprudential transformation in "The Rule of Law as a Law of Rules" and *A Matter of Interpretation*, with a determination to integrate it into judicial opinions after *Romer*. See Antonin Scalia, *A Matter of Interpretation: Federal Courts and the Law* (Princeton, NJ: Princeton University Press, 1997); Antonin Scalia,

"The Rule of Law as a Law of Rules," *University of Chicago Law Review* 56 (Fall 1989): 1175–88. I would like to thank Dr. Greve for his input on this argument. Possible support for this timeline thesis can be found in correspondence between Justice Scalia and (then retired) Justice Blackmun at the end of the October 1995 term (the term during which the Court decided *Romer*). Letter from Justice Blackmun to Justice Scalia, 2 July 1996: "Dear Nino: I know that this has not been an easy year for you. But it is over with, and next October one will be rejuvenated and a new chapter will unfold. As a group or individually, we cannot get discouraged. May the summer be a good one for you"; letter from Justice Scalia to Justice Blackmun: "Dear Harry: How kind of you to write the nice note you did! You are right that I am more discouraged this year than I have been at the end of any of my previous nine terms up here. I am beginning to repeat myself, and don't see much use in it any more. I hope I will feel better in the fall. A cheery note from an old colleague—and one whom, God knows, I was not always on the same side with—sure does help. Many thanks—and have a pleasant summer," Box 1408, HAB-LOC.

163. 539 U.S. at 586 (Scalia, J., joined by Rehnquist, CJ., and Thomas, J., dissenting); 539 U.S. at 578.

164. For particularly good scholarly analyses of the opinion, see Tribe, "The 'Fundamental Right,'" and the following trio of articles and responses: Randy E. Barnett, "Justice Kennedy's Libertarian Revolution: *Lawrence v. Texas*," *Cato Supreme Court Review* (2003): 21–41; Dale Carpenter, "Is *Lawrence* Libertarian?," *Minnesota Law Review* 88 (May 2004); 1140–70; Randy E. Barnett, "Grading Justice Kennedy: A Reply to Professor Carpenter," *Minnesota Law Review* 89 (May 2005); 1582–90.

165. 539 U.S. at 586, 599 (Scalia, J., joined by Rehnquist, CJ., and Thomas, J., dissenting).

166. 539 U.S. at 567.

167. *Kennedy Sup. Ct. Nomination Hearings*, 149.

168. Ibid., 179–80.

169. 539 U.S. at 578–79.

170. 478 U.S. at 196; 539 U.S. at 599 (Scalia, J., joined by Rehnquist, CJ., and Thomas, J., dissenting).

171. 539 U.S. at 562 (italics added).

172. Katherine M. Franke, "The Domesticated Liberty of *Lawrence v. Texas*," *Columbia Law Review* 104 (June 2004): 1399.

173. 539 U.S. at 578, quoting *Planned Parenthood v. Casey*, 505 U.S. 833, 847 (1992) (italics added).

174. 539 U.S. at 567.

175. Earl M. Maltz, "Anthony Kennedy and the Jurisprudence of Respectable Conservatism," in *Rehnquist Justice: Understanding the Court Dynamic*, ed. Earl M. Maltz (Lawrence: University Press of Kansas, 2003), 153.

176. 539 U.S. at 571. As Professor Ward observes: "Perhaps the most remarkable aspect of Kennedy's opinion [in *Lawrence*] was his lengthy discussion of the history of laws regarding sexual conduct." Ward, "Gay Rights Jurisprudence," 17.

177. 539 U.S. at 571, quoting 505 U.S. at 850.

178. This desire also appears to have greatly affected Justice Kennedy's call to the American Bar Association to create a commission to produce recommendations pertaining to incarceration and sentencing standards. See Anthony M. Kennedy, "Speech at the American Bar Association Annual Meeting," 9 August 2003 (revised 14 August 2003) (paginated transcript on file at the Public Information Office, United States Supreme Court), 8; "ABA News Conference: The Justice Kennedy Commission Report on Incarceration," (C-SPAN, June 23, 2004).

179. 509 U.S. 312 (1993).

180. *Heller* conference notes, 24 March 1993; first draft, Justice Kennedy's *Heller* dissent, 14 June 1993; memo from Justice White to Justice Kennedy, 15 June 1993, Box 624, HAB-LOC.

181. The main difference in the wording of the final opinion was the change from "strict" to "heightened scrutiny." First draft, Kennedy *Heller* dissent, 18, 14 June 1993, Box 624, HAB-LOC; 509 U.S. at 319.

182. A year earlier, White castigated the majority (for whom Justice Kennedy wrote) in *National Railroad Passenger Corporation v. Boston & Maine Corp.* for its reliance on the "post hoc rationalization of Government lawyers attempting to explain a gap in the reasoning and fact finding of the Interstate Commerce Commission." 503 U.S. 407, 425 (1992) (White, J., joined by Blackmun and Thomas, JJ., dissenting). See Helen J. Knowles, "A Dialogue on Liberty: The Classical Liberal and Civic Educational Principles of Justice Kennedy's Vision of Judicial Power" (Ph.D. dissertation, Boston University, 2007), 307–10.

183. First four drafts of Justice Kennedy's *Heller* opinion, 17, 22, and 23 June 1993; memo from Justice Scalia to Justice Kennedy, 21 June 1993; first draft, Justice White's *Heller* opinion concurring in part and concurring in the judgment, 23 June 1993; Box 624, HAB-LOC.

184. 509 U.S. at 321–28.

185. John C. Jeffries Jr., *Justice Lewis F. Powell, Jr.* (New York: Charles Scribner's Sons, 1994), 521–30.

186. Justice Kennedy, quoted in Rosen, "Agonizer," 90.

Chapter 4

1. *Metro Broadcasting v. FCC*, 497 U.S. 547, 637 (1990) (Kennedy, J., joined by Scalia, J. dissenting).

2. *Metro Broadcasting* conference notes, 30 March 1990, Box 558, Harry A. Blackmun Papers, Manuscript Division, Library of Congress, Washington, DC. [hereafter HAB-LOC].

3. Ibid.

4. 497 U.S. at 631 (Kennedy, J., joined by Scalia, J., dissenting).

5. *Metro Broadcasting* conference notes.

6. 323 U.S. 214, 216 (1944).

7. Paul Brest, "In Defense of the Antidiscrimination Principle," *Harvard Law Review* 90 (November 1976): 6.

8. Memo from Justice Powell to the Court, 3n2, 5 January 1978, Box 260, HAB-LOC.

9. The "angriest dissenting opinion" refers to Justice Rehnquist's opinion in *United Steelworkers of America v. Weber*, 443 U.S. 193, 219 (1979) (Rehnquist, J., joined by Burger, CJ., dissenting). See Henry J. Abraham and Barbara A. Perry, *Freedom and the Court: Civil Rights & Liberties in the United States*, 8th ed. (Lawrence: University Press of Kansas, 2003), 491. For Nazi Germany and apartheid South Africa references, see 497 U.S. at 633n1 (Kennedy, J., joined by Scalia, J., dissenting); on eviscerating a precedent, see Stephen J. Breyer, "Hand-Down Statement, *Parents Involved in Community Schools v. Seattle School District No. 1*, No. 05-908, Thursday, June 28, 2007, Breyer, J., dissenting," http://www.scotusblog.com/movabletype/archives/Breyerr%20bench%20statement%206-28-07.pdf (accessed 3 July 2007).

10. Lazarus went on to say: "I admire the intellectually purity of Justice Scalia's thinking, even while disagreeing passionately with his conclusions." Memo from Edward Lazarus to Justice Blackmun, 20 December 1988, Box 517, HAB-LOC. He was talking about Justice Scalia's opinion concurring in the judgment in *Richmond v. Croson*, 488 U.S. 469, 520 (1989) (Scalia, J., concurring in the judgment). While Justice Kennedy agreed with much of the content of this concurrence, he wrote separately to distance himself from his colleague's absolutist language: "A rule of automatic invalidity for racial preferences in almost every case would be a significant break with our precedents that require a case-by-case test, I am not convinced we need adopt it at this point." 488 U.S. at 519 (Kennedy, J., concurring in part and concurring in the judgment).

11. Anne Wortham, "Individualism versus Racism," in *The Libertarian Alternative: Essays in Social and Political Philosophy*, ed. Tibor R. Machan (Chicago: Nelson-Hall, 1974), 405.

12. David Boaz, *Libertarianism: A Primer* (New York: Free Press, 1998), 229.

13. Recall that in the previous chapter we saw that Kennedy has not confined his use of Harlan's *Plessy* dissent to opinions in race-related cases. He opened his opinion in *Romer v. Evans* with one of the most famous phrases from the dissent: "One century ago, the first Justice Harlan admonished this Court that the Constitution 'neither knows nor tolerates classes among citizens.'" 517 U.S. 620, 623 (1996) (quoting *Plessy v. Ferguson*, 163 U.S. 537, 559 (1896) (Harlan, J., dissenting)).

14. *Parents Involved in Community Schools v. Seattle School District No. 1*; *Meredith v. Jefferson County Board of Education*, 127 S. Ct. 2738, 2796, 2797 (2007) (Kennedy, J. concurring).

15. Memo from Justice Blackmun to the Court, 1 May 1978, 6, Box I:441, Papers of William J. Brennan, Jr., Manuscript Division, Library of Congress, Washington, D.C. [hereafter WJB-LOC].

16. Quoted in Bill Maxwell, "Our Constitution Should Be Celebrated," *St. Petersburg Times (FL)*, 17 September 2006, 3(P).

17. 163 U.S. 537, 559 (1896) (Harlan, J., dissenting); 60 U.S. (19 How.) 393 (1857).

18. Quoted at 163 U.S. at 540.

19. United States Senate, Committee on the Judiciary, *Hearings on the Nomination of Anthony M. Kennedy to be Associate Justice of the Supreme Court of the United States*, 100th Cong., 1st sess., 14–16 December 1987, 201.

20. 163 U.S. at 559 (Harlan, J., dissenting).

21. Andrew Kull, *The Color-Blind Constitution* (Cambridge, MA: Harvard University Press, 1992), 6.

22. Brief for Plaintiff in Error in *Plessy*, quoted in Kull, *Color-Blind*, 119.

23. Ibid., 34. The document was the *Report of the Minority of the Committee of the Primary School Board, on the Caste Schools of the City of Boston; With Some Remarks on the City Solicitor's Opinion.*

24. *Kennedy Sup. Ct. Nomination Hearings*, 150.

25. Kull, *Color-Blind.*

26. As defined by the FCC, minorities were "those of Black, Hispanic Surnamed, American Eskimo, Aleut, American Indian and Asiatic American extraction." FCC policy statement quoted at 497 U.S. at 554n1.

27. 497 U.S. at 557.

28. *Statement of Policy on Minority Ownership of Broadcasting Facilities*, 68 F. C. C. 2d 979, 980-981 (footnotes omitted), quoted at 497 U.S. at 556.

29. 497 U.S. at 558–59. That minority ownership could trump community ties raised an interesting issue that Kennedy noted during oral argument when he expressed concern that one of the answers from Margaret Polivy, the attorney arguing for the private respondent, led to the conclusion that "there's no correlation required between the race of the owners and the racial composition of the community that it serves." Transcript of Oral Argument, 42, *Metro Broadcasting v. FCC* (No. 89-453), 1990 U.S. Trans Lexis 190, 28 March 1990. Audio recording available at "Oyez: *Metro Broadcasting Inc. v. FCC*, 497 U.S. 547 (1990), U.S. Supreme Court Oral Argument," http://www.oyez.org/cases/1980-1989/1989/1989_89_453/argument/ (accessed 11 June 2008).

30. "The Constitution's guarantee of equal protection binds the Federal Government as it does the States, and no lower level of scrutiny applies to the Federal Government's use of race classifications. . . .'It would be unthinkable that the same Constitution would impose a lesser duty on the Federal Government.' Consistent with this view, the Court has repeatedly indicated that 'the reach of the equal protection guarantee of the Fifth Amendment is coextensive with that of the Fourteenth.'" 497 U.S. at 604–5, quoting from *Brown v. Board of Education*, 347 U.S. 483, 500 (1954) and *United States v. Paradise*, 480 U.S. 149, 166, n16 (1987) (plurality opinion).

31. 497 U.S. at 568 (citations omitted) (quoting *Regents of the University of California v. Bakke*, 438 U.S. 265, 311–13 (1978)).

32. 497 U.S. at 564–66.

33. 497 U.S. at 637 (Kennedy, J., joined by Scalia, J., dissenting).

34. *Metro Broadcasting* Oral Argument, 29. Also see Scalia's comments at 34–36, 44–45. The closest Kennedy came, during oral argument, to publicizing his views was when he asked David M. Armstrong, counsel for the FCC: "Well, in your view, then, could the FCC require that every broadcast station in the United States devote one

hour a week to minority—the expression of minority views? . . . Assuming we can define that." *Metro Broadcasting* Oral Argument, 30.

35. *Metro Broadcasting* conference notes, 30 March 1990, Box 558, HAB-LOC.

36. Thomas M. Keck, *The Most Activist Supreme Court in History: The Road to Modern Judicial Conservatism* (Chicago: University of Chicago Press, 2004), 232; Thomas M. Keck, "From *Bakke* to *Grutter*: The Rise of Rights-Based Conservatism," in *The Supreme Court and American Political Development*, eds. Ronald Kahn and Ken I. Kersch (Lawrence: University Press of Kansas, 2006), 428.

37. For an interesting discussion of some of the complexities of this issue, see Jennifer Jackson Preece, *Minority Rights: Between Diversity and Community* (Cambridge: Polity, 2006), particularly chapter 3.

38. 497 U.S. at 632 (Kennedy, J., joined by Scalia, J., dissenting).

39. First draft, Justice Kennedy's *Metro Broadcasting* dissent, 25 June 1990, Box 558, HAB-LOC.

40. As he did seven years later in *Romer v. Evans*, 517 U.S. 620 (1996).

41. 497 U.S. at 631–32 (Kennedy, J., joined by Scalia, J., dissenting).

42. Ibid., 634–35.

43. Ibid., 635.

44. Ibid., 637–38.

45. 488 U.S. 469 (1989). First draft, Justice O'Connor's opinion for the Court in *Croson*, 28 October 1988; first draft, Justice Kennedy's opinion concurring in part and concurring in the judgment in *Croson*, 17 January 1989; both in Box 469, TM-LOC.

46. *Croson* conference notes, 7 October 1988, Box 517, HAB-LOC; 488 U.S. at 493 (italics added). As political scientist Tom Keck reminds us, it is significant that Scalia wrote separately in *Croson*. His decision to concur only in the judgment was one of his efforts to "express . . . impatience with her [O'Connor's] approach" in race-dependent cases, an impatience that would later be shared and expressed by Justice Thomas. Keck, "From *Bakke* to *Grutter*," 427. Scalia's opinion can be found at 488 U.S. at 520 (Scalia, J., concurring in the judgment).

47. *Rice v. Cayetano*, 528 U.S. 495, 523 (2000).

48. Neil A. Lewis, "An Ultimate Capital Insider—John Glover Roberts," *New York Times*, 20 July 2005, 1(A).

49. Comments of Ted Olson, Transcript of Oral Argument, 1, *Rice v. Cayetano*, (No. 98-818), 1999 U.S. Trans Lexis 71, 6 October 1999. Audio recording available at "Oyez: *Rice v. Cayetano*, 528 U.S. 495 (2000), U.S. Supreme Court Oral Argument," http://www.oyez.org/cases/1990-1999/1999/1999_98_818/argument/ (accessed 11 June 2008).

50. Haw. Rev. Stat. § 10-3 (1993), quoted at 528 U.S. at 508 (italics added).

51. 528 U.S. at 515.

52. Ibid., 499.

53. Ibid., 509–10.

54. 146 F.3d 1075, 1079 (CA9 1998), quoted in Ibid., 511.

55. In a 2006 interview, Kennedy was asked about the following passage from his opinion in *Cayetano*: "When the culture and way of life of a people are all but engulfed by a history beyond their control, their sense of loss may extend down through generations; and their dismay may be shared by many members of the larger community. As the State

of Hawaii attempts to address these realities, it must, as always, seek the political consensus that begins with a sense of shared purpose. One of the necessary beginning points is this principle: The Constitution of the United States, too, has become the heritage of all the citizens of Hawaii." 528 U.S. at 524. In response, Kennedy said: "What I tried to do in that sentence is to set up the equation within which we can begin thinking about this and evolving the necessary standards to ensure that there is a respect and an allegiance for the Constitution on the ground that it is committed to protecting human freedom." Quoted in Liam Skilling, "Features: Justice Anthony M. Kennedy," *Hawaii Bar Journal* (February 2007): 32. It is unsurprising that, a few months later, Justice Kennedy used very similar language to open his concurring opinion in *Parents Involved* (which is discussed in detail later in this chapter). He observed: "The Nation's schools strive to teach that our strength comes from people of different races, creeds, and cultures uniting in commitment to the freedom of all." 127 S. Ct. at 2788 (Kennedy, J., concurring).

56. *Kennedy Sup. Ct. Nomination Hearings*, 149.

57. 528 U.S. at 511–12.

58. Ibid., 512.

59. "Super-duper" is a reference to Senator Specter's description of *Roe v. Wade* during the nomination hearings of John Roberts. Adam Liptak, "Roberts Drops Hints in 'Precedent' Remarks," *New York Times*, 18 September 2005, 30(1).

60. 377 U.S. 533, 562 (1964).

61. 528 U.S. at 523.

62. Ibid., 524, 515.

63. Ibid., 517 (italics added).

64. Ibid., 523–24.

65. Memo from Chief Justice Burger to the Court, 21 October 1977, WJB I:441, WJB-LOC.

66. Ronald Dworkin, "The *Defunis* Case: The Right to Go to Law School (1976)," in *Affirmative Action: Social Justice or Reverse Discrimination?*, ed. Francis J. Beckwith and Todd E. Jones (Amherst, NY: Prometheus, 1997), 73.

67. Lyndon Baines Johnson, "To Fulfill These Rights: Commencement Address at Howard University (1965)," in *Affirmative Action: Social Justice or Reverse Discrimination?*, ed. Francis J. Beckwith and Todd E. Jones (Amherst, NY: Prometheus, 1997), 57.

68. The term "Liberal of 1960" is taken from the title of William Nelson's excellent essay about Byron White, one of President Kennedy's two Supreme Court appointments, who, like Kennedy, shared liberal values that could later be characterized as more moderate or conservative than liberal: William E. Nelson, "Byron White: A Liberal of 1960," in *The Warren Court in Historical and Political Perspective*, ed. Mark Tushnet (Charlottesville: University Press of Virginia, 1993), 139–54.

69. Lyndon B. Johnson, "Executive Order 11246—Equal Employment Opportunity," John T. Woolley and Gerhard Peters, *The American Presidency Project* [online]. Santa Barbara, CA: University of California (hosted), Gerhard Peters (database), http://www.presidency.ucsb.edu/ws/index.php?pid=59153 (accessed 17 August 2007).

70. Johnson, "To Fulfill These Rights: Commencement Address." On the relationship of this speech to the Moynihan Report, see Kull, *Color-Blind*, 186.

71. Johnson, "To Fulfill These Rights: Commencement Address," 57.

72. Ibid., 62.

73. Memo from Justice Thurgood Marshall to the Court, 3, 13 April 1978, Box I: 441, WJB-LOC.

74. For excellent overviews of the changes in political attitudes toward affirmative action in the 1960s and 1970s, see Thomas Sowell, "From Equal Opportunity to 'Affirmative Action,'" in *Affirmative Action: Social Justice or Reverse Discrimination?*, ed. Francis J. Beckwith and Todd E. Jones (Amherst, NY: Prometheus, 1997), 99–120; Kull, *Color-Blind*, chapter 11.

75. 438 U.S. 265 (1978).

76. William Greider, "The Scene; An Hour of History, Yes, But Without the Thunderclap," *Washington Post*, 29 June 1978, 1(A).

77. Memo from Justice Powell to the Court, 21 June 1978, Box I:442, WJB-LOC.

78. 438 U.S. at 274.

79. Ibid., 289, 288, 291.

80. Ibid., 289–90 (italics added), quoting *Shelley v. Kraemer*, 334 U.S. 1, 22 (1948).

81. Keck, "From *Bakke* to *Grutter*." For an excellent, detailed analysis of the different forces that contributed to the successful establishment of a network of legally oriented conservative interest groups, see Steven M. Teles, *The Rise of the Conservative Legal Movement* (Princeton, NJ: Princeton University Press, 2008).

82. Powell said: "The denial to respondent of this right to individualized consideration without regard to his race is the principal evil of petitioner's special admissions program." 438 U.S. at 318n52.

83. Kennedy was able to refer the senators to his opinion in *Bates v. The Pacific Maritime Association*, 744 F.2d 705 (CA 9) (1984). However, reading this decision reveals little about Kennedy's substantive views on race-based laws; as he noted in his testimony, the case simply involved a question of whether a consent decree entered into by an employer, requiring the adoption of affirmative action hiring practices, was still binding on the employer to whom the business was subsequently sold (the employees, equipment, and premises remained the same)—the court held that it was. *Kennedy Sup. Ct. Nomination Hearings*, 183.

84. Linda Greenhouse, "Hearings to Begin for Court Nominee," *New York Times*, 14 December 1987, 1(A); *Kennedy Sup. Ct. Nomination Hearings*, 182.

85. *Kennedy Sup. Ct. Nomination Hearings*, 182.

86. Ibid., 182 (italics added).

87. Remarks of Justice Kennedy, Transcript of Oral Argument, 5, *Grutter v. Bollinger* (No. 02-241), 2003 U.S. Trans Lexis 26, 1 April 2003. Audio recording available at "Oyez: *Grutter v. Bollinger*, 539 U.S. 306 (2003), U.S. Supreme Court Oral Argument," http://www.oyez.org/2000-2009/2002/2002_02_241/argument (accessed 11 June 2008).

88. "A Question of Fairness" (NBC News, June 6, 2003).

89. 539 U.S. 244 (2003). Gratz was joined as petitioner by Patrick Hamacher, another white Michigan resident denied admission to the University of Michigan.

90. 539 U.S. at 270.

91. 539 U.S. 306, 346 (2003) (Scalia, J., joined by Thomas, J., concurring in part and dissenting in part). The extent to which it is possible to reconcile *Gratz* and *Grutter* has

already been the subject of extensive academic commentary. For example, see Joel L. Selig, "The Michigan Affirmative Action Cases: Justice O'Connor, *Bakke* Redux, and the Mice That Roared but Did Not Prevail," *Temple Law Review* 76 (2003): 579–94; Paul R. Baier, "Of *Bakke*'s Balance, *Gratz* and *Grutter*: The Voice of Justice Powell," *Tulane Law Review* 78 (2004): 1955–2007; Martin H. Belsky, "Accentuate the Positive, Eliminate the Negative, Latch on to the Affirmative [Action], Do Mess with Mr. In-Between," *Tulsa Law Review* 39 (2003): 27–48.

92. 539 U.S. at 316.

93. Ibid., 334.

94. Ibid., 332.

95. Ibid., 337.

96. 515 U.S. 200, 204 (1995).

97. 515 U.S. at 239 (Scalia, J., concurring in part and concurring in the judgment). He referred readers to *Richmond v. J. A. Croson Co.*, 488 U.S. 469, 520 (1989) (Scalia, J., concurring in judgment).

98. *Adarand Constructors v. Pena*, 515 U.S. 200, 237 (1995).

99. 539 U.S. 306 at 326–27.

100. Letter from Justice Powell to Chief Justice Burger, 5 June 1980 (italics added), Box 248, TM-LOC.

101. 539 U.S. at 387 (Kennedy, J., dissenting).

102. Barbara A. Perry, *The Michigan Affirmative Action Cases* (Lawrence: University Press of Kansas, 2007), 50–51, 96; John C. Jeffries Jr., *Justice Lewis F. Powell, Jr.* (New York: Charles Scribner's Sons, 1994), 506–8; Joan Biskupic, *Sandra Day O'Connor: How the First Woman on the Supreme Court Became Its Most Influential Justice* (New York: Ecco, 2005), 174–77.

103. *Grutter* Oral Argument, 25.

104. Ibid., 30–31.

105. Ibid., 5.

106. 539 U.S. at 393 (Kennedy, J., dissenting).

107. Ibid., 389.

108. Akhil Reed Amar and Neal Kumar Katyal, "*Bakke*'s Fate," *UCLA Law Review* 43 (August 1996): 1774.

109. Ken Gormley, "Affirmative Action, for the Time Being," http://aad.english.ucsb.edu/docs/op81.html (accessed 11 June 2008). For an excellent discussion of Cox's argument in *Bakke*, see Ken Gormley, *Archibald Cox: Conscience of a Nation* (Reading, MA: Perseus, 1997), 401–5.

110. Memo from Chief Justice Burger to the Court, 6, 21 October 1977, Box I:441, WJB-LOC.

111. Memo from Justice Powell to the Court, 6–7, 5 January 1978, Box 260, HAB-LOC.

112. Memo from Justice Blackmun to the Court, 1 May 1978, Box I:441, WJB-LOC.

113. 539 U.S. at 343. According to Jeffrey Toobin, O'Connor wrote the twenty-five years passage and then instructed her clerk to insert it into the draft opinion. Jeffrey Toobin, *The Nine: Inside the Secret World of the Supreme Court* (New York: Doubleday, 2007), 224–25. In addition to encountering the skepticism of her colleagues regarding

her statement about rising test scores since 1978, significant conflicting data on this point were presented in amicus briefs in both support and opposition of petitioner Grutter. Interestingly, the only brief that specifically spoke to grades during the twenty-five year period from 1978–2003 seemed to suggest that the improvements had *not* occurred. Brief of the New York State Black and Puerto Rican Legislative Caucus as Amicus Curiae, 18, *Grutter v. Bollinger* (No. 02-241), 2002 U.S. Briefs 241.

114. 539 U.S. at 346 (Ginsburg, J., joined by Breyer, J., concurring).

115. 539 U.S. at 386–87 (Rehnquist, CJ., joined by Scalia, Kennedy, and Thomas, JJ., dissenting).

116. 539 U.S. at 348 (Scalia, J., joined by Thomas, J., concurring in part and dissenting in part).

117. 539 U.S. at 351 (Thomas, J., joined by Scalia, J. (in part), concurring in part and dissenting in part) (italics added).

118. 539 U.S. at 394 (Kennedy, J., dissenting) (italics added).

119. 347 U.S. 483 (1954).

120. Justice Kennedy, quoted in Stuart Taylor Jr., Evan Thomas, and Katie Connolly, "The Power Broker; In an Exclusive Interview, Justice Kennedy Discusses Life, Center Stage," *Newsweek*, 16 July 2007, 36.

121. Gerald N. Rosenberg, *The Hollow Hope: Can Courts Bring About Social Change?* (Chicago: University of Chicago Press, 1991), chapter 1.

122. Justice Kennedy quoted in Taylor, Thomas, and Connolly, "The Power Broker."

123. Breyer Hand-Down Statement.

124. Heather K. Gerken, "Justice Kennedy and the Domains of Equal Protection," *Harvard Law Review* 121 (November 2007): 106.

125. 127 S. Ct. at 2789 (Kennedy, J., concurring in part and concurring in the judgment).

126. 127 S. Ct. at 2836 (Breyer, J., joined by Stevens, Souter, and Ginsburg, JJ., dissenting).

127. 127 S. Ct. at 2743.

128. Austin Sarat and Thomas R. Kearns, "Beyond the Great Divide: Forms of Legal Scholarship and Everyday Life," in *Law in Everyday Life*, ed. Austin Sarat and Thomas R. Kearns (Ann Arbor: University of Michigan Press, 1995), 22, 58.

129. Jeffrey Rosen, "Supreme Leader: The Arrogance of Justice Anthony Kennedy," *New Republic*, 18 June 2007, 21.

130. Ibid.

131. For an excellent overview of the history of Sacramento, including insight into race relations over the course of time, see Steven M. Avella, *Sacramento: Indomitable City* (Charleston, SC: Arcadia, 2003). Thank you to Pat Johnson, at the Sacramento Archives and Museum Collection Center, for recommending various research sources.

132. H. N. Hirsch, *A Theory of Liberty: The Constitution and Minorities* (New York: Routledge, 1992), 2–3.

133. 127 S. Ct. at 2791 (Kennedy, J., concurring in part and concurring in the judgment), quoting 127 S. Ct. at 2768.

134. 127 S. Ct. at 2791 (Kennedy, J., concurring in part and concurring in the judgment). In this respect, Kennedy would likely agree with the need—that Justice Breyer

identified in dissent—of detailing in "exceptional length" the history of the school districts' efforts to combat racial segregation. 127 S. Ct. at 2800 (Breyer, J., joined by Stevens, Souter, and Ginsburg, JJ., dissenting). For this discussion in Breyer's opinion, see 127 S. Ct. at 2802–9 (Breyer, J., joined by Stevens, Souter, and Ginsburg, JJ., dissenting).

135. 127 S. Ct. at 2791–92 (Kennedy, J., concurring in part and concurring in the judgment).

136. Ibid., 2792, 2797.

137. Ibid., 2789.

138. Ibid., 2788, 2797, 2791.

139. Ibid., 2790. It is interesting to note that in dissent Justice Breyer argued that the case be remanded so as to give the school districts the opportunity to address the unanswered questions about the specifics of administering the plans. 127 S. Ct. at 2829 (Breyer, J., joined by Stevens, Souter, and Ginsburg, JJ., dissenting).

140. Ibid., at 2817, 2819–20 (italics added).

141. 127 S. Ct. at 2793 (Kennedy, J., concurring in part and concurring in the judgment).

142. 490 U.S. 642 (1989); 490 U.S. 755 (1989); 490 U.S. 900 (1989); 491 U.S. 701 (1989); 491 U.S. 164 (1989). Abraham and Perry, *Freedom and the Court,* 501.

143. Linda Greenhouse, "The Year the Court Turned to the Right," *New York Times,* 7 July 1989, 1(A).

144. Jan Crawford Greenburg, *Supreme Conflict: The Inside Story of the Struggle for Control of the United States Supreme Court* (New York: Penguin, 2007), 144.

Chapter 5

1. United States Senate, Committee on the Judiciary, *Hearings on the Nomination of Anthony M. Kennedy to be Associate Justice of the Supreme Court of the United States,* 100th Cong., 1st sess., 14–16 December 1987, 113.

2. 410 U.S. 113 (1973).

3. First draft, Chief Justice Rehnquist's opinion for the Court in *Casey,* Box 602, Harry A. Blackmun Papers, Manuscript Division, Library of Congress, Washington, D.C. [hereafter HAB-LOC].

4. Handwritten note from Justice Kennedy to Justice Blackmun, 29 May 1992; memos between Justices Stevens, O'Connor, Kennedy, and Souter, 3, 12, 18, 19, 22 June 1992; Box 601, HAB-LOC.

5. 505 U.S. 833, 966 (1992) (Rehnquist, CJ., joined by White, Scalia, and Thomas, JJ., concurring in the judgment in part, and dissenting in part).

6. 505 U.S. at 846.

7. Ibid., 877.

8. Justice Kennedy quoted in Jan Crawford Greenburg, *Supreme Conflict: The Inside Story of the Struggle for Control of the United States Supreme Court* (New York: Penguin, 2007), 177.

9. Jonah Goldberg, "Justice Kennedy's Mind," *National Review Online*, 9 March 2005.

10. "Denying the Right to Choose," *New York Times*, 19 April 2007 26(A).

11. Richard A. Epstein, "Substantive Due Process by Any Other Name: The Abortion Cases," *Supreme Court Review* 1973 (1973): 159–85; Richard A. Epstein, "Of Same Sex Relationships and Affirmative Action: The Covert Libertarianism of the United States Supreme Court," *Supreme Court Economic Review* 12 (2004): 87.

12. Epstein, "Of Same Sex Relationships and Affirmative Action," 87.

13. Quoted in Stuart Taylor, "Newest Judicial Activists Come from the Right," *New York Times*, 8 February 1987, 24(A).

14. Epstein, "Of Same Sex Relationships and Affirmative Action," 88.

15. Jan Narveson, "Liberty and Equality—A Question of Balance?" in *Liberty and Equality*, ed. Tibor R. Machan (Stanford, CA: Hoover Institution Press, 2002), 41.

16. David Boaz, *Libertarianism: A Primer* (New York: Free Press, 1998), 230.

17. *Gonzales v. Carhart*,127 S. Ct. 1610, 1634 (2007).

18. *Kennedy Sup. Ct. Nomination Hearings*, 201; "Posing for Posterity: An Investiture Tradition," *Docket Sheet of the Supreme Court of the United States* 24, no. 3 (Winter 1988): 4.

19. There is no shortage of literature on the right to privacy. In the last ten years alone, over 150 American or Canadian law review articles have included in their titles either "right of privacy" or "right to privacy." Lexis-Nexis search, 30 July 2007. This should not surprise us. After all, it is the title of the 1890 *Harvard Law Review* article by Samuel D. Warren and future Supreme Court Justice Louis D. Brandeis that one scholar has called "the most influential law review article of all." Samuel D. Warren and Louis D. Brandeis, "The Right to Privacy," *Harvard Law Review* 4 (1890): 193–220; Harry Kalven Jr., "Privacy in Tort Law—Were Warren and Brandeis Wrong?" *Law & Contemporary Problems* 31 (1966): 327. For a summary of other descriptions of this article's significance, see Benjamin E. Bratman, "Brandeis and Warren's *The Right to Privacy* and the Birth of the Right to Privacy," *Tennessee Law Review* 69 (2002): 623–51. It is important to understand, however, that this literature does not refer to one single right. While the right to privacy obviously means many different things to many different people, it also has multiple legal meanings. Unlike the informational right inherent in the Fourth Amendment ("The right of the people to be secure in their persons, houses, papers, and effects, against unreasonable searches and seizures, shall not be violated, and no Warrants shall issue, but upon probable cause, supported by Oath or affirmation, and particularly describing the place to be searched, and the persons or things to be seized"), and in tort law (limiting "the ability of others to gain, disseminate, or use information about oneself"), the substantive right "immuniz[es] certain conduct—such as using contraceptives, marrying someone of a different color, or aborting a pregnancy—from state proscription or penalty." It is the substantive right to privacy that abortion law addresses. Jed Rubenfeld, "The Right of Privacy," *Harvard Law Review* 102 (1989): 740.

20. Terence Moran, "Kennedy's Constitutional Journey," *Legal Times*, 6 July 1992, 20.

21. *Griswold v. Connecticut*, 381 U.S. 479, 527 (1965) (Stewart, J., joined by Black, J., dissenting).

22. 367 U.S. 497 (1961).
23. 381 U.S. at 484.
24. Ibid., 509–10 (Black, J., joined by Stewart, J., dissenting).
25. 367 U.S. 497, 548–49 (1961) (Harlan, J., dissenting).
26. Ibid., 542, 545–46.
27. 381 U.S. at 500 (Harlan, J., concurring in the judgment).
28. 381 U.S. at 486–87 (Goldberg, J., joined by Warren, CJ., and Brennan, J., concurring).
29. 381 U.S. at 502 (White, J., concurring in the judgment).
30. 405 U.S. 438 (1972).
31. The marital status of the woman was unclear: "The Court of Appeals below described the recipient of the foam as 'an unmarried adult woman.' However, there is no evidence in the record about her marital status." 405 U.S. at 440n1.
32. Ibid., 453.
33. Ibid., 453.
34. Letter from Justice Brennan to Justice Douglas, 30 December 1971, 7; *Summaries and History of Opinions of Justice Brennan*, case history of *Eisenstadt*; Boxes I:285 and II:6, papers of William J. Brennan Jr., Manuscript Division, Library of Congress, Washington, D.C. [hereafter WJB-LOC]; Linda Greenhouse, *Becoming Justice Blackmun: Harry Blackmun's Supreme Court Journey* (New York: Times Books, 2005), 86. Also see Bob Woodward and Scott Armstrong, *The Brethren: Inside the Supreme Court* (New York: Simon & Schuster, 1979), 175–76.
35. *Doe* was reargued in October 1972 and was decided with *Roe v. Wade* in January 1973.
36. Letter from Justice Brennan to Justice Douglas, 30 December 1971, 5–6.
37. 410 U.S. 179 (1973); 410 U.S. 113 (1973).
38. 410 U.S. at 210–11 (Douglas, J., concurring).
39. Ibid., 211–13.
40. *Bowers* conference notes, Box 451, HAB-LOC.
41. Anthony M. Kennedy, Judge, Unenumerated Rights and the Dictates of Judicial Restraint, 10, Speech, Canadian Institute for Advanced Legal Studies, The Stanford Lectures, Palo Alto, CA, 24 July–1 August 1986, *Committee on the Judiciary*, Judiciary Nominations files, A. Kennedy, Sup. Court, 100th Congress, Records of the Senate, Record Group 46, National Archives, Washington, DC [hereafter Sen. RG46-NAB].
42. *Kennedy Sup. Ct. Nomination Hearings*, 164, 231–32.
43. Ibid., 164.
44. Ibid., 86; Judge Kennedy's Comments at the Ninth Circuit Judicial Conference, Hawaii, 21 August 1987, 5, Sen. RG46-NAB; Jeffrey Toobin, "Swing Shift; How Anthony Kennedy's Passion for Foreign Law Could Change the Supreme Court," *New Yorker*, 12 September 2005, 42–51.
45. 367 U.S. at 542 (Harlan, J., dissenting).
46. Ibid., 542–43.
47. Stephen M. Griffin, *American Constitutionalism: From Theory to Politics* (Princeton, NJ: Princeton University Press, 1996), 172 (but generally see 170–82).
48. 491 U.S. 110 (1989).

49. Ibid., 127n6.

50. 491 U.S. at 137 (Brennan, J. joined by Marshall, and Blackmun, JJ., dissenting), quoting *Moore v. East Cleveland*, 431 U.S. 494, 549 (1977) (White, J., dissenting).

51. 491 U.S. at 132 (O'Connor, J., joined by Kennedy, J., concurring in part), citations omitted.

52. Originally, in November 1988, both O'Connor and Kennedy indicated their willingness to join Scalia's opinion very shortly after the first draft of that opinion was circulated; and Kennedy was still prepared to sign on to that opinion in its entirety as late as 1 June 1989, when the fifth draft was circulated. By this time, however, O'Connor had already drafted a concurrence opting out of Scalia's footnoted paean to history. On 12 June, three days before the decision announcement, Justice Kennedy finally wrote to O'Connor to tell her that he was joining her concurring opinion. Memo from Justice O'Connor to Justice Scalia, 23 November 1988, Box 515, HAB-LOC; first and fifth drafts of Justice Scalia's *Michael H.* opinion, 22 November 1988 and 1 June 1989; memo from Justice Kennedy to Justice Scalia, 28 November 1988; second and third drafts of Justice O'Connor's *Michael H.* concurrence, 30 May and 13 June 1989; memo from Justice Kennedy to Justice O'Connor, 12 June 1989, Box 468 Thurgood Marshall Papers, Manuscript Division, Library of Congress, Washington, DC [hereafter TM-LOC].

53. *Kennedy Sup. Ct. Nomination Hearings*, 230.

54. Ibid., 139 (italics added).

55. Griffin, *American Constitutionalism*, 172–73.

56. Letter from Justice Kennedy to Justice Blackmun, 23 January 1992, Box 589, HAB-LOC.

57. Letter from Stephanie Dangel to Justice Blackmun, 24 April 1992, Box 589, HAB-LOC.

58. 504 U.S. 191, 198–211 (1992).

59. Dane A. Cameron, "The Kennedy Appointment" (paper presented at the annual meeting of the Western Political Science Association, Salt Lake City, UT, 30 March–1 April 1989), 12–13.

60. David G. Savage, "The Rescue of *Roe vs. Wade*: How a Dramatic Change of Heart by a Supreme Court Justice Affirmed the Right to Abortion—Just When the Issue Seemed Headed for Certain Defeat," *Los Angeles Times*, 13 December 1992, 1(A), 22(A).

61. Daniel A. Farber, "Abortion after *Webster*," *Constitutional Commentary* 6 (1989): 225–30.

62. 492 U.S. 490 (1989).

63. Memo from Anne Dupre to Justice Blackmun, 18 December 1989, Box 545, HAB-LOC.

64. *Webster* conference notes, Box 536, HAB-LOC.

65. 492 U.S. at 520, quoted in Farber, "Abortion after *Webster*," 227.

66. Ibid.

67. *Webster* conference notes, Box 536, HAB-LOC.

68. Her position in the case changed several times. Memo from Justice O'Connor to Chief Justice Rehnquist, 8 December 1989: "I have spoken to John [Paul Stevens]

about his views in these cases since his memo of yesterday. As your assignment reflects, I am presently in the unhappy position of adopting a disposition which is supported by no other justice. John's views are close to my own in these two cases, and, if I understand his approach correctly, I think I can agree with it. This leads me to change my vote to reverse in 88-1125 and still to affirm in 88-1309," Box 500, TM-LOC; memo from Justice O'Connor to the conference, 11 June 1990: "I am circulating today an opinion concurring in part and dissenting in part from John's opinion in these cases. At the end of the day, I am back where I started. I agree with John that subdivision 2, the 2-parent notification, is invalid. But I agree with Tony [Kennedy] that subdivision 6, the 2-parent notification plus judicial bypass, passes constitutional muster," Box 499, TM-LOC. And there is considerable evidence that the more liberal justices knew it was important to make every effort to accommodate her concerns so as to ensure her support. As Justice Brennan wrote to Justice Marshall, "Sandra has for the first time joined us in holding invalid a law regulating abortion." Memo from Justice Brennan to Justice Marshall, 13 June 1990, Box 499, TM-LOC. Also see the memos between Justices Brennan, Marshall, Blackmun, and Stevens, 15 and 18 June 1990, Box 499, TM-LOC; and the memo from Anne Dupre to Justice Blackmun, 15 March 1990: "I have talked extensively with JPS' clerk (Lewis Liman) regarding this case. From what I can gather JPS is walking a very fine line to try to draw SOC away from the conservatives. As we have discussed, JPS is probably the only one who could succeed in reaching SOC. I see no need to castigate him if he can get SOC to strike down any statute that has the word 'abortion' in it. It looks unreasonable, I think, to get so worked up if the statute is to be struck down," Box 545, HAB-LOC.

69. *Bellotti v. Baird*, 443 U.S. 622, 640–41 (1979) quoting *Planned Parenthood v. Danforth*, 428 U.S. 52, 91 (1976) (Stewart, J., concurring), quoted at *Hodgson v. Minnesota*, 497 U.S. 417, 480 (1990) (Kennedy, J., joined by Rehnquist, CJ., and White and Scalia, JJ., concurring in the judgment in part and dissenting in part).

70. 497 U.S. at 481 (Kennedy, J., joined by Rehnquist, CJ., and White and Scalia, JJ., concurring in the judgment in part and dissenting in part).

71. Letters from Justices Marshall and Brennan to Chief Justice Burger, 23 November 1976, Box 249, HAB-LOC. They were referring to *Moore v. City of East Cleveland*, 431 U.S. 494 (1977).

72. 497 U.S. at 501 (Kennedy, J., joined by Rehnquist, CJ., and White and Scalia, JJ., concurring in the judgment in part and dissenting in part).

73. Ibid., 496.

74. *Akron Center* conference notes; memo from Justice Stevens to Justice Kennedy, 19 June 1990, Box 544, HAB-LOC; first, second, and third drafts of Justice Kennedy's opinion in *Akron Center*; memo from Justice O'Connor to Chief Justice Rehnquist, 8 December 1989; memo from Justice Stevens to Justice Kennedy, 16 January 1990; memo from Justice O'Connor to Justice Kennedy, 19 March 1990; Box 498, TM-LOC.

75. 497 U.S. at 519–20.

76. First, second, and third drafts of Justice Kennedy's opinion in *Akron Center*, Box 498, TM-LOC.

77. Memo from Anne Dupre to Justice Blackmun, 29 November 1989, Box 545, HAB-LOC. It is reasonable to assume that Dupre was referring to the article in the

Washington Post: Al Kamen and Ruth Marcus, "2 Cases May Clarify O'Connor's Murky Views on Abortion," *Washington Post*, 27 November 1989, 1(A).

78. For an overview discussion of this history of using the undue burden test, see Valerie J. Pacer, "Salvaging the Undue Burden Standard—Is It a Lost Cause? The Undue Burden Standard and Fundamental Rights Analysis," *Washington University Law Quarterly* 73 (1995): 296–301.

79. *City of Akron v. Akron Center for Reproductive Health*, 462 U.S. 416, 461–62 (1983) (O'Connor, J., joined by White and Rehnquist, JJ., dissenting); *Thornburgh v. American College of Obstetricians and Gynecologists*, 476 U.S. 747, 828–32 (1986) (O'Connor, J., joined by Rehnquist, J., dissenting).

80. See, for example, Linda Greenhouse, "Abortion Case May Be Central in Confirmation," *New York Times*, 1 November 2005, 1(A); Jim Wooten, "Bush Makes Meticulous Pick for Court," *Atlanta Journal-Constitution*, 1 November 2005, 15(A); Charles Babington, "As Democrats Lead Opposition, GOP Moderates May Control Vote," *Washington Post*, 1 November 2005, 9(A); Jonathan H. Adler, "Samuel Alito," *Wall Street Journal*, 1 November 2005, 16(A).

81. 18 Pa. Cons. Stat. § 3203 (1990), quoted at 505 U.S. at 879.

82. 947 F.2d 682, 719 (1991) (Alito, Circuit Judge, concurring in part and dissenting in part).

83. 505 U.S. at 877.

84. 505 U.S. at 844, 901 (italics added).

85. Jeffrey Rosen, "The Agonizer," *New Yorker*, 11 November 1996, 87–88; first draft, joint opinion in *Casey*, Box 602, HAB-LOC.

86. 505 U.S. at 984–85 (Scalia, J., joined by Rehnquist, CJ., and White and Thomas, JJ., concurring in the judgment in part and dissenting in part); see Mark Tushnet, *A Court Divided: The Rehnquist Court and the Future of Constitutional Law* (New York: W. W. Norton, 2005), 215 (describing it as "sonorous—and almost meaningless").

87. Greenburg, *Supreme Conflict*, 176, 182.

88. Nancy Kassop, "From Arguments to Supreme Court Opinions in *Planned Parenthood v. Casey*," *PS: Political Science and Politics* 26 (1993): 56.

89. 505 U.S. at 846.

90. Ibid., 847.

91. Ibid.

92. *Kennedy Sup. Ct. Nomination Hearings*, 86.

93. 505 U.S. at 848, quoting 367 U.S. at 543 (Harlan, J., dissenting).

94. 367 U.S. at 542 (Harlan, J., dissenting); 505 U.S. at 849.

95. 367 U.S. at 542 (Harlan, J., dissenting); 505 U.S. at 850.

96. 505 U.S. at 851; for Scalia's description, see *Lawrence v. Texas*, 539 U.S. 558, 588 (2003) (Scalia, J., joined by Rehnquist, CJ., and Thomas, J., dissenting).

97. 505 U.S. at 852.

98. Ibid.

99. Ibid.

100. Ibid.

101. Ibid.

102. 410 U.S. 113, 159 (1973) (citations omitted).

103. 505 U.S. at 852–53 (italics added).

104. Ibid., 872.

105. Ibid., 873, 877.

106. Anonymous justice quoted in Savage, "The Rescue of *Roe v. Wade*," 1(A).

107. 492 U.S. at 557 (Blackmun, J., joined by Brennan and Marshall, JJ., concurring in part and dissenting in part).

108. 505 U.S. at 923 (Blackmun, J., concurring in part, concurring in the judgment in part, and dissenting in part).

109. For example, see Joan Biskupic, "Court Takes Cases on Abortion, Gays; 'Partial Birth' Procedure, Boy Scouts at Issue," *Washington Post*, 15 January 2000, 1(A); Linda Greenhouse, "Justices to Rule on Law That Bans Abortion Method," *New York Times*, 15 January 2000, 1(A).

110. 530 U.S. 914 (2000) (recall, from chapter 2, that *Hill v. Colorado*, 530 U.S. 703 (2000) was decided on the same day).

111. Neb. Rev. Stat. Ann. §§ 28-328(1), 28-326(9) (Supp. 1999), quoted at 530 U.S. at 921–22.

112. 530 U.S. at 945. Many of the supporters of the Nebraska law, and partial-birth abortion bans in general, argue that there is less need to ban D&E abortions because the procedure is not as gruesome as the D&X procedure, which is often depicted as bordering on infanticide. However, as Justice Stevens observed in his *Stenberg* concurrence: "The notion that either of these two equally gruesome procedures performed at this late stage of gestation is more akin to infanticide than the other, or that the State furthers any legitimate interest by banning one but not the other, is simply irrational." 530 U.S. at 946–47 (Stevens, J., joined by Ginsburg, J., concurring).

113. 530 U.S. at 949 (O'Connor, J., concurring).

114. 505 U.S. at 879 (quoting *Roe*, 410 U.S. at 164–65) (emphasis added).

115. 530 U.S. at 930–31, quoting *Brief of Petitioners*, 48.

116. 530 U.S. at 946 (Stevens, J., joined by Ginsburg, J., concurring).

117. 539 U.S. at 578.

118. Edward Lazarus, "Court Crackup," *Washington Post*, 25 July 2000, 23(A); Linda Greenhouse, "The Supreme Court: The Nebraska Case: Court Rules that Governments Can't Outlaw Type of Abortion," *New York Times*, 28 June 2000, 1(A).

119. 530 U.S. at 956 (Kennedy, J., joined by Rehnquist, CJ., dissenting).

120. 530 U.S. at 929.

121. Greenburg, *Supreme Conflict*, 178.

122. 505 U.S. at 844; 530 U.S. at 979 (Kennedy, J., joined by Rehnquist, CJ., dissenting).

123. 530 U.S. at 956 (Kennedy, J., joined by Rehnquist, CJ., dissenting), citation omitted.

124. Ibid. Also see pages 960, 961: "*Casey* is premised on the States having an important constitutional role in defining their interests in the abortion debate." Given Kennedy's commitment to the protection of states' rights, it is unsurprising that he opened his *Stenberg* dissent by emphasizing the interests in the abortion debate held by the nation's fifty sovereignties. After all, federalism is a subject about which Kennedy has

spoken often and passionately throughout his judicial career. See, for example, Anthony M. Kennedy, Judge, Rotary Speech, 1, Sacramento Chapter of the Rotary Club, Sacramento, CA, 15 October 1987; "Federalism: The Theory and the Reality," Speech, Historical Society for the United States District Court for the Northern District of California, San Francisco, CA, 26 October 1987; Sen. RG46-NAB; *U.S. Term Limits v. Thornton*, 514 U.S. 779, 838–39 (1995) (Kennedy, J., concurring).

125. 530 U.S. at 956–57 (Kennedy, J., joined by Rehnquist, CJ., dissenting).

126. 530 U.S. at 923; 530 U.S. at 957 (Kennedy, J., joined by Rehnquist, CJ., dissenting).

127. 530 U.S. at 957 (Kennedy, J., joined by Rehnquist, CJ., dissenting).

128. Steven G. Calabresi, "Substantive Due Process after *Gonzales v. Carhart*," *Michigan Law Review* 106 (2008): 1520.

129. 127 S. Ct. at 1640 (Ginsburg, J., joined by Stevens, Souter, and Breyer, JJ., dissenting), quoting 505 U.S. at 844, *Eisenstadt v. Baird*, 405 U.S. 438, 453 (1972), and 505 U.S. at 851–52.

130. 127 S. Ct. at 1640 (Ginsburg, J., joined by Stevens, Souter, and Breyer, JJ., dissenting).

131. John T. Woolley and Gerhard Peters, "William J. Clinton, Message to the House of Representatives Returning Without Approval Partial Birth Abortion Legislation, 10 April 1996," *The American Presidency Project*, Santa Barbara: University of California (hosted), Gerhard Peters (database), http://www.presidency.ucsb.edu/ws/index.php?pid=52655&st=&st1= (accessed 2 July 2008).

132. Garrett Epps and Dahlia Lithwick, "The Sphinx of Sacramento," *Slate.com*, 27 April 2007, http://www.slate.com/id/2165133/ (accessed 9 July 2008).

133. 127 S. Ct. at 1619.

134. 127 S. Ct. at 1619–23, 1627–32. It is interesting to note that in the fall of 2007, during an interview with Jeffrey Rosen for a feature article in the *New York Times Magazine*, Justice Stevens described the PBABA as a "*silly* statute" that was "a distressing exhibition by Congress." In the grand scheme of abortion law, however, Stevens believed that the decision to uphold the law in *Carhart* was not "all that important" because it restricted only one type of abortion, a method that was very rarely used. Justice Stevens quoted in Jeffrey Rosen, "The Dissenter," *New York Times Magazine*, 23 September 2007, 54.

135. Calabresi, "Substantive Due Process," 1521.

136. Kevin M. Stack, "The Practice of Dissent in the Supreme Court," *Yale Law Journal* 105 (1996): 2240; Patricia M. Wald, "The Rhetoric of Results and the Results of Rhetoric: Judicial Writings," *University of Chicago Law Review* 62 (1995): 1412. For additional discussions of the different windows into judges' legal souls that separate and majority opinions provide, see William J. Brennan Jr., "In Defense of Dissents," *Hastings Law Journal* 37 (1986): 435; William H. Rehnquist, "The Supreme Court: Past and Present," *American Bar Association Journal* 59 (1973): 363; R. Dean Moorhead, "Concurring and Dissenting Opinions," *American Bar Association Journal* 38 (1952): 822.

137. 530 U.S. at 963 (Kennedy, J., joined by Rehnquist, CJ., dissenting).

138. 127 S. Ct. at 1633.

139. 127 S. Ct. at 1632–33, quoting Congressional Findings (14)(N), in notes following 18 U.S.C. § 1531 (2000 ed., Supp. IV), p. 769.

140. My use here of "unborn child" instead of "fetus" simply reflects the fact that in using dignity language to describe the PBABA, the law's supporters are very likely to try and humanize their rhetoric using references to "children."

141. Quoted in Linda Greenhouse, "In Reversal of Course, Justices, 5–4, Back Ban on Abortion Method," *New York Times*, 18 April 2007, 1(A).

142. 505 U.S. at 882.

143. 505 U.S. at 883–84, quoting 18 Pa. Cons. Stat. §3205 (1990).

144. 127 S. Ct. at 1634.

145. Ibid.

146. Mark Tushnet, quoted in Carl M. Cannon, "Anthony Kennedy," *California Journal* 28 (November 1997).

147. Robin West, "The Supreme Court, 1989 Term: Foreword: Taking Freedom Seriously," *Harvard Law Review* 104 (1990): 103–6.

Conclusion

1. Anthony M. Kennedy, "Speech at the American Bar Association Annual Meeting," 9 August 2003 (rev. 14 August 2003) (paginated transcript on file at the Public Information Office, United States Supreme Court), 1–2.

2. Anthony M. Kennedy, Judge, "Federalism: The Theory and the Reality," 14, Speech, Historical Society for the United States District Court for the Northern District of California, San Francisco, CA, 26 October 1987, *Committee on the Judiciary*, Judiciary Nominations files, A. Kennedy, Sup. Court, 100th Congress, Records of the Senate, Record Group 46, National Archives, Washington, D.C.

3. Jeffrey Rosen, "The Agonizer," *New Yorker*, 11 November 1996, 85.

4. Justice Kennedy, quoted in Bob Egelko, "Justice Kennedy Wins ABA's Highest Award," *San Francisco Chronicle*, 14 August 2007, 2(B); "Dialogue on Freedom Summary," http://www.abavideonews.org/ABA243D/DOF_summary.html (accessed 6 June 2008).

5. Della Thompson, ed., *The Concise Oxford Dictionary of Current English*, 9th ed. (Oxford: Clarendon Press, 1995), 875.

6. "The Role of the Judiciary in Promoting the Rule of Law" (C-SPAN, November 10, 2005); Justice Kennedy quoted in Charles Lane, "Justice Kennedy's Future Role Pondered; High-Profile Activities Spark Talk About Aims," *Washington Post*, 17 June 2002, 1(A).

7. *Ashcroft v. Free Speech Coalition*, 535 U.S. 234, 253 (2002).

8. Ibid.

9. Kennedy, "Speech at the American Bar Association Annual Meeting," 10.

10. Jan Crawford Greenburg, *Supreme Conflict: The Inside Story of the Struggle for Control of the United States Supreme Court* (New York: Penguin, 2007), 177.

11. Mark Graber quoted in Caryn Tamber, "MD Supreme Court Briefs: September 29, 2006," *Daily Record*, 29 September 2006.

12. Justice Kennedy quoted in Stuart Taylor Jr., Evan Thomas, and Katie Connolly, "The Power Broker; In an Exclusive Interview, Justice Kennedy Discusses Life, Center Stage," *Newsweek*, 16 July 2007, 36–37.

13. For a variety of views about the relative impact of Chief Justice Roberts and Justices Kennedy and Alito, see Linda Greenhouse, "Clues to the New Dynamic on the Supreme Court," *New York Times*, 3 July 2007, 11(A); Linda Greenhouse, "In Steps Big and Small, Supreme Court Moved Right," *New York Times*, 1 July 2007, 1(A); David G. Savage, "High Court Has Entered a New Era; The Chief Justice, with Help from Fellow Bush Appointee Alito, Carries Big Rulings to the Right—a Generational Shift," *Los Angeles Times*, 1 July 2007, 1(A); Robert Barnes, "A Rightward Turn and Dissension Define Court This Term," *Washington Post*, 1 July 2007, 7(A), Erwin Chemerinsky, "Conservative Justice; Forget the Promises—Roberts and Alito Delivered High Court Ideology." *Los Angeles Times*, 29 June 2007, 35(A).

14. Linda Greenhouse, "On Court That Defied Labeling, Kennedy Made the Boldest Mark," *New York Times*, 29 June 2008, 1(A); "A Supreme Court on the Brink," *New York Times*, 3 July 2008, 22(A).

15. "SCOTUSblog Super Stat Pack—OT07 Term Recap," http://www.scotusblog.com/wp/wp-content/uploads/2008/06/superstatpack07.pdf (accessed 10 July 2008).

16. Lee Epstein and Tonja Jacobi, "Super Medians," *Stanford Law Review* 61(2008): 41.

17. Comments of Judge Wilkinson in "A Tribute to Justice Lewis F. Powell, Jr.," *Harvard Law Review* 101 (1987): 420.

18. Greenburg, *Supreme Conflict*, 182.

19. Michael W. McConnell, quoted in Richard C. Reuben, "Man in the Middle," *California Lawyer*, October 1992, 36; Mark Tushnet, *A Court Divided: The Rehnquist Court and the Future of Constitutional Law* (New York: W. W. Norton, 2005), 63.

20. Jason DeParle, "In Battle to Pick Next Justice, Right Says, Avoid a Kennedy," *New York Times*, 27 June 2005, 1(A).

21. Greenhouse, "In Steps Big and Small," 1(A).

22. Steven G. Calabresi, "Substantive Due Process after *Gonzales v. Carhart*," *Michigan Law Review* 106 (2008): 1530.

23. *12 Angry Men*, DVD, directed by Sidney Lumet (1957; MGM Vintage Classics, 2001).

24. Quoted in "Chief Justice Says His Goal Is More Consensus on Court," *New York Times*, 22 May 2006, 16(A). The Chief Justice made this call for consensus during his commencement address at Georgetown University Law Center in May 2006. For analysis, see Cass R. Sunstein, "The Minimalist; Chief Justice Roberts Favors Narrow Court Rulings that Create Consensus and Tolerate Diversity," *Los Angeles Times*, 25 May 2006, 11(B).

25. Taylor, Thomas, and Connolly, "Power Broker," 36–37.

26. Kennedy, "Speech at the American Bar Association," 1–2; Tony Mauro, "Justice Kennedy to ABA: 'The Work of Freedom Has Just Begun.'" *Legal Times*, 14 August 2007; Justice Kennedy quoted in "A Justice Among Us," *Vanderbilt Magazine* (Winter 1997): 2.

Bibliography

"ABA News Conference: The Justice Kennedy Commission Report on Incarceration." C-SPAN, June 23, 2004. http;//www.cspan.org.

Abraham, Henry J., and Barbara A. Perry. *Freedom and the Court: Civil Rights and Liberties in the United States.* 8th ed. Lawrence: University Press of Kansas, 2003.

"Academy of Achievement Interview, Anthony Kennedy, 23 June, 2005." http://www.achievement.org/autodoc/printmember/ken0int-1 (accessed 13 June 2007).

Adler, Jonathan H. "Samuel Alito." *Wall Street Journal*, 1 November 2005, 16(A).

Amar, Akhil Reed. "Justice Kennedy and the Ideal of Equality." *Pacific Law Journal* 28 (Spring 1997): 515–32.

Amar, Akhil Reed, and Neal Kumar Katyal. "*Bakke*'s Fate." *UCLA Law Review* 43 (August 1996): 1745–80.

Ashley, W. J., ed. *John Stuart Mill, Principles of Political Economy with Some of Their Applications to Social Philosophy.* New York: A. M. Kelley, 1965.

Avella, Steven M. *Sacramento: Indomitable City.* Charleston, SC: Arcadia, 2003.

Babington, Charles. "As Democrats Lead Opposition, GOP Moderates May Control Vote." *Washington Post*, 1 November 2005, 9(A).

Baier, Paul R. "Of *Bakke*'s Balance, *Gratz* and *Grutter*: The Voice of Justice Powell." *Tulane Law Review* 78 (June 2004): 1955–2007.

Barnes, Robert. "A Rightward Turn and Dissension Define Court This Term." *Washington Post*, 1 July 2007, 7(A).

———. "Chief Justice Counsels Humility; Roberts Says Lawyers Must Put Themselves in Judges' Shoes." *Washington Post*, 6 February 2007, 15(A).

Barnett, Randy E. "Scrutiny Land." *Michigan Law Review* 106, no. 8 (June 2008): 1479–1500.

———. "Grading Justice Kennedy: A Reply to Professor Carpenter." *Minnesota Law Review* 89 (May 2005): 1582–90.

———. *Restoring the Lost Constitution: The Presumption of Liberty*. Princeton, NJ: Princeton University Press, 2004.

———. "The Moral Foundations of Modern Libertarianism." In *Varieties of Conservatism in America*, edited by Peter Berkowitz, 51–74. Stanford, CA: Hoover Institution Press, 2004.

———. "Justice Kennedy's Libertarian Revolution: *Lawrence v. Texas*." *Cato Supreme Court Review* (2003): 21–41.

———. *The Structure of Liberty: Justice and the Rule of Law*. New York: Oxford University Press, 1998.

———. "Getting Normative: The Role of Natural Rights in Constitutional Adjudication." *Constitutional Commentary* 12 (1995): 93–122.

———, ed. *The Rights Retained by the People: The History and Meaning of the Ninth Amendment*. Vol. 2. Fairfax, VA: George Mason University Press, 1993.

———. "A Ninth Amendment for Today's Constitution." *Valparaiso University Law Review* 26 (1991): 419–35.

———. "Unenumerated Constitutional Rights and the Rule of Law." *Harvard Journal of Law and Public Policy* 14 (1991): 615–44.

———, ed. *The Rights Retained by the People: The History and Meaning of the Ninth Amendment*. Vol. 1. Fairfax, VA: George Mason University Press, 1989.

Barron, David "Fighting Federalism with Federalism: If It's Not Just a Battle between Federalists and Nationalists, What Is It?" *Fordham Law Review* 74 (March 2006): 2081–121.

———. "Constitutionalism in the Shadow of Doctrine: The President's Non-Enforcement Power." *Law & Contemporary Problems* 63 (2000): 61–106.

Belsky, Martin H. "Accentuate the Positive, Eliminate the Negative, Latch on to the Affirmative [Action], Do Mess with Mr. In-Between." *Tulsa Law Review* 39 (2003): 27–48.

Bentham, Jeremy. "Anarchical Fallacies; Being an Examination of the Declaration of Rights Issued During the French Revolution." In *Nonsense Upon Stilts: Bentham, Burke and Marx on the Rights of Man*, edited by Jeremy Waldron, 46–69. London: Methuen, 1987.

Bernstein, David E. *You Can't Say That!: The Growing Threat to Civil Liberties from Antidiscrimination Laws*. Washington, DC: CATO Institute, 2003.

BeVier, Lillian R. "Rehabilitating Public Forum Doctrine: In Defense of Categories." *Supreme Court Review* 1992 (1992): 79–122.

Biskupic, Joan. *Sandra Day O'Connor: How the First Woman on the Supreme Court Became Its Most Influential Justice*. New York: Ecco, 2005.

———. "Court Takes Cases on Abortion, Gays; 'Partial Birth' Procedure, Boy Scouts at Issue." *Washington Post*, 15 January 2000, 1(A).

———. "Gay Rights Case Closely Watched at High Court." *Washington Post*, 10 October 1995, 1(A).

Boaz, David. *Libertarianism: A Primer*. New York: Free Press, 1998.

Bork, Robert H. *The Tempting of America: The Political Seduction of the Law*. New York: Free Press, 1990.

Bottum, Joseph. "Social Conservatism and the New Fusionism." In *Varieties of Conservatism in America*, edited by Peter Berkowitz, 31–47. Stanford, CA: Hoover Institution Press, 2004.

Boudin, Michael. "Commentary." *New York University Law Review* 70 (June 1995): 772–79.

Bratman, Benjamin E. "Brandeis and Warren's *The Right to Privacy* and the Birth of the Right to Privacy." *Tennessee Law Review* 69 (2002): 623–51.

Brennan, William J., Jr. "In Defense of Dissents." *Hastings Law Journal* 37 (1986): 427–38.

Brest, Paul. "In Defense of the Antidiscrimination Principle." *Harvard Law Review* 90 (November 1976): 1–54.

Breyer, Stephen J. "Hand-Down Statement, *Parents Involved in Community Schools v. Seattle School District No. 1*, No. 05-908, Thursday, June 28, 2007, Breyer, J., Dissenting." http://www.scotusblog.com/movabletype/archives/Breyerr%20bench%20statement%206-28-07.pdf (accessed 3 July 2007).

Brown, Chris. *Sovereignty, Rights and Justice: International Political Theory Today.* Cambridge, MA: Polity, 2002.

Brust, Richard. "The Man in the Middle." *ABA Journal* 89 (October 2003): 24–25.

Butler, Paul. "Racially Based Jury Nullification: Black Power in the Criminal Justice System." *Yale Law Journal* 105 (December 1995): 677–725.

Calabresi, Steven G. "Substantive Due Process after *Gonzales v. Carhart.*" *Michigan Law Review* 106 (2008): 1517–41.

———. "The Libertarian-Lite Constitutional Order and the Rehnquist Court: Reviewing the New Constitutional Order. By Mark Tushnet." *Georgetown Law Journal* 93 (2005): 1023–60.

Cameron, Dane A. "The Kennedy Appointment." Paper presented at the annual meeting of the Western Political Science Association, Salt Lake City, UT, 30 March–1 April 1989.

Cannon, Carl M. "Anthony Kennedy." *California Journal* 28 (November 1997).

Carpenter, Dale. "Is Lawrence Libertarian?" *Minnesota Law Review* 88 (May 2004): 1140–70.

Carter, Terry. "Crossing the Rubicon." *California Lawyer*, October 1992, 39–40, 103–4.

Chemerinsky, Erwin. "Conservative Justice; Forget the Promises—Roberts and Alito Delivered High Court Ideology." *Los Angeles Times*, 29 June 2007, 35(A).

"Chief Justice Says His Goal Is More Consensus on Court." *New York Times*, 22 May 2006, 16(A).

Clayton, Cornell W., and Howard Gillman, eds. *Supreme Court Decision-Making: New Institutionalist Approaches.* Chicago: University of Chicago Press, 1999.

Clemon, U. W., and Bryan K. Fair. "Lawyers, Civil Disobedience, and Equality in the Twenty-First Century: Lessons from Two American Heroes." *Alabama Law Review* 54 (2003): 959–83.

Colucci, Frank J. "Still Struggling: Anthony Kennedy and Abortion." Paper presented at the Annual Meeting of the Midwest Political Science Association, Chicago, 4–6 April 2008.

———. "The Jurisprudence of Justice Anthony Kennedy." PhD Dissertation, University of Notre Dame, 2004.

Cordray, Richard. "Justice White and the Exercise of Judicial Power: Justice White and the Democratic-Republicans." *University of Colorado Law Review* 74 (Fall 2003): 1319–26.

Corwin, Edward S. "The 'Higher Law' Background of American Constitutional Law." *Harvard Law Review* 42 (1928): 149–85, 365–409.

———. "The Basic Doctrine of American Constitutional Law." *Michigan Law Review* 12 (1914): 247–76.

Cosgrove, Kenneth M. *Branded Conservatives: How the Brand Brought the Right from the Fringes to the Center of American Politics.* New York: Peter Lang, 2007.

Curtis, Michael Kent. *No State Shall Abridge: The Fourteenth Amendment and the Bill of Rights.* Durham, NC: Duke University Press, 1986.

Cushman, Barry. *Rethinking the New Deal Court: The Structure of a Constitutional Revolution.* New York: Oxford University Press, 1998.

Dailey, John Daniel, and Paul Farley. "Colorado's Amendment 2: A Result in Search of a Reason." *Harvard Journal of Law and Public Policy* 20 (Fall 1996): 215–68.

Delgado, Richard, and David H. Yun. "Pressure Valves and Bloodied Chickens: An Analysis of Paternalistic Objections to Hate Speech Regulation." *California Law Review* 82 (1994): 871–92.

"Denying the Right to Choose." *New York Times*, 19 April 2007, 26(A).

DeParle, Jason. "In Battle to Pick Next Justice, Right Says, Avoid a Kennedy." *New York Times*, 27 June 2005, 1(A).

"Dialogue on Freedom Summary." http://www.abavideonews.org/ABA243D/DOF_summary.html (accessed 6 June 2008).

"Dialogue on Freedom: What is a Dialogue on Freedom?" http://www.abanet.org/dialogue/whatis.html (accessed 25 February 2005).

Ditslear, Corey. "Building New Measures of Supreme Court Ideology: Clerk Selection as an Indicator of Preferences." Paper presented at the Annual Meeting of the American Political Science Association, Washington, DC, 1–4 September 2005.

Ditslear, Corey, and Lawrence Baum. "Selection of Law Clerks and Polarization in the U.S. Supreme Court." *Journal of Politics* 63 (2001): 869–85.

Do, Long X. "Jury Nullification and Race-Conscious Reasonable Doubt: Overlapping Reifications of Commonsense Justice and the Potential Voir Dire Mistake." *UCLA Law Review* 47 (August 2000): 1843–83.

Dorf, Michael C. *No Litmus Test: Law versus Politics in the Twenty-first Century.* Lanham, MD: Rowman & Littlefield, 2006.

Downs, Donald Alexander. *Restoring Free Speech and Liberty on Campus.* New York: Cambridge University Press, 2005.

Duncan, Craig. "The Errors of Libertarianism." In *Libertarianism: For and Against*, edited by Craig Duncan and Tibor R. Machan. 45–64. Lanham, MD: Rowman & Littlefield, 2005.

Duncan, Craig, and Tibor R. Machan. *Libertarianism: For and Against.* Lanham, MD: Rowman & Littlefield, 2005.

Dworkin, Ronald. "The *Defunis* Case: The Right to Go to Law School (1976)." In *Affirmative Action: Social Justice or Reverse Discrimination*, edited by Francis J. Beckwith and Todd E. Jones, 70–89. Amherst, NY: Prometheus, 1997.

———. *Taking Rights Seriously*. Cambridge, MA: Harvard University Press, 1977.

Egelko, Bob. "Justice Kennedy Wins ABA's Highest Award." *San Francisco Chronicle*, 14 August 2007, 2(B).

Epps, Garrett, and Dahlia Lithwick. "The Sphinx of Sacramento." *Slate.com*, 27 April 2007. http://www.slate.com/id/2165133/ (accessed 9 July 2008).

Epstein, Lee, and Tonja Jacobi. "Super Medians." *Stanford Law Review* 61(2008): 37–99.

Epstein, Lee, and Jack Knight. *The Choices Justices Make*. Washington, DC: CQ Press, 1997.

Epstein, Lee, Andrew D. Martin, Kevin M. Quinn, and Jeffrey A. Segal. "Ideological Drift Among Supreme Court Justices: Who, When, and How Important?" *Northwestern University Law Review* 101 (March 2007): 127–31.

Epstein, Lee, and Jeffrey A. Segal. "The Rehnquist Court and the First Amendment: Trumping the First Amendment?" *Washington University Journal of Law & Policy* 21 (2006): 81–121.

Epstein, Lee, Thomas G. Walker, Nancy Staudt, Scott Hendrickson, and Jason Roberts. *The U.S. Supreme Court Justices Database* (2007). http://epstein.law.northwestern.edu/research/justicesdata.html (accessed 7 September 2007).

Epstein, Richard A. *How Progressives Rewrote the Constitution*. Washington, DC: CATO Institute, 2007.

———. "Of Same Sex Relationships and Affirmative Action: The Covert Libertarianism of the United States Supreme Court." *Supreme Court Economic Review* 12 (2004): 75–113.

———. "Skepticism and Freedom: The Intellectual Foundations of Our Constitutional Order." *University of Pennsylvania Journal of Constitutional Law* 6 (2004): 657–83.

———. *Skepticism and Freedom: A Modern Case for Classical Liberalism*. Chicago: University of Chicago Press, 2003.

———. "A Rational Basis for Affirmative Action: A Shaky but Classical Liberal Defense." *Michigan Law Review* 100 (August 2002): 2036–61.

———. *Principles for a Free Society: Reconciling Individual Liberty with the Common Good*. Cambridge, MA: Perseus, 1998.

———. *Simple Rules for a Complex World*. Cambridge, MA: Harvard University Press, 1995.

———. "Property, Speech, and the Politics of Distrust." *University of Chicago Law Review* 59 (1992): 41–89.

———. *Takings: Private Property and the Power of Eminent Domain*. Cambridge, MA: Harvard University Press, 1985.

———. "Substantive Due Process by Any Other Name: The Abortion Cases." *Supreme Court Review* 1973 (1973): 159–85.

Etienne, Margareth. "Parity, Disparity, and Adversariality: First Principles of Sentencing." *Stanford Law Review* 58 (2005): 309–22.

"Excerpts from the Bork Hearing: Pinning Down His Positions." *New York Times*, 17 September 1987, 10(B).

Farber, Daniel A. "Free Speech without Romance: Public Choice and the First Amendment." *Harvard Law Review* 105 (1991): 554–83.
———. *The First Amendment.* 2nd ed. New York: Foundation, 2003.
———. "Abortion after *Webster.*" *Constitutional Commentary* 6 (1989): 225–30.
Farber, Daniel A., and John E. Nowak. "The Misleading Nature of Public Forum Analysis: Content and Context in First Amendment Adjudication." *Virginia Law Review* 70 (1984): 1219–66.
"Federal Judges Convene Civic Education Summit." *Third Branch* 34, no. 6 (June 2002).
"Fiscal Year 2009 Supreme Court Budget—House Appropriations Committee Meeting." C-SPAN, March 30, 2008, http://www.cspan.org.
Foley, Elizabeth Price. *Liberty for All: Reclaiming Individual Privacy in a New Era of Public Morality.* New Haven, CT: Yale University Press, 2006.
Foner, Eric. *The Story of American Freedom.* New York: W. W. Norton, 1998.
Franke, Katherine M. "The Domesticated Liberty of *Lawrence v. Texas.*" *Columbia Law Review* 104 (June 2004): 1399–426.
Fried, Charles. *Modern Liberty and the Limits of Government.* New York: W. W. Norton, 2007.
Friedman, Lawrence. "The Limitations of Labeling: Justice Anthony M. Kennedy and the First Amendment." *Ohio Northern University Law Review* 20 (1993): 225–62.
Fuller, Lon L. *The Morality of Law,* revised ed. New Haven, CT: Yale University Press, 1969.
Galanter, Marc. "Why the 'Haves' Come out Ahead: Speculations on the Limits of Legal Change." *Law and Society* 9 (1974): 95–160.
Gallagher, Maggie. "Here Comes the Judge." *National Review,* 18 December 1987, 33, 59–60.
Garnett, Richard W. "William H. Rehnquist: A Life Lived Greatly, and Well." *Yale Law Journal* 115 (2006): 1847–55.
The Gauer Distinguished Lecture in Law and Public Policy, Vol. 1: The Constitution and the Spirit of Freedom by Anthony M. Kennedy Associate Justice Supreme Court of the United States of America. Washington, DC: National Legal Center for the Public Interest, 1990.
Gauthier, David. *Morals by Agreement.* New York: Oxford University Press, 1986.
Gerhart, Peter M. "The Two Constitutional Visions of the World Trade Organization." *University of Pennsylvania Journal of International Economic Law* 24 (Spring 2003): 1–75.
Gerken, Heather K. "Justice Kennedy and the Domains of Equal Protection." *Harvard Law Review* 121 (November 2007): 104–30.
Gerring, John. "Ideology: A Definitional Analysis." *Political Research Quarterly* 50, no. 4 (1997): 957–94.
Gillman, Howard, and Cornell Clayton, eds. *The Supreme Court in American Politics: New Institutionalist Interpretations.* Lawrence: University Press of Kansas, 1999.
Ginsburg, Ruth Bader. "Remarks on Writing Separately." *Washington Law Review* 65 (1990): 133–50.
Goldberg, Jonah. "Justice Kennedy's Mind." *National Review Online,* 9 March 2005.

Goldstein, Amy, and Charles Lane. "At D.C. School, Justice Kennedy and Teens Explore U.S. Values." *Washington Post*, 29 January 2002, 17(A).

Goldstein, Joel K. "The New Constitutional Vice Presidency." *Wake Forest Law Review* 30 (Fall 1995): 505–61.

Goldstein, Robert Justin. *Flag Burning and Free Speech: The Case of Texas v. Johnson.* Lawrence: University Press of Kansas, 2000.

Goodell, William. "Letter XXIII: All Theories of Government, Under All Forms, Preclude the Idea of Power to Legalize Slavery, but Imply the Obligation of Suppressing It.—Concluded." *National Era*, 7 December 1854.

Gormley, Ken. "Affirmative Action, for the Time Being." http://aad.english.ucsb.edu/docs/op81.html (accessed 11 June 2008).

———. *Archibald Cox: Conscience of a Nation.* Reading, MA: Perseus, 1997.

Gould, Jon B. *Speak No Evil: The Triumph of Hate Speech Regulation.* Chicago: University of Chicago Press, 2005.

Graber, Mark A. *Dred Scott and the Problem of Constitutional Evil.* New York: Cambridge University Press, 2006.

———. "Popular Constitutionalism, Judicial Supremacy, and the Complete Lincoln-Douglas Debates." *Chicago-Kent Law Review* 81 (2006): 923–51.

———. "Social Democracy and Constitutional Theory: An Institutional Perspective." *Fordham Law Review* 69 (April 2001): 1969–87.

Greenburg, Jan Crawford. *Supreme Conflict: The Inside Story of the Struggle for Control of the United States Supreme Court.* New York: Penguin, 2007.

Greenhouse, Linda. "On Court That Defied Labeling, Kennedy Made the Boldest Mark." *New York Times*, 29 June 2008, 1(A).

———. "Clues to the New Dynamic on the Supreme Court." *New York Times*, 3 July 2007, 11(A).

———. "In Steps Big and Small, Supreme Court Moved Right." *New York Times*, 1 July 2007, 1(A).

———. "In Reversal of Course, Justices, 5–4, Back Ban on Abortion Method." *New York Times*, 18 April 2007, 1(A).

———. "Abortion Case May Be Central in Confirmation." *New York Times*, 1 November 2005, 1(A).

———. *Becoming Justice Blackmun: Harry Blackmun's Supreme Court Journey.* New York: Times Books, 2005.

———. "The Supreme Court: The Nebraska Case: Court Rules that Governments Can't Outlaw Type of Abortion." *New York Times*, 28 June 2000, 1(A).

———. "Justices to Rule on Law That Bans Abortion Method." *New York Times*, 15 January 2000, 1(A).

———. "The Year the Court Turned to the Right." *New York Times*, 7 July 1989, 1(A).

———. "Justices, 5–4, Back Protesters' Right to Burn the Flag." *New York Times*, 22 June 1989, 1(A).

———. "Hearings to Begin for Court Nominee." *New York Times*, 14 December 1987, 1(A).

Greider, William. "The Scene; An Hour of History, Yes, But Without the Thunderclap." *Washington Post*, 29 June 1978, 1(A).

Greve, Michael S. "New Scalia Positivism." Panel presentation at the Annual Meeting of the American Political Science Association, Chicago, 2–5 September 2004.

Griffin, Stephen M. *American Constitutionalism: From Theory to Politics.* Princeton, NJ: Princeton University Press, 1996.

Gunther, Gerald. "Foreword: In Search of Evolving Doctrine on a Changing Court: A Model for a Newer Equal Protection." *Harvard Law Review* 86 (November 1972): 1–48.

Harlan, John M., II. "The Role of Oral Argument." In *Judges on Judging: Views from the Bench*, edited by David M. O'Brien, 104–7. Washington, DC: CQ Press, 2004.

Hayek, Friedrich A. *Law, Legislation and Liberty. Vol. 1: Rules and Order.* Chicago: University of Chicago Press, 1973.

———. *The Constitution of Liberty.* Chicago: University of Chicago Press, 1960.

Henrie, Mark C. "Understanding Traditionalist Conservatism." In *Varieties of Conservatism in America*, edited by Peter Berkowitz, 3–30. Stanford, CA: Hoover Institution Press, 2004.

Heyman, Steven J. *Free Speech and Human Dignity.* New Haven, CT: Yale University Press, 2008.

Hirsch, H. N. *A Theory of Liberty: The Constitution and Minorities.* New York: Routledge, 1992.

Hobbes, Thomas. *Leviathan.* Edited by Richard Tuck. New York: Cambridge University Press, 1996.

Institute for Justice, Brief of the Institute for Justice as Amicus Curiae in Support of Petitioners, *Lawrence v. Texas*, No. 02-102, 2002 U.S. Briefs 102.

Irons, Peter. *The Courage of Their Convictions: Sixteen Americans Who Fought Their Way to the Supreme Court.* New York: Penguin, 1990.

Jackson, Robert H. *The Global Covenant: Human Conduct in a World of States.* Oxford: Oxford University Press, 2000.

Jeffries, John C., Jr. *Justice Lewis F. Powell, Jr.* New York: Charles Scribner's Sons, 1994.

Johnsen, Dawn E. "Ronald Reagan and the Rehnquist Court on Congressional Power: Presidential Influences on Constitutional Change." *Indiana Law Journal* 78 (Winter/Spring 2003): 363–412.

Johnson, Lyndon Baines. "To Fulfill These Rights: Commencement Address at Howard University (1965)." In *Affirmative Action: Social Justice or Reverse Discrimination?*, edited by Francis J. Beckwith and Todd E. Jones, 56–63. Amherst, NY: Prometheus, 1997.

Johnson, Timothy R., Paul J. Wahlbeck, and James F. Spriggs II. "The Influence of Oral Arguments on the U.S. Supreme Court." *American Political Science Review* 100, no. 1 (February 2006): 99–113.

"A Justice Among Us." *Vanderbilt Magazine* (Winter 1997): 2.

Kahn, Ronald, and Ken I. Kersch, eds. *The Supreme Court and American Political Development.* Lawrence: University Press of Kansas, 2006.

Kalven, Harry, Jr. "Privacy in Tort Law—Were Warren and Brandeis Wrong?" *Law & Contemporary Problems* 31 (1966): 326–41.

Kamen, Al. "Court Nullifies Flag-Desecration Laws; First Amendment is Held to Protect Burnings During Political Demonstrations." *Washington Post*, 22 June 1989, 1(A).

———. "Ginsburg Acknowledges He Smoked Marijuana; Judge Says Use Was Occasional in '60s, '70s." *Washington Post*, 6 November 1987, 1(A).

Kamen, Al, and Ruth Marcus. "2 Cases May Clarify O'Connor's Murky Views on Abortion." *Washington Post*, 27 November 1989, 1(A).

Kassop, Nancy. "From Arguments to Supreme Court Opinions in *Planned Parenthood v. Casey*." *PS: Political Science and Politics* 26 (1993): 53–58.

Keck, Thomas M. "From *Bakke* to *Grutter*: The Rise of Rights-Based Conservatism." In *The Supreme Court and American Political Development*, edited by Ronald Kahn and Ken I. Kersch, 414–42. Lawrence: University Press of Kansas, 2006.

———. *The Most Activist Supreme Court in History: The Road to Modern Judicial Conservatism*. Chicago: University of Chicago Press, 2004.

Kennedy, Anthony M. "Comments." *The Supreme Court of the United States*. York Associates Television. Video.

Kennedy, Anthony M., "Justice Kennedy Address." C-SPAN, August 13, 2006. http://www.cspan.org.

———. "Speech at the American Bar Association Annual Meeting," 9 August 2003, revised 14 August 2003. Paginated transcript on file at the Public Information Office, U.S. Supreme Court.

———. Judge, Pre-Supreme Court Nomination Speeches, Judiciary Nominations files, Sup. Court, 100th Cong., Records of the Senate, Record Group 46, National Archives, Washington, DC.

———. "Federalism: The Theory and the Reality," Speech, Historical Society for the U.S. District Court for the Northern District of California, San Francisco, 26 October 1987.

———. "Rotary Speech," Sacramento Chapter of the Rotary Club, Sacramento, CA, 15 October 1987.

———. "Judge Kennedy's Comments at the Ninth Circuit Judicial Conference, Hawaii, 21 August 1987.

———. "Unenumerated Rights and the Dictates of Judicial Restraint," Speech, Canadian Institute for Advanced Legal Studies, The Stanford Lectures, Palo Alto, CA, 24 July–1 August 1986.

———. "Rotary Speech," Sacramento Chapter of the Rotary Club, Sacramento, CA, February 1984.

———. "Patent Lawyers Speech," Los Angeles Patent Lawyers Association, Los Angeles, February 1982.

———. "McGeorge Commencement Speech," McGeorge School of Law of the University of the Pacific Commencement, Sacramento, CA, 30 May 1981.

Kenworthy, Tom. "Colorado Springs Culture Wars; After Years of Conservatism, a March Toward Middle Ground Is Picking Up Speed in the 'Vatican of Evangelical Christianity,'" *Washington Post*, 18 November 1997, 3(A).

Knowles, Helen J. "Clerkish Control of Recent Supreme Court Opinions? A Case Study of Justice Kennedy's Opinion in *Gonzales v. Carhart*," *Georgetown Journal of Gender and the Law* 10 (forthcoming, 2009).

———. "A Dialogue on Liberty: The Classical Liberal and Civic Educational Principles of Justice Kennedy's Vision of Judicial Power." PhD Dissertation, Boston University, 2007.

———. "From a Value to a Right: The Supreme Court's Oh-So-Conscious Move from 'Privacy' to 'Liberty.'" *Ohio Northern University Law Review* 33 (2007): 595–621.

———. "May It Please the Court?: The Solicitor General's Not So 'Special' Relationship—Archibald Cox and the 1963–1964 Reapportionment Cases." *Journal of Supreme Court History* 31, no. 3 (July 2006): 279–97.

Kramer, Larry D. *The People Themselves: Popular Constitutionalism and Judicial Review.* New York: Oxford University Press, 2004.

Kull, Andrew. *The Color-Blind Constitution.* Cambridge, MA: Harvard University Press, 1992.

Kymlicka, Will. *Contemporary Political Philosophy: An Introduction.* 2nd ed. Oxford: Oxford University Press, 2002.

L'Heureux-Dube, Claire. "The Importance of Dialogue: Globalization, the Rehnquist Court, and Human Rights." In *The Rehnquist Court: A Retrospective*, edited by Martin H. Belsky, 234–52. Oxford: Oxford University Press, 2002.

Lane, Charles. "Attacks Led to 'Dialogue' for Justice Kennedy." *Washington Post*, 26 January 2002, 11(A).

———. "Justice Kennedy's Future Role Pondered; High-Profile Activities Spark Talk About Aims." *Washington Post*, 17 June 2002, 1(A).

Laslett, Peter, ed. *John Locke, Two Treatises of Government.* Cambridge: Cambridge University Press, 1989.

Lazarus, Edward. "Court Crackup." *Washington Post*, 25 July 2000, 23(A).

Lee, Rex E., and Richard G. Wilkins. "On Greatness and Constitutional Vision: Justice Byron R. White." *Brigham Young University Law Review* 1994 (1994): 291–312.

Leonard, Arthur S. "Kennedy and the Gays, Again." *New York Native*, 7 December 1987, 18.

Levinson, Sanford. *Constitutional Faith.* Princeton, NJ: Princeton University Press, 1988.

Lewis, Neil A. "An Ultimate Capital Insider—John Glover Roberts." *New York Times*, 20 July 2005, 1(A).

Lichtman, Steven B. "The Justices and the Generals: A Critical Examination of the U.S. Supreme Court's Tradition of Deference to the Military, 1918–2004." *Maryland Law Review* 65 (2006): 907–64.

Liptak, Adam. "Roberts Drops Hints in 'Precedent' Remarks." *New York Times*, 18 September 2005, 30(1).

Lynch, Brendan P. "Personal Injuries or Petty Complaints?: Evaluating the Case for Campus Hate Speech Codes: The Argument from Experience." *Suffolk University Law Review* 32 (1999): 613–46.

Macedo, Stephen. *The New Right v. The Constitution.* Washington, DC: CATO Institute, 1987.

Maltz, Earl M. "Anthony Kennedy and the Jurisprudence of Respectable Conservatism." In *Rehnquist Justice: Understanding the Court Dynamic*, edited by Earl M. Maltz, 140–56. Lawrence: University Press of Kansas, 2003.

Maltzman, Forrest, James F. Spriggs, and Paul J. Wahlbeck. *Crafting Law on the Supreme Court: The Collegial Game.* New York: Cambridge University Press, 2000.

Martin, Andrew D., Kevin Quinn, and Lee Epstein. "The Median Justice on the United States Supreme Court." *North Carolina Law Review* 83 (June 2005): 1275–317.

Mauro, Tony. "Justice Kennedy to ABA: 'The Work of Freedom Has Just Begun.'" *Legal Times*, 14 August 2007.

———. "A Lost Chance to Be the Chief." *Legal Times*, 7 March 2005, 1.

———. "Court Shows Interest in International Law." *New York Law Journal*, 14 July 2003, 1.

———. "Visiting Justices Get an Earful in London." *Legal Times*, 31 July 2000, 10.

Maveety, Nancy. "The Rehnquist Era and the Court's Commentators." Paper presented at the Annual Meeting of the American Political Science Association, Washington, DC, 1–4 September 2005.

Maxwell, Bill. "Our Constitution Should Be Celebrated." *St. Petersburg Times (FL)*, 17 September 2006, 3(P).

McElroy, Wendy. *The Debates of Liberty: An Overview of Individualist Anarchism, 1881–1908.* Lanham, MD: Lexington, 2003.

McIntosh, Wayne V., Cynthia L. Cates, Michael Evans, and Rebecca Thorpe. "Textualism v. Active Liberty: Testing the Doctrinal Approaches of Justice Scalia and Breyer." Paper presented at the UK American Politics Group Annual Conference, Institute for the Study of the Americas, University of London, 3–5 January 2008.

Melone, Albert P. "Revisiting the Freshman Effect Hypothesis: The First Two Terms of Justice Anthony Kennedy." *Judicature* 74 (1990): 6–13.

Merrill, Thomas W. "The Constitution and the Cathedral: Prohibiting, Purchasing, and Possibly Condemning Tobacco Advertising." *Northwestern University Law Review* 93 (1999): 1143–204.

Michelman, Frank I. "Symposium: Reason, Passion, & the Progress of Law: Remembering and Advancing the Constitutional Vision of Justice William J. Brennan." *Harvard Civil Rights–Civil Liberties Law Review* 33, no.2 (Summer 1998): 325–32.

Milbank, Dana. "And the Verdict on Justice Kennedy Is: Guilty." *Washington Post*, 9 April 2005, 3(A).

Moorhead, R. Dean. "Concurring and Dissenting Opinions." *American Bar Association Journal* 38 (1952): 821–24.

Moran, Terence. "Kennedy's Constitutional Journey." *Legal Times*, 6 July 1992, 1, 20–21.

Murdoch, Joyce, and Deb Price. *Courting Justice: Gay Men and Lesbians v. the Supreme Court.* New York: Basic Books, 2001.

Murphy, Walter F. "Constitutions, Constitutionalism, and Democracy." In *Constitutionalism and Democracy: Transitions in the Contemporary World*, edited by Douglas Greenberg, Stanley N. Katz, Melanie Beth Oliviero, and Steven C. Wheatley, 3–25. New York: Oxford University Press, 1993.

———. *Elements of Judicial Strategy.* Chicago: University of Chicago Press, 1964.

Murray, Donald R. "The President's Message: A Call to Action: Please Join Us in This Vital 'Dialogue on Freedom.'" *Montana Lawyer* 27 (April 2002): 4–5, 11.

Narveson, Jan. "Liberty and Equality—A Question of Balance?" In *Liberty and Equality*, edited by Tibor R. Machan, 35–59. Stanford, CA: Hoover Institution Press, 2002.

———. *The Libertarian Idea*. Toronto: Broadview, 2001.

NBC News. "A Question of Fairness." June 6, 2003.

Nelson, William E. "Byron White: A Liberal of 1960." In *The Warren Court in Historical and Political Perspective*, edited by Mark Tushnet, 139–54. Charlottesville: University Press of Virginia, 1993.

Neuborne, Burt. "First Amendment." *Touro Law Review* 6 (1989): 113–36.

Neveril, Edward J. "'Objective' Approaches to the Public Forum Doctrine: The First Amendment at the Mercy of Architectural Chicanery." *Northwestern University Law Review* 90 (1996): 1185–253.

Newman, Stephen L. *Liberalism at Wits' End: The Libertarian Revolt Against the Modern State*. Ithaca, NY: Cornell University Press, 1984.

Nozick, Robert. *Anarchy, State, and Utopia*. New York: Basic Books, 1974.

Nunziato, Dawn C. "The Death of the Public Forum in Cyberspace." *Berkeley Technology Law Journal* 20 (2005): 1115–71.

O'Connor, Sandra Day, and H. Alan Day. *Lazy B: Growing Up on a Cattle Ranch in the American Southwest*. New York: Random House, 2002.

The Oxford American Dictionary and Language Guide. New York: Oxford University Press, 1999.

Pacer, Valerie J. "Salvaging the Undue Burden Standard—Is It a Lost Cause? The Undue Burden Standard and Fundamental Rights Analysis." *Washington University Law Quarterly* 73 (1995): 295–32.

Peppers, Todd C. *Courtiers of the Marble Palace: The Rise and Influence of the Supreme Court Law Clerk*. Stanford, CA: Stanford University Press, 2006.

Perry, Barbara A. *The Michigan Affirmative Action Cases*. Lawrence: University Press of Kansas, 2007.

Perry, H. W. Jr., and L. A. Powe Jr. "The Political Battle for the Constitution." *Constitutional Commentary* 21 (Winter 2004): 641–96.

Pollack, Louis H. "Professional Attitude." *ABA Journal* 84 (August 1998): 66–68.

Pope, James Gray. "Labor's Constitution of Freedom." *Yale Law Journal* 106 (January 1997): 941–1031.

"Posing for Posterity: An Investiture Tradition." *Docket Sheet of the Supreme Court of the United States* 24, no. 3 (Winter 1988): 1, 4, 7.

Post, Robert C. "Between Governance and Management: The History and Theory of the Public Forum." *UCLA Law Review* 34 (1987): 1713–835.

Preece, Jennifer Jackson. *Minority Rights: Between Diversity and Community*. Cambridge: Polity, 2006.

Pritchett, C. Herman. "The Development of Judicial Research." In *Frontiers of Judicial Research*, edited by Joel Grossman and Joseph Tanenhaus, 27–42, New York: Wiley, 1969.

———. *The Roosevelt Court: A Study in Judicial Politics and Values, 1937–1947*. New York: Macmillan, 1948.

Rae, Douglas, Douglas Yates, Jennifer Hochschild, Joseph Morone, and Carol Fessler. *Equalities*. Cambridge, MA: Harvard University Press, 1981.

Raz, Joseph. "Free Expression and Personal Identification." In *Free Expression: Essays in Law and Philosophy*, edited by W. J. Waluchow, 1–29. Oxford: Clarendon Press, 1994.

———. *The Authority of Law: Essays on Law and Morality*. Oxford: Clarendon Press, 1979.

"Records Spotlight Kennedy Lobbying." *New York Times*, 15 November 1987, 31.

Rehnquist, William H. "The Supreme Court: Past and Present." *American Bar Association Journal* 59 (1973): 361–63.

Reinhold, Robert. "Restrained Pragmatist Anthony M. Kennedy." *New York Times*, 12 November 1987, 1(A).

Reuben, Richard C. "Man in the Middle." *California Lawyer*, October 1992, 35–38, 103.

Rodgers, Daniel T. *Contested Truths: Keywords in American Politics Since Independence*. New York: Basic, 1987.

"The Role of the Judiciary in Promoting the Rule of Law." C-SPAN, November 10, 2005. http://www.cspan.org.

Rosen, Jeffrey. "The Dissenter." *New York Times Magazine*, 23 September 2007, 50–56, 72, 76, 78–79, 81.

———. "Supreme Leader: The Arrogance of Justice Anthony Kennedy." *New Republic* 18 June 2007, 16–22.

———. "The Agonizer." *New Yorker*, 11 November 1996, 82–90.

Rosenberg, Gerald N. *The Hollow Hope: Can Courts Bring About Social Change?* Chicago: University of Chicago Press, 1991.

Rosenkranz, Joshua E. "Remembering and Advancing the Constitutional Vision of Justice William J. Brennan, Jr.: Foreword." *New York Law School Law Review* 43 (1999): 1–7.

Rossiter, Clinton. *Conservatism in America*. New York: Knopf, 1955.

Rossotti, Jack E., Laura Natelson, and Raymond Tatalovich. "Nonlegal Advice: The Amicus Briefs in *Webster v. Reproductive Health Services*." In *Judicial Politics: Readings from Judicature*, edited by Elliott E. Slotnick, 193–96. Washington, DC: CQ Press, 2005.

Rubenfeld, Jed. "The Right of Privacy." *Harvard Law Review* 102 (1989): 737–807.

Sarat, Austin, and Thomas R. Kearns. "Beyond the Great Divide: Forms of Legal Scholarship and Everyday Life." In *Law in Everyday Life*, edited by Austin Sarat and Thomas R. Kearns, 21–61. Ann Arbor: University of Michigan Press, 1995.

Savage, David G. "High Court Has Entered a New Era; The Chief Justice, with Help from Fellow Bush Appointee Alito, Carries Big Rulings to the Right—a Generational Shift." *Los Angeles Times*, 1 July 2007, 1(A).

———. *Turning Right: The Making of the Rehnquist Supreme Court*. New York: John Wiley & Sons, 1992.

———. "The Rescue of *Roe vs. Wade*: How a Dramatic Change of Heart by a Supreme Court Justice Affirmed the Right to Abortion—Just When the Issue Seemed Headed for Certain Defeat." *Los Angeles Times*, 13 December 1992, 1(A), 22(A).

Scalia, Antonin. *A Matter of Interpretation: Federal Courts and the Law*. Princeton, NJ: Princeton University Press, 1997.

———. "Of Democracy, Morality and the Majority (Rome Address Transcript)." *Origins* 26, no. 6 (1996): 81, 83–90.

———. "The Rule of Law as a Law of Rules." *University of Chicago Law Review* 56 (Fall 1989): 1175–88.

———. "The Judges Are Coming." *Congressional Record.* 96th Cong., 2nd sess., 1980. Vol. 126, pt 14.

"SCOTUSblog Super Stat Pack—OT07 Term Recap." http://www.scotusblog.com/wp/wp-content/uploads/2008/06/superstatpack07.pdf (accessed 10 July 2008).

Segal, Jeffrey A., and Harold J. Spaeth. *The Supreme Court and the Attitudinal Model Revisited.* New York: Cambridge University Press, 2002.

Selig, Joel L. "The Michigan Affirmative Action Cases: Justice O'Connor, *Bakke* Redux, and the Mice That Roared but Did Not Prevail." *Temple Law Review* 76 (2003): 579–94.

Shapiro, Fred R. *The Oxford Dictionary of American Legal Quotations.* New York: Oxford University Press, 1993.

Shapiro, Ian. *The Evolution of Rights in Liberal Theory.* Cambridge: Cambridge University Press, 1986.

Sherry, Suzanna. "Hard Cases Make Good Judges." *Northwestern University Law Review* 99 (2004): 3–31.

Silverstein, Mark. *Constitutional Faiths: Felix Frankfurter, Hugo Black, and the Process of Judicial Decision Making.* Ithaca, NY: Cornell University Press, 1984.

Silverstein, Mark, and William Haltom. "You Can't Always Get What You Want: Reflections on the Ginsburg and Breyer Nominations." *Journal of Law and Politics* 3 (Summer 1996): 459–79.

Skilling, Liam. "Features: Justice Anthony M. Kennedy." *Hawaii Bar Journal* (February 2007): 30–32.

Smith, William Raymond. "The Rhetoric of the Declaration of Independence." *College English* 26, no. 4 (January 1965): 306–9.

Sowell, Thomas. "From Equal Opportunity to 'Affirmative Action.'" In *Affirmative Action: Social Justice or Reverse Discrimination?*, edited by Francis J. Beckwith and Todd E. Jones, 99–120. Amherst, NY: Prometheus, 1997.

Spooner, Lysander. "An Essay on the Trial by Jury (1852)." In *The Collected Works of Lysander Spooner: Vol. 2, Legal Writings (I)*, edited by Charles Shively. Weston, MA: M&S Press, 1971.

Stack, Kevin M. "The Practice of Dissent in the Supreme Court." *Yale Law Journal* 105 (1996): 2235–59.

Stern, Nat. "State Action, Establishment Clause, and Defamation: Blueprints for Civil Liberties in the Rehnquist Court." *University of Cincinnati Law Review* 57 (1989): 1175–242.

Stevens, John Paul. "Learning on the Job." *Fordham Law Review* 74 (March 2006): 1561–67.

Stone, Geoffrey R. "Content Regulation and the First Amendment." *William & Mary Law Review* 25 (1983): 189–252.

Strasser, Mark. "Unconstitutional? Don't Ask; If It Is, Don't Tell: On Deference, Rationality, and the Constitution." *University of Colorado Law Review* 66 (1995): 375–460.

Strauss, David A. "Persuasion, Autonomy, and Freedom of Expression." *Columbia Law Review* 91 (1991): 334–71.

Sunstein, Cass R. "The Minimalist; Chief Justice Roberts Favors Narrow Court Rulings that Create Consensus and Tolerate Diversity." *Los Angeles Times*, 25 May 2006, 11(B).

———. "On Marshall's Conception of Equality." *Stanford Law Review* 44 (Summer 1992): 1267–75.

"A Supreme Court on the Brink." *New York Times*, 3 July 2008, 22(A).

"Symposium: To What Extent Should the Interpretation and Application of Provisions of the U.S. Constitution be Informed by Rulings of Foreign and International Tribunals: University of Hawai'i Law Review Symposium: Comments of Justice Ruth Bader Ginsburg." *University of Hawai'i Law Review* 26 (2004): 335–36.

Tamanaha, Brian Z. *On the Rule of Law: History, Politics, Theory*. Cambridge: Cambridge University Press, 2004.

Tamber, Caryn. "MD Supreme Court Briefs: September 29, 2006." *Daily Record*, 29 September 2006.

Taylor, Stuart. "When High Court's Away, Clerks' Work Begins." *New York Times*, 23 September 1988, 7(B).

———. "Which Way Will Kennedy Tilt the Bench?" *New York Times*, 7 February 1988, 4(4).

———. "Newest Judicial Activists Come from the Right." *New York Times*, 8 February 1987, 24(A).

Taylor, Stuart Jr., Evan Thomas, and Katie Connolly. "The Power Broker; In an Exclusive Interview, Justice Kennedy Discusses Life, Center Stage." *Newsweek*, 16 July 2007, 36–37.

Teles, Steven M. *The Rise of the Conservative Legal Movement*. Princeton, NJ: Princeton University Press, 2008.

Thompson, Della, ed. *The Concise Oxford Dictionary of Current English*. 9th ed. Oxford: Clarendon Press, 1995.

Tilman, Rick. *Ideology and Utopia in the Social Philosophy of the Libertarian Economists*. Westport, CT: Greenwood, 2001.

Toobin, Jeffrey. *The Nine: Inside the Secret World of the Supreme Court*. New York: Doubleday, 2007.

———. "Swing Shift; How Anthony Kennedy's Passion for Foreign Law Could Change the Supreme Court." *New Yorker*, 12 September 2005, 42–51.

Tribe, Laurence H. "*Lawrence v. Texas*: The 'Fundamental Right' That Dare Not Speak Its Name." *Harvard Law Review* 117 (April 2004): 1893–955.

———. "Structural Due Process." *Harvard Civil Rights Civil Liberties Law Review* 10 (1975): 269–321.

"A Tribute to Justice Lewis F. Powell, Jr." *Harvard Law Review* 101 (1987): 417–20.

Trussell, Trait, and Colleagues at the Commission on the Bicentennial of the United States Constitution to Everett C. Ladd, 10 April 1987; Decision Memos (March–April 1987) file; Office of the Chairman, Correspondence of the Chairman, 1985–1991, Correspondence thru Equal Justice Under Law, Box 1 NN3-220-92-004 H.M. 1992; Records of Temporary Committees, Commissions & Boards: Commission on the Bicentennial of the U.S. Constitution, Record Group 220; National Archives and Records Administration at College Park, MD.

Tuck, Richard, ed. *Thomas Hobbes, Leviathan.* New York: Cambridge University Press, 1996.

Tushnet, Mark. *A Court Divided: The Rehnquist Court and the Future of Constitutional Law.* New York: W. W. Norton, 2005.

———. "Kormendy Lecture Series: Understanding the Rehnquist Court." *Ohio Northern University Law Review* 31 (2005): 197–210.

12 Angry Men, DVD. Directed by Sidney Lumet. 1957; MGM Vintage Classics, 2001.

U.S. Senate, Committee on the Judiciary. Hearings on the Nomination of Anthony M. Kennedy to be Associate Justice of the Supreme Court of the United States. 100th Cong., 1st sess., 14–16 December 1987.

———. Committee on Rules and Administration. Testimony of Michael C. Munger, Hearings on Political Parties in America. 5 April 2000, http://rules.senate.gov/hearings/2000/04500munger.htm (accessed 1 July 2008).

Volokh, Eugene. "The Rehnquist Court: Pragmatism vs. Ideology in Free Speech Cases." *Northwestern University Law Review* 99 (2004): 33–46.

———. "How the Justices Voted in Free Speech Cases, 1994–2000." *UCLA Law Review* 48 (2001): 1191–202.

Wald, Patricia M. "The Rhetoric of Results and the Results of Rhetoric: Judicial Writings." *University of Chicago Law Review* 62 (1995): 1371–419.

Ward, Artemus. "The 'Good Old #3 Club' Gets a New Member." *Journal of Supreme Court History* 33, no. 1 (March 2008): 110–19.

———. "The Gay Rights Jurisprudence of Anthony Kennedy: An Institutional Analysis." Paper presented at the annual meeting of the Midwest Political Science Association, Chicago, 15–18 April 2004.

Ward, Artemus, and David L. Weiden. *Sorcerers' Apprentices: 100 Years of Law Clerks at the United States Supreme Court.* New York: New York University Press, 2006.

Warren, Samuel D., and Louis D. Brandeis. "The Right to Privacy." *Harvard Law Review* 4 (1890): 193–220.

Waters, Melissa A. "Mediating Norms and Identity: The Role of Transnational Judicial Dialogue in Creating and Enforcing International Law." *Georgetown Law Journal* 93 (2005): 487–574.

West, Robin. "The Supreme Court, 1989 Term: Foreword: Taking Freedom Seriously." *Harvard Law Review* 104 (1990): 43–106.

Whitman, James Q. *Harsh Justice: Criminal Punishment and the Widening Divide between America and Europe.* Oxford: Oxford University Press, 2003.

Williams, Geraint, ed. *John Stuart Mill, Utilitarianism, On Liberty, Considerations on Representative Government, Remarks on Bentham's Philosophy.* London: Everyman, 1993.

Woodward, Bob, and Scott Armstrong. *The Brethren: Inside the Supreme Court.* New York: Simon & Schuster, 1979.

Woolley, John T., and Gerhard Peters. "Speech of Senator John F. Kennedy, Commodore Hotel, New York, NY, Acceptance of Party Nomination, September 14th, 1960." *The American Presidency Project.* Santa Barbara: University of California (hosted), Gerhard Peters (database). http://www.presidency.ucsb.edu/ws/?pid=74012 (accessed 9 April 2008).

———. "Lyndon B. Johnson, Executive Order 11246—Equal Employment Opportunity." *The American Presidency Project.* Santa Barbara, CA: University of California (hosted), Gerhard Peters (database), http://www.presidency.ucsb.edu/ws/index.php?pid=59153 (accessed 17 August 2007).

———. "William J. Clinton, Message to the House of Representatives Returning Without Approval Partial Birth Abortion Legislation, 10 April 1996." *The American Presidency Project.* Santa Barbara: University of California (hosted), Gerhard Peters (database), http://www.presidency.ucsb.edu/ws/index.php?pid=52655&st=&st1= (accessed 2 July 2008).

Wooten, Jim. "Bush Makes Meticulous Pick for Court." *Atlanta Journal-Constitution*, 1 November 2005, 15(A).

Wortham, Anne. "Individualism versus Racism." In *The Libertarian Alternative: Essays in Social and Political Philosophy*, edited by Tibor R. Machan, 403–7. Chicago: Nelson-Hall, 1974.

Yalof, David Alistair. *Pursuit of Justices: Presidential Politics and the Selection of Supreme Court Nominees.* Chicago: University of Chicago Press, 1999.

Zuckert, Michael P. *Natural Rights and the New Republicanism.* Princeton, NJ: Princeton University Press, 1994.

Index

About the Author

Helen J. Knowles is assistant professor of political science at the State University of New York, Oswego. In 2006, she received the U.S. Supreme Court Historical Society's Hughes-Gossett Award presented by Chief Justice John Roberts for her *Journal of Supreme Court History* article about Solicitor General Archibald Cox and the 1963–1964 reapportionment cases. Other articles have been published in *Slavery & Abolition, Ohio Northern University Law Review, First Amendment Law Review*, and the *Journal of Legal Education.* Her current research focuses on the constitutional theory and jurisprudence of the U.S. Supreme Court.